850 Intriguing Questions about Judaism

850 Intriguing Questions about Judaism

True, False, or In Between

Ronald L. Eisenberg

ROWMAN & LITTLEFIELD
Lanham • Boulder • New York • London

Published by Rowman & Littlefield
A wholly owned subsidiary of The Rowman & Littlefield Publishing Group, Inc.
4501 Forbes Boulevard, Suite 200, Lanham, Maryland 20706
www.rowman.com

Unit A, Whitacre Mews, 26-34 Stannary Street, London SE11 4AB

British Library Cataloguing in Publication Information Available

Library of Congress Cataloging-in-Publication Data

Eisenberg, Ronald L., author.
850 intriguing questions about Judaism : true, false, or in between / Ronald L. Eisenberg.
pages cm
Includes bibliographical references and index.
ISBN 978-1-4422-3946-3 (hardback : alk. paper) — ISBN 978-1-4422-3947-0 (ebook) 1. Judaism—
Miscellanea. I. Title. II. Title: Eight hundred fifty intriguing questions about Judaism.
BM51.E37 2015
296—dc23
2015006592

♾ ™ The paper used in this publication meets the minimum requirements of American
National Standard for Information Sciences Permanence of Paper for Printed Library
Materials, ANSI/NISO Z39.48-1992.

Printed in the United States of America

To Zina, Avlana, and Cherina

Contents

Preface

Both Jews and non-Jews have misconceptions about Judaism. Some seemingly unusual ideas about Jewish history, teachings, and practices are actually true, whereas some ostensibly reasonable and popularly believed concepts are patently false. In many cases, notions regarding Judaism are neither true nor false and actually require a nuanced explanation.

850 Intriguing Questions about Judaism: True, False, or In Between explores a wide range of aspects of Judaism, framed as a series of questions, a substantial number of which do not have a clear-cut yes or no answer. This work contains more than 850 questions, organized into 13 chapters, or categories, that cover a broad range of topics in Jewish life, history, and practice. Each chapter opens with a list of questions, so that readers can ponder the answers before delving into the text. Afterward, the reader will find each question and its answer, with a small designation indicating whether the question is true (T), false (F), or neither (N), meaning a nuanced answer.

Many of the questions deal with subtopics and could be placed in more than one category. For example, the question "Is there significance to the four cups of wine at the Tu b'Shevat seder?" appears in "Sabbath and Festivals," but also could have been listed in the chapter on "Food." *850 Intriguing Questions about Judaism: True, False, or In Between* features a question index organized by key words and arranged in alphabetical order, listing all pages on which the relevant questions appear. For example, a reader interested in questions related to Passover could choose to look at all the questions for the entire chapter on Sabbath and festivals, or quickly search the index to find Passover-related questions dealing with such topics as Haggadah, seder, *matzah*, *chametz*, *afikoman*, and various Passover songs.

In addition to a bibliography of major sources, this work includes a list of abbreviations for books of the Bible and Talmud, and a glossary. As in many texts, a distinction is made between the term Rabbi (capitalized for those of the Talmudic era) and rabbi (lowercase for those of subsequent eras).

850 Intriguing Questions about Judaism: True, False, or In Between is designed to appeal to all Jews interested in broadening their Jewish horizons, and to anyone who wants to learn more about the many facets and diversity of Jewish thought and practice.

Abbreviations

Ar.	Arachin
ARN	Avot d'Rabbi Nathan
Av. Zar.	Avodah Zarah
Avot	Pirkei Avot
BB	Bava Batra
B.C.E	Before the Common Era
Bek.	Bechorot
Betz.	Beitzah
Ber.	Berachot
Bik.	Bikurim
BK	Bava Kama
BM	Bava Metzia
C.E.	Common Era
Chron.	Chronicles
Dem.	Demai
Deut.	Deuteronomy
Deut. R.	Deuteronomy Rabbah
Eccles.	Ecclesiastes
Eccles. R.	Ecclesiastes Rabbah
Eduy.	Eduyot

Er.	Eruvin
Esth.	Esther
Esth. R.	Esther Rabbah
Exod.	Exodus
Exod. R.	Exodus Rabbah
Ezek.	Ezekiel
Gen.	Genesis
Gen. R.	Genesis Rabbah
Git.	Gittin
Hab.	Habbakuk
Hag.	Haggai
Hag.	Hagigah
Hal.	Hallah
Hor.	Horayot
Hos.	Hosea
Hul.	Hullin
Isa.	Isaiah
Jer.	Jeremiah
Jon.	Jonah
Josh.	Joshua
JT	Jerusalem Talmud
Judg.	Judges
Ker.	Keritot
Ket.	Ketubot
Kid.	Kiddushin
Kil.	Kilayim
Lam.	Lamentations
Lam. R.	Lamentations Rabbah
Lev.	Leviticus
Lev. R.	Leviticus Rabbah
Mak.	Makot
Mal.	Malachi

Mech.	Mechilta
Me'il	Meilah
Meg.	Megillah
Men.	Menachot
Mic.	Micah
Mid.	Middot
Mid. Ps.	Midrash Psalms
Mik.	Mikva'ot
MK	Mo'ed Katan
Nah.	Nahum
Naz.	Nazir
Ned.	Nedarim
Nid.	Niddah
Num.	Numbers
Num. R.	Numbers Rabbah
Obad.	Obadiah
OH	Orach Hayim
PdRE	Pirkei de-Rabbi Eliezer
PdRK	Pesikta de-Rabbi Kahana
Pes.	Pesachim
Pes. Rab.	Pesikta Rabbati
Prov.	Proverbs
Ps.	Psalms
RH	Rosh Hashanah
Ruth R.	Ruth Rabbah
Sam.	Samuel
Sanh.	Sanhedrin
Sem.	Semachot
Shab.	Shabbat
Shek.	Shekalim
Shev.	Shevuot
Sifra Ked.	Sifra Kedoshim

Sot.	Sotah
Suk.	Sukkah
Taan.	Ta'anit
Tam.	Tamid
Tanh.	Tanhuma
Ter.	Terumah
Tos.	Tosafot
YD	Yoreh De'ah
Yev.	Yevamot
Zech.	Zechariah
Zeph.	Zephaniah
Zev.	Zevachim

Chapter One

The Bible

Have you ever wondered . . .

1. Was the biblical narrative of Creation based on myths of the Babylonians and other peoples in the ancient Near East?
2. Was Eve the wife of Adam?
3. Was the "mark of Cain" a sign of disgrace?
4. Did Noah take a male and female of all animals with him in the ark?
5. Is Mount Ararat in the Land of Israel?
6. During the Flood, did it rain for exactly 40 days and 40 nights?
7. Is a cubit equal to a foot?
8. Did the firstborn son automatically succeed his father as leader of the family?
9. Is there any significance in the name of Isaac?
10. Did Laban, the brother of Rebecca, warmly embrace his nephew Jacob because he hoped his kinsman would marry one of his daughters, Rachel or Leah?
11. Are all the patriarchs and matriarchs buried in the Cave of Machpelah?
12. Is the listing of the Twelve Tribes of Israel consistent throughout the Bible?
13. Are modern Jews the descendants of the Twelve Tribes of Israel?
14. According to the *aggadah*, was Miriam instrumental in the conception of her brother, Moses?
15. Was Benjamin the only one of the 12 sons of Jacob born in the Land of Canaan?
16. Were the midwives who saved the Israelite newborns actually Jewish?

1

17. Did Jethro save the life of Moses many years before becoming his father-in-law?
18. Did Zipporah save the life of Moses, her husband?
19. Did the covenant between God and the Jewish people take place at Mount Sinai?
20. Is the covenant between God and Israel both conditional and unconditional?
21. When Moses came down from Mount Sinai with the second set of tablets, were there horns arising from his head as in the Michelangelo statue?
22. Was the *Mishkan* considered the "dwelling place" for God?
23. Was the biblical skin disease *tzara'at* leprosy?
24. Could *tzara'at* affect inanimate objects?
25. Was the Nazirite required to bring a sin offering after his period of consecration to God?
26. Did the Nazarite vow not to cut his hair?
27. Was Moses buried in a marked grave on Mount Nebo?
28. Was necromancy ever practiced in Israel?
29. Is the "City of David" a synonym for Jerusalem?
30. Did King David rule for 40 years in Jerusalem, which is known as the "City of David"?
31. Were there two Isaiahs?
32. Is there a chair left empty for Elijah the Prophet at a circumcision?
33. Is there a modern equivalent of the biblical Altar in the Temple?

Was the biblical narrative of Creation based on myths of the Babylonians and other peoples in the ancient Near East? (F)   *False*

Rather than the pagan idea of a primordial realm that contained the elements of all being and led to the birth of sexually differentiated gods who then procreated to produce the full panoply of deities, the Israelite view presented a single God, the source of all being, who causes everything to appear from nothing (*creatio ex nihilo*). In both the biblical and Babylonian accounts, the final act of the creative process is the human being. However, unlike the Babylonian myth, in which human beings are created merely to build shrines and worship the gods, attending to their every physical need, the Bible views man as the pinnacle of Creation, a creature who represents a unique combination of animalistic traits with the nobility of a soul that elevates him to be created in the image of God. In the Babylonian epic of creation, the deities relaxed after their creative activities and held a huge feast, whereas in Genesis, God's rest set an orderly pattern for the future conduct of mankind, making the Sabbath holy.

Was Eve the wife of Adam? (N)   N e i t h~

According to Jewish folklore, the first wife of Adam was actually Lilith. She was known as an evil spirit and natural enemy of newborns. This led to the development of various customs designed to protect new mothers and their babies.

Was the "mark of Cain" a sign of disgrace? (F)

The "mark of Cain" (Gen. 4:15) was actually an indication of Divine protection, for "if anyone kill Cain, sevenfold vengeance shall be taken on him." The *aggadah* offered various suggestions as to the precise nature of this sign: "God made the sun shine upon him [as a sign of Divine benevolence]; He caused Cain to develop *tzara'at* [flaky white skin disease, mistranslated as leprosy, which would cause others to avoid him]; He gave him a vicious dog [to scare away anyone who would attack him]; He made Cain a sign to others [a warning to murderers and an indication of the saving power of repentance]. In addition, God suspended the punishment of Cain until [some future time when] the Flood came and drowned him" (Gen. R. 22:12). Another explanation was that "God took one of the twenty-two letters [*aleph-bet*] from which the Torah was written and placed it on Cain's arm, so that he would not be killed" (Yalkut Shimoni, Gen. 38).

Did Noah take a male and female of all animals with him in the ark? (N)

When God sent the great Flood to destroy the entire human race because of their sinfulness, Noah took a male and female of every "unclean" species of living creature to allow for their regeneration (Gen. 6:20). However, he took seven pairs of each type of "clean" animal to provide for sacrifices to God after the Deluge (Gen. 7:2).

Is Mount Ararat in the Land of Israel? (F)

The mountain range where Noah's ark came to rest after the Flood (Gen. 8:4) is located in eastern Turkey, near the point where the borders of Turkey, Iran, and Armenia meet.

During the Flood, did it rain for exactly 40 days and 40 nights? (N)

The text describes that torrential rains fell for 40 days and 40 nights (Gen. 7). However, in the Bible, the number 40 is used to indicate a substantial time. For example the Israelites were condemned to wander in the wilderness for 40 years after the episode of the spies. Moses remained on Mount Sinai twice for 40 days, while receiving the first and second tablets of the Ten Commandments (Exod. 24:18; Deut. 10:10). King David ruled for 40 years (2 Sam. 5:4), as did his son Solomon (1 Kings 11:42).

Is a cubit equal to a foot? (F)

Many biblical measurements of length are given in cubits, which is the distance between the elbow and the tip of the middle finger. In an average man, a cubit equals about 18 inches (1.5 foot or 45 cm.).

Did the firstborn son automatically succeed his father as leader of the family? (N)

The Bible (Deut. 21:17) endorsed the principle of primogeniture, meaning that the firstborn of the father received a double share in the estate. This may have reflected the requirement that the eldest son provide for his mother and any unmarried female members of the family. Nevertheless, the father could choose a son other than the firstborn for leadership—an option that occurred frequently in the stories of the Patriarchs. Thus Abraham selected Isaac over Ishmael, and Isaac gave the primary blessing to Jacob rather than Esau (albeit through a skillful subterfuge engineered by his wife, Rebecca). Jacob gave the primacy of the tribes to Judah rather than Reuben, his firstborn, and Joseph arranged for his younger son Ephraim to be favored over the older Menashe.

Is there any significance in the name of Isaac? (T)

According to the Bible, Sarah was almost 90 years old and had given up hope of ever bearing a child. When she overheard an angel of the Lord informing Abraham that within a year she would have a son, Sarah laughed with disbelief at the news (Gen. 18:9–14). Therefore, their son was named Isaac (*Yitzhak*, Hebrew for "he will laugh"), for "God has brought me laughter; everyone who hears will laugh with me" (Gen. 21:6). However, another rabbinic explanation of the name *Yitzhak* comes from numerology. The first letter, *yud*, has a numerical value of 10, which refers to the 10 trials with which Abraham (Isaac's father) was tested. The second letter, *tzadi*, has a numerical value of 90, the age of Sarah when she gave birth to Isaac. The third letter, *chet*, equals eight, referring to the eighth day on which Isaac was circumcised (Gen. 21:4). The final letter, *kuf*, has a numerical value of 100, the age of Abraham when his son Isaac was born (Num. R. 18:21).[1]

Did Laban, the brother of Rebecca, warmly embrace his nephew Jacob because he hoped his kinsman would marry one of his daughters, Rachel or Leah? (F)

According to the Rabbis, Laban's motivation was pure greed. Years before, Eliezer (servant of Abraham) had come to Mesopotamia to find a wife for Isaac. Seeing the gold nose ring and bracelets that Eliezer had given Rebecca, Laban was convinced that if his young sister had received such extravagant gifts, how much more expensive tokens would be his. Years later, when Jacob arrived at the home of Laban after escaping the wrath of his brother, Esau, Laban contemplated the riches that Abraham's grandson must be bringing with him since Eliezer, a mere servant, had previously brought with him 10 heavily laden camels (Gen. 24:10). Crestfallen that Jacob was empty-handed, Laban was convinced that he must be hiding money in his cloak or even in his mouth (Gen. R. 70:13). Therefore, "Laban ran to greet him; he embraced him [to feel whether he had any hidden treasures on his person] and kissed him [to see whether Jacob had any jewels hidden in his mouth]" (Gen. 29:13).

Are all the patriarchs and matriarchs buried in the Cave of Machpelah? (F)

The Cave of Machpelah is the grave site in Hebron purchased by Abraham from Ephron the Hittite as a place to bury his wife, Sarah (Gen. 23). Abraham and Sarah, Isaac and Rebecca, and Jacob and Leah are buried in this "Tomb of the Patriarchs," which is housed in a fortress built by Herod that was converted into a mosque following the Muslim conquest of the Land of Israel in the seventh century. However, when traveling from Beit El to Efrat (now Bethlehem), Rachel died while giving birth to her second son, Benjamin (Gen. 35:16–20). The heartsick Jacob buried his beloved Rachel along the road, and the ancient site of her tomb remains revered as an important religious shrine to this day.

Is the listing of the Twelve Tribes of Israel consistent throughout the Bible? (F)

These founders of the Jewish people are listed in two ways in the Bible. Jacob had 12 sons with his wives, Leah and Rachel, and his concubines, Bilhah and Zilpah—Reuben, Shimon, Levi, Judah, Dan, Naphtali, Gad, Asher, Issachar, Zebulun, Joseph, and Benjamin. However, for purposes of settling the Promised Land, Joseph received a double share that was passed on to his sons, Ephraim and Menashe. The post-settlement listing of the Twelve Tribes of Israel excludes Levi, because this tribe inherited the priesthood rather than any of the tribal lands and was scattered among the people.

Are modern Jews the descendants of the Twelve Tribes of Israel? (N)

Jews today are the descendants of the two southern tribes (Judah and Benjamin) plus the *levi'im* (Levites). After the Assyrian conquest of the Northern Kingdom in 721 B.C.E., the 10 tribes of Israel were scattered throughout the empire, assimilated, and lost to history. Over the centuries, various groups have claimed that they are the descendants of these lost tribes.

According to the *aggadah*, was Miriam instrumental in the conception of her brother, Moses? (T)

The Talmud (Sot. 12a) relates that Amram and Jochebed already had two children, Miriam and Aaron, when Pharaoh decreed that all newborn Israelite males would be cast into the Nile. Amram divorced his wife, arguing that there was no point having another child only to see him killed. As "leader of the Sanhedrin and the greatest man of his generation," all the other Israelite men followed his example. Miriam then accused her father of being worse than Pharaoh: "Pharaoh decreed only against the males; you have decreed against the males and the females. Pharaoh only decreed concerning this world; you have decreed concerning this world and the World to Come [i.e., the drowned infants would live again in the future world, but unborn children are denied that bliss]." She added that there was a possibility that Pharaoh's decree might not be carried out, whereas "though you are righteous, it is certain that your decree [not to have children] will be fulfilled." Amram saw the wisdom of his daughter's words and reunited with his wife, and soon afterward Moses was born.

Was Benjamin the only one of the 12 sons of Jacob born in the Land of Canaan? (Y)

Benjamin, the younger son of Rachel, was the only son of Jacob born in the Land of Canaan. All the others were born during the years that Jacob lived in Haran in Mesopotamia, where the patriarch worked for his father-in-law, the wily Laban. En route to Beth El and then to Hebron, the home of his parents, Jacob's beloved Rachel died giving birth to Benjamin (Gen. 35:16-20).

Were the midwives who saved the Israelite newborns actually Jewish? (N)

After Pharaoh's order to kill all the newborn Israelite boys, two Hebrew midwives named Shifra and Puah bravely refused to obey the royal decree. They explained to Pharaoh that the Hebrew women were not like their Egyptian counterparts: "Before the midwife can come to them, they have given birth" (Exod. 1:15–19). According to Midrashic tradition, Shifra and Puah were Jochebed and Miriam, the mother and sister of Moses (Sot. 11b).

Did Jethro save the life of Moses many years before becoming his father-in-law? (T)

A midrash relates how Jethro, the priest of Midian, saved the life of the young Moses. When Pharaoh hugged and kissed the child, Moses took the royal crown and placed it on his own head. The Egyptian sorcerers warned that this act indicated that the boy was destined to take away the kingdom. Some suggested that Moses be executed by the sword, others by fire. But Jethro, who sat among them, argued that the boy simply did not understand what he was doing. He urged Pharaoh to test Moses by placing before him a plate containing gold and glowing coal. "If he reaches for the gold, he has understanding and you will kill him. If he reaches for the coal, he has no understanding and does not deserve the death penalty." The two objects were brought before Moses, who initially reached for the gold. But the angel Gabriel came and pushed away his hand, and Moses burned his fingers on the hot coals (Exod. R. 1:26).

Did Zipporah save the life of Moses, her husband? (T)

According to the Bible, when God was about to kill Moses for failing to circumcise his son, Zipporah averted the imminent death of her husband by circumcising Gershom with a flint (Exod. 4:24–26).

Did the covenant between God and the Jewish people take place at Mount Sinai? (N)

The concept of covenant (*brit* in Hebrew), a special relationship between God and the Jewish people, is a major foundation of the theology of Judaism. The classic covenant between God and Israel took place at Mount Sinai, less than two months after the Exodus from Egypt (Exod. 19). However, periodic renewal of the covenant was a major biblical motif at times of important historical events. In addition to the ceremonies before the entry of the Israelites into the Promised Land and after its conquest, formal renewals of the covenant occurred under Solomon at the dedication of the Temple; Josiah after the discovery of the Book of Deuteronomy and as part of his sweeping religious reforms; and Nehemiah after the return of the people to Zion from Babylonian Exile. Each of these was characterized by a "reaffirmation of faith"—a long sermon to the entire nation that served as a tool to educate the people and renew their connection with both the One God and their national history. At the renewal ceremony before entering Canaan, Moses emphasized the continuity of the covenant throughout the generations, stressing that at Sinai, "it was not with our fathers that the Lord made this covenant." Rather, it was made "with us, the living, every one of us who is here today" (Deut. 5:2–3) and thus was binding upon the Jewish people for all time. Covenants also were made between God and specific human beings—Noah (Gen. 6:18; 9:9–11) and Abraham (Gen. 15). Circumcision is the primary outward sign testifying to the validity of the covenant.

Is the covenant between God and Israel both conditional and unconditional? (T)

The mutual agreement between God and Israel stipulates that when the people perform the will of God, they will enjoy Divine blessings. However, if they disobey the law of God, fail to fulfill the commandments, and lapse into idolatry, they will be cursed and suffer natural and political disasters. This concept of national reward and punishment, associated with the covenant at Mount Sinai and elucidated in the *Tochachah* (two chilling prophecies detailing an extensive list of dire consequences that will befall the Israelites if they spurn God and the *mitzvot*; Lev. 26:3–39; Deut. 28:1–68), is the traditional explanation for the destruction of the First Temple and the Babylonian Exile.

Nevertheless, there is also an unconditional covenant, in which God pledged to David that his dynasty will be everlasting. According to Jewish tradition, the fulfillment of this Divine promise will be the coming of the Messiah, who will be a descendant of King David.

When Moses came down from Mount Sinai with the second set of tablets, were there horns arising from his head as in the Michelangelo statue? (F)

The work of the famed Italian master was based on a mistranslation of the Hebrew word *keren*, which is used in the biblical text. Although it can mean "horn," in this context the term means that the face of Moses emitted a radiance reflecting the afterglow of his encounter with the splendor of the Divine Presence (Exod. 34:29–35). According to one legend, these "rays of glory" arose from the sparks that emanated from the mouth of the *Shechinah* when God taught the Torah to Moses; in another, their origin was a bit of ink left in the pen used by Moses when writing the Torah, which he then passed over his head. A third opinion was that the Divine radiance came from the cave in which Moses hid himself as God said, "When My glory passes, I will place you [Moses] in a cleft of the rock" (Exod. 33:22).

Was the *Mishkan* considered the "dwelling place" for God? (N)

Often translated as "Tabernacle," the *Mishkan* was a portable tent-like structure for the Divine Presence that the Israelites were commanded to build in the wilderness so that God might "dwell among them." It contained an inner chamber (Holy of Holies), which was entered only once a year by the High Priest on the Day of Atonement. Rather than a dwelling place for God, the *Mishkan* was considered by most commentators as a central focus where the people could worship God and receive Divine inspiration,[2] or as a symbol of the historic experience on Mount Sinai (i.e., a "portable Mount Sinai" because it was ringed by the tribes and topped by the cloud of God's Presence). The portable sanctuary was replaced by a permanent structure when King Solomon built the First Temple in Jerusalem.

Was the biblical skin disease *tzara'at* leprosy? (F)

Although often translated as "leprosy," the signs described in the Torah and the reversibility of this skin condition make it doubtful that it refers to that incurable disease. The Rabbis regarded *tzara'at* as a Divine punishment for *lashon ha-ra* (slander or tale-bearing), indicating that such a person is a "moral leper" who must be excluded from the camp of Israel. The prime biblical example was when Miriam developed *tzara'at* after she "spoke against Moses because of the Cushite woman whom he had married" (Num. 12:1).

Could *tzara'at* affect inanimate objects? (T)

Tzara'at could also contaminate garments through contact with an afflicted individual or his sores (Lev. 13:47–59), or affect a house, which might require its partial or even complete demolition (Lev. 14:33–53). This condition was most likely due to a fungus similar to that which causes dry rot, though some have suggested that it represented parasitic insects or a collection of nitrous material that had formed in the walls.[3]

Was the Nazirite required to bring a sin offering after his period of consecration to God? (T)

Literally meaning either one who was "separated" (from the temptations of the environment) or "consecrated" (to God), the Nazirite voluntarily assumed restrictions beyond the obligatory commandments in order to reach an elevated state of holiness. The Nazirite vow was often taken purely for personal reasons, such as thanksgiving for recovery from illness or the birth of a child. The minimum period of the vow was 30 days, but some persisted for years.[4] The Rabbis debated why the Nazirite was required to bring a sin offering after a period dedicated to the Divine service. The most popular view was that the offering of the Nazirite atoned for the sin of rejecting the delights of the world that God had created for human beings, instead misconstruing them as sources of temptation and evil.[5]

Did the Nazarite vow not to cut his hair? (N)

The most famous Nazirite was Samson, whose supernatural strength lay in his unshorn hair. However, in addition to allowing the hair to remain uncut during the period of the vow, the Nazirite also promised to abstain from grapes or grape products, such as wine, and to avoid any contact with a human corpse (Num. 6:1–21).

Was Moses buried in a marked grave on Mount Nebo? (F)

When Moses was about to die, he was permitted to ascend Mount Nebo in the extreme northwest of the mountains of Moab, across the Jordan from Jericho. There God showed him the entire land that constituted the Divine promise to the Patriarchs (Deut. 34:1–3). Moses died at the age of 120, in full command of his faculties ("his eyes were undimmed and his vigor unabated"; Deut. 34:7). His place of burial (by God Himself; Sot. 9b) remained unknown to prevent the possibility of a cult developing in relation to his grave site.

Was necromancy ever practiced in Israel? (N)

Necromancy is a magical practice that purports to foretell the future by communicating with the spirits of the dead. The Bible strictly prohibits necromancy, which it describes as "the sorcery of the *ob* and the *yid'oni*" (translated as "ghosts and familiar spirits"). Necromancy was one of the esoteric arts that were collectively disparaged as "abominations to the Lord." Nevertheless, the Bible does relate an actual account of this practice, when King Saul consulted the witch of En Dor to summon the spirit of the prophet Samuel to learn his fate (1 Sam. 28).

Is the "City of David" a synonym for Jerusalem? (N)

Although this term is generally used as a synonym for Jerusalem, it more precisely refers to the ancient City of David, which was located on a narrow ridge south of the current Old City. On the east it bordered the deep Kidron Valley, the site where the Gihon Spring (Jerusalem's water source) is located. Under King Solomon, the city was extended northward and the valley separating the City of David from Mount Moriah was filled in. This area became the site of many new palaces, and the Temple was built on the summit of Mount Moriah. By medieval times, the southern wall of Jerusalem had been built along the line of the present Old City wall. This excluded the City of David and left the site of biblical Jerusalem uninhabited. Archeological exploration of the City of David began in the middle of the nineteenth century and continues to this day.

Did King David rule for 40 years in Jerusalem, which is known as the "City of David"? (N)

King David ruled for 40 years. However, the first seven and a half years of his reign was in Hebron. Only after that period was David successful in uniting all the Israelite tribes into a single kingdom (2 Sam. 5). He conquered the city of Jerusalem from the Jebusites and made it the national capital, center of worship, and the holy site of the Jewish pilgrimage for about 3,000 years.

Were there two Isaiahs? (N)

The first of the major prophets, Isaiah lived in Judah during the eighth century B.C.E. He attacked the idolatry, moral laxity, and injustice of his time, sternly warning of impending judgment against the Israelites. According to biblical scholars, the second half of the Book of Isaiah (chapters 40–66) was written by an unnamed author (known as "Deutero-Isaiah" or "Second Isaiah") who lived at the end of the Babylonian Exile during the sixth century. Unlike the older prophet, who warned against the destruction of Judah, Second Isaiah predicts the demise of Babylonia and attempts to provide comfort to an exiled, suffering, and despairing people.

Some modern scholars even attribute chapters 56–66 to a third Isaiah (Trito-Isaiah).

Is there a chair left empty for Elijah the Prophet at a circumcision? (N)

A special decorative chair is traditionally left unoccupied and symbolically meant for Elijah the Prophet at the circumcision ceremony. It often is now occupied by the *sandek* (godfather). Elijah is depicted as the protector of the Jewish child, probably based on the biblical story in which he revived the son of a widow (1 Kings 17:17–24). Another reason for the symbolic presence of Elijah at every circumcision is the traditional belief that the prophet will ultimately announce the crowning of the Messiah to redeem humankind.

Therefore, he must appear at each circumcision in order to determine whether this child will be the long-awaited messianic figure.

Is there a modern equivalent of the biblical Altar in the Temple? (T)

The Altar (*Mizbeach*) was the raised surface or platform on which sacrifices were performed in the Sanctuary. There was a bronze altar for burnt offerings and a golden altar for incense. Originally, an altar could be anywhere and sacrifices performed by anyone. Eventually, a sacrificial cult became more institutionalized and limited to special practitioners and specific places. Altars were permanent fixtures in the Jerusalem Temple, which became the only permitted site of sacrificial worship. Over time, the term "altar" came to designate the central location for liturgical functions in the synagogue, such as reading the Torah. After the destruction of the Second Temple, the Rabbis considered the dinner table to be symbolic of the Altar in the Temple (Ber. 55a). Because salt was brought with all offerings, the custom of sprinkling salt on the Sabbath *challah* developed to commemorate the sacrificial system.

NOTES

1. Isaacs, 182–83.
2. *Sefer ha-Chinuch*, cited in Chill, 118.
3. Waskow, 473.
4. Hertz, 592.
5. *Etz Hayim*, 800.

Chapter Two

Literature

Have you ever wondered . . .

1. Does the word "Torah" mean the first five books of the Bible?
2. Do customs have legal status, and are they binding on all Jews?
3. Is "Old Testament" as a term for Scriptures generally accepted by Jews?
4. Do the Hebrew names of the first five books of the Bible reflect their contents?
5. Are the "major" prophets more important than the "minor" prophets?
6. Do Christian and Hebrew Bibles contain the same books?
7. Are the five books of the Writings, called *megillot* (scrolls), read in the synagogue on specific occasions?
8. Were the vowels, punctuation, and musical markings for chanting the Bible written down in biblical times?
9. Is parallelism the essence of biblical poetry?
10. Is there more than one classical way to interpret the Bible?
11. In the Bible, are there two versions of the Ten Commandments?
12. Is there internal structure to the Ten Commandments?
13. Are the Ten Commandments a central part of the synagogue service?
14. Is there more than one way to chant the Ten Commandments?
15. Does the First Commandment describe God as the Creator of the universe?
16. Does the Sixth Commandment prohibit killing?
17. Did the Rabbis consider as murder any actions not resulting in death?
18. Does the Eighth Commandment apply to stealing money or other valuables?

19. Were the two sets of the Tablets of the Covenant (*luchot ha-brit*) the same?
20. According to Jewish tradition, was the Oral Law part of the Revelation at Sinai?
21. Is *halachah* the same as Jewish law?
22. Is *aggadah* different from *halachah*?
23. Does the term *mishnah* have multiple meanings?
24. Is the Mishnah divided into five books to parallel the first five books of the Bible?
25. Is there a single Talmud?
26. Is the Talmud written in Hebrew?
27. Does page one of each Talmudic tractate summarize what it contains?
28. Are the pages of the Talmud consecutively numbered?
29. Are the interpretations of the later Rabbis more authoritative?
30. Can seemingly contradictory rabbinic interpretations both be valid?
31. Is the Midrash a collection of legends?
32. Is there more than one type of Midrash?
33. Was the *Mishneh Torah* of Maimonides universally acclaimed?
34. Was the *Shulchan Aruch* (Set Table) immediately accepted as the authoritative code of Jewish law?
35. Did major authorities support a standard code of Jewish law?
36. Did the second-century sage Shimon bar Yochai write the *Zohar*?
37. Was the Bible the first book printed in Hebrew?
38. Was "Rashi script" developed by the famous eleventh-century commentator on the Talmud and Bible?
39. Is a yeshivah the same as a *kolel*?
40. Are Jewish studies limited to the Bible and its commentaries?
41. Was the study of Hebrew ever mandatory in American colleges?
42. Over the past century, has there been a shift in the type of academic institutions in the United States engaged in Jewish studies?

Does the word "Torah" mean the first five books of the Bible? (N)

For most Jews, the word "Torah" refers to the first five books of the Bible, or to the scroll read in the synagogue on which these books are contained. The Torah narrative begins with the story of Creation and ends with the death of Moses, as the Israelites are poised to cross the Jordan River into the Promised Land. Interspersed with the ancient historical narrative of the Jewish people are the 613 Divine commandments. In the Torah, the Jewish people develop from a single family into a covenantal people, committed to carrying out these commandments to fulfill the will of God.

However, "Torah" is also an inclusive term used for all of Jewish law and learning. In this expansive definition, the word can be considered as referring to: (a) the *Tanach*, the entire codified Hebrew Bible; (b) the combination of the Written Law (Bible) plus the Oral Law (which according to tradition was also conveyed to Moses at Sinai); (c) the rest of rabbinic literature, including midrash; (d) medieval commentaries on the Bible and Talmud as well as other writings of the period; and (e) everything in Jewish tradition. Thus, all of Judaism is Torah.

Do customs have legal status, and are they binding on all Jews? (N)

Local customs spontaneously developed by the people (not the rabbis), which have become standard practice over time, have been considered in Jewish law as being binding with the force of *halachah*. The expression *Minhag avoteinu, Torah hu* (the custom of our fathers is Torah) means that a community custom (*minhag*) developed by past generations has the highest authority as if it were part of the Torah. Examples of customs that the rabbis tried unsuccessfully to stop are breaking a glass at a wedding and the *Tashlich* ceremony on Rosh Hashanah in which one casts off sins into a river, both of which were accused of being mere superstitious practices.

Many of the differences between Ashkenazic and Sephardic Jews relate to different customs adopted by these two communities. For example, Sephardim have the custom of eating rice on Passover, whereas the Ashkenazic custom is to refrain from this grain. For each community, the respective customs have the force of law.

Is "Old Testament" as a term for Scriptures generally accepted by Jews? (F)

Old Testament is a Christian term that is not accepted in Jewish tradition because it expresses the belief that there is a "New Testament" that has somehow superseded the special Divine relationship with the Jewish people. It also implies that the Bible of the Jews is archaic and irrelevant.

The most frequently employed Hebrew term for the Bible is the acronym *Ta-Na-Kh* (or *Tanach*), which is derived from the initial letters of the names of its three major divisions—Torah (Five Books of Moses), *Nevi'im* (Prophets), and *Ketuvim* (Writings). In English, the Five Books of Moses are known as the Pentateuch, a Greek word meaning "the five-volume [book]." The Rabbis referred to these books as *Chamishah chumshei Torah* (lit., "The Five Fifth-Parts of the Torah"), from which derived the popular abbreviation *Chumash*.

Do the Hebrew names of the first five books of the Bible reflect their contents? (F)

The Hebrew name of each book is actually the initial or first significant word—*Bereshit* (in the beginning), *Shemot* (names), *Vayikra* (and He [God] called), *Bamidbar* (in the wilderness), and *Devarim* (words). The English names for these five books have their origins in the titles prevailing among the ancient Greek-speaking Jews, who translated the Hebrew designations in use among their coreligionists in the Land of Israel. These names are descriptive of the contents or major themes of the respective books:

- Genesis: *Sefer ha-Yetzirah* or *Sefer Beri'at ha-Olam* (Book of the Creation of the World)
- Exodus: *Sefer Yetziat Mitzrayim* (Book of the Exodus from Egypt)
- Leviticus: *Torah Kohanim* (Book of the Priestly Code)
- Numbers: *Chumash ha-Pekudim* (Book of the Census)
- Deuteronomy: *Mishneh Torah* (Repetition of the Torah)

Are the "major" prophets more important than the "minor" prophets? (F)

The three "major" classical prophets are Isaiah, Jeremiah, and Ezekiel; the 12 so-called "minor" prophets are Hosea, Joel, Amos, Obadiah, Jonah, Micah, Nahum, Habakkuk, Haggai, Zephaniah, Zechariah, and Malachi. The popular epithet "minor" is solely a quantitative connotation and is no indication of their relative importance.

Do Christian and Hebrew Bibles contain the same books? (N)

The Christian Bible derived from the "Greek Bible," which was developed by the Jews of Alexandria and the Greek-speaking Diaspora. Although containing all the books of the Hebrew Bible, it differed from the normative Hebrew canon both in the grouping and sequencing of the biblical books. The traditional Jewish Bible contains 24 books. In contrast, most Christian Bibles in English list 39 books, a number obtained by dividing Samuel, Kings, and Chronicles into two books each, separating Ezra and Nehemiah, and counting each of the 12 "minor" prophets individually (though they initially were written on a single scroll and considered as only one book). They also usually include a spectrum of books collectively known as the Apocrypha (hidden books), such as the Books of the Maccabees and the Wisdom of Ben Sira, which were not accepted into the Hebrew Bible.

Are the five books of the Writings, called *megillot* (scrolls), read in the synagogue on specific occasions? (T)

The fourth through eighth books of the Writings section are often grouped together because of the custom of reading them on festivals and fast days: The Song of Songs on Passover, Ruth on Shavuot, Lamentations on Tisha b'Av, Ecclesiastes on Sukkot, and Esther on Purim.

Were the vowels, punctuation, and musical markings for chanting the Bible written down in biblical times? (F)

Torah scrolls have always contained only the consonants of the text. The vowels, accentuation, and melody to be used when chanting the text were handed down orally to each generation. In the seventh through the tenth centuries, textual scholars known as the Masoretes (from a Hebrew root meaning "tradition" or "that which has been transmitted") determined and preserved the authentic (masoretic) text of the Torah and developed a system of vowel-points designed to ensure the correct pronunciation of the individual words. They also introduced cantillation marks (trope), which indicate the proper way of accenting the words, where sentences begin and end, and musical patterns to be used when chanting the text.

Is parallelism the essence of biblical poetry? (T)

Although having some sort of meter or rhythm, the major aspect of biblical poetry is parallelism, the division of a verse into two halves. In the most frequent variety of parallelism, the second half expresses the same ideas as the first but usually in different words that often intensify the meaning. Only in the geonic period (seventh century C.E.) did rhyme become an important feature of Hebrew poetry through the influence of Arabic verse.

Is there more than one classical way to interpret the Bible? (T)

At the end of the thirteenth century, a Bible scholar named Bachya ben Asher noted that there are four ways of interpreting Scripture, which came to be known by the acronym *pardes* (a Hebrew word meaning "orchard" or "Paradise"). This is a mnemonic for the initial letters of the following words:

Peshat: plain, literal meaning of the verse based on its intrinsic language and historical context

Remez: allegorical or symbolic meaning, which is only hinted at in the text

Drash: homiletic interpretation to uncover an ethical or moral lesson thought to be implicit in the text

Sod: secret, esoteric, or mystical interpretation, emphasized by the kabbalists

The most popular methods of exegesis are *peshat* and *drash*, since they are comprehensible to most students.

In the Bible, are there two versions of the Ten Commandments? (N)

Known as *Aseret ha-Dibrot* (lit., "Ten Words/Utterances") in Hebrew and by the Greek word Decalogue, these core moral principles, revealed to the Israelites at Mount Sinai seven weeks after the Exodus from Egypt (Exod. 20:2--14), have become the essential code of human behavior in the Western tradition. However, a second version of the Ten Commandments is found in the Book of Deuteronomy (5:6–18). Most of the differences in wording are minimal, though the second version of the Fourth Commandment requires that the Israelites "observe" rather than "remember" the Sabbath day and makes specific reference to the Exodus from Egypt rather than Creation.

Is there internal structure to the Ten Commandments? (T)

The first four commandments—I am YHVH your God; you shall have no other gods besides me (or make any graven image); you shall not take the name of YHVH in vain; remember the Sabbath day—deal with the relationship between human beings and God. The last five focus on the interactions among fellow human beings—prohibitions against murder, committing adultery, stealing, bearing false witness, and coveting. The Fifth Commandment, describing the relation of children to parents (honor your father and mother), forms a bridge between the two groups.

The first five commandments appear to be addressed specifically to the Israelites, since each contains an additional phrase that provides a reason for observing the commandment and refers to "YHVH your God." In contrast, the last five commandments, which consist entirely of prohibitions, are universal ethical requirements incumbent on all human beings (Pes. Rab. 21:99).

Are the Ten Commandments a central part of the synagogue service? (F)

Although the *kohanim* recited the Ten Commandments daily as part of the Temple service (Tam. 5:1), Israelites outside the Temple were forbidden to do so. This ruling was designed to disprove insinuations by heretical sects (including early Christians) that only the Ten Commandments and not the entire Torah were Divinely revealed at Mount Sinai (Ber. 12a). Therefore, the Ten Commandments were excluded from the liturgy and have never become part of the synagogue service. However, the congregation customarily rises when the Decalogue is read in synagogue twice each year as part of the designated weekly Torah portions, and on the festival of Shavuot commemorating the Revelation at Mount Sinai.

Is there more than one way to chant the Ten Commandments? (T)

The Ten Commandments are unique in that they have two sets of cantillations (the musical notations for reading the Torah). The so-called "upper" set, which represents the traditional manner in which Israel heard the Ten Commandments at Sinai, is used for public reading of the Decalogue in the synagogue. It treats the whole paragraph as one long verse and breaks the four "You shall nots" into individual verses. The "lower" set is used on all other occasions, such as when reading the commandments in private. It breaks the first paragraph into four verses and unites the "You shall nots" into a single verse.

Does the First Commandment describe God as the Creator of the universe? (F)

Rather than Creator of the universe, the First Commandment describes God as the Redeemer from Egypt. Ibn Ezra maintained that the Exodus from Egypt was an event that hundreds of thousands of Israelites actually witnessed (unlike the creation of the world, which occurred well before the advent of human beings), thus enabling them and subsequent generations to believe in a personal God who is involved with His people in their time of need.

Does the Sixth Commandment prohibit killing? (N)

Although often translated as "you shall not kill," the Sixth Commandment actually prohibits murder (Exod. 20:13). Jewish law recognized that there were situations in which it was required to take a human life. These included the obligatory war, the infliction of capital punishment based on judicial decree, and the requirement to kill a pursuer (*rodef*) if there was no other way to save the person being pursued.

Did the Rabbis consider as murder any actions not resulting in death? (T)

The Rabbis extended this commandment by describing many things as "equivalent to murder," such as shaming a fellow human being in public, failing to provide food and safety for travelers, causing loss of livelihood, withholding charity from the poor, slander, and character assassination.

Does the Eighth Commandment apply to stealing money or other valuables? (N)

Although this is the usual interpretation, the Talmud argues that the Eighth Commandment also includes a special type of thief—a kidnapper who forced his victim to work for him and then sold him into slavery. Because the two prohibitions in the Ten Commandments that precede it are against the capital offenses of murder and adultery, the Rabbis reasoned that "you shall not steal" must refer to kidnapping, the only theft for which the perpetrator was liable for the death penalty. [1]

Were the two sets of the Tablets of the Covenant (*luchot ha-brit*) the same? (N)

Grieved over the blasphemy of the Golden Calf, Moses smashed the first pair of tablets containing the Ten Commandments (Exod. 32:19; Deut. 9:17). After Moses pleaded with God to forgive the people, a second set of tablets was written. Although the text was identical, there was one important difference. The first set of tablets was engraved "by the finger of God" (Exod. 31:18), whereas Moses himself was ordered to write the second set (Exod. 34:27–28).

According to Jewish tradition, was the Oral Law part of the Revelation at Sinai? (T)

The first verse in *Pirkei Avot* (Ethics of the Fathers) states that the Oral Law was given to Moses and subsequently transmitted faithfully by the leaders of each generation to their successors—from Moses to Joshua, and then to the elders, the prophets, the men of the Great Assembly, the leaders of the Pharisees, and eventually to the earliest Rabbis.

Is *halachah* the same as Jewish law? (N)

Literally meaning "path" (from the Hebrew verb "to go"), this all-inclusive term refers to the body of law (rules, prohibitions, requirements) and customs that govern every aspect of Jewish life and constitute the essence of Jewish religious and civil practice. In addition to the biblical commandments, *halachah* includes their application to practical situations as interpreted by the Rabbis during the Talmudic period and further developed in *responsa* by the *geonim* and their rabbinic successors. Over time, some long-standing customs in specific communities have become binding with the force of *halachah*.

Is *aggadah* different from *halachah*? (T)

Halachah is distinct from *aggadah*, the nonlegal aspects of the Talmud and Midrash. It includes statements of major moral and ethical principles often elucidated by the use of parables and anecdotes, stories about biblical heroes and the great Rabbis, and Jewish folklore. Rather than being legally binding, *aggadah* serves to explain and clarify Jewish laws and customs, enriching the ethical ideas of the Torah.

Does the term *mishnah* have multiple meanings? (T)

Coming from a Hebrew root meaning "to repeat," the word *mishnah* was originally used as a synonym for each specific *halachah* that developed from multiple sources. These included local laws and customs, historical traditions, priestly rituals, court rulings, and rabbinic pronouncements and decrees. Later, the term Mishnah was applied to the first rabbinic book, the basis for the Talmud, which was compiled in the early third century by Judah ha-Nasi (Judah the Prince). He sifted through, evaluated, and edited the vast number of legal opinions constituting the Oral Law that had been expressed over the centuries in the academies of learning, primarily in the Land of Israel.

Is the Mishnah divided into five books to parallel the first five books of the Bible? (F)

The Mishnah is divided into six "orders"—Zera'im (seeds), Mo'ed (festivals), Nashim (women), Nezikin (damages), Kodashim (holy things), and Tohorot (purities). Each order is divided into various numbers of *massechot* (tractates).

Is there a single Talmud? (N)

Although in general use the term "Talmud" refers to the Babylonian Talmud, there is also a smaller Jerusalem (Palestinian) Talmud.

The Babylonian Talmud (*Talmud Bavli*) is a compendium of the extensive discussions and interpretations of the Mishnah in the great academies of learning by scholars known as *amoraim* (Aramaic for "explainers") from the first half of the third century C.E. to its editing around 500. The final editing was probably completed by the middle of the sixth century by the *Savoraim*, the disciples of the last *amoraim* and their immediate successors. The Babylonian Talmud is a monumental work, aptly termed the "sea of Talmud," which consists of approximately 2.5 million words on 5,894 folio pages. Far more extensive than its Jerusalem counterpart, the Babylonian Talmud is regarded as the most authoritative compilation of the Oral Law. It deals with a wide array of topics ranging from religion and ethics to politics and social problems.

The much smaller Jerusalem Talmud was actually produced in Galilee and completed in the early fifth century by *amoraim* in the Land of Israel. Unlike the numerous tangents and extraneous material in the Babylonian Talmud, which frequently delves into topics in great depth, the discussions in the Jerusalem Talmud are shorter and to the point. The Jerusalem Talmud is primarily concerned with mishnaic interpretation and contains much less aggadic material, reflecting the fact that in the Land of Israel the aggadic element was assembled in special collections, out of which later evolved the Midrash.

Is the Talmud written in Hebrew? (N)

Aramaic is the primary language of the Talmud, the vernacular of the time. The Babylonian Talmud contains a substantial number of words in Hebrew, whereas the Jerusalem Talmud contains words from the Greek dialect prevalent at that time in the Land of Israel. The Mishnah, which is printed in the Talmud and on which its discussions are based, was written in Hebrew.

Does page one of each Talmudic tractate summarize what it contains? (F)

Surprisingly, no Talmudic tractate has a page one. A homiletic explanation for starting each tractate on page two is that the prospective student immediately realizes it is impossible to know everything. A more practical reason is that this reflected the custom of early printers, who devoted page one to a highly decorated title page at the beginning of each volume and routinely began the text with page two.

Are the pages of the Talmud consecutively numbered? (N)

Pages in classic Hebrew books, like the Talmud, are numbered in "leaves" rather than "pages." Therefore, each numbered page has "a" and "b" sides, and this information must be included whenever a reference is made to a Talmudic source.

Are the interpretations of the later Rabbis more authoritative? (N)

The relative standing and authority of earlier and later Rabbis is highly controversial. The Talmud stresses that the worthiness of the generations had decreased as they became further removed in time from Sinai: "If the early authorities were as angels, we are as men; and if they were as men, we are as donkeys" (Shab. 112b). The later geonic literature challenged this view, emphasizing the halachic rule that "the law is in accordance with the later authorities." They argued that this was either because those who came later were "more painstaking in clarifying the *halachah*" or because they had already taken into account the reasoning of their predecessors, as in the well-known proverb, like "a dwarf sitting on the back of a giant."

Can seemingly contradictory rabbinic interpretations both be valid? (T)

Eilu v'eilu is a Talmudic term that is short for *eilu v'eilu, divrei Elohim hayim*, which literally means "these and these are both words of the Living God" (Er. 13b). According to Jewish thought, a search for "truth" requires that an issue be viewed from all sides, rather than by a dry analysis of restrictive definitions. Unlike Greek thought, which tries to arrive at a final answer by means of a priori proof through deductive logic, the Talmud starts with the premise that it is necessary to investigate all arguments (measures of truths) through open investigation—not coming to a final conclusion, but instead exploring all aspects of the issue. Frequently, two opposite views (*eilu v'eilu*) are presented as "words of the Living God" because Divine truth may reside in multiple opinions. Discussions often end with *teiku* (lit., "it remains standing," meaning that we await the final answer). Thus, in analyzing a biblical or mishnaic text, the goal is not to attain the absolute truth, but rather to understand its various meanings; not to freeze the biblical text as a conclusion, but to open it to many interpretations.

Is the Midrash a collection of legends? (N)

Although it does contain legends and folk tales, Midrash (derived from a Hebrew root meaning "to search out") is a genre of rabbinic literature that fills in the gaps of the terse biblical narrative. As an ancient document, the Bible reflects its time of origin, the world of the early history of Israel. By the time of the Rabbis, the social and political situation had dramatically changed and was heavily influenced by Hellenic culture. The Midrash permitted the Rabbis to reread the biblical text according to the values and beliefs of their own era, rendering it more meaningful to contemporary readers.

Is there more than one type of Midrash? (T)

There are several ways to categorize Midrash. Halachic Midrash clarifies and details the particular requirements of biblical laws. For example, it helps one to understand what it means to "love your neighbor" (Lev. 19:18) and how to observe the Sabbath (listing the 39 activities that constituting forbidden "work"). Midrash is also the source for requiring separate dishes for meat and milk, derived from the three identical biblical verses stating that one should "not boil a kid in its mother's milk" (Exod. 23:19; 34:26; Deut. 14:21). The more common aggadic Midrash contains stories and legends that are concerned with the ethical teachings and other topical issues of the nonlegal parts of the Bible.

Homiletic Midrash is structured around sermons expounding verses from the weekly Torah portion or the readings for special Sabbaths and festivals by bringing in verses from elsewhere in the Bible. Rather than explicating the biblical text in an orderly manner, narrative Midrash contains stories and legends about individual Rabbis or biblical characters.

Was the *Mishneh Torah* of Maimonides universally acclaimed? (F)

In his massive 14-volume code of law, Maimonides discussed every conceivable topic of Jewish law in an immensely logical sequence. He collected and digested all Talmudic sources relevant to any given subject and then wrote down a simple statement of the law in the clearest possible language, without any summary of the ancient discussions. Maimonides wrote that the purpose of his code was to make the study of the Talmud unnecessary for those who merely wanted to know the law and how to live as observant Jews. For using this approach, Maimonides was condemned and denounced by many rabbis as a threat to traditional Judaism. Moreover, by making categorical decisions without listing the Talmudic discussions on which they were derived, Maimonides was accused of eliminating minority opinions that otherwise would have provided a basis for future scholars to interpret the law in different ways.

Was the *Shulchan Aruch* (Set Table) immediately accepted as the authoritative code of Jewish law? (F)

Compiled by Joseph Caro in the sixteenth century, the *Shulchan Aruch* is the most influential code of law in modern Jewish life and the last comprehensive one to be written. However, this major code of Jewish law reflected the Sephardic background of the author and was initially not accepted as authoritative by Ashkenazim, since it completely ignored the halachic decisions and customs among the Jews of Germany and Poland. The *Shulchan Aruch* gained universal acceptance through the work of Moses Isserles, a renowned mid-sixteenth century Polish rabbi known as the Rema, who wrote a "Tablecloth" (*Mapah*) for the Set Table that included the distinctive customs of the Jews of Eastern Europe. This composite work has become the functioning code for observant Jews to the present day.[2]

Did major authorities support a standard code of Jewish law? (N)

Some prominent rabbis have voiced strenuous opposition to any code that purported to lay down a definitive version of Jewish law. Although establishing a single objective and authoritative standard of the final halachic position on a given issue can clarify Jewish practice for the masses, codes have some serious inherent problems. Each law code represents the view of a single author and threatens to make it the norm, even though there are equally authoritative precedents on many halachic issues. Moreover, most codes do not document the underlying reasoning process or mention other valid alternatives, and the author often selects a view with a minority (or even no) precedent. Of even more concern is that the historical and social conditions prevalent at the time of the codifier might automatically become the basis for halachic decisions at all later times and places, when conditions are substantially different. Codes tend to freeze Jewish law, preventing the natural organic process of legal development and impeding responses to major societal issues. For example, many women are distressed by the insensitivity of the Orthodox establishment to legitimate concerns of women regarding their role in Jewish practice and the devastating plight of the *agunot*. Consequently, many traditional Jewish authorities consider even the most famous law codes to be only guides, and not binding.

Did the second-century sage Shimon bar Yochai write the *Zohar*? (N)

Known as the "Book of Splendor," the *Zohar* is the principal kabbalistic book and the basis for all subsequent Jewish mystical works. Its central tenet is that human actions such as good deeds, prayer, and mystical meditation can impact the Divine world, thus promoting a harmonious union between the "upper" and "lower" spheres that increases the flow of Divine energy to the human world. Conversely, sinful and unrighteous behavior impedes this life-giving flow. According to tradition, this immense mystical commentary on the Pentateuch and parts of the Writings, written in both Hebrew and Aramaic and consisting of some 20 separate treatises, is attributed to the second-century rabbinic authority Shimon bar Yochai and his colleagues and disciples. However, most scholars now attribute the *Zohar* to Moses de León, who lived in the late thirteenth century.

Was the Bible the first book printed in Hebrew? (F)

The first Hebrew books—Rashi's commentary on the Pentateuch and Jacob ben Asher's *Arba'ah Turim*—appeared in 1475, within 20 years after the invention of printing.

Was "Rashi script" developed by the famous eleventh-century commentator on the Talmud and Bible? (F)

Rashi script is the term for the semi-cursive form of Hebrew writing used for printing the biblical and Talmudic commentaries of Rashi. His clear and explicit explanations, incorporating both literal and midrashic interpretations, have become the standard guide for every Bible student. However, this script was not used by the preeminent sage himself. Instead, it was developed by Daniel Bomberg, a fifteenth-century Christian printer from Venice, to distinguish Rashi's commentaries from the actual text of the Bible and Talmud. It was used in the first printed Hebrew book, a Bible with Rashi's commentary.

Is a yeshivah the same as a *kolel*? (N)

Derived from a Hebrew root meaning "to sit" and literally an "academy," a yeshivah is a Jewish school or seminary of higher learning where students intensively study Torah, Talmud, and rabbinic literature. A *kolel* is a similar institute of advanced Talmudic studies for married students, whereas the term *yeshivah* has traditionally been applied to academies for students who are not married.

Are Jewish studies limited to the Bible and its commentaries? (N)

Traditionally based in *yeshivot*, for centuries Jewish studies referred predominantly to analysis of codes and Talmudic precedents as preparation for rabbinic ordination. In early America, the Bible was an important area of study in Christian denominational colleges (especially Ivy League schools). Modern Jewish studies have been profoundly influenced by the "science of Judaism" (*Wissenschaft des Judentums*), which utilized critical methods and such scholarly tools as demography and social and economic history. Today, the field of Jewish studies has greatly expanded to include such areas as Jewish history and literature, religious studies, Near Eastern languages, and Jewish arts.

Was the study of Hebrew ever mandatory in American colleges? (T)

In early America, the study of Hebrew was mandatory in some colleges, especially Ivy League colleges. This reflected the idea that to be a cultured person, one needed to learn the major classical languages (Latin, Greek, and Hebrew). Moreover, knowing biblical Hebrew increased one's ability to understand the Hebrew Bible, which was considered the basis for understanding Christianity.

Over the past century, has there been a shift in the type of academic institutions in the United States engaged in Jewish studies? (T)

In the first half of the twentieth century, Jewish studies in the United States were confined primarily to such Jewish institutions as rabbinical seminaries and Hebrew colleges. With the rise of "ethnic studies" in the 1970s, Jewish studies became recognized as an academic field of interest in major American universities.

NOTES

1. *Stone Chumash*, 412.
2. Holtz, 161–62.

Chapter Three

History

Have you ever wondered . . .

1. Was Aramaic a language spoken by the Israelites at the time of King David?
2. After the Exodus, did Jews return to Egypt during the Persian period?
3. Was there always a single head of the Jewish community in Babylonia from the sixth to eleventh centuries C.E.?
4. Was Judah, the son of Mattathias of Modi'in, given the name "Maccabee" as a testament to his great strength?
5. Is the Western Wall (*Kotel ha-Ma'arivi*) the only remaining portion of the Second Temple?
6. Was the Sanhedrin and Jewish learning saved from destruction by a clever ruse when Jerusalem fell to the Romans in 70 C.E.?
7. Did most of a Turkish tribe ever convert to Judaism?
8. Was the experience of the Khazar conversion the subject of a modern novel?
9. Did a Jew ever lead one Arab army against another?
10. Can old religious books and articles be simply thrown away?
11. Were Ashkenazic Jews in the Middle Ages and early modern period organized under a quasi-governmental authority?
12. In the *kehilla*, was there an opportunity for upward social and economic mobility?
13. Is "Marranos" the preferred name for Spanish Jews who were forcibly converted to Christianity but continued to practice their Judaism in secret?
14. Did Jews enthusiastically welcome the Enlightenment?
15. Did Napoleon attempt to revive the Sanhedrin in France?

16. Did the Reform movement advocate small changes in traditional *halachah*?
17. Did the Reform movement reject the concept of Jews being in exile?
18. Was Modern Orthodoxy a reaction to the concepts of the Enlightenment?
19. Was the Baal Shem Tov a religious scholar?
20. Has Hasidism had a revival in the last 50 years?
21. Was Hasidism accepted by the traditional Jewish community?
22. Is anti-Semitism an ancient term for hatred of the Jews?
23. Did the Dreyfus Affair play a major role in the development of political Zionism?
24. Was Zionism a unified movement?
25. Was the establishment of the Pale of Settlement initially motivated by economics?
26. Did the Nazis develop the earliest Jewish ghettos?
27. Did all sides accept the United Nations Partition of 1947 that divided Mandatory Palestine into Arab and Jewish states?
28. Soon after the War of Independence in Israel, did Jews take up arms against other Jews?

Was Aramaic a language spoken by the Israelites at the time of King David? (F)

Aramaic is an ancient Semitic tongue that was the official language of the Persian Empire. It became the vernacular of the Israelites who were exiled to Babylonia after the destruction of Jerusalem in 586 B.C.E.—about 400 years after King David ruled in the Land of Israel. During the Second Temple period, Aramaic replaced Hebrew as the medium of everyday speech. Aramaic also is the primary language of both the Jerusalem and Babylonian Talmuds (except for the Mishnah, which is in Hebrew), the Midrash, and the authorized translation of the Bible known as Targum Onkelos.

After the Exodus, did Jews return to Egypt during the Persian period? (T)

During the Persian occupation of Egypt, a military garrison of Jewish soldiers was stationed in Elephantine, an island in the middle of the Nile River. The Elephantine papyri—a collection of legal documents and letters written in Aramaic and dealing with such material as marriage and divorce, commerce, and inheritance—document this flourishing community, which maintained its own temple. Even after the expulsion of the Persians from Egypt, the Jewish garrison continued to serve on Egypt's southern frontier.

Was there always a single head of the Jewish community in Babylonia from the sixth to eleventh centuries C.E.? (F)

For centuries, this center of Jewish life had separate political and religious leaders. The exilarch was the political head of the Jewish community. Known in Aramaic as *Resh Galuta* (head of the exile), the office was hereditary, with the holder traditionally being a member of the House of David who wielded considerable power. Recognized by the established royal court, the exilarch was the chief tax collector among the Jews, appointed judges, and oversaw the criminal justice system in his community. The g*eonim* were the heads of the academies of Sura and Pumbedita. Known for their scholarship and wisdom, the *geonim* were considered the intellectual leaders of the entire Diaspora, and their decisions in all religious matters had absolute legal validity in most Jewish communities. Similar weight was given to their *responsa*, replies to written questions sent to them from all parts of Babylonia and throughout the world.

Was Judah, the son of Mattathias of Modi'in, given the name "Maccabee" as a testament to his great strength? (N)

After the death of his father, who initiated the successful guerilla war against the Syrian-Greeks that is celebrated in the festival of Chanukah, Judah assumed leadership of the band. He waged a brave and brilliant campaign that eventually led to the defeat of the forces of Antiochus Epiphanes, the liberation of Jerusalem, and the rededication of the Temple (165 B.C.E.). The name "Maccabee" is derived from the Hebrew word *makav* (hammer), and thus may have been a testament to his great strength. Another explanation is that Maccabee is an acrostic for the first letters of the Hebrew words *Mi chamocha ba'elim Adonai* ("Who is like You, O Lord, among the mighty"; Exod. 15:11), which is recited daily before the morning and evening *Amidah* and as part of the Song at the Sea (*Shirat ha-Yam*).

Is the Western Wall (*Kotel ha-Ma'arivi*) the only remaining portion of the Second Temple? (F)

Popularly known as the *Kotel*, the Western Wall is part of the Herodian retaining wall surrounding and supporting the Temple Mount, rather than a part of the Temple itself. It was formerly called the Wailing Wall by European observers, because for centuries Jews came here to bewail the loss of their Temple. The holiest of Jewish sites, the Western Wall is a major venue for prayers day and night. Many place private petitions on bits of paper stuffed into the cracks of the massive stone blocks.

Was the Sanhedrin and Jewish learning saved from destruction by a clever ruse when Jerusalem fell to the Romans in 70 C.E.? (T)

According to legend, during the Roman siege of Jerusalem, Yochanan ben Zakkai summoned his nephew, Abba Sikra (a zealot leader), and asked how long he would allow the people of Jerusalem to die of hunger before he would surrender to the Romans. Abba Sikra replied that even suggesting peace to his fellow zealots would result in his death. When Yochanan ben Zakkai asked how he might leave the city to save himself and others, the two devised a plot. Pretending to be dead, Yochanan ben Zakkai escaped from the city in a coffin carried by trusted disciples, since the Romans respected the Jewish law that did not permit a body in the city of Jerusalem to remain unburied overnight. Making his way to the camp of the Roman general Vespasian, Yochanan ben Zakkai predicted that Vespasian would soon become Emperor of Rome. When this transpired, Vespasian granted Yochanan ben Zakkai's request for permission to gather a small community of sages and organize a school at Yavneh. The Sanhedrin was reestablished, with Yochanan Ben Zakkai as its head, and Yavneh remained the seat of Jewish scholarship and culture until the Bar Kochba revolt (132–135 C.E.).

Did most of a Turkish tribe ever convert to Judaism? (T)

At some point during the eighth century, the royalty and nobility of the Khazars, a semi-nomadic Turkish tribe from Central Asia, converted to Judaism. Part of the general population followed, and Judaism became the state religion. The power of the Khazars declined in the tenth and eleventh centuries, and they disappeared from history following the Mongol invasion of 1237.

Was the experience of the Khazar conversion the subject of a modern novel? (F)

Judah Halevi, a famed Spanish poet, philosopher, and physician, wrote *The Kuzari* in the early twelfth century. Officially known as the *Book of Refutation and Proof on Behalf of the Despised Religion*, this philosophical work depicts an imaginary discussion at the court of the Khazar king, who had a dream in which an angel appeared and said, "Your intention is pleasing to God, but your actions are not pleasing." Although the king responded with a sincere increased diligence in pursuing the established forms of Khazar worship, the dream with its disturbing message continually recurred. This prompted the king to examine other religions and sects to discover which encompassed actions that were most pleasing to the Divine. Convinced of the inadequacy of philosophy and the superiority of revelation, the king investigated Christianity and Islam, but both of these faiths claimed that their religion was the culmination of a prophetic tradition dating back to the experiences of biblical Israel. Ultimately, the king spoke to a Jewish sage, who explained that the special relationship between God and the Jews resulted not from one revelation to a single person but to the 600,000 Israelites who came out of Egypt, as well as from a series of miraculous events occurring over the lifetimes of an entire people. Convinced by the sage's description of these unique aspects of his faith, the Khazar king and his people converted to Judaism.

Did a Jew ever lead one Arab army against another? (T)

During the Middle Ages, *nagid* (prince) was the name for the head of the Jewish community in Islamic countries. The most famous was Shmuel ha-Nagid (993–ca. 1055), vizier of Granada, statesman, poet, and scholar. His meteoric rise and political and military career mark the highest achievement of a Jew in medieval Muslim Spain. Ironically, much of his work as vizier involved leading the army of Granada, which was constantly at war with Seville, which was also controlled by Muslims.

Can old religious books and articles be simply thrown away? (F)

Torn prayer books, Bibles, and other holy texts, as well as religious articles such as *tefillin* and *tzitzit* that have deteriorated and can no longer be used, must be disposed of in a way that shows respect for the name of God contained within them. An ancient tradition is to place these items in a special storeroom in a synagogue called a *genizah* (lit., "hidden away"). The contents of the *genizah* are removed periodically and reverently buried in the cemetery. The most famous *genizah* was in Cairo, which also held a wide variety of "secular" documents that revealed otherwise unknown aspects of the economic, social, and family life of Jews in medieval Egypt.

Were Ashkenazic Jews in the Middle Ages and early modern period organized under a quasi-governmental authority? (T)

The *kehilla* was a community structure, developed in the Middle Ages, which was based strictly on "tradition" (i.e., Torah as interpreted by the rabbis). The *kehilla* was a paradigmatic insular community that had minimal interaction with the outside world, except for the *stadlan*, who served as the official "ambassador" to the non-Jewish population. Granted a charter by the civil authorities, the *kehilla* was responsible for keeping order and providing taxes through its officials and the regulations they imposed. It had the power to impose *cherem* (shunning), which would subject an offender and his family to economic and social isolation as punishment for refusing to obey rabbinic authority. With the development of nation-states and Jews becoming subject to their laws, the *kehilla* was no longer granted autonomy within the larger community and thus lost its civil authority and its reason for existence.

In the *kehilla*, was there an opportunity for upward social and economic mobility? (N)

The *kehilla* was a tightly stratified society, with each person having a predefined role that prevented all possibilities for upward social and economic mobility. The sole exception was rabbinic scholarship, which allowed a poor but intelligent boy to be ordained as a rabbi and marry into the leadership of the community.

Is "Marranos" the preferred name for Spanish Jews who were forcibly converted to Christianity but continued to practice their Judaism in secret? (F)

During the late Middle Ages, tens of thousands of Jews and their descendants in Spain and Portugal were forcibly converted to Christianity but continued to practice their Judaism in secret. Those "crypto-Jews" who were caught by the Inquisition, the church body charged with uprooting heresy, were ruthlessly tortured and burned at the stake in a ceremony known as the *auto-da-fé*. Because *Marranos* stems from a Spanish word meaning "swine," *Conversos* is much preferred to the other disparaging term.

Did Jews enthusiastically welcome the Enlightenment? (N)

The Enlightenment was an era of great social and cultural changes that began in Western Europe in the late seventeenth century. An age of rationalism and unparalleled scientific achievement, the Enlightenment led philosophers in England and France to question the existing order dominated by the church, the state, and the privileged aristocracy. It introduced new concepts of freedom, natural human rights, religious tolerance, equality, and reliance on reason rather than tradition. Jewish proponents of this movement (*maskilim*) welcomed this opportunity to explore the language, manners, and culture of their Gentile neighbors and immerse themselves in secular knowledge. However, others challenged this belief, attacking it as a threat to Jewish traditions and institutions. Indeed, acceptance of Enlightenment thinking did result in widespread assimilation in Western and Central Europe. Many Jews, deciding that the opening of new opportunities required them to renounce their Judaism, became baptized as Christians, considering this their ticket to societal advancement in the arts and the professions. In Eastern Europe, the Enlightenment aided the rise of the Zionist and Jewish socialist movements.

Did Napoleon attempt to revive the Sanhedrin in France? (N)

In an attempt to integrate French Jews into society, Napoleon convened an Assembly of Jewish Notables (July 26, 1806 to April 6, 1807) to "revive among Jews the civil morality weakened during their long debasement." In a speech to the assembly, Napoleon attacked the Jews as "a nation within a nation" that must be reformed so that Jews would become "loyal French citizens of the Mosaic faith." Twelve questions were posed to the delegates, the responses to which emphasized the loyalty and patriotism of French Jews. To confer legitimacy on the responses, Napoleon convened a largely rabbinic French Sanhedrin of 71 members—a mere caricature of the supreme judicial, religious, and political body in the Land of Israel during the Roman and Byzantine periods—to translate the resolutions passed by the Assembly of Jewish Notables into Jewish religious imperatives that would cause the Jews to "look upon France as their Jerusalem." Despite the goodwill exhibited by the Sanhedrin, Napoleon passed discriminatory legislation against the Jews, thereby betraying the hopes of the Sanhedrin that their responses would lead to religious equality, which was only attained in 1830 under King Louis Philippe.

Did the Reform movement advocate small changes in traditional *halachah*? (F)

The Reform movement, which developed in nineteenth-century Germany and was rooted in the Enlightenment era and the age of political emancipation, rejected the authority of *halachah*. It championed the idea of personal autonomy in deciding which religious observances to follow, thus maintaining the right to modify Jewish traditions to increase their contemporary relevance. It developed the concept of "ethical monotheism" based on the moral and ethical teachings of the Hebrew prophets, emphasized *tikun olam* (repairing the world) as the dominant means of service to God, and deemphasized the ritual aspects of Judaism. Reform dramatically shortened the worship service and introduced the use of the organ, prayers, and a sermon in the vernacular, and the confirmation ceremony.

Did the Reform movement reject the concept of Jews being in exile? (T)

Rather than the classical rabbinic teaching that the Jews were in exile, the Reform movement argued that the dispersion of Jews to be a "light among the nations" was necessary for them to fulfill their messianic duty of spreading the teachings of ethical monotheism. Indeed, the houses of worship of Reform Jews were often called "Temples," indicating their utter rejection of the hope for a return to the Land of Israel and rebuilding the Temple in Jerusalem.

Was Modern Orthodoxy a reaction to the concepts of the Enlightenment? (N)

The Modern Orthodox movement, founded in the late nineteenth century by Samson Raphael Hirsch, was at its core a reaction to the Reform movement. It attempted to harmonize traditional observance (*halachah*) and values with the secular modern world. This philosophy has been termed *Torah im derech eretz* (Torah with the way of the Land). As opposed to the ultra-Orthodox, the goal of Modern Orthodoxy is to develop Torah-observant Jews who are nevertheless comfortable participating and contributing to modern society.

Was the Baal Shem Tov a religious scholar? (F)

The charismatic founder of the mystical religious movement known as Hasidism in eighteenth-century Poland, the Baal Shem Tov (lit., "master of the good name" or "miracle worker") found his religious feelings within the marvels of the natural world, which he perceived as physical manifestations of the all-pervasive Divine spirit. The Baal Shem Tov stressed devotion to

God through song, music, and dance. He taught that joyful, enthusiastic, and sincere worship, even that of an unlearned person, finds more favor in the eyes of God than elite scholarship and knowledge of the Law.

Has Hasidism had a revival in the last 50 years? (T)

With an increased emphasis on study and halachic observance, Hasidism has enjoyed renewed popularity. Lubavitch Hasidism (Chabad), inspired by Menachem Mendel Schneerson, has become an international movement. Today, the ultra-Orthodox Hasidim are distinguished by their modest dress, exuberant worship, and devotion to a leader known as a *tzadik* or *rebbe*.

Was Hasidism accepted by the traditional Jewish community? (F)

The Hasidic emphasis on simple piety and emotions rather than traditional scholarship, as well as giving Kabbalah precedence over halachic studies, incited strenuous objections from the Vilna Gaon, the major figure of the *mitnagdim* (lit., "those opposed [to Hasidism]"). He strenuously objected to the singing of wordless melodies (*nigunim*) in prayer services and the seemingly excessive veneration of their leaders. The Vilna Gaon and other *mitnagdim* stressed the strict observance of all the details and minutiae of *halachah*, convinced that the undermining of a single precept of the Written or Oral Law was a blow to the foundations of the Torah as a whole. The *mitnagdim* issued several bans of excommunication against the Hasidim.

Is anti-Semitism an ancient term for hatred of the Jews? (F)

Although the concept of hatred of the Jews has existed for more than 2,000 years, as exemplified by Haman in the Book of Esther and then by the Catholic Church ever since it rose to power in the Roman Empire during the reign of Constantine (early fourth century), the term "anti-Semitism" was coined in Germany in 1879 in a pamphlet by William Marr, who preached a "racial scientific" rather than religious anti-Semitism. In the Middle Ages, anti-Semitism led to discrimination, persecution, forced conversion, and expulsion. In its most virulent form in Nazi Germany, anti-Semitism began with degrading the Jews by removing their civil, political, social, economic, and religious rights, before eventually murdering them.

Did the Dreyfus Affair play a major role in the development of political Zionism? (T)

The trial and subsequent attempts at exoneration of Alfred Dreyfus, a Jewish officer on the General Staff of France accused of treason, developed into a political event that had repercussions throughout France and the Jewish world. The son of a wealthy, assimilated family, in 1894 Dreyfus was falsely accused and found guilty of writing documents divulging French military secrets to Germany and sentenced to life imprisonment on Devil's Island. The Dreyfus affair increasingly developed into a cause célèbre involving all strata of French society. Those on the political right generally believed in Dreyfus's guilt, while most on the left considered him innocent. More than a decade later, Dreyfus was cleared of all charges, restored to the army, raised to the rank of major, and decorated with the Legion of Honor.

Jews everywhere were shocked that the affair could take place in liberal France, and that so many of its citizens harbored such virulent hatred toward them. The Jewish victim in this case was completely assimilated, seeming to prove clearly that this was no defense against anti-Semitism. Covering the Dreyfus trial for an Austrian newspaper was the equally assimilated Theodor Herzl. This shocking experience led Herzl to embrace Zionism and devote his life to the political establishment of a Jewish state.

Was Zionism a unified movement? (F)

There were multiple, often incompatible, approaches to Zionism. The *political* Zionists, led by Theodor Herzl, concentrated all efforts on securing a charter to establish a Jewish state in Palestine. They were convinced that the practical work of mass settlement would come once legal guarantees had been achieved through the support of a major world power. The *cultural* Zionists, championed by Ahad Ha-Am, advocated restoration of the Land of Israel as a cultural and spiritual center, imbued with the ideals of the Hebrew prophets, which would serve and inspire the entire Jewish people both in the national homeland and throughout the Diaspora. For *labor* Zionists, neither political nor cultural Zionism seemed to be a realistic alternative, especially since they did not address the urgent need to appeal to the increasing number of young Jews who were joining the growing socialist and communist movements in Eastern Europe. To meet this challenge, labor Zionism emerged as the dominant activist force, setting up a host of settlements on a communal basis, with thousands of workers tilling the land and building a national infrastructure. Almost exclusively secular, labor Zionism saw itself as a revolutionary movement that would not only change the situation of the land, but also transform the traditional Jewish social and economic structure and the character of the entire Jewish people. The *practical* Zionists (Lovers of Zion) stressed settlement in Palestine, convinced that the presence of a large number of Jews in the land would give greater weight to the political efforts of the movement. The *religious* Zionists, under the leadership of Abraham Isaac Kook, the first Ashkenazic Chief Rabbi of Palestine, wanted to build the land according to the Torah and tradition, unlike the secular pioneers who regarded religion as obsolete and adherence to the *mitzvot* as an obstacle to building the land according to socialist principles. Finally, the *revisionist* Zionists represented a political movement that was both anti-socialist and militantly nationalistic. It criticized the official Zionist policy as too conciliatory toward Britain, and advocated the speedy creation of a Jewish state on both sides of the Jordan River.

Was the establishment of the Pale of Settlement initially motivated by economics? (T)

The Pale of Settlement was the name for an area within the borders of the czarist Russian Empire where Jews were officially permitted to live. It included territory of present-day Latvia, Lithuania, Ukraine, Moldova, Belarus, and Poland. The Pale of Settlement was established by Catherine the Great in 1791, in response to pressure to rid Moscow of Jewish business competition and their "evil influence" on the susceptible Russian masses. Subsequent czars reduced the area of the Pale (only 4 percent of imperial Russia), where more than 90 percent of the Jews of the Russian Empire were forced to live in poverty in what was effectively a large-scale ghetto.

Did the Nazis develop the earliest Jewish ghettos? (F)

The ghetto was a compulsory residential quarter of a city or town, generally walled, where Jews were required to live. The term derives from the foundry (*geto*) section in Venice into which Jews were segregated about 1516. During the sixteenth and seventeenth centuries, ghettos were established throughout Central and Southern Europe. Although Jews in ghettos enjoyed some autonomy, were free to practice their religion, and enjoyed a strong sense of community, the physical barriers separating them from the rest of the population seriously limited their educational, economic, and political opportunities. Moreover, as the ghettos became increasingly overcrowded and Christian rulers imposed heavier taxes, the Jews were reduced to desperate poverty. Ghettos largely disappeared as Jews were steadily emancipated in the nineteenth century, but were reimposed in some towns and cities (such as Warsaw) under Nazi rule.

Did all sides accept the United Nations Partition of 1947 that divided Mandatory Palestine into Arab and Jewish states? (F)

After the British formally announced the decision to relinquish their Mandate over Palestine, a United Nations Committee of Inquiry recommended partitioning the country into separate Arab and Jewish states, with Jerusalem to be governed by an international authority. On November 29, 1947, a majority of UN members voted to approve this compromise solution. This was accepted by the *yishuv* (government of the Jews of Palestine before the establishment of the State of Israel), but rejected by the Arabs of Palestine and surrounding Arab states.

Soon after the War of Independence in Israel, did Jews take up arms against other Jews? (T)

The focus of this tragic episode was the *Altalena*, a cargo ship carrying munitions and fighters for the paramilitary Irgun, which anchored off the coast of Israel in June 1948, just after the beginning of the War of Independence. The Haganah, by then the official army of the State of Israel, refused to allow the *Altalena* to land and unload its cargo because of the fear that the Irgun would start a revolt to topple the provisional government. After fruitless negotiations, David Ben Gurion ordered the Haganah to sink the ship. For decades, the *Altalena* affair remained a major source of bitter controversy in Israeli political discourse. Proponents of Ben Gurion's actions praised them as essential in establishing the government's authority and discouraging factionalism and the formation of a rival army. Opponents, led by Menachem Begin, condemned the unnecessary violence and claimed that opportunities for a peaceful resolution were intentionally frustrated by Ben Gurion and top Haganah officers.

Chapter Four

Theology

Have you ever wondered . . .

1. Are the biblical statements ascribing the physical attributes of God meant literally?
2. Are Jews required to "fear" God?
3. Does the requirement to "love" God mean fulfilling the commandments?
4. Is the statement to love God the most frequent commandment in the Bible?
5. Is *Adonai* pronounced as written?
6. Is *Elohim* a plural word in Hebrew?
7. Does the word *Elohim* refer to God?
8. Are there other biblical names for God based on *El*?
9. Did the Rabbis of the Talmud develop additional names for God?
10. Is it permissible to write the Hebrew names of God?
11. Is it permitted to use the name of God other than in a religious context?
12. Is the biblical version of Creation compatible with the theory of evolution?
13. Do Jews believe that God limited Himself to allow space for the creation of the world?
14. Does Lurianic Kabbalah posit a primordial catastrophe that altered the destiny of the newly created universe?
15. In classic Jewish tradition, does *tikun olam* mean social justice?
16. Like Christianity, does Judaism have a creed?
17. Do Jews believe in a Holy Spirit?
18. Is there a Jewish view of the existence of evil?

19. Do Jews believe in "original sin"?
20. Do Jews believe in Satan?
21. Do Jews believe in Revelation?
22. Was the major role of the Hebrew prophet to predict the future?
23. Were some of the biblical prophets women?
24. Was there a standard type of sacrifice in the Temple?
25. Were there restrictions regarding what could or could not be brought with offerings?
26. Does the Bible provide specific reasons for the sacrificial system?
27. Were the motivations different for Israelite and pagan sacrifices?
28. Since the destruction of the Temple in Jerusalem, are there remnants of sacrifices in Jewish life?
29. Is there a tradition of asceticism in Judaism?
30. Do Jews believe and trust in miracles?
31. Are Jews supposed to rely on miracles?
32. Has there been a difference between "official" versus "folk" religion in Judaism?
33. Are religious controversies characteristic of the modern period?
34. Is the Jewish concept of redemption different from that of Christians?
35. Does Judaism believe in the coming of a Messiah?
36. In Judaism, is the Messiah depicted as Divine?
37. Should Jews simply wait for the coming of the Messiah?
38. With the arrival of the Messiah, will human beings no longer have to take care of the world?
39. Is there a Jewish tradition of two Messiahs, rather than only one?
40. Does the term "Armageddon" come from a Hebrew place-name?
41. Have there been "false messiahs"?
42. Does the Bible provide a description of the Messianic Age?
43. Do some modern Jews believe that there is a harbinger of the Messianic Age?
44. Does Judaism accept the idea of Messianic Jews?

Are the biblical statements ascribing the physical attributes of God meant literally? (F)

According to traditional Jewish belief, God is non-corporeal. All statements in the Bible ascribing physical attributes to God are mere metaphors attempting to describe an otherwise incomprehensible Deity. An excellent example of striking anthropomorphic metaphors that draw on biblical and midrashic sources is *An'im Zemirot* (Let me chant sweet hymns). Also known as *Shir ha-Kavod* (Song of Glory), it exalts the power and magnificence of God. It was written by Judah the Pious, a twelfth-century German mystic who was the central figure of the Hasidei Ashkenaz. In traditional Ashkenazic synagogues, *An'im Zemirot* is recited in front of the open ark at the conclusion of the *Musaf* (additional) service on the Sabbath and festivals, with a child often leading the congregational singing.

Are Jews required to "fear" God? (N)

In the verse, "You shall fear the Lord your God" (Deut. 6:13; 10:20), the phrase *yirat Hashem* is often translated as "fear" of God. Maimonides related this to the rabbinic doctrine of reward and punishment, an integral part of traditional Judaism and the 11th of his Thirteen Principles of Faith. However, this term has negative connotations, which conflict with the commandment to "love God," as expressed in the *Shema* (Deut. 6:5). Abraham Joshua Heschel preferred to translate *yirat Hashem* as "awe" (or "reverence") of God. The realization that God is the foundation of the world leads to an overwhelming sense of awe and the holiness of God. For Heschel, "awe" of God was a term almost equivalent to the English word "religion," for which there is no true Hebrew equivalent.

Does the requirement to "love" God mean fulfilling the commandments? (N)

The biblical verse, "And you shall love [*v'ahavta*] the Lord your God . . ." (Deut. 6:5), means performing God's commandments. However, this is out of pure love—an intense desire to fulfill the Divine will and the highest level in the human being's relationship with God—rather than because of fear of punishment or the inducement of a reward. People who are motivated by fear may abandon a task if it becomes too difficult to perform, whereas those who act based on love are prepared to make substantial sacrifices for the objects of their affection.[1]

Is the statement to love God the most frequent commandment in the Bible? (F)

The commandment, "You shall love the stranger (*ger*), for you were strangers in the land of Egypt," is the most frequently repeated, occurring 36 times in the Torah. This commandment required the Israelites to protect those who were born elsewhere but reside in the Land of Israel. The explicit reason for this commandment was that Jews—because of their bitter experience in Egypt, long history of persecution, and desire to remain a holy people—should be especially sensitive to the suffering of aliens and therefore obliged to love them simply because they are fellow human beings and creations of God.

Is *Adonai* pronounced as written? (F)

Adonai is the holiest and most distinctly Jewish name of God, which is written in the Hebrew Bible as the four consonants YHVH. Referred to as the Tetragrammaton, according to tradition it was regularly pronounced with the

proper vowels by all Israelites until the destruction of the First Temple in 586
B.C.E. However, its use was eventually restricted to the *Kohen Gadol* (High
Priest) in the Holy of Holies on Yom Kippur, and to other *kohanim* when
reciting the Priestly Blessing during the daily services in the Temple. When
the Second Temple was destroyed, the word lost its vocalization. By the time
of the Talmud, the term *Adonai* was generally substituted for YHVH, as is
still the custom in the standard prayer formula, "*Baruch Ata Adonai.*"

Is *Elohim* a plural word in Hebrew? (T)

Paradoxically, this second most common biblical term to designate the
One God of Israel is in the plural form, which has been interpreted to illus-
trate the idea of the innumerable examples of God's majesty and the many
facets of the Deity.

Does the word *Elohim* refer to God? (N)

Although by far the most common usage, in the Bible the word sometimes refers to princes, judges, and even pagan gods.

Are there other biblical names for God based on *El*? (T)

El is the oldest of the names of God. It is often incorporated in biblical
names as the first element (Elijah, Elisha, Elihu) or, more commonly, at the
end (Israel, Ishmael, Samuel). It also appears as the first element in compound names of the Divine, such as *El Elyon* (Most High God) and *El
Shaddai* (God Almighty).

Did the Rabbis of the Talmud develop additional names for God? (T)

The Rabbinic names for God include:

*   *Ha-Kadosh baruch hu* (the Holy One, praised be He)
*   *Ribbono shel Olam* (Sovereign of the Universe)
*   *Ha-Makom* (lit., "the place," meaning the Omnipresent)
*   *Ha-Rachaman* (the All-Merciful, from the Hebrew word *rechem* meaning
    womb)—used particularly in the Grace after Meals
*   *Avinu Malkeinu* (Our Father our King)—especially in prayers on the High
    Holy Days
*   *Avinu she-ba-Shamayim* (Our Father in Heaven)—as in the opening of the
    modern prayer for the State of Israel
*   *Melech ha-Olam* (Ruler of the Universe)—in the formula of all blessings
*   *Shechinah* (Divine Presence)—often depicted as the feminine aspect of
    God.

Is it permissible to write the Hebrew names of God? (N)

The Rabbis prohibited writing the name of God, except in sacred texts,
lest any paper on which it was casually written might later be defaced,

obliterated, or destroyed accidentally. Some very traditional Jews will not even write the English word "God," preferring instead to use the spelling "G-d."

Is it permitted to use the name of God other than in a religious context? (N)

To avoid saying the sacred name *Adonai*, itself a substitute for YHVH, Jews began using *ha-Shem* (lit., "the name"), thus emphasizing the prohibition against pronouncing the Tetragrammaton. Today, some traditional Jews use the term *Adoshem*, derived from a combination of *Adonai* and *ha-Shem*, as a substitute for speaking either of these names or, in writing, to avoid risking the erasure or defacement of God's name.

Is the biblical version of Creation compatible with the theory of evolution? (N)

According to the evolutional theory promoted by Charles Darwin, all plant and animal species have successively progressed from lower to higher forms through a struggle for survival accompanied by a series of mutations, natural selection, and survival of the fittest. Initially, traditional Judaism utterly rejected this theory as incompatible with the biblical description of God creating the world in six days (Gen. 1). However, some scholars have reconciled evolution and the account in Genesis by figuratively interpreting the six days of Creation, while others have argued that evolution is part of the Divine plan.

Do Jews believe that God limited Himself to allow space for the creation of the world? (N)

An essential concept of Kabbalah, based on the thought of famed sixteenth-century mystic Isaac Luria from Safed, is *tzimtzum* (lit., "contraction"), the self-limitation of God to provide space for the creation of a finite independent world. According to this idea, the primeval act of creation by God was the contraction, concealment, and withdrawal of the Infinite Divinity in order to allow for a "conceptual space" in which a finite, seemingly independent world could exist. Only after this act of contraction did God turn outward, sending into the primeval void created by *tzimtzum* a thread of the light of Divine Essence, from which emanated the *sefirot* (the unfolding of the Divine personality, the inner life of God).

Does Lurianic Kabbalah posit a primordial catastrophe that altered the destiny of the newly created universe? (T)

According to this stream of Jewish mysticism, the Divine light originating from *Ein Sof* (hidden aspect of the infinite God) and flowing from orifices in the head of *Adam Kadmon* (Primordial Man, symbolizing the linking of God, Man, and the world) was trapped in vessels representing the 10 *sefirot* (Divine Emanations). However, these vessels (especially the lower seven) were too weak to contain the intense light of *Ein Sof* and broke. Many of the Divine sparks fell and were trapped by the realm of darkness in shells (*klipot*) caused by sins. Therefore, the task of human beings is to perform *mitzvot* and good deeds to redeem these sparks, thus allowing the sparks to return to their original source and repair the world (*tikun olam*).

In classic Jewish tradition, does *tikun olam* mean social justice? (F)

Literally "repair of the world," *tikun olam* is a powerful mystical concept attesting to the central role of human beings, who are crucial in maintaining both the natural world and the upper Divine world of the *sefirot*. This idea reached its climax in the kabbalistic system of Isaac Luria, which posits that through good deeds and repentance, human beings are capable of assisting God by elevating the holy sparks entrapped in the *klipot* (husks) in this material world and restoring them to their original Divine source. This would mend the world, overcome evil, restore cosmic harmony, and ultimately usher in the Messianic Age, thus completing and perfecting the work of Creation. Modern liberal streams of Judaism have extended the classic definition of *tikun olam* to mean the pursuit of social justice and care for the environment, which for some congregations has become the essence of Judaism.

Like Christianity, does Judaism have a creed? (N)

Although popular in Christianity, a concise formula expressing a fundamental and authoritative system of beliefs is not a basic idea in Judaism. Judaism has never developed a single binding catechism, instead permitting a spectrum of different formulations of belief as long as they are compatible with the overall Torah system of the Written and Oral Law. Rather than expressing obedience to a creed, traditional Judaism stresses performance of *mitzvot*, so that a person is judged by actions rather than on professions of belief. During the Middle Ages, several rabbinic authorities attempted to establish a set of uniformly accepted beliefs. By far the most enduring has been the Thirteen Principles of Faith developed by Maimonides in the twelfth century.

Do Jews believe in a Holy Spirit? (N)

Unlike the Christian view of the Holy Spirit as a separate aspect of the trinity, the Hebrew term *ru'ach ha-kodesh* (translated as "holy spirit") refers to the Divine power that inspires human beings, especially in the context of the gift of inspired speech conferred on the prophets. Jewish thought links communion with the holy spirit to the striving for moral and spiritual perfection through religious study, prayer, and the performance of deeds of loving-kindness.

Is there a Jewish view of the existence of evil? (N)

The existence of evil and the problem of theodicy have been vexing theological problems throughout Jewish history. Unlike polytheistic religions, which posited separate deities for good and evil, the Bible clearly states that both were created by God, who is termed "the Former of light and the Creator of darkness, the Master of peace and Creator of evil" (Isa. 45:7). For the medieval philosophers, who tried to minimize the problem, evil did not really exist and was merely "the absence of the good." The mystics offered several explanations for evil, such as an intrinsic flaw in the work of Creation (due to the breaking of the vessels) and dilution of the Divine flow from *Ein Sof* to our world, where God's presence is represented by the *Shechinah* rather than the omnipotent Divine Being of the philosophers. Following the Holocaust, philosophers and theologians sought to grapple anew with the problem of evil. While some reformulated traditional explanations, others took a more radical course, even advancing new ideas of the nature of God.

Do Jews believe in "original sin"? (F)

After Adam and Eve ate the forbidden fruit, they were expelled from the Garden of Eden. Men were forced to work for their bread, women were fated to suffer pain in childbirth, and human beings became mortal. However, Jews reject the Christian doctrine of "original sin," which maintains that the "fall of man" caused a fundamental change in human nature, so that all Adam's descendants are born in sin and can only be redeemed by Divine grace. Instead, Jews believe in the concept of reward and punishment, which is repeatedly expressed in the Torah and rabbinic literature. This maintains that God rewards those who observe the Divine commandments and punishes those who intentionally disobey them.

Do Jews believe in Satan? (N)

Rather than a demonic creature who is the personification of evil and the enemy of God, the biblical word *satan* is merely a common noun that means "adversary," "accuser," or "hinderer." The role of Satan is to make things difficult for human beings, so that they can overcome temptations and their evil inclinations and eventually succeed in accomplishing the tasks that God has prepared for them. Thus, Satan convinces God to test the faithfulness of Job. In a Talmudic legend, it is Satan who challenged God to put Abraham to the test of the *Akedah* (binding of Isaac) to prove the patriarch's allegiance (Sanh. 89b). Nevertheless, throughout the Bible, Satan is clearly subordinate to God and unable to act without Divine permission. Only in the Talmud and Midrash does Satan emerge as a distinct entity, often called "Samael," who is identified with the *yetzer ha-ra* (the inclination toward evil) and the Angel of Death. According to the Rabbis, the purpose of the sounding of the shofar on Rosh Hashanah is "to confuse the Accuser [Satan]" (RH 16b), to prevent him from bringing any charges against the Jews before God on the Day of Judgment.

Do Jews believe in Revelation? (N)

Although the concept of revelation is a core Jewish belief, there is a broad diversity of views on the precise meaning of the term. According to the Torah, by far the most significant Divine revelation occurred when God revealed the Ten Commandments to the Israelites as they camped at the foot of Mount Sinai. At the same time, God gave Moses the Oral Law, which was handed down through the generations. According to this Orthodox view, Divine revelation ended with the death of Malachi, the last biblical prophet (fifth century B.C.E.). Consequently, the closer the proximity to the initial source of revelation (Sinai), the higher the authority.

Some Jews believe in *continuous* revelation, the theological concept that although Sinai and the prophets represented the major revelations, some important revelations have occurred after that and will always occur in the future. As Rabbi Judah Loew of Prague noted, the conclusion of both Torah blessings is in the present tense (*notein ha-Torah*), implying that the act of revelation is a continuing outpouring. This idea is generally accepted by the Conservative movement, which maintains that, since the end of the prophetic age, revelation continues through the people of Israel rather than through individuals. Thus, Zechariah Frankel stated, "Judaism is the religion of the Jews." As Orthodox scholars have observed, a potential problem is that what the Jewish people accept at a given period as the will of God may be wrong. Nevertheless, those who believe in continuous revelation see it as a Divine unfolding of God's will in human history.

Reform Judaism traditionally favored the theological concept of *progressive* revelation, which argues that not only has revelation continued to this day, but it is now of a higher quality. Thus, the greatest act of revelation was not Sinai, but will be the Messianic Age at the end of time. Since we are closer to that time and "know more," we now have higher authority and thus a higher degree of revelation. This approach is based on the Hegelian and Darwinian concept that there is inevitable progress as things evolve. Consequently, more has been revealed to those living today than to any past generation, and thus we now have more access to truth. This concept of revelation is the only one not found in classical Jewish sources, and it makes Jews vulnerable to claims by Christians, Muslims, and even Baha'i that later revelations have superseded those made to the Jews. After the Holocaust, the Reform movement abandoned a strict view of progressive revelation, since it was difficult to claim that history was indeed moving toward a better state.

Was the major role of the Hebrew prophet to predict the future? (F)

The biblical prophet was a messenger of God. Unlike the pagan prophet and diviner, who answered the inquiries of human beings and manipulated the deity on their behalf, the biblical prophet conveyed the Divine will to human beings. Even the popular prophets who were healers and wonder workers were viewed as merely performing the will of God, rather than demonstrating any inherent powers. The prophets described in vivid terms the dire consequences of failing to fulfill the Divine commandments and perpetuating injustice by neglecting the poor and the weak, permitting the greed and corruption of the wealthy and powerful, and believing that God could be satisfied by sacrifices alone. They warned the people that violating the covenant and continuing to behave in a manner unacceptable to God would inevitably lead to destruction, captivity, and exile. Indeed, the ancient Israelites did experience these cataclysmic developments at the hands of the Assyrian and Babylonian Empires. The prophets, however, balanced their message of doom with the promise of ultimate redemption and restoration, which did occur following the Babylonian Exile.

Were some of the biblical prophets women? (T)

The Bible explicitly labels four women as prophetesses—Miriam (Exod. 15:20), Deborah (Judg. 4:4), Huldah (2 Kings 22:14), and Noadiah (Neh. 6:14). Rabbinic tradition added three others—Hannah, Abigail, and Esther—and the Talmud replaced Noadiah with Sarah in its list of the seven prophetesses.

Was there a standard type of sacrifice in the Temple? (F)

The Israelites could bring five major types of offerings to God—burnt, meal, peace, sin, and guilt—and the Torah provides precise regulations concerning how each was to be offered, what part of them was to be burnt, and what portion was to be eaten. There were two basic classifications of offerings. The *voluntary* offerings (*nidava*) consisted of the burnt (*olah*), meal (*mincha*), and peace (*sh'lamim*) offerings that an individual *could* bring should he so desire. The *obligatory* offerings (*chovah*) consisted of the sin (*chatat*) and guilt (*asham*) offerings that an individual *must* bring if he had transgressed certain commandments. The voluntary offerings reflected the individual's desire to *improve* his relationship with God, whereas the obligatory offerings were designed to *amend* the relationship with God should it be tainted by sin.

Were there restrictions regarding what could or could not be brought with offerings? (T)

Salt had to be brought with every offering. This commandment is recalled today by sprinkling salt over the *challah* on the Sabbath eve, since the dinner table is considered to be symbolic of the Altar in the Temple. Because idolaters only offered leavened bread and seasoned their sacrifices with honey (a favorite food of their gods), the Israelites were forbidden from offering leaven and honey.

Does the Bible provide specific reasons for the sacrificial system? (F)

The sacrifices are among the commandments known as *chukim*, Divine requirements for which there are no explanations. However, these rituals were designed to allow the Israelites to offer themselves, body and soul, to the will of God. In his *Guide of the Perplexed*, Maimonides wrote that the laws of sacrifices were ordained by the Torah as concessions to the universal ancient Near Eastern custom of bringing offerings to various pagan deities. Abravanel supported this thesis, noting that the Israelites at such an early stage in their historical development would not have comprehended any type of worship other than that practiced by the surrounding Canaanite cultures. For Nachmanides, animal sacrifices stressed that the sinner would have forfeited his own life had strict justice been applied. Only Divine grace permitted the sinner to substitute the life of an animal for his own. *Sefer ha-Chinuch* argued that the sight of a living creature being completely consumed on the Altar was a vivid image of what would happen to the sinful soul, overwhelmed by selfish and animalistic desires, if it did not repent.

Were the motivations different for Israelite and pagan sacrifices? (T)

The Hebrew word often translated as offerings is *korban*, which derives from the root meaning "to draw near." This implies the sacrifices were gifts to God that would allow the Israelites to draw nearer to the Divine Presence. This is a striking contrast to contemporaneous pagan religions, in which sacrifices were offered to nourish or bribe their gods.

Since the destruction of the Temple in Jerusalem, are there remnants of sacrifices in Jewish life? (N)

Although the elaborate system of sacrifices has been disbanded, during the *musaf* (additional) services on the Sabbath and festivals, traditional congregations recite descriptions of the required offerings for that specific day. They pray that God will return the Jewish people to the Land of Israel and permit them to rebuild the Temple in Jerusalem, where they will once again be able to perform the sacrificial rites. The Conservative prayer book also calls for the return of the dispersed Jews to the land where their ancestors sacrificed the various offerings, but not for a resumption of the sacrificial service. The biblical verses detailing the specific sacrifice for the day are included in small print, with the instructions "some congregations add." The Reform prayer book makes no mention of the ancient sacrificial system.

Instead of the sacrificial system, the Rabbis prescribed certain practices to take the place of these offerings. The most important of these are prayer, study of Torah (especially those portions concerned with sacrifices), fasting, and charity.

Is there a tradition of asceticism in Judaism? (N)

Asceticism is a regimen of denying physical or psychological desires to avoid the temptations and distractions that hinder spiritual development. This might include frequent fasting, not drinking wine, wearing rough clothing, and distancing oneself from contact with other people. Although never a strong force in normative Judaism, which respects the human body and emphasizes moderation, Jewish groups utilizing ascetic practices included the Nazirites and Rechabites of the Bible, the Essenes during late Second Temple times, the Avelei Zion and the Hasidei Ashkenaz in the Middle Ages, and the devotees of some forms of kabbalistic thought.

Do Jews believe and trust in miracles? (N)

Miracles are extraordinary events attributed to Divine intervention, in which an omnipotent God sets aside the established order of nature. Nevertheless, the Rabbis feared that such departures from the natural order might be seen as evidence that Creation was somehow imperfect. Therefore, they taught that the miracles recorded in the Bible were preordained from the beginning of the world. "At the Creation, God made a condition with the sea that it should divide for the passage of the Israelites [as they escaped from slavery in Egypt]; . . . with the sun and moon to stand still before Joshua; with the ravens to feed Elijah; to not harm Hananiah, Michael, and Azariah; with the lions not to hurt Daniel; with the heavens to open before Ezekiel; and with the fish to spew out Jonah" (Gen. R. 5:5).

Are Jews supposed to rely on miracles? (F)

The Rabbis condemned anyone who placed himself in a position in which he had to depend on a miracle to rescue him: "One may not rely on a miracle" (JT Yoma 1:4). In a classic story, R. Huna had stored wine in a dilapidated house with walls that threatened to collapse at any moment. He wanted to remove the wine, but was afraid to enter it. So he took R. Adda bar Ahava into that house and kept him occupied with a legal discussion until he had time to remove the wine. As soon as they left, the walls collapsed. When R. Adda bar Ahava realized what had happened, he was angry (Taan. 20b), since he agreed with R. Yannai's famous warning: "A person should never stand in a dangerous place and declare, 'A miracle will befall me.' Perhaps a miracle will not take place. And if a miracle does occur, it will be deducted from his merits [i.e., reward in the World to Come]" (Shab. 32a).

Nevertheless, the Talmud relates numerous miraculous events. The Rabbis emphasized that, though often unaware, we are surrounded by miracles on a daily basis. The workings of the human body, the beauty and harmony of nature, and the very gift of life are miraculous. As the Midrash observes, "How many miracles does God perform for man, of which man does not know?" (Exod. R. 24:1).

Has there been a difference between "official" versus "folk" religion in Judaism? (T)

Throughout history, the "official" and "folk" religion constituted two, often differing, expressions of Jewish living. The canonical texts of the Bible, Talmud, and Codes reflect the official representation of Judaism and Jewish living. However, some scholars have suggested that these represent an ideal model of Jewish living for future generations (i.e., what the rabbis wanted observed), rather than a true history of how Jews actually lived and believed at the time. According to this view, when later Jews compared themselves to this ideal, though not practiced, model, they felt guilty about their lower level of observance.

In contrast, "folk" religion is what the people actually practice. Archeology and obscure manuscripts indicate the presence of a vibrant folk religion in ancient Israel. For example, the official religion prohibited all forms of witchcraft, yet Saul consulted the witch of En Dor. Pig bones were found in a Jewish house in Galilee, and Jewish women worshipped Babylonian gods in biblical times. Although the Maccabees were fighting against foreign influences in Jewish life, a substantial percentage of the soldiers killed wore idolatrous amulets to protect them—a clear example of magic in folk religion. Moreover, "incantation books" (a form of folk magic) were frequently found in ancient Israelite homes.

Are religious controversies characteristic of the modern period? (N)

As with all religions, Judaism has experienced sectarian disputes. Today, there are conflicts between the ultra-Orthodox and more liberal Jewish movements. However, religious conflicts have involved Jews for centuries. Examples include the differences between the Pharisees and Sadducees in the late Second Temple period; the Rabbinites and Karaites in the eighth century; and the Hasidim and Mitnagdim in the eighteenth century.

Is the Jewish concept of redemption different from that of Christians? (T)

The Jewish concept of personal redemption is different from the Christian idea of salvation, since Jews reject the belief that humans are born condemned by original sin and require a messianic figure to "save" them. Traditional Jews also believe in a communal redemption in the Messianic Age, an era of universal peace and justice when the Temple will be rebuilt and those Jews dispersed throughout the world will be gathered to the Land of Israel. God is described as the "Redeemer of Israel" in the daily liturgy.

Does Judaism believe in the coming of a Messiah? (T)

Absolute trust in the ultimate coming of the Messiah is a core belief in Judaism and one of Maimonides's Thirteen Principles of Faith. Faith in, and hope for, the Messiah sustained Jews throughout centuries of suffering and persecution. Yearning for the coming of the Messiah plays a major role in Jewish festivals and liturgy. The song *Eliyahu ha-Navi* (Elijah the Prophet, the herald of the Messiah) is sung at *Havdalah*, when according to tradition the Messiah will come; at every circumcision, since this Jewish child may be the long-awaited Messiah; and at the Passover seder, the festival of redemption.

Some Jews view the Messiah not as a human agent but in more figurative terms as a time when justice, mercy, and peace will prevail throughout the world.

In Judaism, is the Messiah depicted as Divine? (F)

In Jewish tradition, the term "Messiah" (from the Hebrew word *mashiach*, meaning "anointed king") always applies to a human agent of Divine redemption. The concept of a Divine "savior," whose self-sacrifice will save mortals from the punishment merited by their sins, is a purely Christian idea that has no foundation in Jewish thought.

Should Jews simply wait for the coming of the Messiah? (F)

Normative Judaism teaches that one should work actively to hasten the arrival of the Messiah by doing everything possible to perfect the world, rather than simply waiting passively for the Messiah to come. The Talmud states, "The Messiah will come if every Jew observes the Sabbath twice in a row" (Shab. 118b). According to tradition, the Messiah will only come when we are ready. The Talmud relates that R. Joshua ben Levi found Elijah the Prophet, disguised as a filthy beggar, sitting at the gates of Rome. He asked, "When will you come and proclaim the Messiah?" Elijah replied, "Today, if you will only hear his voice" (Sanh. 98a).

With the arrival of the Messiah, will human beings no longer have to take care of the world? (F)

Even the advent of the Messiah will not relieve human beings of responsibility for taking care of the world. This is perfectly illustrated by the statement of R. Yochanan ben Zakkai: "If you are planting a tree, and you hear that the Messiah has come, finish planting the tree and then go greet him" (ARN 31).

Is there a Jewish tradition of two Messiahs, rather than only one? (T)

The Messiah is usually envisioned as a single king from the House of David (*Mashiach ben David*), who will defeat the enemies of Israel, bring the Jewish people back from exile, rebuild the Temple and reinstitute the sacrificial cult, and establish a kingdom of God on earth. However, in the Book of Zechariah, there is mention of two messianic figures, a king (9:9) and a priest (6:13). The Talmud (Suk. 52a) discusses a second Messiah (*Mashiach ben Joseph*), who will precede the messianic king and be killed in an epic battle with the enemies of God and Israel.

Does the term "Armageddon" come from a Hebrew place-name? (N)

Armageddon refers to the apocalyptic battle prior to the Messianic Age at the end of days, when the forces of evil will be utterly destroyed by the forces of good. The term is also used popularly to refer to any great loss of life in battle, or even to the use of weapons of mass destruction. First used in the Christian Bible, the word "Armageddon" probably derives from the Hebrew phrase *Har Megiddo* (Mountain of Megiddo), which is situated in the southern Jezreel Valley and overlooks the site of many decisive battles in ancient times.

Have there been "false messiahs"? (T)

Throughout the Middle Ages and early modern times, Jews speculated extensively on the apocalyptic end of days, attempting to determine exactly when the Messiah would appear. Periodically, self-proclaimed "messiahs" attracted thousands of followers, whose hopes were subsequently dashed when their messianic claims proved to be false. The most infamous was Shabbetai Tzvi in the seventeenth century, who proclaimed himself the Messiah in the synagogue at Smyrna (today in Turkey) and attracted thousands of followers. With the Jewish world in a frenzy of excitement, Shabbetai Tzvi traveled to Constantinople to claim his kingdom from the sultan. Promptly arrested, he converted to Islam under threat of death. This apostasy was a devastating blow; many disillusioned Jews converted with him, while others were left depressed and demoralized.

Does the Bible provide a description of the Messianic Age? (T)

The Messianic Age is to be characterized by universal peace and justice, which the Bible describes as a time when "the wolf shall live with the sheep, and the leopard lie down with the kid; the calf with the young lion shall grow up together, and a little child shall lead them" (Isa. 11:6). It will be a time when "every man shall sit under his vine and under his fig tree, and none shall make him afraid" (Mic. 4:4). According to traditional Jewish belief, the Messiah will be a descendant of King David. Under his rule, the city of Jerusalem and the Temple will be rebuilt, and all Jews throughout the world will be gathered to the Land of Israel.

Do some modern Jews believe that there is a harbinger of the Messianic Age? (T)

In the prayer for Israel in most prayer books, the establishment of the State in 1948 is called *reishit tz'michat g'ulateinu* (the beginning of the dawn of our redemption). Contemporary religious Zionists have embraced this idea, viewing the establishment of the State of Israel as the inauguration of the messianic process.

Does Judaism accept the idea of Messianic Jews? (F)

So-called Messianic Jews are those who were born Jewish or converted to Judaism and acknowledge their Jewish ethnicity, but believe that Jesus was the Messiah. The state of the world is clearly inconsistent with the biblical prophecy that universal peace and justice will be a distinguishing feature of the Messianic Age. Traditional Judaism rejects Jesus as the Messiah and thus is completely opposed to the concept of Messianic Jews.

NOTE

1. *Stone Chumash*, 973; Donin, *To Pray as a Jew*, 150.

Chapter Five

Mitzvot

Have you ever wondered . . .

1. Is a *mitzvah* a good deed?
2. Are the 613 *mitzvot* found and listed in the Torah?
3. Did the Rabbis establish seven *mitzvot* in addition to those found in the Torah?
4. Are some *mitzvot* more important than others?
5. Does the Torah offer specific reasons for the commandments?
6. Is merely performing the *mitzvot* sufficient?
7. Is *kavanah* necessary to fulfill a *mitzvah*?
8. Is it a *mitzvah* to donate stolen money to a Jewish charity?
9. Does observance of the *mitzvot* require a belief in God?
10. Are men and women equally responsible for performing the *mitzvot*?
11. Are women forbidden from performing the time-bound commandments for which they are not required?
12. Can a woman who assumes a *mitzvah* as her duty perform this commandment on behalf of the congregation?
13. Are men obligated to observe more commandments because they are intrinsically more holy?
14. According to the Rabbis, are non-Jews subject to any specific laws?
15. According to Jewish tradition, is it permitted to violate any of the commandments to preserve life?
16. Is a person required to sacrifice one's life rather than be forced to publicly violate a religious law?

Is a *mitzvah* a good deed? (N)

Although the term is often used in the context of an action that brings joy or comfort to another (e.g., "do a *mitzvah* by taking care of your sister while I am shopping"), strictly speaking a *mitzvah* is a Divinely mandated religious commandment rather than a voluntary act of kindness or compassion.

Are the 613 *mitzvot* found and listed in the Torah? (N)

The Torah is the source of the commandments, though it does not specifically enumerate them. The first mention of a precise number of commandments appears in a fourth-century Talmudic statement that "613 commandments were communicated to Moses; 365 negative commandments, corresponding to the number of days [in the solar year], and 248 positive commandments, corresponding to the number of parts of the human body" (Mak. 23b).

During the Talmudic period, there was no attempt to precisely enumerate each individual commandment. The major monumental work listing and elucidating the meaning of the commandments was *Sefer ha-Mitzvot* (Book of the Commandments) of Maimonides, the major Jewish philosopher of the Middle Ages. The thirteenth-century *Sefer ha-Chinuch* (Book of Education) arranged the commandments according to the order in which they appear in the Torah, so that they could be studied along with the weekly reading in the synagogue. In the nineteenth century, the Chofetz Chaim (Israel Meir ha-Cohen) wrote the *Sefer ha-Mitzvot ha-Katzar* (Short Book of the Commandments), which includes a listing of those positive and negative commandments that are still applicable today.

Did the Rabbis establish seven *mitzvot* in addition to those found in the Torah? (T)

These rabbinic commandments include:

- Washing hands before eating (Eduy. 5:6)
- Lighting Sabbath candles (Shab. 20b)
- Reciting the *Hallel* psalms of praise on festival days (Ber. 14a; Pes. 117a)
- Lighting Chanukah candles (Shab. 23a)
- Reading the Scroll of Esther on Purim (Meg. 7a)
- Making an *eruv* (to alleviate some Sabbath restrictions concerning the limitation of movement and transfer of objects) (Er. 21b)
- Saying a blessing of thanksgiving before experiencing pleasure in worldly items (such as for specific foods) (Ber. 35a)

Are some *mitzvot* more important than others? (N)

Some of the commandments were classified as *mitzvot kallot* (less important; lit., "light") or *mitzvot chamurot* (more important), with violations of some even being subject to the death penalty. However, in *Pirkei Avot* (2:1), the Rabbis stressed that Jews should "be as scrupulous in performing a 'minor' *mitzvah* as in a 'major' one, for you do not know the reward given for the respective *mitzvot*."

Does the Torah offer specific reasons for the commandments? (N)

Why should Jews observe the commandments? Are they to be obeyed merely because they represent the will of God, or because they possess some intrinsic meaning designed to spiritually improve the person who performs them, or for both reasons? Surprisingly, the Torah provides specific reasons for very few of the commandments. Classic examples are the prohibition against oppressing a stranger, which is repeated 36 times in the Torah and is based on the verse, "for you were strangers in the land of Egypt" (Exod. 22:20), implying that the Israelites had learned firsthand the need to be sensitive to the plight of strangers in their midst; and the reward of long life for honoring parents (Exod. 20:12). Broad reasons given for observing the entire gamut of positive and negative commandments include ensuring the holiness of the nation, upholding the everlasting legal covenant, sustaining the love relationship between God and Israel, the concept of reward and punishment, sanctifying the name of God, and leading a wise and moral life.

Is merely performing the *mitzvot* sufficient? (F)

The Rabbis stressed that performance of the commandments is not merely a mechanical ritual or the discharge of a burdensome obligation, but rather an infinitely rich and rewarding experience within the reach of every individual. Instead of a thoughtless matter of routine, religious observance requires *constant* and careful consideration, since the greater the devotion with which the *mitzvot* are carried out, the greater the reward and spiritual satisfaction. [1]

The observant Jew is urged to go beyond the call of duty in fulfilling a *mitzvah* (glorifying the *mitzvah*), to not bargain over the price when buying something pertaining to a *mitzvah* (love of the *mitzvah*), to feel joy in having the privilege of such opportunities to serve God and perform the commandments with enthusiasm, an uplifted heart, at the earliest possible moment, and with conscious purpose (*kavanah*).

Is *kavanah* necessary to fulfill a *mitzvah*? (N)

The Hebrew word *kavanah* means "devotion, intent, conscious purpose," which describes the state of mind required for praying or performing a *mitzvah*. When a *mitzvah* entails the performance of a specific act (such as eating unleavened bread on Passover), one who merely performs the act without conscious purpose technically fulfills the obligation. However, where no specific act is required, there must be a conscious awareness of fulfilling one's duty. In a Talmudic example, "If a man is passing behind a synagogue, or if his house adjoins the synagogue, and he hears the sound of the shofar, or the reading of the Scroll of Esther, then if he listens with attention he fulfills his obligation, but otherwise he does not" (RH 27b). The blessing recited before performing a *mitzvah* not only offers praise to God, but also reminds the individual of the importance of the sanctified act.

Is it a *mitzvah* to donate stolen money to a Jewish charity? (F)

The Hebrew phrase, *mitzvah ha-ba'ah b'averah* (lit., "one that comes with sin") means that a *mitzvah* must never be performed with the profits of a transgression. For example, one does not fulfill the obligation of taking up the four species on Sukkot by using a stolen *lulav*. As the Talmud asks, "If one has stolen a measure of wheat and has ground, kneaded and baked it, and set apart the *challah*, how can he recite a blessing over it? It would not be a blessing, but rather a blasphemy!" (Sanh. 6b).

Does observance of the *mitzvot* require a belief in God? (T)

The fundamental essence of Judaism is a belief in God, who is omniscient, omnipresent, omnipotent, and the Creator of everything in existence. This is clearly stated in the first of the Ten Commandments, "I am the Lord your God, who brought you out of the land of Egypt . . ." (Exod. 20:2). Belief in the One God is a prerequisite for the acceptance of all of the other commandments, because a denial of the existence of God would render observance of the other Divinely mandated commandments irrelevant.

Are men and women equally responsible for performing the *mitzvot*? (N)

The great majority of *mitzvot* apply equally to men and women. Obvious exceptions are those *mitzvot* that are gender-based, such as circumcision and the laws regarding menstruation. Although women are obligated to observe virtually all the negative commandments, they are not required to perform those positive commandments that are "time-bound." The most common explanation for this distinction is that it reflects the traditional domestic role of women in society. Occupied with the responsibilities of a housewife and mother, the imposition of time-bound *mitzvot* would be an unreasonable burden.

The Talmud lists five specific time-bound positive commandments for which women are not obligated—dwelling in the sukkah and taking up the *lulav* (four species) on Sukkot; hearing the shofar on Rosh Hashanah and Yom Kippur; wearing *tzitzit* (fringes); and putting on *tefillin*. (Elsewhere, women are also exempted from counting the Omer and from reciting the *Shema*, though they still have an obligation to pray at their own time and in private.) Nevertheless, some time-bound positive commandments are obligatory for women, such as observing the Sabbath, rejoicing on festivals, eating *matzah* on Passover, fasting on Yom Kippur, lighting the Chanukah lights, and assembling to hear the reading of the Torah. Conversely, women are exempt from some positive commandments that are not time-bound, such as the study of Torah, procreation, and the redemption of the firstborn son.

Are women forbidden from performing the time-bound commandments for which they are not required? (N)

In describing the time-bound positive commandments that were not obligatory for women, the Mishnah uses the term "exemption." This raises the question of whether women "may" perform these *mitzvot* if they so choose. In practice, women have voluntarily assumed most of the time-dependent *mitzvot* as if they were obligatory, and most rabbinic authorities have not only sanctioned this but consider it praiseworthy. The only exceptions among Orthodox women are the *mitzvot* of *tallit* and *tefillin*, but even these are permitted in liberal, egalitarian communities.

Can a woman who assumes a *mitzvah* as her duty perform this commandment on behalf of the congregation? (N)

This is an extremely controversial issue. According to Rabbenu Tam, once a woman takes on a *mitzvah* by assuming the obligation, she is just as accountable as a man for all aspects and implications of the new duty. If this point of view is accepted, a woman would be able to perform this commandment on behalf of the congregation. Except for a few recent opinions, the general consensus in traditional circles has been that women may *not* discharge men's obligations for *mitzvot* they have taken upon themselves because they are fulfilling them voluntarily rather than as a Divinely mandated responsibility. One concept underlying this decision is *k'vod ha-tzibbur*. Literally translated as "honor of the community," this means that having a woman discharge a *mitzvah* for men would cast doubt on the education and piety of the male members of the congregation, putting them to shame by implying that none of them was capable of performing this function. In egalitarian Conservative and Reform synagogues, women can read the Torah and lead prayer services, thus discharging *mitzvot* for men.

Are men obligated to observe more commandments because they are intrinsically more holy? (F)

One of the reasons for observing the commandments is that they foster a sense of discipline and responsibility. Some rabbis have argued that it is because women have greater innate spirituality that they need to fulfill fewer *mitzvot* to achieve spiritual perfection.

According to the Rabbis, are non-Jews subject to any specific laws? (T)

The rabbis derived seven basic laws that were binding on all human beings and constituted the fundamental precepts required for the establishment of a civilized society. They are termed the "Noahide laws" since they are to be observed by all people on earth, whom the Torah describes as descended from the three sons of Noah (Gen. 9:19). The Noahide laws include (1) the establishment of courts of justice, and the prohibition of (2) idolatry, (3) blasphemy, (4) murder, (5) incest and adultery, (6) robbery, and (7) eating flesh cut from a live animal. Although Israelites in the Land were obliged to carry out all 613 commandments in the Torah, observance of the seven Noahide laws was all that was required of non-Jews who lived among them or attached themselves to the Jewish community. In this way, non-Jews could assure themselves of a place in the World to Come.

According to Jewish tradition, is it permitted to violate any of the commandments to preserve life? (N)

The sanctity of human life is a supreme value in Judaism, based on the biblical concept of humans being created "in the image of God" (Gen. 1:27) and the Talmudic dictum that "one who destroys a single soul is regarded as having destroyed an entire world, and one who preserves one life is as if he preserved an entire world" (Sanh. 4:5, 37a). Even desecration of the Sabbath is permitted for the preservation of life. According to the Rabbis, if a Jew is forced to transgress any of the negative commandments on pain of death, he may violate the law rather than surrender his life, in accordance with the principle, "You shall therefore keep My statutes, and My ordinances, which if a man do he shall *live* by them" (Lev. 18:5). However, there are three specific exceptions—the commandments on idolatry, unlawful sexual intercourse (incest, adultery), and murder.

Is a person required to sacrifice one's life rather than be forced to publicly violate a religious law? (N)

The answer to this question depends on whether a reasonable onlooker would deem such an action as meaning that one was renouncing Judaism. The Talmud distinguishes between a Jew being compelled to light a fire in a church (permitted, since the motivation was merely to provide warmth, rather than force him to be associated with idolatrous worship) and one ordered to cut grass to feed cattle on the Sabbath (forbidden, because the intention was to force the Jew to violate his religion).

NOTE

1. Maimonides, *The Commandments*, 281–88.

Chapter Six

Ethical Living

Have you ever wondered ...

1. Is there a tradition that the world continues only because of the existence of a specific number of righteous people?
2. Is *gemilut chasadim* a core social value in Judaism?
3. Are there specific actions that are considered as *gemilut chasadim*?
4. Does *tzedakah* mean "charity"?
5. Is there a difference between the Jewish ideal of *tzedakah* and the Christian concept of "charity"?
6. Is *gemilut chasadim* greater than *tzedakah*?
7. Are the poor required to give *tzedakah*?
8. Should Jews give *tzedakah* only to fellow Jews?
9. Should one accept *tzedakah* when in need of it?
10. Is the more *tzedakah* one gives the better?
11. Are all types of *tzedakah* equally good?
12. Is *tzedakah* an individual responsibility?
13. Is visiting the sick a core aspect of righteous Jewish living?
14. According to Jewish tradition, is it always a good time to visit the sick?
15. Is it permitted to visit the sick on the Sabbath?
16. Does the physical act of visiting the sick fulfill the *mitzvah*?
17. In the prayer for the sick, is a person's usual Hebrew name used?
18. Did a lack of hospitality lead directly to the destruction of the Second Temple?
19. Is the virtue of hospitality mentioned at the Passover seder?
20. It is possible for human beings to fulfill the biblical commandment to "fear the Lord your God, to walk in all of His ways" (Deut. 10:12)?

21. Does *derech eretz* mean living correctly?
22. Is washing hands before eating bread at the beginning of a meal done for hygienic reasons?
23. Is washing the hands only done before meals?
24. Are there halachic requirements for washing the hands other than before and after meals?
25. Is a menstruating woman "unclean"?
26. Is a menstruating woman permitted to use makeup or wear jewelry or colorful clothes, even though this might arouse her husband who is forbidden to have relations with her during that time?
27. Do Orthodox men touch their wives in public when they are menstruating?
28. Did the Rabbis enforce separation during menstruation only because it is biblically mandated?
29. Is there variation in the time a woman is ritually impure after childbirth?
30. Do all women immerse themselves in a *mikveh* after menstruation?
31. Is immersing in a *mikveh* restricted to women?
32. Does a person have to wash before entering the water of a *mikveh*?
33. Does Judaism have a holistic view toward health?
34. Do human beings have a religious responsibility to take care of their health?
35. Does taking a bath have religious significance?
36. Is smoking permitted by Jewish law?
37. Does the Bible encourage Jews to become physicians?
38. Does Judaism praise the efforts of physicians as members of an honorable profession?
39. Did Maimonides, the most illustrious Jewish philosopher of the Middle Ages, write about health?
40. Are there any "Jewish diseases"?
41. Are some people more important than others?
42. Is one's teacher considered more important than one's father?
43. In Jewish law, may one life be destroyed to save others?
44. In allocating scarce resources, must all share equally even if it results in none of them surviving?
45. Is Jewish law based on rights?
46. Do the Bible and Talmud provide for a sophisticated legal system?
47. Does the majority rule?
48. Does Jewish law use the jury system?
49. Did the Rabbis have a specific set of questions to ask witnesses?
50. Is the testimony of a single witness sufficient at a traditional Jewish trial?
51. In Jewish law, may a murderer be killed without trial?

52. Under biblical law, could an Israelite who murdered another pay a monetary penalty if the family of the victim agreed?
53. In biblical law, did an Israelite who accidently killed another escape punishment?
54. In Jewish law, is a homeowner permitted to kill a burglar?
55. Does Jewish law make an exception for acting under duress?
56. In traditional Jewish law, is an intoxicated person responsible for his actions?
57. Is a person who causes damage when sleepwalking responsible for his actions?
58. Is a person who injures another only responsible for paying the victim's medical bills?
59. In classic Jewish law, could anyone be a witness?
60. Under biblical law, was perjury punishable by more than a fine?
61. Is a Jew exonerated by a court of law freed from punishment?
62. Are Jews expected to conform to local laws?
63. Does Judaism favor capital punishment?
64. Does the State of Israel permit capital punishment?
65. Does Judaism have a concept of vicarious punishment?
66. Are Jewish ethics different from secular Western ethics?
67. Does human decision-making ever contradict apparent Divine law?
68. In Jewish thought, is the human being inherently good?
69. Does Jewish ethics believe in free will?
70. Does Jewish law have a negative view of becoming wealthy?
71. Does Judaism accept the concept of caveat emptor ("let the buyer beware")?
72. When bargaining with a seller, can a buyer falsely claim that he can purchase similar merchandise cheaper at another store?
73. Do workers have rights in traditional Jewish law?
74. In Jewish law, is it permitted to walk into an expensive store simply to discover the price of an object?
75. When advertising a product, it is fair to attack the competition to increase sales?
76. Does Jewish law prohibit cross-dressing?
77. Does Judaism favor the literal concept of "an eye for an eye"?
78. Does Jewish law believe in the principle of "finders keepers"?
79. Can a person keep some found property?
80. In traditional Jewish law, can daughters inherit from the father's estate?
81. Is the legal concept of negligence part of biblical law?
82. Is ritual impurity the same as being dirty?
83. Was the source of ritual impurity coming into contact with a dead body?

84. Could ritual impurity be passed from one person to another?
85. Could ritual impurity be removed by taking a bath at home?
86. In Jewish law, is a person permitted to do anything to protect another?
87. In biblical times, were all Israelites required to take part in wars against enemies of the nation?
88. Were there rules of cleanliness in an Israelite military camp?
89. Were the Israelites permitted to do whatever was necessary to win a war?
90. Did the Bible permit a father to sell his daughter?
91. Does the Bible permit one Jew to be the slave of another?
92. Could a Jewish servant be harshly treated?
93. Were there limits on how badly a non-Jewish slave could be treated?
94. According to the Bible, must fugitive slaves be returned to their rightful owner?
95. Is the biblical prohibition against "putting a stumbling block before the blind" taken literally?
96. Does *Kiddush ha-Shem* mean martyrdom?
97. Is it a religious duty to kiss such holy objects as the *tallit* and *tefillin*?
98. Are Jews permitted to say whatever they want as long as it is true?
99. Was *lashon ha-ra* considered as serious as murder?
100. Is there any reference to *lashon ha-ra* in the prayers?
101. Is sharing gossip with a spouse considered *lashon ha-ra*?
102. Is the person who relates gossip guilty of a transgression?
103. Is it permissible to make use of *lashon ha-ra*?
104. Are Jews prohibited from charging interest in loans to other Jews?
105. Did the Rabbis change the prohibition against lending at interest?
106. Is it permitted to lend money at interest to non-Jews?
107. Can Jews lend at interest to other Jews today?
108. Is "love your neighbor as yourself" a Christian concept?
109. Is it praiseworthy to love a neighbor more than oneself?
110. Is there a difference between the negative actions of taking revenge and bearing a grudge?
111. May Jews wear all types of clothes?
112. Is there any exception to the ban against *sha'atnez*?
113. Is shaving the beard forbidden according to Jewish law?
114. Is not shaving the beard a sign of mourning?
115. Does Jewish law require standing for an older person?

Is there a tradition that the world continues only because of the existence of a specific number of righteous people? (T)

According to ancient tradition, in every generation there are 36 righteous people (*tzadikim*), unknown to the world and even to themselves, for whose sake the world is sustained. They often are called the *lamed-vavniks*, since the numerical values of the Hebrew letters *lamed* and *vav* are 30 and 6, respectively.

Is *gemilut chasadim* a core social value in Judaism? (T)

Literally "the giving of loving-kindness," yet difficult to define, *gemilut chasadim* is a quintessential and distinctive attribute of the Jew and one of the three characteristics required to be a true member of the Jewish people (Yev. 79a). According to the Midrash, "Whoever denies the duty of *gemilut chasadim* denies the fundamental of Judaism" (Eccles. R. 7:1). *Gemilut chasadim* is listed among the things "that have no fixed measure," for which "man enjoys the fruits in this world, while the principal remains for him in the World to Come" (Shab. 127a). The opening lines of *Pirkei Avot* (1:2) state: "On three things does the [continued] existence of the world depend— Torah, *avodah* [initially the Temple service, later prayer], and *gemilut chasadim*."

Are there specific actions that are considered as *gemilut chasadim*? (N)

The Talmud specifies six traditional kinds of *gemilut chasadim*—clothing the naked, visiting the sick, comforting mourners, extending hospitality to strangers, providing for a bride, and accompanying the dead to the grave. During the Middle Ages, the broad concept of *gemilut chasadim* became restricted to the granting of interest-free loans to the needy. More recently, the term has been expanded to refer not only to free-loan societies, but also to individual acts as well as a wide variety of communal welfare organizations.

Does *tzedakah* mean "charity"? (F)

The Bible repeatedly stresses the obligation to aid those in need, but never designates a special term for this requirement. The Rabbis adopted the word *tzedakah* to apply to charity, primarily in the form of giving gifts to the poor, which they deemed one of the essential *mitzvot* of Judaism. *Tzedakah* literally means "righteousness" or "justice," as in the famous biblical phrase, *tzedek, tzedek, tirdof* ("Justice, justice, shall you pursue"; Deut. 16:20). For the Rabbis, rather than being merely a generous or magnanimous act, *tzedakah* is a religiously mandated duty to provide something to which the needy have a right.

Is there a difference between the Jewish ideal of *tzedakah* and the Christian concept of "charity"? (T)

There is a critical distinction between the Jewish ideal of *tzedakah* and the Christian concept of "charity," which has dominated the connotation of the English word. Charity comes from the Latin *caritas* (love), as does the Greek term *philanthropy* (lit., "love of human beings"). Christianity focuses on charity as motivated by "love" for our fellow human beings, which can be difficult because many of those in need of assistance may appear dirty, diseased, and even dangerous. Judaism takes a more realistic view, requiring one to provide assistance not because one "loves" the person in need of help, but simply because it is "right" that you expend resources for someone in need. This does not mean that Jewish ethics has no concept of love or philanthropy; instead it uses the term *gemilut chasadim*, which implies going above the requirements of the law (i.e., the *tzedakah* that one is obliged to provide) as an act of loving-kindness.

Is *gemilut chasadim* greater than *tzedakah*? (T)

According to the Talmud, *gemilut chasadim* is superior to *tzedakah* in three respects: "Charity can be given only with one's money; *gemilut chasadim*, both by personal service and with money. Charity can be given only to the poor; *gemilut chasadim*, both to rich and poor. Charity can be given only to the living; *gemilut chasadim*, both to the living and the dead [by attending the funeral and the burial]" (Suk. 49b). Thus, helping a blind person across the street is an act of *gemilut chasadim*, though not of charity. A grudging gift to a poor person may qualify as charity, but by adding a sincere smile and a kind word, the same amount is transformed into *gemilut chasadim*. Indeed, the ultimate example of *gemilut chasadim* (termed *chesed shel emet*; the "true" loving-kindness) is giving honor to the dead, since there is no chance that the deceased will ever return the favor. There is no maximum limit on acts of personal service ("with his body") that one can do for another, whereas donations of money and other material goods are restricted to a fifth of one's possessions (JT Pe'ah 1:1, 15b).

Are the poor required to give *tzedakah*? (T)

Every person has a duty to give *tzedakah*. As the Talmud states, "even a poor man who himself subsists on charity should give charity" (Git. 7b).

Should Jews give *tzedakah* only to fellow Jews? (N)

The Rabbis believed that there was a hierarchy in giving *tzedakah*—Jew before Gentile, members of your family before the general poor of your town, and the local poor before those of another city (BM 71a). Nevertheless, according to the *Shulchan Aruch*, this rule does not apply to the poor of the Land of Israel, who have priority over all. The Rabbis stressed the need to give charity to the non-Jewish poor "to preserve good relations," though they strongly urged Jews to refuse financial assistance from non-Jews unless absolutely necessary.

Should one accept *tzedakah* when in need of it? (T)

A Jew should to do everything possible to avoid having to take charity. This means taking any work that is available, even if he thinks it is beneath his dignity. The greatest of the sages adhered to this principle, performing physical labor to support themselves and remain independent. Nevertheless, a person should not feel embarrassed to accept charity when unable to obtain money and support in any other way. Indeed, refusing charity when needed is a sin, and any suffering this entails is equivalent to shedding one's own blood. If a poor man is too proud to accept charity, he can be misled into believing that a gift is really a loan.

Is the more *tzedakah* one gives the better? (N)

The general rabbinic principle is that one is required to give a tenth of one's wealth to charity. However, the Talmud warns against spending more than 20 percent on charity, lest this result in a person becoming dependent on charity himself (Ket. 50a). Of course, it is permissible to give away more the 20 percent of one's possessions upon one's death, since the danger of becoming a burden on the community no longer applies.

Are all types of *tzedakah* equally good? (F)

In his *Mishneh Torah*, Maimonides offered a list of eight degrees of charity. The highest is preventing another person from ever becoming poor, such as by offering him a loan or employment or investing in his business. The second highest level of charity is the rabbinic ideal of giving to the poor in such a way that neither the donor nor the recipient knows the identity of the other (BB 10b). In descending order, the next levels of charity are the donor knows the recipient, but the recipient does not know the donor; the recipient knows the donor, but the donor does not know the recipient; giving directly to a poor person without being asked; giving only after being asked; giving cheerfully but less than one should; and giving grudgingly.

Is *tzedakah* an individual responsibility? (N)

Every person has a duty to give to charity. Nevertheless, convinced that "all Jews are responsible for each other" (Shev. 39a), the Rabbis stressed that charity not only is required of the individual Jew but also is an obligation of the entire community. In addition to maintaining the poor, the communal charitable fund was also used to redeem captives, dower poor brides, and establish soup kitchens. The longer a person lived in the town, the greater the extent of his obligation to share in the charitable needs of the community.

Is visiting the sick a core aspect of righteous Jewish living? (T)

Visiting the sick (*bikur cholim*) is a core *mitzvah*, an aspect of righteous living that constitutes the fundamental Jewish concept of *gemilut chasadim*. Just as God observed this *mitzvah* by visiting Abraham when the patriarch was recovering from his circumcision (Gen. 18:1), so human beings are required to emulate this Divine example (Sot. 14a). *Bikur cholim* is listed as one of the deeds for which "man enjoys the fruits in this world, while the principal remains for him in the World to Come" (Shab. 127a). Recognizing the psychological value of convincing a sick person that he or she has not been abandoned to suffer alone, the Rabbis observed that one who visits the sick "takes away a sixtieth of his pain" (Ned. 39b). Conversely, R. Akiva maintained, "He who does not visit the sick is like a shedder of blood" (Ned. 40a). The *mitzvah* of visiting the sick does not merely apply to Jews who are ill; as the Talmud states, one should also "visit the sick of the non-Jew . . . in the interests of peace" (Git. 61a).

According to Jewish tradition, is it always a good time to visit the sick? (F)

The Rabbis believed that one should not visit too early in the morning, when a sick person is often being attended to by a physician, nor too late at night (when the patient is tired). Coming at these times may cause the visitor to "omit to pray for him; during the first three hours of the day his [the invalid's] illness is alleviated [and thus the visitor may think him on the road to recovery]; in the last three hours his sickness is most virulent [and the visitor may feel that prayer is hopeless]" (Ned. 40a). The *Shulchan Aruch* recommends that "relatives and friends are to visit a sick person as soon as he falls ill, while casual acquaintances wait three days. If the malady takes a turn for the worse, all enter immediately" (YD 335). Long visits were discouraged as too taxing for the patient.

Is it permitted to visit the sick on the Sabbath? (N)

The Rabbis disagreed as to whether one was permitted to visit the sick on the Sabbath, the day of joy on which sorrow should not intrude. Beit Shammai prohibited the practice, but the *halachah* agrees with Beit Hillel, which permitted such visits. Indeed, in medieval communities, congregants generally visited the sick after Saturday morning services.

Does the physical act of visiting the sick fulfill the *mitzvah*? (F)

Simply visiting the sick is not sufficient to completely fulfill this *mitzvah*. One who visits the sick must offer spiritual comfort and be attentive to the patient's material needs. Prayers for the sick are vital and may be said in any language. Multiple visits to a patient are permitted as long as they are not too tiring. However, the Talmud cautions against visiting those suffering from bowel trouble, so as not to cause embarrassment, or patients for whom the effort of speaking is too tiring (Ned. 41a). Sick persons should be spared from hearing of the death of a relative or any other bad news, to avoid delaying their recovery because of being "distracted in mind" (MK 26b).

In the prayer for the sick, is a person's usual Hebrew name used? (F)

When reciting the prayer for the sick, the person who is ill is called by his or her first name (and middle name) followed by *ben* (son of) or *bat* (daughter of) and then the first name (and middle name) of the *mother*—not that of the father, which is traditionally used on other occasions. The Rabbis included a prayer for the healing of the sick as the eighth blessing in the daily

Amidah. It praises God as the "faithful, merciful Physician . . . Who heals the sick of His people Israel." The custom of invoking a get-well blessing for the sick in conjunction with the reading of the Torah developed during the Middle Ages. On the Sabbath, the prayer concludes: "It is the Sabbath, when one must not cry out, and recovery will come soon" (Shab. 12a).

Did a lack of hospitality lead directly to the destruction of the Second Temple? (N)

According to the Talmud (Git. 55b–56a), a certain unnamed man had a friend named Kamtza and an enemy named Bar Kamtza. When planning a large banquet, the man instructed his servant to invite Kamtza, but the servant mistakenly asked Bar Kamtza instead. When the host saw his adversary, he furiously demanded that Bar Kamtza leave immediately. The embarrassed guest pleaded to be allowed to remain, even offering to pay for the cost of his dinner. When the host refused, Bar Kamtza raised his offer, first to half and then to the entire expense of the banquet. Eventually, the host ordered his servants to throw Bar Kamtza out of his house. The mortified guest was determined to exact revenge, not merely on his host, but against all of Jerusalem, since many of the leading rabbis of the city had been present at the banquet but none had done anything to prevent his disgrace. Bar Kamtza convinced the Roman emperor that the Jews of Jerusalem were plotting against his rule—thus precipitating the destruction of the Temple due to the lack of hospitality of a nameless host. [1]

Is the virtue of hospitality mentioned at the Passover seder? (T)

Whenever he had a meal, R. Huna "would open the door wide [as an invitation to strangers] and declare, 'Whosoever is in need, let him come and eat'" (Taan. 20b). This Aramaic saying, *"Kol dich'fin yeitei v'yeichul,"* is still recited early during the Passover seder.

It is possible for human beings to fulfill the biblical commandment to "fear the Lord your God, to walk in all of His ways" (Deut. 10:12)? (N)

Rather than taking this verse literally, the rabbinic interpretation is for us to be as much like God as possible, given the limitations of our mortal state. As created in the Divine image, we are challenged to pattern our actions after those of God. As the Talmud observed (Sot. 14a), we should clothe the naked just as God clothed Adam and Eve (Gen. 3:21), visit the sick as God visited Abraham after his circumcision (Gen. 18:3), comfort the mourners as God did for Isaac (Gen. 25:11), and bury the dead as God buried Moses (Deut. 34:6). This duty of imitating God is a fundamental teaching of Judaism. Its classic expression is found in the verse, "You shall be holy, for I the Lord your God am holy" (Lev. 19:2). Unlike paganism, which portrayed its gods in the physical image of man, in Judaism it is man who is made in the image of God (Gen. 1:27).

Does *derech eretz* mean living correctly? (N)

Literally "way of the land," this Hebrew term is used to describe proper behavior that is in keeping with accepted social and moral standards. In rabbinic literature, it refers both to appropriate conduct[2] and a worldly occupation. The motto of Modern Orthodoxy, as expounded by Rabbi Samson Raphael Hirsch, is "Torah together with *derech eretz*" (i.e., the general culture).

Is washing hands before eating bread at the beginning of a meal done for hygienic reasons? (F)

Although washing the hands before eating is now recognized as essential to decreasing infection, the ritual washing of the hands (*netilat yadayim*, lit., "raising the hands") performed by Jews is a religious, not hygienic, act that was instituted by the Rabbis to correct the condition of *tumat yadayim*—their concept of "impurity of the hands." The method of ritual washing is either by immersion up to the wrist or by pouring about one cup of water over both hands from a receptacle with a wide mouth, the lip of which must be undamaged. One custom is to alternately pour water over each hand three times (first washing the right hand by pouring water from a vessel held in the left hand).

Is washing the hands only done before meals? (F)

Although the most commonly observed ritual washing of the hands occurs before eating bread, the Rabbis deemed it to be of at least equal importance to wash the hands after the meal, before saying *Birkat ha-Mazon* (Grace after Meals). This was to remove any traces of "a certain salt of Sodom" that could adhere to the fingers and cause serious injury to the eyes (Hul. 105b). However, no blessing is recited, since this hand washing is done as a precautionary health measure, rather than as a religious obligation.

Are there halachic requirements for washing the hands other than before and after meals? (T)

Washing the hands is required on many other occasions, some of which are motivated by hygienic considerations and others by superstitious beliefs. In many traditional homes, a pitcher and basin are placed next to the bed for immediate washing of the hands after awakening. Washing the hands is required by *kohanim* before reciting the Priestly Blessing during a public prayer service, before eating the *karpas* (greens) at the Passover seder, and after the following activities: going to the toilet; cutting nails; taking off shoes with bare hands; combing the hair; sexual intercourse; touching hairy parts of the body that are usually covered by clothing; bloodletting; touching vermin (or searching clothes for them); and attending a funeral, leaving a cemetery, or departing from a house where a corpse is present.[3]

Is a menstruating woman "unclean"? (F)

Judaism prohibits contact with a menstruating woman, who is termed a *niddah*, a word meaning "separated" or "excluded." The precise word for her condition is *tamei* (ritually impure), meaning that she was prohibited from entering the Temple. The major causes for this ritual contamination were contact with a dead person or animal and the skin disease *tzara'at* (mistranslated as leprosy). This concept of "uncleanness" had no relation to hygiene and, as far as the menstruating woman was concerned, only prohibited her from having sexual relations with her husband.

Is a menstruating woman permitted to use makeup or wear jewelry or colorful clothes, even though this might arouse her husband who is forbidden to have relations with her during that time? (T)

This was a major Talmudic issue, reflecting an inherent conflict between eliminating anything that might result in sexual arousal during the *niddah* period and the need to prevent any long-term harm to the marital relationship due to the enforced period of separation (Shab. 64b). The strict approach of the early sages was overturned by the more permissive statement of R. Akiva: "If so, you make her repulsive to her husband, with the result that he will divorce her."[4] Maimonides went even further, claiming that it is a halachic obligation for a woman to make an effort to dress attractively and adorn herself during her period of separation from her husband.

Do Orthodox men touch their wives in public when they are menstruating? (F)

Although the biblical laws of sexual separation only prohibited intercourse during a woman's menstrual period, subsequent rabbinic rulings have also precluded any physical contact that could conceivably be sexually stimulating. This includes kissing, hugging, or otherwise touching one's spouse during the forbidden days, during which husband and wife sleep in separate beds. This rule led many Orthodox men to protect the privacy and modesty of their wives by never touching them in public (so no one knows whether or not they are in a state of *niddah* at the time). Similarly, they do not shake hands with any woman (not knowing whether or not she is a *niddah*). For the same reason, Orthodox men and women generally do not dance together in public; when doing so, they grasp a handkerchief between them rather than holding hands.[5]

Did the Rabbis enforce separation during menstruation only because it is biblically mandated? (F)

In a Talmudic discussion of this issue, R. Meir considered the period of separation to be of great benefit to the conjugal relations between man and wife. "Being in constant contact with his wife, a husband might develop a loathing towards her. The Torah, therefore, ordained that she be unclean for seven days in order that she shall be beloved by her husband as at the time of her first entry into the bridal chamber" (Nid. 31b). Indeed, many couples renew their sexual relationship each month with an eagerness and passion that is reminiscent of their honeymoon. In addition, the resumption of sexual relations between husband and wife generally occurs near the time when she is most fertile, thus increasing the chance of her becoming pregnant and ensuring the continuity of the Jewish people.

Is there variation in the time a woman is ritually impure after childbirth? (T)

After giving birth to a child, a mother's period of ritual impurity depends on the gender of the baby. According to the Torah (Lev. 12:1–8), a woman who gives birth to a son is a *niddah* for seven days (like a menstruating woman), but she must wait for an additional 33-day period of purification before being permitted to bring a sacrifice to the Temple and regain her ritual purity. Following the birth of a girl, the mother is a *niddah* for 14 days and then must wait an additional 66 days before she is purified. In sum, a woman is deemed ritually impure for 40 days after the birth of a son and twice that (80 days) after the birth of a daughter.

The reason for doubling the impure period after the birth of a girl is unclear. One possibility is that the newborn daughter will one day menstruate and give birth. Another is that the normal period of ritual impurity following childbirth is two weeks, but is reduced after the birth of a son "to allow the mother to attend the *b'rit* [circumcision] in a state of ritual purity, or because the *brit milah* on the eighth day is a purifying rite."[6]

Do all women immerse themselves in a *mikveh* after menstruation? (N)

Literally "a collection [of water]," *mikveh* is the Hebrew term for a ritual bath. Initially a natural, flowing body of water, today most are located indoors and look like small swimming pools, though they are filled with either rainwater or water from a spring or stream. A *mikveh* must contain 40 *se'ah* (about 200 gallons) of clear water and be deep enough to cover the entire body of the person undergoing immersion.

Today, the *mikveh* is most frequently used by an observant woman before resuming sexual relations with her husband after completing the period of separation related to her menstrual cycle. An unmarried woman does not go to the *mikveh* for purification, and she typically performs *tevilah* (immersion) for the first time before her wedding.

Is immersing in a *mikveh* restricted to women? (F)

Some Orthodox Jewish men immerse themselves in the *mikveh* on Fridays and before Jewish holidays (especially Yom Kippur) to stress the transition between regular weekdays and the Sabbath and festivals.[7] Immersion in the *mikveh* is also part of the conversion ceremony of both male and female non-Jews to Judaism.

Does a person have to wash before entering the water of a *mikveh*? (T)

Prior to entering the *mikveh*, it is essential to wash thoroughly. This indicates, both literally and symbolically, that the purpose of immersion is ritual purity rather than physical cleanliness. No object can be interposed between the body and the water of the ritual bath. Therefore, before entering the *mikveh* it is necessary to remove all makeup and nail polish. [8]

Does Judaism have a holistic view toward health? (T)

In Jewish thought, the concept of "health" entails physical, emotional, and spiritual well-being—health of both the body and the soul. This holistic view is evident in the word *shleimut* (completeness), one of the Hebrew terms for health. Another word for health is *beri'ut* (from the root "to create"), which associates health with creating one's life as a work of art. This implies that one can have a disability, such as an amputation or deafness, and yet be considered healthy in terms of productivity and the ability to contribute to society. The Hebrew word for physician (*rofeh*) comes from a root meaning "to ease," indicating that the doctor treating a "dis-ease" is effectively removing some impediment that is preventing the patient from proceeding further in the creation of a whole and fulfilling life. [9]

Do human beings have a religious responsibility to take care of their health? (T)

Judaism teaches that each person is responsible for taking those steps necessary to preserve health, for seeking qualified medical care when needed, and for not endangering himself through lifestyle choices. Because the body is viewed as a vessel for the soul and the instrument through which one worships God and carries out the Divine will, taking proper care of the body is a *mitzvah*, for only a healthy body is capable of sustaining a holy soul.

Does taking a bath have religious significance? (T)

As the "caretaker" of a body on loan from God, it is incumbent on each person to keep the Divine vessel clean (Lev. R. 34:3). Indeed, the Talmud states that a Jew may not live in a town without a bathhouse (BK 46a).

Is smoking permitted by Jewish law? (N)

Although tobacco use is common among traditional Jews, this should not lead to the conclusion that smoking is permitted by Jewish law. The pre-eminent authority who consistently refused to prohibit "active smoking" was Rabbi Moshe Feinstein. He strongly urged Jews to stop smoking and discouraged others from developing the habit. Nevertheless, in a classic *responsum* he maintained that smoking could not be forbidden on purely halachic grounds, based on the concept that people are permitted to take the risk of a specific action if it only entails the possibility of danger and most people are willing to take that risk (i.e., "God protects the simple"). However, medical science has shown that the danger in smoking is inevitable (and also affects those who passively inhale cigarette smoke), not only in terms of lung cancer but also cardiovascular and chronic pulmonary disease. Consequently, based on current research and the argument of Rabbi Feinstein, smoking cigarettes can only be considered a blatant violation of the biblical commandment against harming oneself, and thus prohibited according to Jewish law.

Does the Bible encourage Jews to become physicians? (N)

Based solely on the literal meaning of the biblical text, it is unclear whether human beings are even permitted to treat illness.[10] Sickness is often described as a Divine punishment for sin—either as a specific statement ("King X did . . . and he became sick") or in nonspecific terms ("If you do . . . you will be punished by a certain sickness"). Thus medical care could be interpreted as a human attempt to intervene in Divine actions, a rejection of God's prerogative. Jeremiah (17:14) exclaims, "Heal me, O Lord, and I shall be healed," and the eighth blessing in the *Amidah* describes God as "Who heals the sick of His people Israel"—implying that only God cures those who are to get well and suggesting that humans should not interfere. One Talmudic-era tract states that the physician is counted among the seven professions whose members have no share in eternal bliss, because he is the accomplice of the patient who should leave his destiny to Divine decree (ARN 36:5).[11]

Nevertheless, the Talmud suggests various proof texts that permit the physician to attempt to heal. The most quoted citation refers to the situation in which one person strikes and injures another; the first is required to ensure that his victim is "thoroughly healed" (*rapo y'rapei*; Exod. 21:19). A later verse notes that if a person loses something that you know is his, "you shall restore [the lost property] to him" (Deut. 22:2). Maimonides interpreted this phrase as referring to one's health, implying that it is permissible to provide medical care. Commenting on the well-known phrase, "You should love your neighbor as yourself" (Lev. 19:18), the Rabbis argued that this even permits curative measures that require inflicting a wound in the process. The concept of *pikuach nefesh* associates medical care with the religious requirement of saving a life, implying that the delivery of medical care is legally required. Similarly, one is obliged to "not stand idly by the blood of your neighbor" (Lev. 19:16). The Talmud concludes that human beings and God are partners, not antagonists, in aiding the sick, each playing an important role in the process of health care.

Does Judaism praise the efforts of physicians as members of an honorable profession? (N)

R. Akiva noted that just as a farmer works the soil rather than leaving the growing of crops solely to God, so physicians are required to treat the sick—in order to "cultivate" health. The Talmud even observes that "no Jew may live in a town without a physician" (BK 46a), and if a Jew feels ill, he must immediately consult a doctor.

However, in a bizarre text, the Mishnah states that "the best of doctors go to hell" (Kid. 82a). Taking a cynical or playful view of medical care, the Hasidic Reb Nachman of Bratslav maintained that when God created the Angel of Death, the latter protested that he was being given too much work for one angel; immediately, God assured him: "Don't worry, I have given you helpers called physicians!" In *The Book of Delight*, Joseph ibn Zabara relates that a philosopher went to a physician, who said that the philosopher was so sick there was no reason to treat him; the philosopher recovered and later met the physician in the street. "Have you returned from the next world?" asked the physician. "Yes," replied the philosopher. The physician continued, "What did you see there?" When the philosopher described the terrible punishments visited on physicians because "they kill their patients," the physician was horrified. "Do not feel alarmed," reassured the philosopher, "because I swore to them there that you are no physician!"

In a less satiric vein, Rashi argued that the statement refers to the physician who arrogantly believes that the recovery of a patient was due to his own skill, with God playing no role in the process. Some have suggested that "hell" is the fate of those physicians who are convinced they know everything and never seek the advice of their colleagues. Judah Loew, the Maharal of Prague, said it referred to those doctors who deal only with the physical dimension of medical care and deny the spiritual aspect.

In essence, the Jewish view is that physicians are agents or partners of God. Although given permission to treat patients, physicians should never feel that their power and skill alone has resulted in a cure. The major duty of physicians is to educate their patients in ways to prevent illness and attain health. They must serve as role models for their patients, for as expressed in the ethical will of Dr. Tibbon to his physician son, doctors cannot expect the patient to listen unless they themselves practice what they advise.

Did Maimonides, the most illustrious Jewish philosopher of the Middle Ages, write about health? (T)

As court physician in Fostat (Egypt), Maimonides offered a six-point plan for preventing disease and preserving health, citing the importance of clean air; a high-fiber, low-fat diet; exercise; regular excretion; ample sleep; and regulation of emotions (direct link between body and soul).[12]

Are there any "Jewish diseases"? (N)

As an isolated and inbred community for many centuries, the Ashkenazic Jewish population has a relatively higher incidence of specific hereditary diseases. These include Tay-Sachs disease, Gaucher's disease, breast and ovarian cancer due to a specific gene (BRCA 1 and 2), and several rare neurologic disorders. Genetic diseases prevalent in the Sephardic Jewish community include beta thalassemia; familial Mediterranean fever; glucose-6-phosphate dehydrogenase (G6PD) deficiency, a type of glycogen storage disease; and Wolman disease. Consequently, genetic counseling and testing are recommended when both prospective parents are of either Ashkenazic or Sephardic ancestry.

Are some people more important than others? (N)

An essential view in Jewish thought is the equality of all human life, since every person is created in the "image of God." The Talmud (Sanh. 37b) notes that Adam was created as a single person to teach that anyone who destroys a single person is as if he destroyed an entire world, whereas anyone who sustains one soul is described as if he has sustained an entire world. Therefore, each person must say, "For me the world was created."

Even knowledge of Torah is not seen as grounds for measuring a person's worth. Instead, all human beings are inherently equal, as long as they are trying to do God's will. The Talmud recounts a favorite saying of a Rabbi in Yavneh (Ber. 17a): "I am God's creature, and my fellow [i.e., the *am ha-aretz*, or non-student] is God's creature. My work is in the town, and his work is in the country. I rise early for my work, and he rises early for his work. Just as he does not presume to do my work, so I do not presume to do his work. Will you say, I do much [in the way of Torah] and he does little? [No, for] we have learned, 'One may do much or one may do little; it is all one, so long as each directs his heart to heaven.'"

Is one's teacher considered more important than one's father? (T)

Concerning the relative respect to be paid to a father and to a teacher, the Mishnah says that if a person's father and teacher are taken into captivity (or both were searching for lost property or carrying a heavy burden), he must help his teacher first. "For his father has brought him into the light of this world, while his teacher, who brought him wisdom, has brought him into the light of the World to Come" (BM 2:11).

In Jewish law, may one life be destroyed to save others? (N)

The Talmud declares that one is forbidden to destroy one life in order to save another. A man once came before Rava and stated that the governor of his city had given him the alternative of either killing another person or the governor would kill him. When asked how he should respond, Rava answered him: "Be killed rather than kill. What makes you think your blood is redder than his?" (Pes. 25b).

However, this principle does not necessarily hold when weighing the safety of a social group against the life of one person. Joab, the commander of King David's troops, had pursued Sheba the son of Bichri and besieged him in the town of Abel, demanding that he be delivered to the king's forces or Joab would destroy the entire city. A wise woman of the city gave up

Sheba to Joab, and the city was spared (2 Sam. 20:4–22). The Jerusalem Talmud (Ter. 8:10) cites this case as a guide to the situation in which a group of travelers is stopped by robbers who demand that the travelers give them one of their number so that the rest will be let go (i.e., saving a large number of people by having one person die). The decision is that the travelers must refuse and all submit to be killed, for the shedding of blood is one of three sins (in addition to idolatry and immorality) for which a person must be willing to die rather than commit it. However, the Talmud observes that this wholesale self-sacrifice applies only when the robbers do not specify a particular person and merely say "one of you," for the members of the group have no right to select one of their number arbitrarily and deliver him to death in order to save themselves (since the life of each individual is of inestimable value). However, if the robbers specify a particular person by name, there is no requirement that all be killed for his sake (i.e., it is not the group who have selected him for death).

In allocating scarce resources, must all share equally even if it results in none of them surviving? (F)

In a famous Talmudic case (BM 62a), two men walking (presumably in the desert) have a single pitcher of water that contains enough water to keep only one of them alive long enough to reach safety. If both drink, both will die; if one drinks, he will be saved and the other will die. Ben Petura said: "Let them both die and let not one be a witness to the death of his fellow man" (i.e., the principle of human equality). However the greater authority is R. Akiva, who refutes Ben Petura's opinion and says that the person in possession of the water should drink it all. R. Akiva bases his reasoning on a passage concerning exacting interest from a fellow Jew, where the Torah forbids this practice "so that your brother may live with you" (Lev. 25:36). However, that requires that you must be alive before you care for your brother (somewhat like putting your oxygen mask on first on an airplane before assisting someone else), for otherwise he cannot possibly live *with you*. Consequently, according to R. Akiva, "your life takes precedence." Similarly, although there is an obligation to rescue (based on either "Do not stand idly by the blood of your neighbor" [Lev. 19:16] or "If your neighbor is missing something, you shall restore it to him" [Deut. 22:2]), in a dangerous situation a person must first protect his own life (i.e., one is not allowed to sacrifice his life to save another).

Is Jewish law based on rights? (F)

Unlike Anglo-American law, in which issues are framed in terms of *rights*, Jewish law is based on *obligations*. In a system of rights-based law, it is necessary to first determine the rights of each of the involved parties and assess what happens when these rights conflict. In contrast, under Jewish law the decision in each case must fall into one of three basic categories—

obligatory (*hovah*), in which one must do something (duty); prohibited (*asur*), in which one is strictly forbidden from doing something; and permitted (*reshut*), in which one has the option of doing something as long as there is some precedent in Jewish law allowing the action.

Do the Bible and Talmud provide for a sophisticated legal system? (T)

The classical Jewish legal system incorporated concepts of jurisprudence that remain ideals to the present day. A judge was required to recuse himself from a case if related to a litigant (Sanh. 7a) and to treat everyone equally be before the law (Lev. 19:15), neither favoring a man of high rank and distinction (Shev. 30a-31a) nor deciding in favor of a poor man because of pity and compassion for him (Exod. 23:3; Lev. 19:15). Accepting gifts (bribes) from litigants was expressly forbidden (Exod. 23:8), even if the judge rendered a judgment that "acquits the innocent and condemns the guilty." Rather than being influenced by a past criminal record, a defendant must be judged for the crime for which he is now being tried, not for any past transgressions, for only God may judge all the actions of men, both past and present. [13] A judge must deliberate with care before finally pronouncing his verdict, but may not unduly delay justice. Rather than relying on the opinion of a fellow judge in convicting the guilty or acquitting the innocent, each judge must come to his own conclusion based on an independent understanding of the evidence and the law. Under biblical and Talmudic law, circumstantial evidence was inadmissible in criminal cases, and defendants were forbidden to testify against themselves. Rather than based on lawyers acting as advocates for their clients, the classic Jewish legal system depended on rabbinic scholars asking probing questions of witnesses before rendering a decision.

Does the majority rule? (N)

Based on the verse, "You shall not follow a multitude to do evil" (Exod. 23:2), the Rabbis deduced that one *should* follow the majority when it is a matter of doing "not evil" (i.e., the good). Therefore, one is required to follow the majority if there is a difference of opinion among the rabbis regarding any of the laws of the Torah, and litigants must accept the majority view if there is a difference of opinion in a private lawsuit. However, if the majority of judges or witnesses are agreed on an opinion that another judge knows is unjust, he should not abandon his own view in order to fall in line with the others. Automatically accepting the reasoning of another judge, however brilliant, without arriving at the same conclusion through independent thinking, would establish the dangerous situation in which the opinion of a single judge dictates the decisions of an entire court. [14] In a court, a single person who has honestly and accurately analyzed the case and arrived at the correct opinion, in consultation with God, represents the true majority.

Does Jewish law use the jury system? (F)

Beit din (lit., "house of judgment") is the Hebrew term for a Jewish court of law. It is classically composed of three rabbis, who arbitrate disputes among Jews on a variety of issues in civil law. Today, it primarily focuses on religious matters, such as the granting of a *get* (divorce) or decisions regarding conversion.

In ancient Israel, the highest court was the Great Sanhedrin, which was composed of 71 judges who sat in the Temple in Jerusalem.[15] Jurisdiction over criminal matters, including capital cases, was delegated to Lesser Sanhedrins, consisting of 23 judges (Sanh. 1:4).

Did the Rabbis have a specific set of questions to ask witnesses? (T)

Under Jewish law, judges are required to diligently inquire into the testimony of witnesses and to interrogate them rigorously in the greatest possible detail before giving a verdict or inflicting punishment (Deut. 13:15). Meticulous care is required to prevent a judge from rendering an ill-considered and hasty decision that would harm an innocent person. According to the Rabbis, there were seven inquiries by which witnesses were tested: "In what sabbatical cycle [did the matter under consideration take place]? In what year? In what month? On which day of the month? On what day? At what hour? In what place?" (Sanh. 40a). Failure to provide a reasonable response led to the person's evidence being deemed inadmissible.

Is the testimony of a single witness sufficient at a traditional Jewish trial? (N)

According to traditional Jewish law, the infliction of physical punishment (such as death or lashes) may not be based on the testimony of a single witness, regardless of how trustworthy. In a monetary case, however, if a single witness testified in favor of the plaintiff, the defendant was obligated to take an oath stating that he was not liable. This oath was the strictest in Jewish law, with the defendant required to hold a Torah scroll and invoke the name of God. Taking the oath effectively freed the defendant from all liability; if he refused to take the oath, he was required to pay the claim.[16]

The testimony of a single person, man or woman, is sufficient to decide whether something is ritually permitted or forbidden. This enables a determination whether an item is kosher by either a *mashgiach* (*kashrut* supervisor) in a factory or restaurant, or even a cook in a private kitchen.[17]

In Jewish law, may a murderer be killed without trial? (F)

Regardless of how reprehensible the act, Jewish law requires that a murderer must be accorded "due process of law" and be entitled to a fair trial. Consequently, a person who witnesses a murder could only testify against the perpetrator in court, leaving it to the judges to condemn the accused for any crime he has committed and to decree the appropriate punishment. According to *Sefer ha-Chinuch*, one who violates this commandment, even a witness to the actual crime, and takes the law into his own hands is considered a murderer, and he himself is subject to the death penalty.

Under biblical law, could an Israelite who murdered another pay a monetary penalty if the family of the victim agreed? (F)

The Torah explicitly prohibited the acceptance of "atonement money" (ransom) from someone who had committed willful or unintentional murder (Num. 35:31). As Maimonides noted,[18] "even if the murderer is prepared to give all the treasure in the world, and even if the next of kin of the murdered man is willing to absolve him, the Court is forbidden to accept the ransom. For the soul of the murdered man belongs not to the next of kin, but to God." *Sefer ha-Chinuch* added: "If men in power were permitted to take ransom for intentional or unintentional murder, the strong and the rich would kill their opponents and then offer their ransom; thus men would be in constant warfare, and society would be destroyed."[19]

In biblical law, did an Israelite who accidently killed another escape punishment? (N)

The Israelites were commanded to establish six cities of refuge (three on each side of the Jordan River) to which a person could flee if he unintentionally killed another individual. This injunction also required the building of wide, level roads with appropriate directional signs to these cities, as well as the removal of any obstacles that might hinder the fugitive in his flight (Num. 35:9–34). Every person who killed another, "whether unintentionally or with intent," would immediately flee to a city of refuge to escape the blood avenger (family member of the deceased). From the city of refuge, the individual would be sent to the court for trial. If the killing had been completely accidental, the perpetrator would be absolved of any responsibility and set free, and the blood avenger had no right to harm him. If the killing had been intentional, the murderer properly warned in advance, and his act witnessed by two reliable individuals, the court would order his execution. If the act was unintentional but associated with some culpable carelessness (i.e., involuntary manslaughter), the perpetrator would be exiled to a city of refuge. The court would be responsible for providing safe passage so that the blood avenger could not kill the murderer on the way. A person who had been exiled to a city of refuge by the court was required to remain there until the death of the High Priest.

In Jewish law, is a homeowner permitted to kill a burglar? (N)

A homeowner is permitted to kill a burglar to save his own life, but not if only his property was at risk (Exod. 22:1–2). A burglar who entered a house in the dead of night was presumed to have no hesitation about killing the owner; a homeowner who killed this apparent "pursuer" (*rodef*) would not be guilty of murder but rather be deemed to have acted in self-defense. However, if a burglar broke into a home in broad daylight, it was assumed that the intruder was not planning to physically harm the householder, since he would surely be apprehended. Because in this scenario only his property was at risk and it was not necessary to take a life to protect himself, the homeowner was forbidden to kill the burglar.

Does Jewish law make an exception for acting under duress? (T)

According to the Torah, a person cannot be punished for having committed a sin under duress. In the biblical context, this is illustrated by a distinction between two situations in which a man has sexual intercourse with a betrothed virgin (Deut. 22:23–27). If a man finds her in the city and lies with her, both are condemned to death—the man because he "afflicted the wife of a fellow," and the woman because she did not cry out. Since the attack occurred in the city, where there presumably would be other people around who would have heard her shouts and saved her, the Torah attaches some degree of complicity to her failure to scream for help. However, if a man discovers her in the field and attacks her, only he is executed. The text states that the woman "has committed no capital sin," giving her the benefit of the doubt that "the betrothed girl cried out, but there was no one to save her."

In traditional Jewish law, is an intoxicated person responsible for his actions? (N)

In civil law, the transactions of an inebriated person engaged in buying or selling are legally binding. An exception is made if the person reaches the state of "Lot's drunkenness."[20] The actions of a person who is so drunk that he becomes virtually insane are not legally binding. Nevertheless, regardless of how drunk, a person is completely responsible for any damage that he caused while intoxicated.

Is a person who causes damage when sleepwalking responsible for his actions? (N)

Unlike a drunk, who is guilty of becoming intoxicated, a person who falls asleep has committed no crime. Although he would not be guilty of any crime while sleepwalking, he would still have to pay for any damages that he caused, based on the general Jewish principle that a person is always responsible for his acts.

Is a person who injures another only responsible for paying the victim's medical bills? (F)

According to the Mishnah, a person who injures another becomes liable to him for five items: damages, pain, healing (medical expenses), loss of time from work, and humiliation (BK 85a–b). In Talmudic times, damages were estimated by a calculation of the difference in value between how much he would have been worth as a slave being sold in the marketplace before and after the injury. Pain was calculated by "how much money a man of equal standing would accept to undergo so much pain." To estimate the value of loss of time from work, the injured person was considered "as though he were a watchman in a cucumber field," a job that required the least able person, since even a lame or one-armed person could be employed in this capacity.[21] Humiliation was estimated according to the status of the offender and the injured.

In addition to financial considerations, the person also was required to personally approach the victim and ask for forgiveness.

In classic Jewish law, could anyone be a witness? (F)

Under rabbinic law, 10 types of witnesses were disqualified from testifying in court: (1) women (who were thought to be too emotional to render a reasoned judgment); slaves (because they had not acquired the habit of thinking independently); minors; the mentally retarded; deaf-mutes (who could not hear questions nor speak in response to them); the blind (who clearly could not be "eyewitnesses"); relatives of the parties involved in the case (lest their testimony be biased); those personally involved in the case; a "shameless" person; and a wicked person (such as a compulsive gambler, pigeon racer, thief, or usurer).[22]

Under biblical law, was perjury punishable by more than a fine? (T)

Witnesses who testified falsely were punished by making them suffer what they sought to inflict on others by means of their testimony. If the testimony was calculated to produce a monetary loss or whipping, the court should inflict on the witness a loss of equal value or the identical number of lashes, respectively. If the false testimony was designed to lead to the death of the accused, the guilty party would suffer the same kind of death. Ironically, in capital cases this law was applicable only when the person falsely accused had not been put to death. Once the person falsely accused had been executed, witnesses who were proved to have testified falsely were no longer liable under this law. Instead, their punishment was left to Heaven.

Is a Jew exonerated by a court of law freed from punishment? (N)

The Hebrew term *karet* (extirpation) is used to denote punishment "at the hands of Heaven," in cases when a person cannot be convicted by an earthly court because of the absence of witnesses. The Bible indicates *karet* as the penalty for such deliberate transgressions as idolatry, desecration of the Sabbath, the eating of *chametz* on Passover, incest, and adultery.

Are Jews expected to conform to local laws? (T)

In third-century Babylonia, the prominent sage Samuel developed the concept of *dina d'malchuta dina*, an Aramaic phrase meaning "the law of the state is the law." This halachic rule established that even though Jews had their own civil courts, it was a religious duty for them to obey the laws of the country in which they lived. The only exceptions to this idea were laws that contradicted fundamental Jewish beliefs, such as those advocating murder or theft (Git. 10b; BK 113b).

Does Judaism favor capital punishment? (N)

The Bible prescribes the death penalty for a multitude of offenses, including murder, adultery, blasphemy, profaning the Sabbath, idolatry, incest, striking one's parents, false prophecy, witchcraft, and giving false testimony in capital cases. However, capital punishment was actually imposed only as long as the Temple existed (Sanh. 52b). The Rabbis were generally opposed to capital punishment[23] and made it very difficult to sentence someone to death. According to Talmudic law, two eyewitnesses must testify to the crime, and the perpetrator must have been forewarned concerning both the seriousness of his proposed action and its punishment. Although a majority of one was sufficient to acquit the accused, a plurality of two was required to convict. In addition, the law of evidence and the proof of premeditation in capital cases were made so severe that a verdict of death was almost impossible. In a famous passage, the Talmud brands a Sanhedrin (Great Court) that executed one man in seven years as a "destructive" tribunal. R. Eleazar ben Azariah said "one in 70 years," while R. Tarfon and R. Akiva stated, "Were we members of a Sanhedrin, no person would ever be put to death." However, Rabban Shimon ben Gamaliel offered a contrary and sobering view, retorting that "they would also multiply shedders of blood in Israel! [i.e., they would eliminate the fear of retribution, which is a deterrent to murder]" (Mak. 1:10).

Does the State of Israel permit capital punishment? (N)

The modern State of Israel has no capital punishment except for participation in genocidal activities and under certain conditions of warfare. The only person ever put to death in Israel was Adolph Eichmann in 1962, for his crimes against humanity and the Jewish people during the Holocaust.

Does Judaism have a concept of vicarious punishment? (N)

According to traditional Jewish belief, punishment (and reward) are assigned to people according to their own actions. As the Bible explicitly declares: "Fathers shall not be put to death for their sons, and sons should not be put to death for their fathers; a person shall be put to death only for his own sin" (Deut. 24:16). However, the Second Commandment describes a "jealous God visiting the sins of the fathers upon children to the third and fourth generations" (Exod. 20:6). Faced with this apparent contradiction between the two biblical verses, the Rabbis explained that vicarious punishment for the sins of their fathers only applied to children who realized that what their parents did was wrong but failed to actively protest their actions, thus tacitly approving them, incorporating them into their own lives, and meriting their own individual punishment. Nevertheless, Jewish tradition supports the view of the prophet Ezekiel, who concludes that "the person who sins, only he shall die" (18:4, 20).

Are Jewish ethics different from secular Western ethics? (T)

Jewish ethics is a unique mode of thinking that differs from Western philosophical thought in terms of its basic premises and assumptions. As such, it may lead to disparate conclusions as to whether an act is deemed moral or immoral.

Jewish ethics is a form of religious or theological ethics, which ultimately is "derived from a Divine source and is communicated to human beings in acts of revelation. Therefore, Jewish ethics presupposes that morality ultimately has its origins in a source other than ourselves." This is in contrast to secular ethics, "which maintains that ethics is derived from, and is justified by, autonomous human origins, such as human reason, human emotion, human intuition, and social mores. Moral principles conveyed by revelation may be understood, interpreted, embellished, and applied by utilizing God-given abilities, such as intellect, intuition, experience and emotion"[24] Ultimately, however, Jewish ethics rests on theological presuppositions. In modern times, Jewish ethical concerns have been expanded to such areas as business and medicine.

Does human decision-making ever contradict apparent Divine law? (T)

The classic example is the Talmudic tale of the ritual purity of the oven of Achan (BM 59b). Eliezer ben Hyrcanus called for several miraculous events to prove his point of view—a carob tree uprooting itself and moving 100 cubits, the stream outside the academy changing course, and the walls of the school house falling inward—but these signs failed to persuade the other Rabbis. Finally, Eliezer summoned a voice from Heaven to support his view, and a *bat kol* cried out: "Why do you dispute with Eliezer, seeing that in all matters the *halachah* agrees with him?" Referring to a set of biblical verses, R. Joshua calmly replied: "It [i.e., halachic decision] is not in heaven, we pay no attention to a *bat kol,* for it is written in the Torah at Mount Sinai: 'One must follow the majority' (Exod. 23:2)." Thus, in terms of law as well as ethics, human beings must use their own reasoning and intuition to interpret Divine law in making decisions on specific issues.

In Jewish thought, is the human being inherently good? (N)

Jewish ethics speaks of two complementary polar opposites—the *yetzer ha-ra* and the *yetzer ha-tov*, respectively the inclinations toward evil and good. The Rabbis argued that the human being must have both, since without the *yetzer ha-ra* (which includes survival skills and ambition), a human being could not live. Indeed, the inclination toward evil can be a powerful positive force if channeled correctly. As the Midrash observed, "Were it not for the *yetzer ha-ra* [used here as the sexual urge], no man would build a house, marry a wife, or father children" (Gen. R. 9:7). Moreover, only the existence of the *yetzer ha-ra* gives humans the opportunity to become moral beings, for without an inclination toward evil the concept of "goodness" would have no meaning.

The relative powers of the two inclinations control a person's character. The righteous are swayed by their good inclination and the wicked by their inclination toward evil; "average" people are equally influenced by both (Ber. 61b). "Who is mighty? He who subdues his evil impulse" (Avot 4:1).

Does Jewish ethics believe in free will? (N)

Free will is the theological doctrine that each individual has the ability to make choices that are not pre-determined, and that every person is morally responsible for these choices. The biblical concept of reward and punishment, based on whether one observed the commandments, is founded on this principle. The idea of free will must be reconciled with the concept of determinism, which posits that all events and personal choices and actions are pre-ordained by Divine decree or are the necessary and inevitable results of previous causes. The relative importance of free will and Divine Providence was a critical issue in the debate among the three major Jewish groups during the late Second Temple period. The Sadducees totally rejected the notion of Divine interference in human affairs and deemed free will to be absolute, while the Essenes maintained a belief in complete pre-destination. The Pharisees, whose teachings formed the basis of rabbinic Judaism, took the middle ground, accepting a belief in the foreknowledge of God but emphasizing that each individual possesses free will, which they viewed as indispensable for religious and moral life and as compatible with Divine omniscience.

Nevertheless, some of the Rabbis believed in Divine determinism. R. Hanina said, "No man injures his finger here on earth unless it was decreed for him in heaven" (Hul. 7b). The Rabbis ask why God created all of humanity from a single man. One answer relates directly to the existence of free will and the rejection of pure determinism—so that the righteous could not claim a heredity that would prevent them from sinning, nor the wicked maintain that they had inherited an evil disposition and thus it was useless for them to repent (Sanh. 38a).

Does Jewish law have a negative view of becoming wealthy? (N)

Traditional Judaism does not condemn the pursuit and acquisition of wealth, as long as it operates within the parameters established by Jewish law, morality, and custom and does not detract excessively from the time that a Jew should dedicate to Torah study. As wealth is considered a gift from God, there is also an obligation to conduct business affairs in accordance with the Divine will. Dishonesty in business is not merely a legal crime, but more importantly a religious transgression.

Does Judaism accept the concept of caveat emptor ("let the buyer beware")? (F)

Jewish law places the full responsibility for disclosing defects and other shortcomings on the seller, even in the absence of a written guarantee. Based on the biblical injunction against "placing a stumbling block before the blind" (Lev. 19:14), the Rabbis required that all customers be fully informed about the quality of merchandise (no false advertising). Selling inferior goods as superior quality is not permitted, even if one reduces the price. An ethical seller must also divulge the dangers in such inherently harmful products as cigarettes, liquor, drugs, and weapons not used solely for self-defense.

When bargaining with a seller, can a buyer falsely claim that he can purchase similar merchandise cheaper at another store? (F)

Just as sellers are prohibited from overcharging and making false claims, it is forbidden for a buyer to deliberately mislead a seller by saying that the item is for sale elsewhere at a cheaper price. Similarly if a vendor is ignorant of the true value of an item and is offering it for an obviously low price, the buyer is obliged to make the seller aware of the error. Getting a bargain is a pleasure, but it should not be achieved at the expense of one's ethical values. Thus, both buyers and sellers are forbidden from employing devious business practices.

Do workers have rights in traditional Jewish law? (T)

The Torah requires that Jewish employers treat their workers with dignity and respect and pay them a fair wage (Deut. 24:15). Salaries must be paid promptly; as the Talmud notes, "He who withholds an employee's wages is as though he had taken his life" (BM 112a).

In Jewish law, is it permitted to walk into an expensive store simply to discover the price of an object? (F)

It is forbidden for a person to feign interest in an item by asking a merchant the price of an article or requesting to taste some food, when he has no money or knows that he will not buy it. (It is permissible to inform the seller that you are just browsing.)

Similarly, in a social context it is forbidden as fraud to invite someone to dinner or some event if you know that the other person will not accept.

When advertising a product, it is fair to attack the competition to increase sales? (F)

Although a common business practice, this is forbidden by Jewish law. It is permissible to point out the superiority of one's own product, the reasonableness of the price, and the excellent service provided after the sale, but not to say that the competition is selling an inferior product with poor service at an inflated price. In effect, this would be a violation of the prohibition against *lashon ha-ra* (evil speech)—even if true!

Does Jewish law prohibit cross-dressing? (T)

The Bible explicitly forbids men and women from adopting the attire (or other practices) of the opposite sex (Deut. 22:5). A major reason underlying this prohibition was the desire to avoid the promiscuity that might result from men and women mixing too freely together.

A man was forbidden to be overly concerned with certain aspects of personal grooming, such as not shaving his face to appear feminine or adorning himself with jewelry. Conversely, a woman was not to appear masculine, such as being clad in military armor. According to the Rabbis, other violations of this commandment included a man dying his hair or pulling out gray hairs from his head to retain a youthful appearance.[25] Maimonides maintained that wearing the clothes and adornments of the opposite sex was related to idol worship and designed to arouse sexual desire.[26]

Unlike other biblical prohibitions, the provisions of this rule are affected by the social norms in a given place at a specific time. An excellent example is whether a woman is permitted to wear pants. Until the modern era, virtually no women wore pants, so that Jewish women would be forbidden from wearing such "male" clothing. However, in the Western world today, where many women wear pants, a Jewish woman who wears them would not necessarily violate the biblical prohibition against cross-dressing. Nevertheless, the wearing of pants is strongly discouraged in ultra-traditional Jewish circles because of issues relating to modesty and propriety.[27]

Does Judaism favor the literal concept of "an eye for an eye"? (F)

The classic biblical law of retaliation ("eye for an eye")[28] mandates that the punishment inflicted for bodily injury be precisely the same as the harm caused. This concept was common to all Semitic peoples and well developed by the time of the Code of Hammurabi (1750 B.C.E.). Rejecting a literal interpretation, the Rabbis declared that the law required an individual who injured another to pay the monetary equivalent to the person he had harmed. As the Talmud notes, there are cases in which actually exacting "an eye for an eye" would not constitute true justice. For example, if the victim was already blind in one eye, the injury would have left him totally blind, whereas the aggressor would still be able to see with one eye (and vice versa). Therefore, the Rabbis were convinced that the biblical phrase could only be interpreted as meaning that the aggressor must pay the victim the *worth* of an eye.

Does Jewish law believe in the principle of "finders keepers"? (F)

The Bible explicitly requires that lost property be returned to its rightful owner. Indeed, the finder even must care for the lost article until the owner claims it. Talmudic examples include unrolling and reading a scroll and shaking a garment every 30 days (BM 29b). A person who finds a lost object or animal and does not attempt to return it to its rightful owner is branded as a thief. The finder must make a public announcement and return the item to a person who can describe its identifying signs or provide evidence of ownership.

Can a person keep some found property? (T)

According to Jewish law, a person who finds "ownerless" property (*hefker*) may acquire it by taking possession. Property may become ownerless if the owner renounces it (e.g., putting it in the trash) or has given up hope of recovering something that has been lost (e.g., a dollar bill accidentally dropped in a public place), or if it remains unclaimed for a specific period of time. Similarly, lost property that lacks identifying marks and is found in a public place or appears abandoned (e.g., spilled fruit along a road) is deemed ownerless and can be taken by the finder.

In traditional Jewish law, can daughters inherit from the father's estate? (N)

According to biblical and Talmudic law, daughters were denied a direct share in the inheritance of their father as long as there were sons. The reason was that men were primarily responsible for sustaining their families and thus would be sharing the estate with the women they married. Although a daughter would not directly inherit from her father, she would indirectly inherit from the father of her future husband. As long as daughters were unmarried, however, the cost of supporting them was the first duty of the estate of the deceased. Anything left over went to the sons; if there were nothing extra, the sons were forced to fend for themselves. As the Talmud eloquently states, "If the property is small, the daughters are maintained [from it] and the sons shall go begging" (BB 139b).

What if there were no sons? After hearing that only men were counted in preparation for the distribution of the Promised Land, the five daughters of Zelophehad successfully complained to Moses that, because they had no brothers, their family would be without a share (Num. 27:1–11). Consequently, if there are no sons, the daughters gain title to the estate.

Is the legal concept of negligence part of biblical law? (T)

In Jewish law dating back to the Bible, people are responsible for all damage caused by their property or actions if they fail to take appropriate care to prevent them from becoming dangerous. They are also required to protect property entrusted to them against any foreseeable harm. These are excellent descriptions of the modern legal concept of negligence as a failure to meet the duty of "reasonable care."

As an example, if an ox gored a person or an animal, the degree of punishment depended on whether the owner of the ox was aware of any dangerous tendencies of the animal. If the animal was known to be savage and had caused damage in the past, the owner was considered negligent and held responsible for all damages. However, if the animal had not been in the habit of causing damage, the owner need only pay half (Exod. 21:28–36; 22:4–6).

Similarly, if a person willfully or negligently allowed his cattle to graze in the field or vineyard of another, the owner of the animal was responsible for making restitution for any damage it caused by eating or trampling his neighbor's crops or grapes. However, if the animal merely wandered there without any culpable negligence on the owner's part, or if the animal caused damage in a public thoroughfare (because those who set their things in such a place are themselves guilty of contributory negligence), the owner of the animal was not liable.[29]

If a person kindled a fire in his own field and the wind carried sparks that set fire to a neighboring field, he was liable for negligence and must make full restitution for any damage caused.

Is ritual impurity the same as being dirty? (F)

In the Bible, the concept of ritual impurity had nothing to do with cleanliness or hygiene. A person who touched anything considered ritually unclean (or in certain circumstances, was only near it) was himself rendered ritually impure and subject to all the obligations relating to ritually impure persons. This had no practical significance unless the individual wanted to come into the Sanctuary, touch any holy thing, or eat any hallowed food.

Was the source of ritual impurity coming into contact with a dead body? (N)

The most potent source of ritual impurity was a dead human body (Num. 19:11). It conveyed ritual impurity to anyone or anything that entered or remained within the same tent or under the same roof as a corpse (including household utensils and wearing apparel), even if the person had no direct contact with it. However, among other causes of ritual impurity were contact with the carcasses of animals (Lev. 11:24) and certain creeping creatures (weasel, mouse, great lizard, gecko, land crocodile, lizard, sand lizard, chameleon), which also were prohibited as food (Lev. 11:29–30); and food and drink in an earthen vessel into which one of these dead creatures or their droppings had fallen (Lev. 11:34). The other major causes of ritual impurity included normal discharges from the sexual organs—bleeding related to menstruation or childbirth in women, seminal emissions in men—or discharges related to illness or infection.

Could ritual impurity be passed from one person to another? (T)

A person who had contact with an individual who had become ritually impure became himself ritually impure and could even transmit this state to food and drink. During a woman's menstrual period or after childbirth, anyone who touched her, her bedding, or anywhere she sat would become ritually impure.

Could ritual impurity be removed by taking a bath at home? (F)

For women after menstruation or childbirth (40 days for a son, 80 for a daughter), immersion in a *mikveh* was sufficient to remove the state of ritual impurity. Other ritual impurities could be removed by various combinations of immersion in the *mikveh*, washing clothes, offering sacrifices, and being sprinkled with the ashes of the red heifer.

In Jewish law, is a person permitted to do anything to protect another? (N)

The Rabbis required that one has an obligation to do whatever is necessary to save the life of one who is being pursued and threatened with harm, even going as far as taking the life of the pursuer (*rodef*), without incurring any liability. However, if one can save an endangered person by merely wounding the pursuer, the rescuer must not take his life lest he be considered guilty of murder.[30] This is contrary to American law, in which there is "no affirmative duty to rescue an imperiled party."

Saving the life of the pursued is the basis on which abortion is required if the life of the mother is in danger. In this situation, it is obligatory to save the life of the pregnant woman (the pursued) by destroying the fetus (the pursuer). However, if the child's head has emerged from the womb, it is regarded as alive and may not be harmed, for it is forbidden to destroy one independent life to save another.[31]

In biblical times, were all Israelites required to take part in wars against enemies of the nation? (N)

Although all male Israelites over the age of 20 were to participate in wars against enemies of the nation, the Bible declared that all soldiers who were excessively fearful were not permitted to go into combat (Deut. 20:8), lest they adversely affect the morale of their comrades in arms. However, they were required to help supply food and water to the troops.[32] Three groups of men were required to be excused from battle: a person who had built a house and not dwelled in it; one who had planted a vineyard and not eaten its fruit; and an individual who had betrothed a woman but not yet married her, or a newlywed during his first year of marriage (Deut. 20:5–7). These people were not only freed from actual military service but were allowed to return home.

Were there rules of cleanliness in an Israelite military camp? (T)

The encampment of an Israelite army was to be completely different from that of any other nation. Because Israel's success was in the hands of God, the camp must be a place of purity, free from dirt and waste, as befitting the Divine Presence.[33] One mechanism for ensuring the cleanliness and sanctity of the camp was the command to reserve a place outside the camp where the troops could go to relieve themselves so that God would not "see an unseemly thing among you and turn away from you" (Deut. 23:13). Moreover, each soldier was required to provide himself with a shovel or paddle, in addition to his weapon, so that he could dig up the earth and cover his excrement (Deut. 23:15).

Were the Israelites permitted to do whatever was necessary to win a war? (F)

When besieging a city, the Torah prohibited the Israelites from cutting down fruit trees lest this cause distress and suffering to its inhabitants (Deut. 20:19–20). Even during times of war, Jews must avoid unnecessary destruction and remain conscious of the need to maintain concern for the general welfare, even of their enemies.

Because fruit trees are vital to man, the Rabbis deduced the general principle of *bal tashchit*, the prohibition of wanton destruction of anything valuable to human existence, including vessels, clothing, buildings, springs, and food.[34]

Did the Bible permit a father to sell his daughter? (N)

Under biblical law, an impoverished father did have the right to "sell" his daughter to a wealthy family as a bondwoman until she reached puberty (Exod. 21:7–11). However, this practice was designed to be for *her* benefit, because the Torah commanded that the purchaser or his son was to marry her or be guilty of a "betrayal," though the daughter always retained the right to reject the marriage. In effect, this offered the daughter the possibility of escaping a life of extreme poverty. The girl went free (without any redemption payment) in one of three ways: (a) after six years; (b) with the arrival of the Jubilee Year; or (c) when her puberty began.[35]

If the owner or his son married this Hebrew bondwoman, he was forbidden to treat her any differently than a free woman. Despite her effectively being "purchased" as a wife, she had the same rights to food, clothing, and marital relations as a woman from the highest stratum of Israelite society. These obligations to the former bondwoman persisted even if he later took another wife.[36]

Does the Bible permit one Jew to be the slave of another? (N)

Although the biblical word *eved* is often translated as "slave," as with the Israelites being slaves to Pharaoh in Egypt, in the context of the relationship of one Israelite to another it meant "servant." There were two ways in which a Jew could be sold into indentured servitude. A free man could choose to sell himself to escape from extreme poverty, becoming a member of the household of another and earning his food and shelter through his labor; or a thief might be sold by the court if he was unable to repay his victims. A

Hebrew servant was to serve his master for only six years; in the seventh year he was required to be set free. Thus, servitude was designed to be merely a temporary condition, rather than a permanent state. The master was commanded to give generous gifts to Israelite bondmen when they gained their freedom, thus helping them make a fresh start in life.

Could a Jewish servant be harshly treated? (F)

Strict rules protected the Israelite servant. The master was forbidden to employ a Hebrew bondman in degrading menial tasks and was required to assign him to skilled work or field labor, like hired help. He was prohibited from ordering an Israelite servant to perform tasks that had no useful purpose (like boiling water when there was no need for it) or whose duration was ill-defined (such as to continue digging around a tree until his master returned). Physical abuse was forbidden. Because servant and master were ultimately related, the servant could not be given food or accommodation inferior to that of his master. Kindness and humanity were to characterize the bearing of the Israelite toward his less fortunate brother.[37] Servants were entitled to Sabbath rest, participated in the sacrificial meal on Passover, and were permitted to own and acquire property. In view of all these limitations upon the master, the Talmud ironically observed: "One who buys an Israelite slave buys himself a master!" (Kid. 20a).

Were there limits on how badly a non-Jewish slave could be treated? (T)

Although a non-Jewish slave was considered his master's property and did not enjoy the same privileges as the Israelite indentured servant, Jewish law was sensitive to his needs. A heathen slave was entitled to rest on the Sabbath and was to be set free if he sustained physical injury at the hand of his owner. An Israelite master who killed a heathen slave was even subject to the death penalty.

According to the Bible, must fugitive slaves be returned to their rightful owner? (F)

Unlike the Babylonian Code of Hammurabi, in which aiding and abetting the escape of a runaway slave was a crime punishable by death, the Torah teaches that the Jew should always be merciful in protecting and assisting those who are in need of help. Slaves and prisoners escaping from a besieged enemy city must be given their freedom and allowed to settle wherever they wish in the Land of Israel (Deut. 23:15–16). Sending a man seeking his freedom back to a life of idolatry would be inconsistent with the ideal of sanctity permeating the Israelite camp. The biblical fugitive slave law is in stark contrast to laws existing in the United States before the Civil War, which mandated the return of runaway slaves to their masters.

Is the biblical prohibition against "putting a stumbling block before the blind" taken literally? (N)

In addition to its literal meaning, this biblical commandment (Lev. 19:14) has been interpreted as forbidding one from giving misleading advice to an unsuspecting or uninformed person, especially if you may benefit from his error. Later it was extended to include causing someone to sin, especially the young and innocent and the morally weak. Among the numerous violations of this ethical precept are offering forbidden food to an unsuspecting individual, tempting the Nazirite to break his oath by holding out a cup of wine (Pes. 22b), a borrower offering interest to appeal to the greed of a creditor, and selling a knife or other lethal weapon to a person of dubious or dangerous character.[38] The overall import of this commandment is to stress that each person is responsible for the welfare of others and may not do anything to endanger it.[39] According to *Sefer ha-Chinuch*, the three pillars on which the world is established are truth, shared confidence, and mutual trust.[40]

Does *Kiddush ha-Shem* mean martyrdom? (N)

The ultimate expression of *Kiddush ha-Shem* (lit., "sanctification of the Name [of God]") is martyrdom, in which Jews have given up their lives rather than desecrate the Name of God. According to the rabbis, if a Jew is forced to transgress any of the commandments (except three) at pain of death, he may violate the law rather than surrender his life. However, a Jew is required to sacrifice his life rather than be guilty of the three cardinal sins— idolatry, adultery, and murder.

However, martyrdom is not the only way in which one can sanctify the Name of God. Israel sanctifies God's Name in the liturgy, when Jews recite the *Kaddish* and exclaim, "Magnified and sanctified be His great Name," and when the congregation recites the *Kedushah* and affirms, "We will sanctify Your Name in the world even as they sanctify it in the highest heaven." However, it is more important to hallow the Name of God by moral action, especially by performing acts of justice and compassion in the sight of Gentiles, for people judge Judaism by the conduct of Jews.

Is it a religious duty to kiss such holy objects as the *tallit* and *tefillin*? (N)

It is a widespread custom, though not a religious duty, to kiss holy objects as a way of expressing a depth of reverence and spiritual devotion. Examples include kissing the two ends of the *atarah* (crown) just before donning the *tallit*; *tefillin* when taken out or returned to their bag; the Torah mantle when it passes by in procession in the synagogue; the Torah scroll before one recites the blessings over it (either with the intermediary of the edge of a *tallit* or the sash used to tie the scroll together, but never with the bare hand); a *siddur* (prayer book) and *Chumash* (Five Books of Moses) before putting them away or if they are accidentally dropped on the floor; and the *mezuzah* on the doorpost when entering or leaving a house.

Are Jews permitted to say whatever they want as long as it is true? (F)

There is a strict biblical prohibition against *lashon ha-ra* (lit., "evil speech," often translated as "gossip"), which refers to any derogatory or damaging statement against an individual that, if publicized to others, would cause the subject physical or monetary damage, anguish, or fear. Unlike secular American law, this prohibition applies even when the slanderous or defamatory remarks are true.

Was *lashon ha-ra* considered as serious as murder? (T)

Ibn Ezra noted that the Bible follows the commandment against *lashon ha-ra* with a verse warning against standing idly by the blood of your neighbor, indicating that slander is considered tantamount to murder since both "shed blood" (BM 58b). Indeed, the Rabbis deemed the slanderer worse than a murderer, "since he destroys a man's reputation, which is more precious than his life."[41] As Ecclesiasticus observed, "Many have been killed by the sword, but not so many as by the tongue" (28:18).

Is there any reference to *lashon ha-ra* in the prayers? (T)

According to the Talmud, the destruction of Jerusalem resulted from false charges brought to the Roman authorities by an angry Jew who was insulted by his neighbor (Git. 55b–56a). Those making false accusations to a ruling authority were placed in the category of persons who commit assault with intent to kill, and putting them to death was authorized. The extent to which Jewish communities were endangered throughout the centuries led to the inclusion in the daily *Amidah* of the prayer, "And for slanderers (*malshinim*), let there be no hope." The dangerous temptation of *lashon ha-ra* is also emphasized in the concluding paragraph of the silent *Amidah*, which begins: "My God, guard my tongue from evil and my lips from speaking falsely" (Ps. 34:14).

Is sharing gossip with a spouse considered *lashon ha-ra*? (T)

Even though husband and wife are regarded as a single unit, they are viewed as two separate individuals as far as gossip is concerned. Consequently, the law forbidding *lashon ha-ra* applies.

Is the person who relates gossip guilty of a transgression? (N)

According to the Talmud, *lashon ha-ra* destroys three people—"he who relates [the slander], he who accepts it, and he about whom it is told" (Ar. 15b). The Rabbis urge that, if someone starts speaking *lashon ha-ra*, one should attempt to respectfully and privately tell the individual that this is forbidden speech. Listening intently to *lashon ha-ra* merely encourages a gossip to continue this reprehensible practice. If caught among people who are engaging in *lashon ha-ra* and unable to leave or change the topic, it is necessary to consciously not accept the material as true; not enjoy it (even if it a funny story, because the subject is being shamed); and not pretend by facial expressions or eye contact that one agrees with the import of what is being said. [42]

Is it permissible to make use of *lashon ha-ra*? (T)

Ironically, the Talmud states, "Although one should not believe slander, one should take note of it" (Nid. 61a). This means that on some occasions it is permissible for a person to listen to *lashon ha-ra* when the information might be used for self-protection or the benefit of another (e.g., potential business partner or roommate). However, one is forbidden to accept the material as true, and may only suspect and investigate its accuracy.

Are Jews prohibited from charging interest in loans to other Jews? (N)

The Bible explicitly forbids Jews from lending at interest to a fellow Jew (Exod. 22:24; Lev. 25:35–37). Moreover, Jews are even prohibited from even taking part in a transaction between borrower and lender involving a loan at interest—whether as surety, witness, or notary drawing up the contract between them for payment of the interest on which they have agreed (BM 5:11).

In addition to direct and fixed interest payments (lending four coins and receiving five in return), the Talmud prohibited a broad spectrum of "indirect benefits" that could be offered in lieu of interest (BM 5:11). These included offering a gift when asking for a loan or giving a gift when repaying it (pre- and post-paid interest, respectively) (BM 5:11), allowing the lender to live on the borrower's premises rent-free or at a reduced rent (BM 64b), and a borrower giving a lender valuable information or even "extending a greeting to him if that is not his usual practice" (BM 75b). An indication of how strongly the Rabbis argued against indirect interest is the ruling that, if two people agreed to do work for each other in turn, they had to make certain that the values were identical (since in different seasons the work may be of unequal difficulty), lest the more valuable work be construed as containing a component of forbidden interest (BM 5:10). When borrowing goods that fluctuate in value, the safest approach is to agree that the lender will return goods of the same value, rather than the exact number of the goods that were borrowed.

Did the Rabbis change the prohibition against lending at interest? (N)

As the agrarian society of the biblical Land of Israel was transformed into a more urban economy, lending money at interest became necessary to pre-serve the financial well-being of the Jewish community. Consequently, the Rabbis developed a variety of techniques for circumventing the prohibition against lending at interest. The simplest method was to lend money at interest to a non-Jew, who in turn would lend the money to a Jew (BM 61b). A more ingenious approach was the *heter iskah* (permission to form a partnership). Using a standardized and witnessed legal form, the "lender" would agree to provide a specified amount of money to the "borrower" as a "joint venture." The "borrower" alone would operate the business, pledging to pay a fixed minimum profit (i.e., interest) and guaranteeing the "lender's" capital against all loss. At the agreed time of maturity, the "lender" would recover the initial investment ("loan") plus the promised minimum profit as stipulated in the deed.

Is it permitted to lend money at interest to non-Jews? (T)

Although Jews are forbidden to exact interest on a loan to a fellow Jew, they are permitted to do so when lending money to a non-Jew. Indeed, Maimonides interpreted the biblical verse, "You may lend at interest to foreigners" (Deut. 23:21), as a *command* to exact interest from non-Jews to whom one lends money, whereas virtually all other commentators believed it was merely *permitted* to do so. During the Middle Ages, when Jews (especially in Northern Europe) were excluded from engaging in agriculture and becoming members of craftsmen's guilds, moneylending became a necessary Jewish occupation. Like Shylock in Shakespeare's *The Merchant of Venice*, the image of the greedy, ruthless, and unmerciful Jewish moneylender demanding his "pound of flesh" became a reviled stereotype that contributed to anti-Semitism.

Despite religious prohibitions, Christians eventually also became moneylenders, though it remained the Jews who were associated with the negative stereotypes of this occupation.

Can Jews lend at interest to other Jews today? (N)

Currently, making an interest-bearing business transaction comply with Jewish law merely requires adding the words *al-pi hetter iskah* to the legal document. Nevertheless, there are Hebrew Free Loan Associations in all cities with a substantial number of Jews that offer interest-free loans in accordance with the biblical precept. Interest-free loans are available for emergencies, personal financial challenges, tuition- and education-related costs, debt consolidation, starting a small business, adopting a child, and special medical needs. Loans are also made to Jewish organizations and synagogues. Borrowers typically agree to a specified repayment plan, ranging from two to five years.

Is "love your neighbor as yourself" a Christian concept? (F)

The commandment to "love your neighbor as yourself" is a biblical commandment (Lev. 19:18). This was interpreted as meaning that one must let the honor, property, and desires of other human beings be "as dear to you as your own" (Avot 2:15, 17). R. Akiva termed this commandment as "a fundamental principle of the Torah." His contemporary, Ben Azzai, stressed that it should be read in conjunction with the verse describing human beings as being created in the image of God, so as to emphasize the essential brotherhood of man (*Sifra Kedoshim*). As the Talmud states, "He who elevates himself at the expense of his neighbor has no portion in the World to Come" (JT Hag. 2:1).

The negative form of this commandment is presented in the well-known story of the heathen scoffer who asked Hillel to condense the entire Torah "while standing on one foot" (i.e., in the shortest form possible). Hillel replied, "What is hateful to you do not do to your neighbor," followed by "this is the whole Torah, the rest is commentary; now go and learn!" (Shab. 31a).

Is it praiseworthy to love a neighbor more than oneself? (F)

The commandment is to love your neighbor "as" and not "more than" yourself. Thus, regard for self has a legitimate place. Hillel stated, "If I am not for myself, who will be for me?" just before saying "And if I am only for myself, what am I?"

Is there a difference between the negative actions of taking revenge and bearing a grudge? (T)

According to the Torah, "You shall not take revenge or bear a grudge" (Lev. 19:18). The Rabbis offered the following illustration of these two commandments. A asks B to lend him a sickle, but B refuses. The next day, B asks to borrow A's hatchet. If A replies, "I *will not* lend it to you, just as you refused to lend me your sickle," that is taking revenge. If A replies, "I *will* lend it to you, even though yesterday you refused to lend me your sickle," that is bearing a grudge. [43]

May Jews wear all types of clothes? (N)

A biblical verse that prohibits several types of mixed species as contrary to the Divinely appointed order of nature (Lev. 19:19) includes a ban on fabric made of a mixture of wool and linen (*sha'atnez*). The Rabbis ruled that the law of *sha'atnez* refers only to the weaving together of these two specific animal and vegetable fibers in the same garment. Thus, a linen tie worn with a wool suit is permitted, but a wool suit with linen-threaded buttons is prohibited. The combination of wool and linen may be mixed with cotton, silk, and other fibers in the manufacture of products other than clothing. [44]

While in practice many garments do not have any *sha'atnez* and may be assumed to have none, the particulars vary by garment type. The padding in many garments, such as suits, or the embroidery thread, such as designs on sweaters (men's and women's), may cause *sha'atnez* problems. When buying clothes, traditional Jews first check the fabric list to exclude garments with *sha'atnez*. If the label suggests that the garment may be permitted, it can be taken for testing at a special *sha'atnez* laboratory, which can be found in most cities with a substantial Orthodox community.

Is there any exception to the ban against *sha'atnez*? (T)

Based on the general principle that a positive commandment overrides a negative one, it is permitted to attach woolen *tzitzit* (fringes) to a linen garment, as in the *tallit* (Men. 40a). Similarly, *kohanim* were permitted to wear garments of mixed texture when performing the Torah-mandated priestly service in the Sanctuary (Yoma 69a).

Is shaving the beard forbidden according to Jewish law? (N)

The Bible prohibits shaving the "corners/side-growths" of the beard (Lev. 19:27; 21:5), presumably to distinguish the Israelites from the priests of pagan cults, who ritually shaved certain areas of their faces to designate their sacred status. Moreover, the beard was regarded as a symbol of male attractiveness and virility and a natural feature distinguishing men from women.

Nevertheless, today it is halachically permitted to shave the beard if one uses scissors, a chemical depilatory, or an electric shaver with two cutting edges. Only a razor with a single cutting edge is forbidden, since this is too close to the biblical prohibition against putting a knife to the face.

Is not shaving the beard a sign of mourning? (N)

In biblical times, shaving the head and beard were considered signs of mourning and great sorrow. Ironically, since many Jewish men are now clean-shaven, growing a beard—as opposed to shaving—has become a sign of mourning.

Does Jewish law require standing for an older person? (N)

The verse, "You shall rise before the aged and honor the presence of a sage" (Lev. 19:32), requires showing respect for scholars and the elderly, who in ancient times were honored for their wisdom and life experiences. The rabbinic attitude to the elderly is well expressed in *Pirkei Avot* (4:26), which states: "A person who learns from the young is compared to one who eats unripe grapes and drinks wine from a vat, whereas a person who learns from the old is compared to one who eats ripe grapes and drinks wine that is aged." The Midrash (Lev. R. 25) relates the tale of a king who, when standing up to honor an elderly commoner, would say: "God has chosen to reward him [with long life]; how can I not do the same?"[45]

Although Rashi maintained that the commandment is to rise and honor a sage who is *both* elderly and righteous, the *halachah* disagrees, considering each half of this verse to be a separate commandment. According to this view, it is necessary to rise for and honor any person over the age of 70, even if not learned; and to rise for and honor a sage, even if young.

However, there are exceptions to this rule. All agree that this requirement does not apply when seeing a wicked person.[46] Also, one must not always defer to the views of the elderly. When considering a halachic issue, the most important factor is the strength of a person's proof and analysis, because "a decision of law depends not on the teacher's age but on his reasoning" (BB 142b).

NOTES

1. Telushkin, 534.
2. Torah study is praiseworthy when combined with *derech eretz* (Avot 2:2).
3. Lutske, 279–80.
4. Biale, 162.
5. Dosick, 272.
6. *Etz Hayim*, 650.
7. Telushkin, 619.
8. Dosick, 270.
9. Adapted from lectures by Dr. Byron Sherwin at the Spertus Institute of Jewish Studies in Chicago.
10. Ibid.
11. Preuss, 22–26.
12. Adapted from lectures by Dr. Byron Sherwin at Spertus Institute of Jewish Studies in Chicago.
13. Chill, 96.
14. Ibid., 106.
15. This corresponded to the 70 elders and officers who assisted Moses in dispensing justice during biblical times (Num. 11:16–17).
16. Maimonides, *The Commandments*, 268.
17. *Stone Chumash*, 1037.
18. Maimonides, *Mishneh Torah*, Rotzeach u-Shemirat Nefesh 1:4.
19. *Sefer Ha-Chinnuch*, 275–76.
20. When after the destruction of Sodom and Gomorrah he became so drunk that he committed incest with both of his daughters.
21. The reimbursement for loss of wages sustained during the illness was based on this standard rather than on the victim's previous employment, because the latter had been taken into account in the payment for the value of his lost hand or leg (which made it impossible to continue his former occupation).
22. Chill, 103.
23. All members of a court that pronounced a death sentence were obliged to abstain from eating on the day of execution (Sanh. 63a).
24. Sherwin, *The Nature of Jewish Ethics*, 50.
25. Chill, 454–55.
26. Maimonides, *The Guide of the Perplexed* 3:37.
27. Enkin, "Does the Torah Tell Jewish Women to Wear Dresses and Not Pants?" About.com: Judaism, n.d., http://judaism.about.com/od/orthodoxfaqenkin/f//deut_dress.htm (accessed March 3, 2015).
28. The full phrase is: "Limb for limb, an eye for an eye, a tooth for a tooth; the injury inflicted is the injury to be suffered" (Exod. 21:24).
29. *Sefer Ha-Chinnuch*, 251.
30. Chill, 227–28.
31. Ibid., 228.
32. *Stone Chumash*, 1039.
33. Chill, 471.
34. Tigay, 190.
35. *Stone Chumash*, 419.
36. Ibid., 419.
37. Hertz, 537.
38. Ibid., 500.

39. *Stone Chumash*, 660.
40. Chill, 225.
41. Hertz, 501.
42. "HaLashon," Torah.org, n.d., http://www.torah.org/learning/halashon/ (accessed March 30, 2015).
43. Chill, 232.
44. Kolatch, *The Second Jewish Book of Why*, 286.
45. *Etz Hayim*, 700.
46. *Stone Chumash*, 665.

Chapter Seven

Sabbath and Festivals

Have you ever wondered . . .

1. Are the Sabbath candles kindled at sunset on Friday evening?
2. Are women responsible for lighting the Sabbath candles?
3. Is an extra candle lit for each child in the family?
4. Is the appropriate blessing said before the Sabbath candles are lit?
5. Does the woman bless the candles?
6. Is kindling the Sabbath candles a biblical commandment?
7. Can *Kiddush* be said either in the synagogue or at home?
8. Is a woman prohibited from reciting the *Kiddush* when there is a man present who can do so?
9. Is the *Kiddush* recited while standing?
10. May the *Kiddush* be said if there is no wine?
11. Is there a "Great" *Kiddush*?
12. Does the Hebrew word *challah* refer to the special bread eaten on Sabbaths and festivals?
13. Is the *challah* offering still observed?
14. Does Jewish law forbid work on the Sabbath?
15. Is it permitted to turn on an electric light on the Sabbath?
16. Does an observant Jew in a high-rise building have to walk up and down the stairs on the Sabbath?
17. Can all objects be handled as long as they are not used for prohibited work?
18. Is it permissible to use the services of a non-Jew on the Sabbath?
19. Is it forbidden to carry anything outside of the house on the Sabbath?
20. Is journeying on the Sabbath prohibited under Jewish law?

21. Under Jewish law, is it permissible to drive an automobile on the Sabbath?

22. Is it ever permitted to violate the Sabbath restrictions?

23. Are there laws prohibiting Sabbath activities that are not forbidden in the Torah?

24. Are there specially named Sabbaths during the year?

25. Is the *Oneg Shabbat* after Saturday morning services an old tradition?

26. Is there a tradition of having a "third meal" on the Sabbath day?

27. Is there a standard text for *Havdalah*?

28. Is "profane" a good translation of the Hebrew term *chol* in *Havdalah*?

29. Are the spices a remembrance of incense in the Temple?

30. Is *Havdalah* performed at sunset on Saturday evening?

31. If a person does not recite *Havdalah* on Saturday evening, may it be said at a later time?

32. Is there a special Saturday evening meal associated with King David?

33. Is the Jewish calendar lunar based?

34. Is the additional month decided each year by rabbis knowledgeable in astronomy?

35. Have the names used for the months of the Jewish year changed since early biblical times?

36. Other than Rosh Chodesh, is there a holiday in every month of the Jewish calendar?

37. Are the Jewish and secular calendars numbered differently?

38. Is it permitted to work on the festivals?

39. If a festival occurs on a Friday, is it forbidden to prepare for the Sabbath on that day?

40. Is observance of two days of festivals in the Diaspora a biblical requirement?

41. Do some Jews in the Diaspora not celebrate the second days of festivals?

42. Are the intermediate days of festivals like ordinary days?

43. Is a standard form of *Hallel* recited on festivals?

44. Is *Hallel* recited on all festivals?

45. Is *Hallel* recited on non-religious occasions?

46. Does the term *machzor* refer to the prayer book used on the High Holy Days?

47. Is Rosh Chodesh always the first day of the new month?

48. Is *Birkat ha-Chodesh* recited before each New Moon?

49. Is it customary for women to abstain from work on the first day of the month?

50. Is *Kiddush Levanah* a monthly prayer to the moon?

51. Can *Kiddush Levanah* take place indoors?

52. Are any popular songs associated with *Kiddush Levanah*?

53. Is Elul, the name of the month before Rosh Hashanah, a Hebrew acronym?
54. Is there only one new year in the Jewish calendar?
55. Are there only four days of the week on which Rosh Hashanah can fall?
56. On Rosh Hashanah, are Jews inscribed in either the Book of Life or the Book of Death?
57. Is there a special procedure for Jews asking forgiveness from each other before Rosh Hashanah?
58. Are the standard *challot* baked for the Sabbath used on Rosh Hashanah?
59. Are there special foods associated with Rosh Hashanah?
60. Are some foods avoided on Rosh Hashanah?
61. Are fish eaten on Rosh Hashanah?
62. As on the Sabbath, is taking a nap on Rosh Hashanah a long-standing tradition?
63. Is a *kitel* worn on the High Holy Days?
64. Is the shofar only blown on Rosh Hashanah?
65. Was the shofar still used after the destruction of the Second Temple?
66. Can the shofar be made from the horn of any kosher animal?
67. Are the precise sounds of the shofar indicated in the Bible?
68. Has the place of the shofar service on Rosh Hashanah changed over time?
69. Was having precisely 100 blasts of the shofar on Rosh Hashanah an arbitrary decision?
70. Do Ashkenazim and Sephardim blow the 100 shofar blasts at the same points in the service?
71. Is the shofar always sounded during Rosh Hashanah services?
72. Was *Avinu Malkeinu* written as a prayer for the High Holy Days?
73. Do Jews prostrate their whole bodies during Rosh Hashanah (and Yom Kippur) services?
74. Is it permitted to touch one's head to a stone floor when bowing on the High Holy Days?
75. Was *Tashlich* a ritual devised by the Rabbis?
76. Is *teshuvah* the major focus of the Ten Days of Repentance?
77. Is there a Jewish movement that emphasizes the importance of *teshuvah*?
78. Is Yom Kippur the saddest day of the year?
79. Is Yom Kippur the holiest time of the year?
80. Is fasting the only way that Jews satisfy the Divine command to "afflict your souls" (Lev. 16:29) on Yom Kippur?
81. Should everyone fast on Yom Kippur?
82. Is a six-year-old permitted to fast on Yom Kippur if he wishes?

83. Does Yom Kippur provide atonement for sins?
84. Is *kaparos* a popular custom rather than a ritual instituted by the rabbis?
85. Is *Kol Nidrei* the most important prayer said on Yom Kippur?
86. Was the precise wording of *Kol Nidrei* controversial?
87. Did *Kol Nidrei* assume special significance during the Spanish Inquisition?
88. In the two confessionals that Jews recite multiple times on Yom Kippur, does each person detail the transgressions that he or she has personally committed?
89. Was the ancient rite of Azazel essential to Divine forgiveness of the Israelites?
90. Was the goat designated to Azazel set free?
91. Are there other Days of Atonement each year?
92. Is Sukkot named for the temporary shelters erected for the festival?
93. Can a space with a large overhanging roof over a deck be used as a *sukkah*?
94. Is special material required for the roof of a *sukkah*?
95. Are Jews required to sleep and eat all meals in the *sukkah*?
96. Are newlyweds required to eat in the *sukkah*?
97. Do the four species required by the Bible have underlying meanings?
98. Are *ushpizin* homeless individuals whom we invite into the *sukkah*?
99. Were the Talmudic Rabbis so pious and studious that they would not allow themselves any feats of dexterity?
100. Does Yom Kippur conclude the High Holy Days?
101. Is Shemini Atzeret really the eighth day of Sukkot?
102. Was the Prayer for Rain always recited on Shemini Atzeret?
103. Is Simchat Torah a biblical holiday?
104. Did the celebration of Simchat Torah begin in the Land of Israel?
105. Has there been a standard Torah reading for Simchat Torah?
106. Are the Chanukah candles lit before the Sabbath candles on Friday night?
107. Is there a special way to light the Chanukah candles?
108. Are additional candles placed in the Chanukah menorah and lit in the same direction?
109. Are dreidels used in Israel the same as those in the Diaspora?
110. Does *Maoz Tzur* have only one stanza?
111. Is the popular English hymn "Rock of Ages" a direct translation of *Maoz Tzur*?
112. Is gift giving a traditional part of the celebration of Chanukah?
113. Is the Passover seder the only one celebrated in Jewish tradition?
114. Does the Tu b'Shevat seder represent multiple worlds of Creation?

115. Is there significance to the four cups of wine at the Tu b'Shevat seder?
116. Did the Divine redemption of the Jews of Persia make the Book of Esther a rabbinic favorite?
117. Is the evening reading of *Megillat Esther* the major synagogue ritual of Purim?
118. Is a special *trope* used throughout the reading of the *Megillah*?
119. Is there a biblical source for the noisemaking when the name of Haman is read?
120. Does *Adloyada*, the name of the Tel Aviv parade held each year on Purim, have a rabbinic meaning?
121. Is the tradition of donating three half-dollars to charity just before reading the *Megillah* on Purim eve designed to raise funds for good causes?
122. Are there any other special acts of *tzedakah* related to Purim?
123. Do all Jews celebrate Purim on the same day?
124. Did Esther fast on the day before Purim?
125. Are Esther and Mordecai Hebrew names?
126. Are *hamantashen* the popular Jewish delicacies for Purim?
127. In some years, is there more than one holiday known as Purim?
128. Does the biblical prohibition against eating *chametz* on Passover refer to bread?
129. Is it necessary to have separate pots and dishes for Passover?
130. Is it permissible to keep *chametz* in the home as long as it is not eaten?
131. Is the sale of *chametz* a legally binding contract?
132. Is quinoa permitted on Passover?
133. Is it traditional for firstborn Jews to fast on the day before Passover?
134. Is the seder a narration of the historical account of the Exodus from Egypt?
135. Is *Mitzrayim* the Hebrew word for Egypt?
136. Does the first written Haggadah date back to biblical times?
137. Does Moses play a major role in the Haggadah?
138. Has drinking four cups of wine always been the accepted standard practice?
139. May any type of kosher for Passover wine be used at the seder?
140. Are the Four Questions said even if no child is present?
141. Are the Four Questions really questions?
142. Does the Haggadah answer these questions?
143. Are the words of the wise child diametrically opposite those of the wicked child?
144. Can *matzah* be made from any type of grain?
145. Is *matzah* a symbol of freedom?

146. Is there a single blessing for *matzah* at the seder?
147. Is there a special type of *matzah* for the seder?
148. Did the rabbis praise the efficiency of the first machine for preparing *matzah*?
149. Can any type of *matzah* be used at the seder?
150. Is horseradish the preferred *maror*?
151. Is the sweet *charoset* a symbol of the slavery of the Israelites in Egypt?
152. Is there a standard type of *charoset* for the Passover seder?
153. May the *afikoman* be eaten at any time on seder night?
154. Does the leader of the service drink wine from the Cup of Elijah?
155. Is there a blessing recited over the Cup of Elijah?
156. Is there also a cup of wine for Miriam at the seder?
157. Is *Chad Gadya* ("One Kid") merely a simple folk song?
158. Is *Hallel* recited in the synagogue on Passover?
159. Was the Song of Songs uniformly approved by the Rabbis?
160. Is there any special celebration at the end of Passover?
161. Is the 49-day Omer period a time of semi-mourning?
162. Are there any days of celebration during this period?
163. Is there any special food eaten on Lag ba-Omer?
164. During the Omer period, is it traditional to study a special tractate of the Mishnah every Sabbath?
165. Is the festival of Shavuot a harvest festival?
166. Is it traditional to stay up all night on Shavuot?
167. Are all normal activities permitted on these days before Tisha b'Av?
168. Were the destructions of the Temples the only catastrophes to befall the Jewish people on Tisha b'Av?
169. According to Jewish tradition, will Tisha b'Av always be a day of mourning?

***

Are the Sabbath candles kindled at sunset on Friday evening? (F)

Although the Sabbath begins at sunset, it is customary to light the candles 18 minutes before sunset so as to not desecrate the Sabbath by miscalculating the precise time that night falls and the seventh day begins.

Are women responsible for lighting the Sabbath candles? (N)

The Sabbath is ushered in by lighting at least two candles on Friday evening, corresponding to the slightly different wording in which the Fourth Commandment is phrased—"remember" (Exod. 20:8) and "observe" (Deut. 5:12) the Sabbath day—two phrases that the Talmud relates were miraculously pronounced together by God. The duty to light the Sabbath candles falls equally on men and women. In a family setting, it traditionally has been considered the responsibility of the woman. Indeed, the lighting of Sabbath candles is generally regarded as one of the three "women's commandments," along with observing the laws of family purity through immersion in a ritual bath (*mikveh*) and separating out a portion of dough (*challah*) when baking bread. However, if there is no woman to light the Sabbath candles, this should be done by a man.

Is an extra candle lit for each child in the family? (N)

Although not a halachic requirement, some women light an extra candle for each child in the family. A possible explanation is the law that a person who forgets to light candles on one Sabbath is required to add a candle each week thereafter. Because a woman in the hospital on Sabbath after the birth of her child may have forgotten (or been unable) to light candles, this could be a reason why she would feel required to add an extra candle each Sabbath in the future.

Is the appropriate blessing said before the Sabbath candles are lit? (F)

Unlike most commandments, for which the recitation of a blessing precedes the activity and any benefit that can be derived from it, the lighting of Sabbath candles is performed *before* the blessing is said. Were this not the case, the woman would have effectively welcomed the Sabbath before lighting the candles, which would violate the prohibition against making a fire on that day.

Does the woman bless the candles? (F)

The Yiddish term for the candle lighting ceremony is *bentsch licht*, which is often misunderstood as "blessing the candles." However, the Sabbath candles are not inherently holy or unholy, and the blessing clearly states that God "has sanctified us" by the commandment to kindle the Sabbath lights. Like all *mitzvot*, this ritual is designed to allow us to experience holiness, rather than make any material object holy. [1]

Is kindling the Sabbath candles a biblical commandment? (F)

Never mentioned in the Bible, kindling the Sabbath candles is one of the seven ritual *mitzvot* legislated by the Rabbis.

Can *Kiddush* be said either in the synagogue or at home? (N)

Kiddush (Sanctification) is a prayer recited over a cup of wine to sanctify the Sabbath (or festival) in accordance with the commandment to "Remember the Sabbath day, to keep it holy" (Exod. 20:8). The Talmudic Rabbis debated whether the *Kiddush* over wine should be recited in the synagogue or the home. The decision was that *Kiddush* should be said at the table just before sitting down to eat the Sabbath dinner. However, because the synagogues of Babylonia had annexes that served as community hostels and provided food and lodging for travelers, it became customary to also recite the *Kiddush* in the synagogue at the end of the Friday evening service. This tradition persists among Ashkenazim.

Is a woman prohibited from reciting the *Kiddush* when there is a man present who can do so? (F)

Although women are generally exempt from fulfilling those positive *mitzvot* that depend on a set time, this does not apply to the *Kiddush* (or kindling the Sabbath and festival lights). Because women have an equal obligation to say the *Kiddush*, according to *halachah* they may do so even on behalf of men who are present,[2] though in practice this is only done in an egalitarian setting.

Is the *Kiddush* recited while standing? (N)

Opinions differ as to whether the *Kiddush* should be said while standing or seated at the dinner table. The Sephardic tradition prefers standing during the *Kiddush*, viewing it as a form of testimony to the loving relationship between God and Israel (and in a Jewish court, testimony is always given while standing). Ashkenazim more commonly sit, based on the concept that if the person saying the *Kiddush* is fulfilling the ritual obligation of the others in the room, the people present must sit down together so as to establish themselves as a group. Hasidim tend to follow the kabbalistic tradition, which advocates standing because of the comparison of the Sabbath to a bride and the fact that the wedding blessings are recited while standing.[3] Moshe Feinstein offered an intriguing compromise—recite the *Kiddush* while standing, but drink the wine while sitting down.

May the *Kiddush* be said if there is no wine? (T)

According to the Talmud (Pes. 107a), it is preferable to recite the evening *Kiddush* over a full cup of wine, which symbolizes joy. However, if wine is not available, or if one may not drink it for health reasons, it is permissible to say the *Kiddush* over grape juice or even over the two loaves of bread. In the latter situation, the only differences are that one first washes, then holds the two *challahs* in his hand, and recites the blessing for bread instead of that for wine.

Is there a "Great" *Kiddush*? (T)

This exaggerated title has been given to the *Kiddush* recited before the noon meal on the Sabbath or a festival. It is essentially only the customary blessing over wine with an added appropriate scriptural verse before the blessing. For the Sabbath, one says: "Therefore the Lord blessed the Sabbath day and hallowed it" (Exod. 20:11). For festivals, the additional verse is: "So Moses declared to the Israelites the set times of the Lord" (Lev. 23:44). Some further embellish the *Kiddush* on the Sabbath by adding the prayer *Ve-Shamru*. Alcoholic beverages other than wine (with the appropriate blessing) may be used for this *Kiddush*, for which the name "great" may originally have referred to the amount of drink rather than the length of the prayer. [4]

Does the Hebrew word *challah* refer to the special bread eaten on Sabbaths and festivals? (N)

Most Jews associate the Hebrew word *challah* with the braided bread eaten on Sabbaths and festivals. However, the term also refers to the biblical dough offering set aside for the *kohen* whenever bread was made from one of five kinds of cereal grains—wheat, barley, spelt, oats, and rye. The amount prescribed was 1/24 of the dough for a private person and 1/48 of the dough for a baker (Num. 15:20). [5]

According to *Sefer ha-Chinuch*, this commandment made life easier for the *kohanim*, who spent most of their days performing the Temple service. Rather than requiring the *kohen* to carry out all steps in the process of preparing bread (sifting grain, grinding it into flour, and kneading the dough), all that he needed to do was to take the gift of dough and bake it. [6]

Is the *challah* offering still observed? (N)

According to the Torah, the *challah* offering was only obligatory in the Land of Israel. After the destruction of the Temple, however, the Rabbis declared that this practice would remain in force everywhere. Taking *challah* is still observed by those baking bread in observant Jewish households and kosher bakeries. Because *kohanim* can no longer observe the laws of priestly purity and thus are prohibited from eating anything related to a holy sacrifice, the *challah* is usually wrapped in a piece of foil and burned in the oven.

Does Jewish law forbid work on the Sabbath? (N)

The Bible does not specifically list those types of work that are prohibited on the Sabbath. Because the description of the Sabbath is found in the Bible just before the section dealing with the building of the Tabernacle in the wilderness, which ceased on the Sabbath, the Rabbis concluded that it was the 39 types of labor involved in this construction that were forbidden on the seventh day (Shab. 7:2). In addition, some categories of work have been prohibited because they are not in keeping with enjoyment of the restful spirit of the Sabbath. However, physical work is not uniformly forbidden. Walking up a steep hill to attend synagogue, or even to commune with nature, is permissible, as is carrying heavy objects within the "private domain" of one's own home. One is allowed to serve a Sabbath meal to family and friends and to clean up afterward.

The Sabbath is a time for physical, spiritual, and emotional rejuvenation. For six days, Jews attend to their businesses and to the task of materially changing the world. The seventh day is focused on the inner self, intense study, enjoyment of family, and relationships with others. As Abraham Joshua Heschel said, "Six days we seek to dominate the world; on the seventh day we try to dominate the self."[7]

Is it permitted to turn on an electric light on the Sabbath? (N)

In addition to the general forbidding of all manner of work on the Sabbath, there is a special prohibition against making a fire (Exod. 35:3). The Rabbis considered this to include everything that pertains to the kindling of light, even if no actual work is involved. In modern times, there is a controversy as to whether the switching on of electric lights and appliances is equivalent to making a fire. First, switching on a light does not create electric power; the power exists already. Second, there is no combustion in the filament of an electric light. Nevertheless, Orthodox Jews do not explicitly use electrical appliances on the Sabbath. Refrigerators may be opened and closed provided the interior light bulb is unscrewed for the Sabbath. Lights that have been kindled before the Sabbath, such as the Sabbath candles and lamps, are allowed, as are pre-set burners and ovens for keeping water and previously cooked food warm. Similarly, it is permitted to leave an electric appliance running during the Sabbath and to use a timer to automatically turn an appliance on or off, as long as the timer is set before the Sabbath begins.

Does an observant Jew in a high-rise building have to walk up and down the stairs on the Sabbath? (N)

Traditional Jews do not use elevators on the Sabbath because of the law forbidding operating electric switches on that day. To circumvent this restriction, there has been the development of the Shabbat elevator, which works in a special mode and operates automatically. There are several ways the elevator works—going up and down and stopping at every floor, stopping at alternative floors, or rising to the top floor and stopping while going down—so that people can step in and out without having to press any buttons. Shabbat elevators can be found in areas with large Jewish populations, and a 2001 law passed by the Israeli Knesset mandated that all new residential buildings, and public buildings which have more than one elevator, install a control mechanism for the Sabbath in one of the elevators.

Can all objects be handled as long as they are not used for prohibited work? (F)

Some items that may not be used on the Sabbath may not even be handled on that day, lest one unintentionally perform one of the forbidden types of work. These objects are termed *muktzeh*, meaning to "set aside" or "store away." Among the many things considered *muktzeh* are money and checks; scissors; pencils and pens; battery-operated toys and flashlights; radios and CDs; telephones and computers; and religious objects such as a shofar, *tefillin*, and *lulav*. Even the Sabbath candlesticks are *muktzeh* and thus should not be moved on the Sabbath after the candles have been lit.[8]

Is it permissible to use the services of a non-Jew on the Sabbath? (N)

One mechanism to ease the difficulty of complying with the prohibition against work on the Sabbath was the concept of the *Shabbos goy*—a non-Jew hired by an observant family to perform activities specifically forbidden to Jews on the Sabbath, such as lighting the stove and turning lights on and off. [9] This was considered a valid practice, though it was not permitted to ask a non-Jew to cook, bake, sew, or do any creative activity on the Sabbath that was forbidden for Jews. Today, the need for a *Shabbos goy* has been virtually eliminated by the proliferation of electronic timers.

Is it forbidden to carry anything outside of the house on the Sabbath? (N)

On the Sabbath, it is forbidden to carry any object (even a house key or handkerchief) outside a private domain, though carrying is permitted inside a private residence or a synagogue. The prohibition against carrying was especially difficult for mothers of infants or young children. Forbidden to carry a child outside the house, they were effectively confined to their homes on the Sabbath. [10]

To overcome these restrictions, under certain circumstances the Rabbis permitted the establishment of an *eruv*. Literally meaning "blending" or "intermingling," an *eruv* converts a large public area into a "private domain" where carrying is permitted on the Sabbath. For example, it is forbidden to carry an object from one house to another. However, if all the tenants living around a large courtyard contribute food and place it at a central point before the Sabbath, the entire area is symbolically transformed from a series of individual private homes into one common group dwelling that belongs to the entire community. Today, a common way of making an *eruv* is to extend a wire or nylon cord around the perimeter of a community, by connecting it to telephone or utility poles. In this way the entire area becomes a single domain, in which it is permitted to carry and push baby carriages. In Israel, *eruvim* have been constructed in all cities. In the United States, they have been established in cities that have a substantial Orthodox Jewish population. [11]

Is journeying on the Sabbath prohibited under Jewish law? (N)

Unlike the Karaites, who took the biblical verse "let no person go out of his place on the seventh day" literally and did not allow anyone to leave home on the Sabbath, the Rabbis did not restrict movement within one's town. However, they prohibited Jews from walking more than 2,000 cubits (approximately a half-mile) beyond the town boundaries on the Sabbath, "because traveling interrupts the rest of both man and beast." [12]

As with all of the negative commandments, the prohibition against journeying on the Sabbath is overridden when a life is in danger, or even if there is only possible or potential danger to life. Maimonides [13] noted that it was permissible and even mandatory to exceed the 2,000 cubit limit to rescue one or more Israelites whose lives were in danger from heathens, a flooding river, a collapsed building, or physical or mental illness.

Under Jewish law, is it permissible to drive an automobile on the Sabbath? (N)

Orthodox rabbis forbid driving an automobile on the Sabbath, based on the fact that it involves turning on the ignition, which in turn ignites sparks—an act that violates the Torah law against making a fire on the Sabbath. Conservative rabbis ruled that Jews may drive on the Sabbath, but only to synagogue. This decision was made in response to the migration of Jews to the suburbs, where most no longer live within walking distance of a synagogue. Continuing to forbid driving on the Sabbath would have forced many congregants to remain at home or to pursue non-religious activities. Fearing an erosion of Jewish identity if synagogue attendance dropped precipitously, these rabbis permitted driving as the lesser of two evils. Orthodox rabbis denounced this decision, arguing that Conservative rabbis should instead encourage their congregants to live within walking distance of their synagogues.[14]

In Israel, public transportation does not operate on the Sabbath in Jerusalem and Tel Aviv, but it does run in Haifa.

Is it ever permitted to violate the Sabbath restrictions? (T)

All of the Sabbath restrictions may be violated in order to preserve life (*pikuach nefesh*), based on the verse: "You shall keep My laws and My rules, by the pursuit of which a man shall *live* [and not die]" (Lev. 18:5). Even if one is in doubt as to whether a life will be saved, it is permitted to violate the Sabbath. As the Talmud states, "Violate one Sabbath [in order that someone may live] to observe many Sabbaths" (Yoma 85b). Thus, the deliberate desecration of the Sabbath to save a life is more than outweighed by the potential for future sanctification of the Sabbath and God's Name.

The concept of *pikuach nefesh* is so highly regarded that if a seriously ill person needs food on the Sabbath, the *halachah* requires that one should slaughter an animal and prepare it according to the dietary laws, rather than feed the individual ritually forbidden food.

Are there laws prohibiting Sabbath activities that are not forbidden in the Torah? (T)

To prevent people from accidentally and unintentionally performing an action forbidden by the Torah, the Rabbis decreed that one also must not do anything that: (1) resembles a prohibited act or could be confused with it; (2) reinforces a habit linked with a prohibited act; or (3) usually leads to performing a prohibited act. The rabbinic enactment of measures to prevent these possibilities is termed "putting a fence around the Torah" (Avot 1:1).

For example, the Torah prohibits work on the Sabbath, but a rabbinic decree mandates that one is forbidden from even handling an implement that is used to perform prohibited work, lest he inadvertently violate the Sabbath. Similarly, agreeing to buy something on the Sabbath is prohibited, since one is in the habit of confirming agreements "in writing"; and climbing a tree is forbidden since it may lead to breaking twigs or tearing leaves, which could be construed as "reaping" (i.e., separating part of a growing plant from its source). [15] From the point of view of a traditional Jew, there is no difference between a negative Torah commandment and a rabbinic law putting a fence around the Torah. Both are equally binding and neither can be disregarded on a whim. The difference is generally in the degree of punishment. For example, desecrating the Sabbath was punishable by death under Torah law, while violating a rabbinic law merited a lesser penalty.

Are there specially named Sabbaths during the year? (T)

Some Sabbaths commemorate specific events and are distinguished by variations in the liturgy and special customs. Two of these recur—Shabbat Mevarchim, which immediately precedes each month and announces its date, and Shabbat Rosh Chodesh, when the Sabbath coincides with the New Moon. Others (in chronologic order) are Shabbat Shuvah (Sabbath of Return, between Rosh Hashanah and Yom Kippur); Shabbat Shirah (Sabbath of Song, when the Torah reading includes *Shirat ha-Yam* [The Song at the Sea; Exod. 15:1–18], the prayer of thanksgiving chanted by the Israelites after crossing the Sea of Reeds during the Exodus from Egypt); Shabbat Shekalim (Sabbath of Shekels, which falls on or immediately precedes Adar, the month of Purim); Shabbat Zachor (Sabbath of Remembrance, which immediately precedes the festival of Purim and commands the Israelites to "blot out the memory of Amalek"); Shabbat Parah (Sabbath of the Red Heifer, which immediately precedes Shabbat ha-Chodesh); Sabbath ha-Chodesh (Sabbath of the Month, which falls on or precedes Nisan, the month of Passover); Shabbat ha-Gadol (Great Sabbath, which occurs at the beginning of the week when Passover will be observed); Shabbat Hazon (Sabbath of Vision, which immediately precedes Tisha b'Av); and Shabbat Nachamu (Sabbath of Comfort, which immediately follows Tisha b'Av).

Is the *Oneg Shabbat* after Saturday morning services an old tradition? (N)

Literally meaning "delight in the Sabbath," the term is based on a verse in Isaiah (58:13): "and you shall call the Sabbath a delight [*oneg*], and the holy of the Lord honorable." According to Maimonides, for the Rabbis "delight" meant lighting candles on Friday night, enjoying special delicacies, a minimum of three Sabbath meals, cohabitation with one's spouse, general repose, and added sleep. Traditionally, "honor" implied the duties of bathing immediately before the Sabbath, wearing special Sabbath clothes, and receiving the Sabbath with joy.[16]

The term *Oneg Shabbat* was coined by famed poet Chaim Nachman Bialik to describe a popular study session with the singing of Sabbath songs on Saturday afternoons, which he initiated during the 1920s in Tel Aviv. This custom spread throughout Israel and the Diaspora. Today, *Oneg Shabbat* refers to the informal social gathering often held in synagogue after Sabbath services on Friday night and Saturday morning.

Is there a tradition of having a "third meal" on the Sabbath day? (T)

Se'udah shlishit (lit., "third meal") is eaten before the end of the Sabbath day. The tradition of having a third Sabbath meal (in addition to the first meal on Friday evening and the second after Saturday morning services) derives from the threefold repetition of the word *ha-yom* (today) in the verse, "And Moses said: Eat that [the *manna*] *today*, for *today* is a Sabbath unto the Lord, *today* you shall not find it in the field" (Exod. 16:25). When eaten at home, the third meal is usually simple. When held in the synagogue, it is often sponsored by a member of the congregation in honor of a special event, such as a marriage or *yahrzeit*. Hasidim assemble around the table of the Rebbe for the third meal, sharing a morsel of food and listening to words of Torah wisdom.[17]

Is there a standard text for *Havdalah*? (N)

Havdalah (lit., separation) is the ritual ceremony that marks the conclusion of the Sabbath. It consists of several introductory verses, three blessings—over wine, sweet-smelling spices, and light—and the major blessing that deals with the distinction that God has made "between *kodesh* (holy) and *chol*, between light and darkness, between Israel and the other nations, and between the seventh day and the six working days." However, there is also a version of *Havdalah* that is recited at the conclusion of a festival. If the festival does not fall on a Saturday night, only the blessing over wine and the major blessing are said. The introductory verses and the blessings for spices and light are omitted. If the end of the Sabbath coincides with the beginning of a festival, *Havdalah* is still recited, though the blessing for spices is omitted since a festival (*yom tov*) is regarded as sufficient "fragrance" to compensate for the loss of the Sabbath (Pes. 102b).[18] The main blessing states that God has made a distinction of the transition "between the holy and the holy."

Is "profane" a good translation of the Hebrew term *chol* in *Havdalah*? (F)

Although generally rendered as "profane," the word *chol* does not have the connotation of something evil or depraved. Instead, it actually means "ordinary," as distinct from *kodesh* ("sacred" or "holy"). The implication is that it is necessary to experience the ordinary to fully appreciate the special value of the Sabbath.

Are the spices a remembrance of incense in the Temple? (F)

The fragrant spices serve to refresh and revive the spirit, alleviating the sadness accompanying the end of the Sabbath day. A mystical view is that they offer spiritual compensation for the loss of the additional soul that each observant Jew figuratively possesses on the Sabbath day.[19]

Is *Havdalah* performed at sunset on Saturday evening? (F)

The departure of the Sabbath is delayed until three stars appear in the night sky (about 42 minutes after sunset) on Saturday evening, so that the Sabbath is a 25-hour respite from the pressures of daily life.

If a person does not recite *Havdalah* on Saturday evening, may it be said at a later time? (T)

If one forgets to recite *Havdalah* on Saturday evening or cannot do so because of some special circumstances, it is permissible to perform the ceremony any time through Tuesday of the coming week. However, only the blessing over wine is said.

Is there a special Saturday evening meal associated with King David? (T)

Melaveh malkah (lit., "escorting the Queen") is the festive meal at the close of the Sabbath on Saturday evening. Throughout the ages, many Jews have preferred to eat their main meal after *Havdalah*, when they could have freshly cooked food. Since the rabbis could not prevent this practice, they insisted that this meal be considered a farewell feast in honor of the departing Sabbath Queen. This Saturday evening meal is also associated with King David, the ancestor of the Messiah. The Talmud (Shab. 30a–b) relates that in answer to his plea, "Lord make me know my end" (Ps. 39:5), David was informed that his death would occur on a Sabbath. Therefore, after the conclusion of each Sabbath, King David would celebrate because he knew he would live for at least one more week.[20]

Is the Jewish calendar lunar based? (N)

The Jewish calendar is primarily based on 12 lunar months of 29 or 30 days. However, the lunar year is only 354 days, about 11 days less than the solar year. Without any adjustments the festivals would "wander" and be shifted from their appointed seasons of the year.[21] For example, Passover could fall in the fall, winter, or summer, whereas according to the Torah it must be observed in the spring in Israel (Deut. 16:1). To prevent this, an additional month (Second Adar) is added 7 times in every 19 years.[22] Therefore, the Jewish calendar is actually a lunar-based system that is corrected periodically to match the solar cycle.

Is the additional month decided each year by rabbis knowledgeable in astronomy? (F)

During Temple times, the Sanhedrin was responsible for keeping track of discrepancies in length between the solar and lunar years, intercalating an extra month when needed according to agricultural conditions. As the Sanhedrin was about to be disbanded (mid-fourth century), the patriarch Hillel II established a permanent Jewish calendar based on astronomical calculations to adjust the solar and lunar years, which has been used ever since.

Have the names used for the months of the Jewish year changed since early biblical times? (T)

The Bible refers to the months of the year with simple numbers, based on the first being the spring month in which Passover occurs on the 15th day. Thus Rosh Hashanah, now celebrated as the New Year, was the first day of the seventh month. The names of the months used today [23] are actually of Babylonian origin and came into use among Jews only after the destruction of the First Temple.

Other than Rosh Chodesh, is there a holiday in every month of the Jewish calendar? (F)

Although there are holidays in 11 months, none occurs during the eighth month of Cheshvan (October–November). Consequently, it is often called Mar Cheshvan, based on either of two meanings of the Hebrew word *mar* — "bitter" and "mister." One tradition is that because Cheshvan contains no holiday or special observance, it has a taste of bitterness to it. A more pleasing explanation is that the Rabbis felt sorry for the month because of its lack of any special day, and thus gave it some honor by calling it "Mister Cheshvan." [24]

Are the Jewish and secular calendars numbered differently? (T)

The numbering of years in the Jewish calendar is based on the time since the "Creation of the world" on Rosh Hashanah. To calculate this, the Rabbis combined the life spans of the early generations listed in the Bible—starting with Adam—with the time that had elapsed since then. To determine the current Jewish year, add 3760 to the year in the secular calendar from January to Rosh Hashanah and 3761 from Rosh Hashanah until the end of December. Thus, the first part of the year 2015 would equal 5775 in the Jewish calendar, while it would become 5776 starting on Rosh Hashanah. Although realizing that this number does not accurately reflect the true age of the earth, Jews use it out of respect for their remote ancestors. This is somewhat similar to the subsequent customs of Christians, who date their calendar back to the birth of Jesus, and Muslims, whose calendar dates back to Muhammad's flight from Mecca to Medina.

Is it permitted to work on the festivals? (N)

On festivals, the prohibition is against *m'lechet avodah*, which is generally translated as "laborious or servile work." This contrasts with the more restrictive prohibition, "you shall do no work," which applies to the Sabbath and Yom Kippur. According to Rashi, *m'lechet avodah* means "essential work that will cause a significant loss if it is not performed." Nachmanides considered it "burdensome" work, such as ordinary farm or factory labor; in contrast, a person may engage in "pleasurable work," such as the preparation of food.[25] Whatever the interpretation of the term, all agree that the preparation of food—including such labors as slaughtering, cooking, and baking—is permitted on festivals (other than Yom Kippur) that fall on a weekday, based on the verse, "except for what every person must eat, only that may be done for you" (Exod. 12:16).

If a festival occurs on a Friday, is it forbidden to prepare for the Sabbath on that day? (N)

While preparation of holiday meals is permitted on festivals, it is forbidden to prepare food for another day. Strictly speaking, if a festival occurs on Friday, one would not be permitted to prepare food for the Sabbath. To overcome this problem, the rabbis instituted the *eruv tavshilin*. On the day before the festival, one prepares a special plate consisting of two items of food (such as bread and a piece of fish) for the Sabbath. In this way, a "blending" (*eruv*) of the Sabbath and festival foods occurs, making it permissible to prepare food on Friday for the Sabbath.[26] According to another Talmudic view, the prohibition against preparing food for the Sabbath without an *eruv tavshilin* was intended to stress the importance of the ban against working on a festival to prepare for the subsequent weekdays.[27]

Although the food is prepared for the Sabbath, it technically must be available to be eaten on the festival day itself. Therefore, it should be prepared early enough so that guests coming for the festival would have time to eat it if they arrived before sunset.

Is observance of two days of festivals in the Diaspora a biblical requirement? (F)

In the Diaspora, an extra day is added to each of the biblical festivals of Passover, Shavuot, Sukkot, and Rosh Hashanah. This practice originated because of uncertainty outside of the Land of Israel as to the day on which the Sanhedrin in Jerusalem announced the New Moon (Rosh Chodesh). Thus, a second day was added to each festival to prevent any chance of the people mistakenly failing to celebrate it on the proper date. For almost 1,650 years, there has been a fixed Jewish calendar, based on precise mathematical and astronomical formulations. Even though the exact day of the festival is known in advance, the sages decided to continue the long-standing custom of celebrating second days of festivals in the Diaspora. Yom Kippur was the sole exception, since a double fast day was considered too difficult (though some observed it). Rosh Hashanah, on the other hand, gradually came to be observed as a two-day festival even in the Land of Israel.[28]

Do some Jews in the Diaspora not celebrate the second days of festivals? (T)

In Babylonia, the Talmudic sages contemplated eliminating the second day of festivals as soon as a permanent calendar was fixed, but this never became traditional practice. Today, however, the Reform movement has generally dropped the second day of festivals.

Are the intermediate days of festivals like ordinary days? (N)

The Torah mandates that the pilgrimage festivals of Passover and Sukkot be celebrated for seven days. The first and last days of each holiday are full festival days, when work is forbidden. Except for laws governing the additional sacrifices (cited in the *Musaf* service), nothing is said about how to observe the "mid-festival" days. The intermediate days are still part of the festival, and the obligation to rejoice applies to them. It is customary to greet people by saying *mo'adim l'simcha* (joyous times). In keeping with the Talmudic dictum that two types of rejoicing should not be mixed, marriages may not take place, and mourning is forbidden.

Is a standard form of *Hallel* recited on festivals? (N)

The reciting of *Hallel* (Pss. 113–118) immediately after the morning *Amidah* is a hallmark of the festival liturgy. Expressing thanksgiving and joy for Divine redemption, *Hallel* (lit., "praise") commemorates times of national redemption from danger.

In the Temple, *Hallel* was chanted by levitical choirs only on the first day of Passover and not on Rosh Chodesh. Beginning in the third century C.E., Babylonian Jews initiated the practice of reciting *Hallel* on the last six days of Passover and on the New Moon. To distinguish these new occasions from those on which *Hallel* had been traditionally recited, they omitted the first 11 verses from Psalm 115 and all of Psalm 116. This resulted in the current distinction between the "full" and "half" *Hallel*.[29]

Is *Hallel* recited on all festivals? (F)

Hallel is not said on Rosh Hashanah and Yom Kippur, because the Rabbis deemed it inappropriate to sing psalms of joy when one's fate and destiny are being decided (Ar. 10b). It also is omitted on Purim because, despite the miracle of the day, the Jewish people remained in exile as servants of King Ahasuerus. The deliverance of the Jews was only partial, for they did not gain complete freedom.

Is *Hallel* recited on non-religious occasions? (T)

The jubilance and celebration expressed in *Hallel* make it most appropriate in the modern State of Israel for days of national rejoicing, such as Yom ha-Atzma'ut (Israel Independence Day) and Yom Yerushalayim (Jerusalem Day).

Does the term *machzor* refer to the prayer book used on the High Holy Days? (N)

Although the best-known *machzor* is the one for the High Holy Days of Rosh Hashanah and Yom Kippur, there is also a *machzor* for the three pilgrimage festivals (Passover, Shavuot, Sukkot), as well as separate prayer books for each. The Hebrew word means "return" or "cycle," appropriate since each of these festivals occurs once a year.

Is Rosh Chodesh always the first day of the new month? (N)

If Rosh Chodesh (lit., "head of the month") is a single day, it always is the first day of the month. At times, however, there are two days of Rosh Chodesh. This means that the first day is really the 30th day of the preceding month, with the second day representing the first day of the new month.

Is *Birkat ha-Chodesh* recited before each New Moon? (N)

Birkat ha-Chodesh (lit., "blessing of the new [month]") is the Hebrew term for the public announcement of the name of the new month and the day(s) on which Rosh Chodesh will be celebrated. It is recited on the Sabbath before the New Moon, following the reading of the *haftarah*. Traditionally, the *shaliach tzibbur* (prayer leader) holds the Torah during *Birkat ha-Chodesh* and the congregation rises, a custom that hearkens back to the Sanhedrin's sanctification of the New Moon, which was performed while standing.

There is one exception to the monthly recitation of *Birkat ha-Chodesh*. On the Sabbath preceding Rosh Hashanah (first of Tishrei), this announcement is omitted in order to "confound the heavenly adversary"—to confuse Satan, the Accuser, so that he will be unable to denounce us before the Heavenly Court when our fate for the coming year is being decided.

Is it customary for women to abstain from work on the first day of the month? (T)

There is an ancient tradition of women not working on Rosh Chodesh as a reward for not giving up their jewelry to make the Golden Calf (JT Taan. 1:6, 64c). In certain communities, no work was done; in others, women were permitted to refrain from "heavy" work. In recent years, some women have formed Rosh Chodesh groups to study and celebrate together.[30]

Is *Kiddush Levanah* a monthly prayer to the moon? (F)

Rather than an idolatrous prayer to the moon, *Kiddush Levanah* is a prayer of thanksgiving to God for creating the universe and keeping the cosmos in order, which is recited at the monthly reappearance of the crescent moon. The moon symbolizes the regenerative capacity of the Jewish people, for just as it remains in the skies even though temporarily absent from our view, so the throne of David will eventually reappear with the coming of the Messiah. As a ceremony stressing God as the Creator and Israel's rebirth, *Kiddush Levanah* should be recited joyously, preferably at the conclusion of the Sabbath. It is customary to delay recitation of *Kiddush Levanah* until after Tisha b'Av (9th day of Av) and Yom Kippur (10th of Tishrei), because the gloom of Av and the trepidation associated with the Day of Judgment (Rosh Hashanah) and the Day of Atonement are not conducive to the requisite joy.

Can *Kiddush Levanah* take place indoors? (N)

This sanctification of the moon should be said with a *minyan* under the open sky, when the moon is clearly visible and not hidden by clouds. It can be recited indoors if a person is too ill to go out or if there is danger outside. In such cases, the ceremony should be performed by a window or door with the moon in view.

Are any popular songs associated with *Kiddush Levanah*? (T)

A code message relating the rebirth of the moon, the Davidic dynasty, and the perpetual existence of the Jewish people developed during the Talmudic era. When the Romans ended the authority of the rabbinical court in Jerusalem to consecrate the New Moon, this ceremony had to be carried out clandestinely. Judah ha-Nasi sent an emissary to the place where the *beit din* met, instructing them to sanctify Rosh Chodesh on the 30th day. The return message indicating that this mission had been accomplished contained the watchword *David, Melech Yisrael, chai v'kayam* (David, King of Israel, lives and endures)—a phrase that has become the lyrics of a popular song and is repeated three times during the *Kiddush Levanah* service as a symbol of Israel's renewal and national redemption. Words of another well-known song have entered the *Kiddush Levanah* service and reflect the symbolism of the New Moon—*Siman tov u-mazel tov, yehei lanu u-l'chol Yisrael* (May it be a good sign and good fortune for us and for all Israel), which is sung to celebrate such joyous activities as weddings and bar/bat mitzvah.

Is Elul, the name of the month before Rosh Hashanah, a Hebrew acronym? (T)

The sixth month of the Jewish year (August–September), Elul is primarily a time to prepare for the High Holy Days with its themes of repentance and renewal. The name is a Hebrew acronym for *Ani le-dodi ve-dodi li* (I am my beloved's and my beloved is mine), a verse from Song of Songs (6:3) that is often used in connection with the wedding ceremony. With the "beloved" traditionally referring to God, the Rabbis took this verse to describe the particularly loving and close relationship between God and Israel. Separated from each other during the Three Weeks, Israel and God meet again on Tu b'Av and their love slowly intensifies. The climax of their relationship occurs on Yom Kippur, when Israel is forgiven for the shameful incident of the Golden Calf, which had initially precipitated the process of mourning, repentance, and renewal. [31]

Is there only one new year in the Jewish calendar? (N)

Rosh Hashanah (lit., "head of the year"), which falls on the first and second of Tishrei (September/October), is now celebrated as the beginning of the Jewish New Year. However, the Mishnah (RH 1:1) labeled four different days as "Rosh Hashanah," each relating to specific activities—(a) the first of Nisan for reckoning the reigns of Jewish kings (the date for determining how many years a king has ruled) and for establishing the order of the festivals; (b) the first of Elul for tithing animals; (c) the first of Tishrei for agriculture (Sabbatical years, Jubilee years), passing judgment on humankind, and marking the anniversary of the Creation of the world; and (d) the first (but according to Hillel, the 15th) of Shevat for trees.

Are there only four days of the week on which Rosh Hashanah can fall? (T)

The first day of Rosh Hashanah (first of Tishrei) can never fall on a Wednesday, Friday, or Sunday. If it occurred on a Wednesday, Yom Kippur (10th of Tishrei) would be on a Friday, so that Jews would be unable to prepare for the Sabbath. If it occurred on a Friday, Yom Kippur would be on a Sunday, so that Jews who observe the Sabbath would be unable to get ready for Yom Kippur. Finally, if Rosh Hashanah were on a Sunday, Hoshanah Rabbah (the last day of Sukkot; 21st of Tishrei) would be on a Saturday. This would preclude performance of the major ritual of the day—beating the willows during the synagogue services—which would be forbidden on the Sabbath. [32]

On Rosh Hashanah, are Jews inscribed in either the Book of Life or the Book of Death? (N)

According to tradition, three books are opened in Heaven on Rosh Hashanah: one for the completely wicked, whose bad deeds definitely outweigh their good; one for the completely righteous; and one for the intermediate (average persons). The completely righteous are immediately inscribed in the Book of Life, while the completely wicked are immediately inscribed in the Book of Death. The judgment of all others is suspended from Rosh Hashanah to Yom Kippur, because one can merit being inscribed in the Book of Life through prayer, repentance, and charity. Consequently, it is customary to greet friends on Rosh Hashanah with *leshanah tovah tikateivu* (may you be inscribed [in the Book of Life] for a good year). On Yom Kippur, the greeting is *g'mar chatimah tovah* (may the final sealing be good).

Is there a special procedure for Jews asking forgiveness from each other before Rosh Hashanah? (T)

Hatarat nedarim (absolution of vows) is a practice among traditional Jews seeking forgiveness from one another on the day before Rosh Hashanah. One person asks three others to serve as a *beit din* (religious court) to grant forgiveness for any unfulfilled vows from the past year. In turn, each of the four asks the other three to serve as the *beit din*.[33]

Are the standard *challot* baked for the Sabbath used on Rosh Hashanah? (F)

The *challot* used on Rosh Hashanah are traditionally round. This symbolizes both a royal crown, which is consistent with the day's ubiquitous motif of the Kingship of God, as well as the cyclical and eternal nature of life, expressing the hope that the coming year will be complete and unbroken by tragedy. In some communities, the *challot* are decorated in the form of a ladder to symbolize our spiritual striving, like the ladder connecting Heaven and earth in Jacob's dream (Gen. 28:10–22), and the recurring theme that on this day the destiny of each person is decreed—whether to ascend the ladder of life and find success in the year to come, or to descend and suffer an unfortunate fate. Another popular style for the *challot* on both Rosh Hashanah and Yom Kippur is a bird shape. Originating in eighteenth-century Ukraine, the symbolism of the *faigele* (little bird) is: "May our sins be carried away by the bird, and may she fly with our prayers for salvation straight up to God."

Are there special foods associated with Rosh Hashanah? (T)

Pomegranates are a popular fruit for Rosh Hashanah because they contain numerous seeds that symbolize the hopes for fertility and the privilege of performing abundant good deeds. The pomegranate is also said to contain 613 seeds, the precise number of commandments in the Torah. Carrots are frequently served because the Yiddish word for them, *meirin* (more), indicates our desire for a year filled with blessings. They also are a symbol of prosperity, since when sliced they appear like golden coins. Apples dipped in honey are eaten in the hope for a sweet New Year. Other foods frequently eaten on Rosh Hashanah are pumpkins, fenugreek, leeks, beets, and dates, because they grow in profusion and are symbols of prosperity (Hor. 12a).[34]

Are some foods avoided on Rosh Hashanah? (T)

Many Jewish recipes avoid nuts (*egoz*) on Rosh Hashanah, because the Hebrew word (if spelled without the final silent *aleph*) has a numerical value (17) equal to that of "sin" (*chet*). Moreover, nuts are said to increase phlegm and the flow of saliva, which interfere with recital of the prayers.[35] Other foods generally not eaten on Rosh Hashanah include sour and bitter foods (pickles, lemons, vinegar, horseradish), and black-colored food (black olives and dark raisins).

Are fish eaten on Rosh Hashanah? (N)

Some Jews avoid eating fish on Rosh Hashanah, because in Hebrew the word fish (*dag*) is close to *da'ag* (worry). Nevertheless, many Sephardic Jews eat fish heads on this holiday to symbolize their wish to head their community in righteousness, hoping that they will be "the head and not the tail." Another custom in some communities is to eat the head of a sheep, as a reminder of the binding of Isaac.[36]

As on the Sabbath, is taking a nap on Rosh Hashanah a long-standing tradition? (F)

Conversely, there is a custom to refrain from sleeping on the afternoon of Rosh Hashanah, using the time instead to study Torah or recite psalms in synagogue. This is based on a statement in the Jerusalem Talmud: "If one sleeps at the beginning of the year [Rosh Hashanah], his good fortune likewise sleeps."

Is a *kitel* worn on the High Holy Days? (N)

A Yiddish word meaning "gown," *kitel* refers to a simple white robe, representing purity and forgiveness of sin, which is traditionally worn on Rosh Hashanah and Yom Kippur. The *kitel* is often worn by a groom on his wedding day, a father at the circumcision of his son, the person conducting the Passover seder, and the prayer leader during the solemn prayers for dew on Passover and rain on Shemini Atzeret. It is also used as a shroud.

Is the shofar only blown on Rosh Hashanah? (F)

On Rosh Hashanah, the Torah explicitly commands the sounding of the shofar, the most recognizable symbol of the day (Lev. 23:24). In fact, the name Rosh Hashanah does not appear in the Torah at all. Instead, the holiday is referred to as *Yom Teruah* (Day of Blowing). However, the use of the shofar was not limited to this day. The shofar was blown to mark the giving of the Torah at Mount Sinai (Exod. 19:16) and the razing of walls of Jericho during the Israelite conquest of the Promised Land (Josh. 6:20). A great blast of the shofar was also sounded every 50th year on Yom Kippur to mark the beginning of the Jubilee Year, when slaves were freed and all land reverted to its original owners (Lev. 25:8–10).[37] An echo of this ancient practice is the long blast of the shofar (*tekiah gedolah*) at the conclusion of the *Ne'ilah* service that marks the end of Yom Kippur.

Was the shofar still used after the destruction of the Second Temple? (N)

After the biblical period, the shofar no longer was used in Jewish priestly, military, and civil ceremonies. However, the shofar was blown on fast days, to announce a death, and at funerals; a special black shofar was used to proclaim an excommunication from the Jewish community.[38] According to the Talmud, six blasts of the shofar were blown on Friday afternoon (Shab. 35b). At the first sounding, the laborers in the fields ceased their work. At the second, shops were closed and city laborers stopped working. The third signaled that it was time to kindle the Sabbath lights. The final three blasts of the shofar formally ushered in the Sabbath. Today, the shofar is sounded daily at the conclusion of the morning service during the month of Elul, except on the Sabbath and the day before Rosh Hashanah.

Can the shofar be made from the horn of any kosher animal? (N)

According to the Talmud, the ritual commandment to hear the sound of the shofar on Rosh Hashanah can be fulfilled using a shofar made from an antelope, gazelle, goat, mountain goat, or ram (RH 27a). However, it explicitly forbids using a cow's horn, because "our advocate on Rosh Hashanah should not be a reminder of the Golden Calf, our great sin and accuser." We do not want our past transgressions to bias God against forgiving our current sins ("the accuser may not act as defender" [RH 26a]). The Rabbis strongly recommended the use of a ram's horn as a shofar, because of its association with the story of the *Akedah* (Binding of Isaac; RH 16b). A ram's horn is also desirable because it is curved, which is symbolic of our bowing in submission to God's will (RH 26b).

Are the precise sounds of the shofar indicated in the Bible? (F)

The Torah refers to two different sounds of the shofar—*tekiah* and *teruah* (Num. 10:5–8). According to the Mishnah, the *tekiah* is a long blast and the *teruah* equals "three *yevavot*," a wavering, crying blast (RH 4:9). Although the Talmudic sages prescribed three sets of shofar sounds, based on the word *teruah* being mentioned three times in the Torah (Lev. 23:24; 25:5–9; Num. 29:1), they disagreed as to whether the *teruah* should be a wailing, moaning, undulating sound (*shevarim*) of three broken notes, or a series of quick sobs (*teruah*) in at least nine staccato notes. Since a crying person may make both of these sounds, it was unclear what God wanted. The final decision was to use all three possible combinations—the first set of sounds should include both *shevarim* and *teruah*, while the other two sets should contain only one or the other.

Has the place of the shofar service on Rosh Hashanah changed over time? (T)

The Rabbis originally decreed that the shofar be blown during the main service of Rosh Hashanah, which in their day was the morning service. Later, this practice was changed, so that the sounding of the shofar and the reading of the biblical verses connected to it were postponed until much later in the day during the *Musaf* (additional) service. An explanation for this delay is that on one occasion the Romans, assuming that the early morning shofar blast was a signal for an uprising against them, attacked the Jews and killed them. Although the historical accuracy of the claim is in doubt, it is indisputable that the shofar, like the trumpet of the Romans, was an instrument used to signal battle as in the story of Joshua and the walls of Jericho. Consequently, the decision was made to sound the shofar later in the day to prevent any misunderstanding, for at that time it could only be construed as part of a religious ritual.[39]

Moving the shofar service from the *Shacharit* service to the *Musaf* presented the problem that the main *mitzvah* of the day was not performed until a relatively late hour. To solve this difficulty, the Rabbis added an additional blowing of the shofar in the morning at the conclusion of the Torah service (without any recitation of biblical verses).[40]

Was having precisely 100 blasts of the shofar on Rosh Hashanah an arbitrary decision? (F)

The Rabbis decided on having exactly 100 shofar blasts, either because this is the number of sobs of Sisera's mother or the number of letters in her lament for her son as recounted in the Song of Deborah (Judg. 5:28). This was designed to show that, just as Jews were sensitive to the tears of the mother of an archenemy, so we hope God will be sensitive to our tears and judge us mercifully on the High Holy Days.

Do Ashkenazim and Sephardim blow the 100 shofar blasts at the same points in the service? (N)

Today, 30 sounds are blown after the Torah reading and 30 during the reader's repetition of the *Musaf Amidah*—10 at the conclusion of each of its three major sections (*Malchuyot, Zichronot, Shofarot*). Another 30 sounds of the shofar are blown either during the silent *Musaf Amidah* (Sephardim) or during the full *Kaddish* at the end of the *Musaf* service (Ashkenazim). Sephardim sound the final 10 blasts during the *titkabeil* portion of the full *Kaddish* at the end of the *Musaf* service; Ashkenazim do so after the *Mourners' Kaddish*. The morning and *Musaf* sets of shofar blasts end with a *tekiah gedolah*.[41]

Is the shofar always sounded during Rosh Hashanah services? (F)

A vexing question for the Rabbis was whether the shofar should be blown if Rosh Hashanah fell on the Sabbath. When this occurred, the shofar was blown in the Temple but not in the countryside. After the Temple was destroyed, there was a difference of opinion among the major Rabbis. Fearing that an inexperienced blower might go for help to a more experienced person, thus violating the law of carrying on the Sabbath, they eventually concluded that the shofar should not be blown on the Sabbath (the current practice). This decision was based on the two descriptions of Rosh Hashanah in the Bible—*Yom Teruah* (Num. 29:1) and *Yom Zichron Teruah* (Lev. 23:24)—respectively "the day of blowing" and "the day of remembering the blowing." The former was deemed to mean any day but the Sabbath, when the shofar would actually be *blown*, while the latter was considered as referring to the Sabbath, when all we do is *remember* the sound of the shofar and not blow it.

Was *Avinu Malkeinu* written as a prayer for the High Holy Days? (F)

Avinu Malkeinu (Our Father, our King) are the opening words of a penitential prayer that originally was recited on fast days as a plea for rain. It now is found in an expanded version after the repetition of the *Amidah* in the morning and afternoon services during the Ten Days of Repentance from Rosh Hashanah through Yom Kippur. In the Ashkenazic tradition, *Avinu Malkeinu* is not recited on the Sabbath, except during the concluding *Ne'ilah* service on Yom Kippur, both because penitential prayers are not said on that day and because its original association with fast days makes it unsuitable for the Sabbath, which is dedicated to joyful experiences.[42] The core of *Avinu Malkeinu* is an appeal to God to "inscribe" (and on Yom Kippur, "seal") us in the book of (a) a good life, and for (b) redemption and salvation, (c) sustenance and prosperity, (d) merit, and (e) forgiveness and pardon—not because of our personal merits, but rather on behalf of the martyrs of Israel and because of God's own unfailing compassion.

Do Jews prostrate their whole bodies during Rosh Hashanah (and Yom Kippur) services? (N)

Prostrating the whole body, indicating total submission to the will of God, was closely associated with the ancient Temple service. However, the practice has been abandoned almost entirely in modern times, possibly because it is associated with other religions. Today, prostration is restricted to once during the *Aleinu* during the *Musaf Amidah* on Rosh Hashanah and three times during the *Avodah* service on Yom Kippur in the Ashkenazic ritual. At these times, it is customary for prayer leaders to actually kneel down and touch their heads to the floor. In some synagogues, all members of the congregation prostrate themselves.

Is it permitted to touch one's head to a stone floor when bowing on the High Holy Days? (F)

The Bible prohibited the Israelites from having a special "kneeling stone" like that on which pagan worshipers would kneel as they prayed before their idols (Lev. 26:1). This was interpreted as forbidding prostrating oneself on a stone floor, even if worshiping God. The Rabbis extended this prohibition to include kneeling outside of the Temple. However, the *Shulchan Aruch* states that it is permissible to kneel on the High Holy Days in synagogue if you put an intervening substance between your knees and the stone floor. Therefore, those who kneel and touch their head to the floor traditionally place a cloth or piece of paper underneath their knees and head, since many synagogues (especially in Israel) have stone or tile floors.

Was *Tashlich* a ritual devised by the Rabbis? (F)

Tashlich is the ceremony on the afternoon of the first day of Rosh Hasha-nah in which Jews recite special penitential prayers and psalms and throw crumbs or small pieces of bread into a body of water (river, reservoir, lake, or ocean) to symbolically cast away their sins. It is postponed to the second day of Rosh Hashanah if the first day falls on the Sabbath, because of the pro-scription against carrying on that day. The name derives from the verse in Micah (7:19): "You will cast (*v'tashlich*) all their sins into the depths of the sea.

Tashlich was not a ritual devised by the Rabbis, but rather a popular folk practice that was eventually accepted by rabbinic authorities after they had fought against it as a superstitious custom designed to propitiate the spirits of the rivers on critical days of the year.[43] The Rabbis feared that Jews would consider this ceremony sufficient to absolve them of their sins, rather than appreciating the need to change their conduct and return to God's path.

Is *teshuvah* the major focus of the Ten Days of Repentance? (T)

Teshuvah (repentance) is a prerequisite for Divine forgiveness, which requires a combination of genuine remorse for the wrong committed and evidence of changed behavior. From the Hebrew root *shuv* (return), it encom-passes both a turning away from evil and a turning toward good. A central biblical concept, *teshuvah* is the theme of the Ten Days of Repentance and a core of the prayers on Yom Kippur.

Is there a Jewish movement that emphasizes the importance of *teshu-vah*? (T)

The Talmudic dictum, "Repent one day before your death" (Shab. 153a), means it is necessary to spend every day in repentance, for none knows which day will be their last. This concept was championed by the Musar movement, founded by Rabbi Israel Salanter in Lithuania during the mid-nineteenth century, which focused on ethics, moral instruction, and character development. It identified and inculcated traits that would strengthen obser-vance through regular spiritual exercises. The Musar movement stressed the powerful role of human actions, teaching that monitoring one's behavior is the persistent task of the Jew, day after day, year after year. This turning inward to scrutinize one's deeds and motives gave the follower of the Musar movement a heightened self-awareness. In Musar *yeshivot*, spiritual develop-ment went hand in hand with intellectual growth.

Is Yom Kippur the saddest day of the year? (F)

Although Yom Kippur (Day of Atonement) is the most solemn day in the Jewish calendar, it is not a day of sadness or mourning. That distinction belongs to Tisha b'Av, which commemorates the destruction of the First and Second Temples. According to the Mishnah, during Temple times Yom Kip-pur afternoon was one of the most joyful times of the year. When the Temple ritual ended in the early afternoon, the solemn mood of the Day of Atonement evaporated and the people began to celebrate the assumed Divine forgiveness. Young women would dress in white and go out into the fields to dance, and the young men would come and choose their brides (Taan. 4:8). Consequently, the Torah reading for the afternoon of Yom Kippur, which deals with forbidden sexual relations, was chosen to remind the people of their moral responsibility, so that they would not to be carried away during this time of dancing and courtship.

Is Yom Kippur the holiest time of the year? (F)

Although there is no biblical ranking of the relative holiness of various holidays, an indication can be inferred by the number of people called up to the Torah and the punishment decreed for violating the commandments related to the day. On Yom Kippur, there are six *aliyot*, one more than any other festival. However, on the Sabbath (and if Yom Kippur falls on a Sabbath), seven people are called up to the Torah. The type of court administering a punishment for breach of a commandment gives an indication of its severity. Violating the laws of Yom Kippur and the Sabbath both merited the death penalty. Desecration of the Sabbath was punished with stoning, administered by an earthly court (reflecting a more serious crime), whereas the punishment for violating the prohibitions of Yom Kippur was only administered by the Divine court (deemed to be a less serious offense). Therefore, the weekly Sabbath is generally considered the holiest day(s) of the year.

Is fasting the only way that Jews satisfy the Divine command to "afflict your souls" (Lev. 16:29) on Yom Kippur? (N)

The major prohibition on Yom Kippur is against eating and drinking. This is unlike most fast days (other than Tisha b'Av), which last only from dawn to dusk. According to the Mishnah, in addition to fasting, the duty of afflicting the soul also requires the prohibition of (a) bathing for pleasure; (b) anointing the body with oil; (c) wearing leather shoes; and (d) engaging in sexual relations (Yoma 8:1). By abstaining from basic needs, Jews demonstrate that they can conquer all physical cravings and overcome the bodily appetites that are the principal source of sin. We attempt to enter a purely spiritual realm, to be as pure as angels, so as to merit Divine forgiveness. The custom of wearing white garments on Yom Kippur emphasizes our otherworldly, angelic qualities on this day.[44]

Should everyone fast on Yom Kippur? (N)

Fasting is an integral part of the observance of Yom Kippur. Nevertheless, based on the principle *of pikuach nefesh* (saving of life), a sick person whose health would be jeopardized by fasting (such as a diabetic, or a woman within three days of giving birth)[45] is obligated to eat and forbidden to fast. Even a healthy person, seized by a fit of "ravenous hunger" that causes faintness, must be fed on Yom Kippur with whatever food is available until he recovers. Although the Talmud states that "a sick person is fed at the word of experts" (Yoma 83a), the decision whether to fast on Yom Kippur generally depends on the subjective opinion of the patient who claims the need to eat, even if contradicted by 100 physicians. This is based on the verse in Proverbs (14:10): "The heart alone knows its own bitterness." Conversely, a patient must eat if a doctor declares that it is essential for health, even if he or she thinks it is not necessary. [46]

The Rabbis ruled that a patient who must take food and drink on Yom Kippur is required to recite the usual blessings before and after the meal. In the Grace after Meals, there is even the addition of a phrase referring to "this fast day of Yom Kippur!"

Is a six-year-old permitted to fast on Yom Kippur if he wishes? (F)

According to tradition, children under the age of nine are not allowed to fast. Over that age, they should be encouraged to fast for a longer period each year. They are not expected to fast for all of Yom Kippur until they have reached their religious maturity.

Does Yom Kippur provide atonement for sins? (N)

The process of repentance that culminates on Yom Kippur brings pardon *only* for sins between human beings and God (*bein adam la-Makom*). For transgressions between one human being and another (*bein adam la-chavero*), Yom Kippur does not secure atonement unless one has sought forgiveness from the other person and redressed any wrongs (Yoma 85b). [47] If necessary, the Talmud states that one must attempt three times to seek forgiveness from another. [48] If forgiveness is not granted—itself a grave sin—the burden of seeking exoneration is removed from the transgressor.

Is *kaparos* a popular custom rather than a ritual instituted by the rabbis? (T)

Literally "atonements," but in the sense of "ransom," this Yiddish term refers to the custom on the day before Yom Kippur in which the sins of a person are symbolically transferred to a fowl (a cock for a male; a hen for a female). While the fowl is swung around the head three times, a prayer is recited to transfer any misfortune that might otherwise befall the person in punishment for sins. These birds, never offered in the Temple, were selected so that no suspicion would arise that one was attempting the strictly forbidden practice of re-creating a Temple sacrifice. After the ceremony, it is customary to donate the fowl to the poor. Today, money is often substituted for the live bird.

Many major rabbinic authorities, both medieval and modern, have strenuously opposed the *kaparos* ceremony, attacking it as a superstitious ritual and decrying the belief that one may substitute the death of an animal for one's own life. Nevertheless, the ceremony appealed strongly to the masses and has survived in traditional households.[49]

Is *Kol Nidrei* the most important prayer said on Yom Kippur? (N)

Kol Nidrei ("All Vows"), chanted by the *hazzan* in a haunting melody on Yom Kippur eve, is not a prayer. Rather, it is a declaration that all personal vows, oaths, and promises made to God unwittingly, rashly, or unknowingly—and which cannot be fulfilled—be considered null and void. A legal formula written in Aramaic, *Kol Nidrei* is associated with several legal customs. As only a *beit din* (court composed of three persons) could abrogate a vow, two people holding Torah scrolls stand on either side of the *hazzan*. *Kol Nidrei* is repeated three times, because in Jewish law a court releasing someone from a vow was required to declare "you are released" three times. Considered a "legal procedure," *Kol Nidrei* must be chanted before sundown while it is still daylight, since a Jewish court could not make decisions at night.

Was the precise wording of *Kol Nidrei* controversial? (T)

The recitation of *Kol Nidrei* is first mentioned in *responsa* of the Babylonian *geonim* beginning in the eighth century. Although popular with the masses, the rabbis rejected it as an invalid practice that made light of vows. This primarily related to the initially accepted version that invoked Divine pardon, forgiveness, and atonement for those sins "from the *previous* Yom Kippur until *this* Yom Kippur" (i.e., the *past* year). In the twelfth century, French and German scholars reworded this phrase to read "from *this* Yom Kippur until the *next* Yom Kippur" (i.e., the *coming* year). Ashkenazim have adopted this formulation, while Sephardim generally accept the earlier geonic version.

Anti-Semites have frequently used *Kol Nidrei* as evidence of the worthlessness of Jewish oaths and proof that Jews could not be trusted. Therefore, the rabbis have taken great pains to stress that the *Kol Nidrei* formulation relates *only* to vows and promises to God and was never meant to apply to oaths taken before secular courts of law.

Did *Kol Nidrei* assume special significance during the Spanish Inquisition? (T)

Even though the Jews of Spain were forced to deny their faith and assume the rites and rituals of the Catholic Church, many continued to practice their religion in secret. *Kol Nidrei* provided a welcome opportunity for solemnly renouncing the vows that they had made under duress.[50]

In the two confessionals that Jews recite multiple times on Yom Kippur, does each person detail the transgressions that he or she has personally committed? (F)

Some Rabbis maintained that it was necessary to specify exactly those sins that one had committed. R. Akiva disagreed, arguing persuasively that a general confession was sufficient. In Talmudic times, any expression of confession sufficed. During the geonic period, however, the rabbis formulated texts that served as the basis of the two set forms of confession that are recited today—*Al Het* and *Ashamnu*. Both of these confessions are expressed in the plural, as is customary in Jewish liturgy, in keeping with the concept of the collective responsibility that Jews have for one another. Each Jew confesses not only those sins that he or she has committed personally, but for every transgression that may have been committed by anyone in the congregation. Therefore, the congregation rises to recite the confessions in unison. At the mention of each transgression, all worshipers symbolically express their remorse by tapping their chests, since the heart was long regarded as the source of consciousness. Pointing to oneself physically connects everyone to each transgression, for even if one did not commit a specific sin, he or she could have done it.

Was the ancient rite of Azazel essential to Divine forgiveness of the Israelites? (F)

Azazel was the name either of a demon or the place to which one of the goats was sent as part of the Temple service on Yom Kippur. The Bible states that Aaron would cast lots upon two goats to select one as a sin-offering for the Lord and the other for Azazel (Lev. 16:8–10). Because this ritual took place only *after* the people had been forgiven, it appears that the goat for Azazel was merely a symbolic rite, emphasizing a cleansing of sins that had already taken place.

Was the goat designated to Azazel set free? (N)

The biblical text mandates that the goat sent to Azazel be set free. However, during Talmudic times it was hurled to its death from a rocky precipice and the scarlet thread attached to its horns miraculously turned white, indicating that God had accepted the atonement of the people of Israel.[51]

Are there other Days of Atonement each year? (N)

Yom Kippur Kattan, literally "little Day of Atonement," is a partial or complete fast observed on the day before each New Moon. The custom was introduced by Rabbi Moses Cordovero, a sixteenth-century kabbalist in Safed. He and his mystical colleagues believed that each New Moon was a time of forgiveness from sins. Therefore, by repenting fully on the preceding day, one can enter the new month in a spirit of renewal. On Yom Kippur Kattan, special penitential psalms are added to the usual prayers. While popular in past centuries in Europe, Yom Kippur Kattan is infrequently observed today and is not even mentioned in the *Shulchan Aruch*, the authoritative Code of Jewish Law.

Is Sukkot named for the temporary shelters erected for the festival? (N)

This festival of thanksgiving, celebrating the joy of the harvest, is named for the temporary shelters (*sukkot*; singular, *sukkah*) in which the Israelites dwelled as they wandered through the wilderness (Lev. 23:42). However, the Talmud (Suk. 11b) records a dispute as to whether the *sukkot* mentioned in the Torah were actual or metaphysical booths, the latter referring to the protective "clouds of glory" that accompanied and sheltered the Israelites during their 40-year journey.[52] Some believe that they originated from the temporary shelters in which workers would live in the fields and vineyards during the harvest season. Even when no longer in common use, these booths remained a religious symbol of God's special care for the Jewish people.[53]

Can a space with a large overhanging roof over a deck be used as a *sukkah*? (F)

The Talmud prescribes precise rules for constructing a *sukkah*.[54] One of these mandates is that it be built under the open sky, not under a tree or inside a house (or an overhanging roof).

Is special material required for the roof of a *sukkah*? (T)

The roof of the *sukkah* is covered with *s'chach*, typically consisting of cut branches or bamboo sticks, arranged so that there is more shade (covered space) than sunshine inside the *sukkah* during the day (Suk. 9b–10a).

Are Jews required to sleep and eat all meals in the *sukkah*? (N)

During the festival of Sukkot, Jews regard the *sukkah* as their principal abode, with the house merely a temporary residence (Suk. 2:9). According to the Talmud, it is forbidden to eat any major meal or to sleep outside the *sukkah*, though the Rabbis did permit "casual" eating (of a small quantity, such as a piece of fruit) and drinking of water elsewhere (Suk. 26a). Modern rabbinic authorities, cognizant of the cold and rainy climates to which Jews have wandered during their long exile, have permitted sleeping and eating inside the house when the weather is bad. Not only is a person not obliged to sleep or eat in the *sukkah* when rain penetrates the roof, but one is forbidden to do so, for it is improper to insist on carrying out a religious duty from which there is an exemption.

Are newlyweds required to eat in the *sukkah*? (F)

Newlyweds and members of the wedding party are exempt from the requirement to eat in the *sukkah*, probably based on the principle of not mixing two kinds of joy (the wedding and the *sukkah*). Moreover, the Rabbis may have felt that the *sukkah* was not the most comfortable spot for the couple to spend their wedding night, and this exemption continues for the traditional seven days of celebration after the wedding.

Do the four species required by the Bible have underlying meanings? (T)

During Sukkot, the four species—*etrog* (citron), *lulav* (palm tree), myrtle (*hadas*), and willow (*aravah*)—are waved in all four directions of the compass, as well as up and down, to demonstrate the omnipresence of God. Then they are carried in procession around the synagogue during the festival (except on the Sabbath). Although the Bible gives no reason for their use, the Midrash offers several moral and homiletic interpretations of the symbolic meaning of the four species. They are said to correspond to the human body (the *etrog* resembles the heart, the *lulav* is like the spine, the *myrtle* resembles the eyes, the *willow* is like the lips) and to the four types of Jews that differ with respect to scholarship (taste) and good deeds (pleasant aroma) but must be united in the community of Israel, so that the failings of one are compensated for by the virtues of the others (Lev. R. 30:12).

Are *ushpizin* homeless individuals whom we invite into the *sukkah*? (F)

Ushpizin, an Aramaic word meaning "guests," refers to the seven biblical personalities whom, according to the Lurianic kabbalistic tradition, Jews invite to visit the *sukkah* during the seven days of Sukkot. Each of these "guests" is symbolic of one of the *sefirot* (Divine Emanations)—Abraham (*Chesed*, loving-kindness); Isaac (*Gevurah*, strength); Jacob (*Tiferet*, beauty); Moses (*Netzach*, victory); Aaron (*Hod*, splendor); Joseph (*Yesod*, foundation); and David (*Malchut*, sovereignty). In our time, there are various "lists" of guests, including their female counterparts.

Were the Talmudic Rabbis so pious and studious that they would not allow themselves any feats of dexterity? (F)

The Talmud states that one who had not seen the ceremony of the water drawing in the Temple on Sukkot had never witnessed real joy (Suk. 5:1). It reports that Rabban Shimon ben Gamaliel "used to take eight lighted torches [and juggle them in the air], catching one and throwing another [so that none touched the ground]. When he prostrated himself, he used to dig his two thumbs in the ground, bend down [while still leaning on them], kiss the ground, and raise himself up again [by these two fingers while doing a headstand], a feat which no other man could accomplish" (Suk. 53a). Other reported feats of incredible dexterity were the juggling of eight knives, glasses of wine (without spilling any), and eggs (without breaking any).

Does Yom Kippur conclude the High Holy Days? (N)

Yom Kippur is the last of the Ten Days of Repentance and traditionally the day on which the Book of Life is sealed for the coming year. Nevertheless, some consider Hoshanah Rabbah, the seventh and last day of Sukkot, as the conclusion of the High Holy Day period, the last time that unfavorable judgments can be averted before the final seal is placed. Hoshanah Rabbah is the day when Jews beat willow branches from the *lulav* against the ground near the Altar, symbolizing the casting away of sins. The *Zohar* states that "the seventh day of the festival [i.e., Hoshanah Rabbah] is the close of the judgment of the world, and writs of judgment issue from the Sovereign." Consequently, it is a custom for Jews to wish each other a *pikta tava*, an Aramaic phrase that literally means a "good note" and refers to a favorable judicial decree from the Divine court.

Is Shemini Atzeret really the eighth day of Sukkot? (N)

Although often considered as the eighth day of Sukkot, Shemini Atzeret is actually an independent festival. It marks the conclusion of the festivities and observances of Sukkot—though none of the Sukkot ceremonies apply to it—and as such was selected as the day for the recitation of *Yizkor*, the memorial service that is recited on the final day of all three pilgrimage festivals. Because *atzeret* comes from a root meaning "to hold back," the Rabbis deemed that God instituted this holiday so that all those who made the pilgrimage to Jerusalem for Sukkot would remain with Him in the city for one additional day.

Was the Prayer for Rain always recited on Shemini Atzeret? (F)

The hallmark of the service on Shemini Atzeret is the Prayer for Rain.[55] The sages decreed that it should be recited during Sukkot, the pilgrimage festival that falls closest to the rainy season in Israel. However, because of the obligation to dwell in the *sukkah*, rainfall would make it uncomfortable or impossible to fulfill this *mitzvah*. This desire for good weather while in the *sukkah*, so that the people could fully experience the Hebrew expression for the festival (*zeman simchatnu*, "the season of our joy"), led the Rabbis to designate that the Prayer for Rain be postponed until Shemini Atzeret.

Is Simchat Torah a biblical holiday? (F)

Literally meaning "Rejoicing in the Torah," Simchat Torah is the final day of the series of festivals associated with Sukkot, but it is not mentioned in the Bible. Rather than a separate festival, during Talmudic times Simchat Torah was simply referred to as the second day of Shemini Atzeret (Meg. 31a). Similarly, it was called Shemini Atzeret in both the prayers and the *Kiddush* recited on this day. In Israel, Simchat Torah is celebrated on the same day as Shemini Atzeret (22nd of Tishrei); in the Diaspora, it falls on the next day (23rd of Tishrei) and concludes the Sukkot season.

Did the celebration of Simchat Torah begin in the Land of Israel? (F)

On Simchat Torah, the annual cycle of reading the Torah scroll is completed and immediately begun again. The unique celebrations associated with Simchat Torah first developed during the geonic period, with the wide acceptance of the Babylonian custom of completing the reading of the Torah in one year. This was in contrast to the triennial cycle followed in the Land of Israel.

Has there been a standard Torah reading for Simchat Torah? (N)

Originally, only the last two chapters of the Torah were selected as the portion for this day. However, it later became customary to also read the first chapter of Genesis on Simchat Torah, so as to prevent Satan from arguing that the Jews were celebrating only because they had finally finished the Torah and did not want to start reading it again.

Are the Chanukah candles lit before the Sabbath candles on Friday night? (T)

The Chanukah candles are lit before the Sabbath candles, to avoid violating the ban against lighting a fire on the seventh day.

Is there a special way to light the Chanukah candles? (N)

Although there is now a standard order for lighting the Chanukah candles, this was a controversial issue during Talmudic times. Lighting the eight-branched menorah on the Festival of Lights is a rabbinically ordained commandment (Shab. 23a). The first reference states: "One light must be kindled in each house; the zealous require one light for each person; the extremely zealous add a light for each person each night" (Shab. 21b). The Talmud then discusses the controversy concerning the number of candles that should be lit. Beit Shammai declared that eight candles should be lit on the first night, and thereafter they should be reduced by one on each successive day. As usual, the *halachah* follows Beit Hillel, which argued for lighting one candle on the first night, two on the second night, and so forth. This view was based on the principle that in matters of holiness, one should increase rather than diminish.

Are additional candles placed in the Chanukah menorah and lit in the same direction? (F)

The current practice is to insert the candles in the menorah from right to left, with the newest addition on the left, but to light them from left to right, with the newest addition kindled first.

Are dreidels used in Israel the same as those in the Diaspora? (F)

The dreidel is a four-sided top, inscribed with Hebrew letters, which is one of the best-known symbols of Chanukah. Dreidel is a Yiddish word derived from the German *drehen* (to turn). In medieval Germany, dice had four letters inscribed on their sides—N, G, H, and S—respectively representing the words *nichts* (nothing), *ganz* (all), *halb* (half), and *shtell arein* (put in). After throwing the dice, the player would do the action indicated by the letter that appeared face upward. Jews transformed the dice into a spinning top and translated the letters into their Hebrew equivalents—*nun, gimel, hei, and shin*—which form an acronym for the phrase *nes gadol hayah sham* (a great miracle happened there) and are used throughout the Diaspora. In modern Israel, the letter *shin* is replaced by a *pei* (the first letter of the word *po,* meaning "here"), so that the phrase becomes "a great miracle happened *here*."

Does *Maoz Tzur* have only one stanza? (F)

Maoz Tzur (Mighty Rock [of my salvation]) is the most popular of the Chanukah songs traditionally sung after kindling the festival lights. Composed in thirteenth-century Germany, the opening stanza is a plea for the reestablishment of the Temple, the rededication of the Altar, and the restoration of the sacrificial rites. Concluding with the phrase *chanukat ha-Mizbeach* (dedication of the Altar), this stanza is the most often sung. However, *Maoz Tzur* actually has six stanzas, with the second through fourth praising God for delivering the Jewish people from various tribulations—Egyptian bondage, the destruction of the First Temple and the Babylonian Exile, and Haman's plot in Persia.[56] The fifth stanza summarizes the miracle of Chanukah, which commemorates the miraculous victory of the Maccabees over the Syrian-Greek army. A final stanza, which is generally regarded as a later addition by a different author and contains a strong plea for Divine vengeance against Israel's foes, was subject to censorship by Christian authorities.

Is the popular English hymn "Rock of Ages" a direct translation of *Maoz Tzur*? (F)

The revenge motif explicit in *Maoz Tzur* troubled some segments of the Jewish community. In the nineteenth century, two well-known American rabbis, Marcus Jastrow and Gustav Gottheil, composed a considerably toned-down English version to the same melody, which they entitled "Rock of Ages."

Is gift giving a traditional part of the celebration of Chanukah? (N)

As the commemoration of a post-biblical event, for more than 2,000 years Chanukah was only a minor holiday in the Jewish calendar. In many communities, it became traditional to give gifts of coins (Chanukah *gelt*) to children. This may have been related to the minting of coins for currency by the Maccabees after restoring political autonomy to the Jewish people. In Eastern Europe, the family customarily gathered together on the fifth night of Chanukah to give children coins as a reward for their diligence in Torah study. In the United States, Chanukah has often been transformed into a "Jewish alternative" to the unrelated winter holiday of Christmas. To emulate, or compete with, their Christian neighbors, many Jewish parents began giving gifts to their children on each night of Chanukah.

Ironically, the widespread gift giving of Chanukah in emulation of Christmas is a complete perversion of the original concept of the festival—a celebration of the heroic victory against the Hellenizing forces of assimilation.

Is the Passover seder the only one celebrated in Jewish tradition? (F)

Attempting to stimulate the flow of positive Divine energy into the world, the sixteenth-century kabbalists of Safed created a seder for Tu b'Shevat (January–February), which was loosely modeled after the Passover seder. It involved eating symbolic fruits and nuts, especially those native to the Land of Israel.

Does the Tu b'Shevat seder represent multiple worlds of Creation? (T)

According to the Kabbalists, there were four worlds or levels of Creation—*asiyah, yetzirah, beri'ah,* and *atzilut,* which are symbolized by various fruits and nuts consumed at the Tu b'Shevat seder. The lowest of the four worlds is *asiyah* (action), the realm of physical reality that requires full protection. This world is represented by fruits and nuts that have tough, inedible outer shells, such as pomegranates, walnuts, almonds, pine nuts, chestnuts, hazelnuts, coconuts, Brazil nuts, pistachios, pecans, bananas, and melons. The next level is *yetzirah* (formation), similar to Plato's "forms" and the ideal version of our world, symbolized by fruits that have inedible pits inside but whose outsides can be eaten, such as olives, dates, cherries, hackberries, jujubes, persimmons, apricots, peaches, loquats, and plums. The next-to-the-highest level is *beri'ah* (creation), symbolized by fruits that have neither pits on the inside nor shells on the outside and thus are totally edible even though they have small seeds, such as grapes, figs, apples, *etrogim* (citrons), lemons, pears, raspberries, blueberries, carobs, and quinces. The highest of the four worlds of Creation is *atzilut* (emanation), which is purely spiritual and cannot be symbolized in any material way.

Is there significance to the four cups of wine at the Tu b'Shevat seder? (T)

Beginning with a cup of white wine, participants at a Tu b'Shevat seder add increasing amounts of red wine so that the next three cups are pink, deep rose, and almost completely red. This sequence symbolizes the gradual transition of the land "from the cold whiteness of winter through the pale buds of spring into the full-blooming flowers of summer and the striking colors of the leaves before they fall from the trees in autumn."[57] The four cups also represent the four letters of the Tetragrammaton (YHVH), the most holy Name of God.

Did the Divine redemption of the Jews of Persia make the Book of Esther a rabbinic favorite? (F)

Unlike Passover, which celebrates God's direct intervention in freeing the Israelites from bondage and leading them out of Egypt, the name of God is never mentioned in the *Megillah,* the scroll that is read on Purim. This seriously troubled the Rabbis, some of whom refused to admit the Book of Esther into the Jewish canon. The Jews neither plead to God to save them in times of peril nor have a celebration of thanksgiving to God for their deliverance. In addition, the violent tone of the concluding chapters, with the Jews eventually triumphing over their enemies, led the Rabbis to fear that the Book of Esther might arouse the hatred and suspicion of non-Jews. Nevertheless, it was finally admitted as part of the biblical canon, and the story of Purim was interpreted as a model of God's hidden hand in history. An entire tractate of the Mishnah (*Megillah*) is devoted to the details of observing this holiday, especially to the rules governing the reading of the Scroll of Esther.

Is the evening reading of *Megillat Esther* the major synagogue ritual of Purim? (N)

Originally, the *Megillah* was only read during the day, which remains halachically as the primary time for fulfilling this *mitzvah*. However, it eventually became traditional to also read the *Megillah* at night, when the attendance is far higher.

Is a special *trope* used throughout the reading of the *Megillah*? (N)

Although there is a special *trope* used for reading the Scroll of Esther, there are several important variations. The four verses of "redemption" (2:5; 8:15,16; 10:3) are enthusiastically recited aloud by the congregation and then repeated by the reader. It is customary for the reader's voice to become louder for those verses that mark the decisive moments in the story (1:22; 2:4, 17; 4:14; 5:4; 6:1). Verse 2:6 is chanted using the *trope* of the Book of Lamentations, since it describes the destruction of Jerusalem. Traditionally, the short lines listing the 10 sons of Haman (9:7–9) are recited in one breath, because they were hanged together.

Is there a biblical source for the noisemaking when the name of Haman is read? (T)

The custom for the congregation to make noise during each of the 54 times that the name of Haman is read in the *Megillah* fulfills the biblical commandment to "blot out the name of Amalek" (Deut. 25:19), the ancestor of Haman. While any kind of noisemaking device is acceptable, including booing and stamping one's feet on the floor, it is traditional to use a *grager* (rattle) for this purpose. Some even write the name Haman on the soles of their shoes, so as to literally blot out the name as they stomp their feet.[58]

Does *Adloyada*, the name of the Tel Aviv parade held each year on Purim, have a rabbinic meaning? (T)

In modern Israel, a prominent feature of Purim observance in Tel Aviv is the huge parade of costumed revelers called *Adloyada*. This term derives from the statement of Rav (Meg. 7b), the renowned scholar of the Babylonian Talmud, mandating that a person get so drunk ("mellowed with wine") on Purim that "he does not know" (*ad lo yada*) the difference between "'Cursed is Haman' and 'Blessed is Mordecai.'" According to *gematria*, the Hebrew letters of these two phrases—*arur Haman* and *baruch Mordecai*—

have the identical numerical value (502). In Eastern Europe, this command to become inebriated was observed so well that a proverb described a foolish person as one "who gets drunk all year and stays sober on Purim."[59]

Is the tradition of donating three half-dollars to charity just before reading the *Megillah* on Purim eve designed to raise funds for good causes? (F)

This custom actually symbolizes the three times that the Torah commands the Israelites to contribute a half-shekel for the upkeep of the Tabernacle (Exod. 30:13, 15). Donated during the month of Adar, in which Purim falls, the half-shekels were affordable even by the poor and used to purchase the animals that were offered twice daily by the *kohanim* on behalf of the Jewish people.[60] The qualification that "the rich shall not pay more and the poor shall not pay less" indicated that the Tabernacle belonged to the entire community, without regard to wealth or social status, since all are equal in the eyes of God. The half-shekel tax is also a moral lesson, teaching that one Jew alone is only half a Jew; he or she must join with another Jew to become a complete individual.[61]

Are there any other special acts of *tzedakah* related to Purim? (T)

Mishlo'ach manot (often abbreviated as *shalach manot*) is the tradition of sending gifts (lit., "portions") to friends and acquaintances. Because the word *manot* is in the plural, it became traditional to send at least two kinds of food to at least two people. Similarly, there is the practice of sending *matanot la-evyonim* (gifts to the poor) to at least two needy people, so that they also can share in the joy of the Purim festival. In most communities, this is accomplished through contributions to charities that care for impoverished Jews.[62]

Do all Jews celebrate Purim on the same day? (N)

Almost all Jews celebrate Purim on the 14th of Adar. However, the Jews of Shushan, the Persian capital, continued to battle against their enemies for an extra day and did not rest until the 15th of Adar, when they celebrated their deliverance. Because Shushan was a walled city, the Rabbis ruled that Jews living in all cities that had a fortified outer wall around them at the time of Joshua would observe Purim on that day. Therefore, in modern Israel, Purim is celebrated on the 15th of Adar in Jerusalem (a walled city in ancient times), whereas in Tel Aviv and elsewhere the festival is observed on the 14th of the month. In leap years, when there is an extra month of Adar, Purim is celebrated in Second Adar so that the festival always falls one month before Passover.

Did Esther fast on the day before Purim? (F)

Purim is preceded by the Fast of Esther, which recalls the three-day fast by the Jews of Persia to lend support to Queen Esther. Because the fate of her people was at stake, Esther was preparing to enter King Ahasuerus's presence without prior permission, an act punishable by death. Ironically, the fast mentioned in the *Megillah* actually occurred during Passover of the previous year, when Esther first learned about the nefarious plot to kill the Jews, rather than just prior to the climactic events in the Purim story. Indeed, on the 13th of Adar that year, the Jews were fighting against their enemies. When Purim falls on a Sabbath, the fast is moved back to Thursday, since fasting is not permitted either on the Sabbath (except on Yom Kippur), a day of joy, or on Friday, when one is preparing for the Sabbath.

Are Esther and Mordecai Hebrew names? (N)

The Hebrew name of the heroine of the Purim story is Hadassah (myrtle), though non-Jews called her Esther, a name seemingly derived from Ishtar, the Persian equivalent of Venus, the goddess of beauty. Yet an alternative explanation is that the name Esther derives from the Hebrew word *seter* (hidden), a foreshadowing of her ability to disguise her Jewish identity until she had won the heart of King Ahasuerus and thus was in a position to save her people from destruction.[63]

Although the name Mordecai bears a close resemblance to Marduk, the chief god in the Babylonian pantheon, the Talmud interprets his name as coming from the two Hebrew words *mor* (myrrh) and *decai* (pure), which reflect his noble character.

Are *hamantashen* the popular Jewish delicacies for Purim? (N)

Hamantashen (lit., "Haman's pockets") are triangular stuffed pastries that are traditionally eaten by Ashkenazic Jews on Purim. One explanation is that they represent the bribes filling the pockets of this corrupt villain of the Purim story. Although there are many delectable variations with puréed dried fruits, *hamantashen* are traditionally filled with *mohn* (Yiddish for "poppy seeds"), a word that sounds like the Hebrew pronunciation of the second syllable of the name Haman. *Hamantashen* are sometimes called "Haman's hat," and in medieval depictions this Persian villain is often anachronistically portrayed wearing a three-cornered hat popular in Europe at that time.

Among Sephardim, however, a popular pastry is the ear-shaped cookies known as *oznei Haman* (Haman's ears). This name is said to have derived from the former practice of cutting off the ears of criminals before hanging them—appropriate since Haman and his 10 sons were hanged at the conclusion of the Book of Esther.

In some years, is there more than one holiday known as Purim? (T)

In a leap year when there are two months of Adar, Purim is celebrated during the second, so that the festival always occurs one month before Passover. The 14th day of the first Adar in a leap year is known as Purim Kattan (little Purim). Although there are no specific observances, fasting and funeral eulogies are prohibited and *Tachanun* is not recited. Some Jewish communities also observe a Purim Kattan for specific dates when they were saved from catastrophic danger, complete with celebrations patterned on the original Purim.

Does the biblical prohibition against eating *chametz* on Passover refer to bread? (N)

The Hebrew term *chametz* means all leavened products. This is a memorial of the Exodus, when the Israelites "took their dough before it was leavened" (Exod. 12:34) and left Egypt in great haste. The criterion for rendering grain *chametz* is that it "ferments" on decomposition. Those grains such as rice and millet that decompose by "rotting" were not regarded as coming within the prohibition of *chametz* (Pes. 35a). Nevertheless, Ashkenazic (but not Sephardic) authorities not only forbid the use of rice and millet on Passover, but extend the prohibition to a group of foods termed *kitniyot* (generally translated as "legumes"), which includes beans, peas, corn, lentils, buckwheat, and, according to some authorities, peanuts.

Is it necessary to have separate pots and dishes for Passover? (N)

Because pots in which *chametz* has been cooked absorb and retain some of it—"imparting a flavor" into any other food cooked in them—those that have been used during the year are forbidden for use during Passover unless they have been rigorously cleansed in accordance with halachic requirements. For the same reason, separate dishes must be used for Passover. However, this is not required for non-permeable glass, which can be soaked and washed in order to be permissible for Passover use.

Is it permissible to keep *chametz* in the home as long as it is not eaten? (N)

The Bible forbids even the mere possession of *chametz* during Passover. However, disposing of this material could produce serious financial hardship when large quantities of foodstuffs are involved, or where *chametz* is used for business purposes. To alleviate this problem, the Rabbis devised the legal formula of "selling" the *chametz* to a non-Jew before Passover and then "buying" it back after the festival had concluded. This initially involved the physical transfer from Jew to non-Jew "in the marketplace" (Pes. 13a). Today, it is accomplished in writing. The parties agree on a price and a down payment is made by the non-Jew. The sale is often done through a rabbi, who is given power of attorney to act as the agent in the transaction. After Passover, the agent buys back the *chametz* and symbolically restores it to the original owners.[64]

Is the sale of *chametz* a legally binding contract? (T)

The sale is a formal legal document. Although there is the presumption that the non-Jew who buys the *chametz* will sell it back after Passover, there is legally no obligation to do so.

Is quinoa permitted on Passover? (T)

One food that is now sanctioned on Passover, even for Ashkenazim, is quinoa.[65] A member of the goosefoot family, named for its three-lobed leaves, quinoa is distinguished by its curly halo when cooked. It was never included in the prohibition against *kitniyot*, since the rabbis were unaware of the existence of this Incan staple. Quinoa is as versatile as rice and is naturally a complete protein.

Is it traditional for firstborn Jews to fast on the day before Passover? (N)

The Fast of the Firstborn (*Taanit Bechorim*) is observed on the 14th of Nisan, the day before Passover, to commemorate and express gratitude to God for sparing the firstborn Israelites during the 10th plague in Egypt. As one of the minor fast days, it begins at sunrise, rather than the previous night. Many of those who observe it take advantage of the halachic principle that Torah study can supersede and cancel the fast. Whenever the study of a Jewish text is completed, such as a tractate of Talmud, it is customary to have a *siyum* (completion)—a celebration of the special occasion with food and drink. Therefore, the tradition has evolved to finish the study of a tractate of Talmud on the morning before Passover, when a festive meal (*seudat mitzvah*, meal in honor of a *mitzvah*) is arranged in the synagogue. For those firstborns who participate, the meal associated with the *siyum* breaks the fast.[66]

Is the seder a narration of the historical account of the Exodus from Egypt? (N)

The seder (lit., "order") is the special home ceremony held on the first night of Passover (also the second in the Diaspora) that fulfills the biblical injunction that parents inform their children of the miraculous deliverance from Egypt. Rather than a mere history lesson, the Talmud states that "in every generation one is obligated to look upon oneself as if he or she personally had gone forth out of Egypt" (Pes. 116b). Rituals designed to enable participants in the seder to experience directly the joy of freedom include reclining in one's chair (as did free Roman citizens), eating *matzah* (consumed by the slaves at their moment of freedom), and drinking four cups of wine. Conversely, inviting in the poor, tasting the bitter herbs, and the tradition among some of adding a fourth *matzah* for those Jews who are still oppressed are actions that remind us of the bitterness of the slavery and repression suffered by our ancestors.

Is *Mitzrayim* the Hebrew word for Egypt? (N)

Mitzrayim, the Hebrew word for the country in northeastern Africa where the Israelites were enslaved for centuries, comes from a root meaning "narrow." Therefore, the idea of "being in Mitzrayim" was interpreted as referring not only to the physical land of Egypt, but also metaphorically as a spiritual and religious constriction due to the idol worship and overemphasis on the afterlife in that country.

Does the first written Haggadah date back to biblical times? (F)

The Haggadah (lit., "telling") is the book that contains the prayers, blessings, legends, commentaries, psalms, and songs traditionally recited at the Passover seder. The word derives from the phrase *ve-higad'ta [le-vincha]* (And you shall *tell* your child [on that day]: "it is because of that which the Lord did for me when I came forth out of Egypt") (Exod. 13:8). The oldest published version of the Haggadah is in the prayer book of Saadiah Gaon from the tenth century. The Haggadah is by far the single book most widely read by Jews, having appeared in more than 3,500 editions.

Does Moses play a major role in the Haggadah? (F)

Despite being the major biblical figure and the hero who led the Israelites out of Egypt during the Exodus, Moses is not mentioned in the classic Haggadah.[67] Faced with the horrors of the Crusades, the medieval rabbis introduced a new element into the Haggadah—Divine justice and revenge—which has been neutralized in many contemporary versions.[68] A link was forged between what God *did* to the Egyptians and what God *will do* to the nations that have oppressed the Jews in the final Messianic redemption. God will be the only actor in the final vengeance, just as God was responsible for the first partial redemption of the Exodus. With no room for human efforts in the process, Moses was eliminated from the Haggadah.

Has drinking four cups of wine always been the accepted standard practice? (N)

Today, each participant at the Passover seder drinks four cups of wine. During Talmudic times, the general consensus among the Rabbis (Exod. R. 6:4) was that the four cups of wine reflect the four different expressions of Divine deliverance used in the Torah in relation to the redemption of Israel (Exod. 6:6–7).[69] According to some opinions, however, there was also a requirement to drink a fifth cup at the seder in commemoration of the Divine pledge in the next verse, "and I will *bring you* [into the land]" (Exod. 6:8). Others maintained that no fifth cup should be drunk, since this Divine promise of the return of the Jewish people to the Land of Israel was still to be fulfilled. The ultimate rabbinic decision was to not drink a fifth cup; however, because the *halachah* was in doubt, Jews pour it and leave it on the table to await the coming of the prophet Elijah and the final fulfillment of the Divine pledge in the Messianic Age. Thus, the Cup of Elijah symbolizes both our hope that he will come soon—perhaps even on this Passover night—and our trust that the Messiah will bring the ingathering of the exiles, the reestablishment of Jewish sovereignty over the Land of Israel, and fulfillment of the Divine promise to return the people to their land.[70] Now that the State of

Israel exists, some rabbis have advocated drinking five cups of wine at the seder, arguing that God's pledge has indeed been fulfilled.[71]

May any type of kosher for Passover wine be used at the seder? (N)

Red wine is preferred (Pes. 108b), though white wine was often used in Europe because of blood libel accusations against the Jews.

Are the Four Questions said even if no child is present? (T)

The four questions asked at the beginning of the Passover seder are popularly known by the first words of the introductory line—*Mah nishtanah* (What is different [about this night from all other nights]?). Although now usually asked by the youngest participant, during geonic and early medieval times, *Mah nishtanah* was probably recited by the person conducting the seder. Today, it is usually asked by the youngest participant, while in some households all of the children get a turn. If there is no child present at the seder table, an adult asks the questions. At any seder, the questions must be asked and answered, even if one is alone so that the questioner and answerer are the same person.

Are the Four Questions really questions? (N)

The first word of the Four Questions (*Mah*) can also be an exclamation, as in its usage in *Mah Tovu* (How goodly [are your tents, O Jacob]), the hymn that opens the morning service. Therefore, some prefer to translate *Mah nishtanah* as "How different [is this night from all other nights]!"

Does the Haggadah answer these questions? (N)

The answers to the first two questions (*matzah, maror*) appear in the Haggadah. However, the third and fourth questions (dipping, reclining) are not specifically answered in the text.

Several reasons are offered for the two "dippings"—the *karpas* in salt water and the bitter herbs in *charoset*. The simplest is that although dipping once was a routine culinary practice, this deliberate departure from customary eating habits was designed to arouse the curiosity of children and prompt them to ask questions. According to some commentators, dipping twice alludes to two historical events that are associated with the Egyptian experience. After selling Joseph into slavery, his brothers dipped his "coat of many colors" into blood in order to convince Jacob that a wild beast had devoured his favorite son. That deed ultimately led to the Egyptian exile because, as viceroy of Egypt, Joseph dispensed the food that Jacob and his family required during the seven years of famine. The second dipping was the Divine command that the Israelites dip a bunch of hyssop into the blood of the Passover offering and then smear the blood on their doorposts to signify that those inside the house should remain unharmed while the first-born Egyptians were being killed in the 10th plague.[72] Reclining dramatizes the status of Jews as free human beings, reflecting the custom of the upper classes to eat their great banquets while reclining on couches, their left arm on the cushions while their right hand held food or wine.

Are the words of the wise child diametrically opposite those of the wicked child? (N)

At the seder, it is traditional to contrast the insightful questions of the wise child (*hacham*), designed to gain a deeper understanding of the proper way to observe the commandments relating to Passover, with those of the wicked child (*rasha*), who effectively excludes himself from the community. Nevertheless, the biblical text quotes the wise child as saying, "What are the statutes, laws, and ordinances that the Lord our God has commanded you [*etchem*]" (Deut. 6:20)—which sounds similar to the tenor of the wicked child. However, the Jerusalem Talmud changed the last word to *otanu* (us) to sharpen the difference between the two children. Which was the original reading? The Talmudic version is the same as that in the Septuagint (Greek translation of the Bible from the first century B.C.E., much earlier than the Haggadah), indicating that there may have been a scribal error in what became the "authoritative" text.

Can *matzah* be made from any type of grain? (F)

Unleavened bread made from flour and water is the quintessential symbol of Passover. Only grains capable of fermentation are valid for the manufacture of *matzah*. This applies to the five species indigenous to the Land of Israel—wheat, barley, spelt, rye, and oats—although wheat is most commonly used.

Is *matzah* a symbol of freedom? (N)

Matzah has a paradoxical symbolism in the Passover story. The flat shape is a reminder that the former Israelite slaves left Egypt for freedom so quickly that their bread did not have time to rise (Exod. 12:39). Conversely, *matzah* is described as *lechem oni* (bread of affliction) (Deut. 16:3), the minimal food provided for the Jewish slaves when they labored for Pharaoh.

Is there a single blessing for *matzah* at the seder? (F)

Two blessings are made over the *matzah* at the seder—the generic one for eating "bread," and the specific one for eating unleavened bread on the festival.

Is there a special type of *matzah* for the seder? (N)

Some Jews prefer to use a special *shmurah* (lit., "guarded") *matzah* for Passover, especially at the seder. The preparation of *shmurah matzah* is closely supervised from the time the wheat is harvested until it comes out of the oven. This is in contrast to ordinary Passover *matzah*, which is supervised starting with the milling of the wheat. Rather than the uniform square sheets of manufactured *matzah*, handmade *shmurah matzah* is uneven and round, resembling the *matzah* baked in ancient times. It is generally more expensive because of the labor involved.[73]

Did the rabbis praise the efficiency of the first machine for preparing *matzah*? (N)

Developed in the 1850s, this machine provoked an intense halachic controversy. It was designed to push the kneaded dough between two metal rollers, from which it emerged thin, perforated, and round. As the machine reused the corners of dough that were cut off to make the *matzot* round, it was feared that these bits might become leavened before finally being incorporated into a sheet of *matzah* ready for baking. This dilemma was solved by a later machine, which produced square *matzot* with no leftover dough. Another rabbinic complaint was that these machines endangered the livelihood of those who earned money before Passover by working in a *matzah* bakery, which would require fewer manual workers. However, this was rejected by the vast majority of authorities, who lauded the efficiency of the new *matzah*-making process and wondered why the same concern had not been expressed for scribes who had been displaced by the printing press.[74]

Can any type of *matzah* be used at the seder? (N)

Matzah used for Passover is produced under exacting standards that require the flour and water mixture be processed in less than 18 minutes, the time assumed to allow leavening to take place. Therefore, for Passover use, it is essential to purchase a package that specifically states that the *matzah* is kosher for Passover.

Some have questioned whether *matzah* made from flour mixed with grape juice, oil, or eggs instead of water may be used on Passover. Although in the absence of mixing with water there is, strictly speaking, no fermenting, the Talmud considered such *matzah* to be forbidden at the seder since it constitutes "rich *matzah*" (*matzah ashirah*) rather than the required "bread of affliction" (Pes. 36a). According to *halachah*, only the sick or the aged are permitted to eat these enriched types of *matzah* at the seder.

Is horseradish the preferred *maror*? (N)

Maror (bitter herb) is eaten at the seder to remember the bitterness the Israelites experienced during their period of slavery in Egypt. Although the Bible does not specify the plant by name, the Jerusalem Talmud describes *maror* as a "bitter vegetable with a silvery appearance that has sap" (Pes. 2:5, 29c). Many Ashkenazic Jews today use horseradish for *maror*. However, the Rabbis suggested romaine lettuce as a bitter herb, since its stem has a milky sap and because the taste, like the experience of the Jews in Egypt, is initially sweet but then turns bitter. In addition, this variety of lettuce starts as a very soft plant, but in time its core hardens, symbolizing the insidious entrapment of the Israelites by the Egyptians. Initially the Egyptians took a soft approach, hiring the Israelites as highly paid workers; but then they hardened their grasp on the Israelites as they gradually converted them into slaves.

Is the sweet *charoset* a symbol of the slavery of the Israelites in Egypt? (N)

Charoset, traditionally a paste made of fruit, nuts, spices, and wine, is considered to be symbolic of the mixture of clay and straw from which the enslaved Israelites made bricks. However, as with other symbols of Passover, *charoset* has a dual meaning. Ashkenazic Jews typically include apples, which the Talmud deemed symbolic of fertility as in a verse from Song of Songs, "Under the apple tree I roused you" (8:5). According to tradition, when Pharaoh ordered the killing of the firstborn males, the men refused to have sexual relations with their wives. Consequently, the women took the men outside the town and seduced them under the apple trees. When it was time to be born, the children were delivered under the same trees and left in the fields where they remained hidden. Then breasts grew from the rocks and the babies would suck milk and honey from them until weaned. In this way, the apple symbolizes the birth of the next generation, which eventually was liberated from slavery in Egypt during the Exodus.

Is there a standard type of *charoset* for the Passover seder? (F)

The ingredients of *charoset* vary widely among different communities. Ashkenazic Jews typically use chopped apples, walnuts, cinnamon, and red wine; Sephardim tend to use ingredients that grew in the Land of Israel during biblical times, such as dates, figs, and almonds. North Africans also include pine nuts, hard-boiled eggs, ginger, and cinnamon. Yemenites add chili pepper, whereas some Israelis mix in dates, bananas, candied orange peel, and orange juice. [75]

May the *afikoman* be eaten at any time on seder night? (F)

Early in the Passover seder, the leader breaks the middle of the three *matzot* into two pieces and hides the larger half. This portion of *matzah* is known as the *afikoman*, and the seder cannot conclude until all guests have eaten a piece of it. Since the destruction of the Second Temple, the broken half of the middle *matzah* has come to replace and symbolize the Passover sacrifice, which was the last item eaten at the seder during Temple times. Consequently, nothing may be eaten or drunk after the *afikoman* (Pes. 119b–120a), except for water and the required last two cups of wine. As with the Passover sacrifice, the *afikoman* must be consumed before midnight. [76]

Does the leader of the service drink wine from the Cup of Elijah? (F)

The Cup of Elijah is a large goblet filled with wine, which is placed on the table at the Passover seder but is not drunk. It symbolizes the hope that the prophet will come soon as the herald of the Messiah.

Is there a blessing recited over the Cup of Elijah? (N)

Although no blessing is said, once the Cup of Elijah has been poured, it is customary to open the front door and recite a prayer asking God to "pour out Your wrath upon the nations that do not recognize You and upon the kingdoms that do not invoke Your Name." This custom dates back to the Middle Ages, when the Passover season was an especially difficult time for Jews because of the proximity to Easter and the threat of a blood libel. During this period of danger, Jews would open their doors to foil such a plot.

Is there also a cup of wine for Miriam at the seder? (N)

At Passover seders in households with a strong feminist bent, a new tradition has developed of adding a cup (parallel to the Cup of Elijah) as a symbol of the contributions of the prophetess Miriam, the sister of Moses. Miriam's Cup is filled with water, rather than wine, to symbolize the miracle of Miriam's well, which brought forth water to sustain the Israelites for 40 years during their wandering in the wilderness after the Exodus.

Is *Chad Gadya* ("One Kid") merely a simple folk song? (N)

This popular Aramaic song, which traditionally concludes the seder, relates in 10 stanzas what happens to a little goat that was bought by a father for two coins (*zuzim*). The goat was eaten by a cat, which was bitten by a dog, which was beaten by a stick, which was burned by fire, which was quenched by water, which was drunk by an ox, which was butchered by the slaughterer (*shochet*), who was killed by the Angel of Death, who in punishment was destroyed by God. Each stanza repeats the previous verses and closes with the refrain, *chad gadya, chad gadya.*

Although deceptively simple and appearing to have no relation to Passover, commentators consider *Chad Gadya* to have a deep hidden meaning that reflects the underlying medieval Ashkenazic theme of ultimate justice and final revenge, with God reigning supreme. The classic interpretation of the song is as an allegory of Jewish history, in which God originally "acquired" the people (the kid) with two coins (the tablets of the covenant). The Jews then became the subjects of various nations that conquered each other in turn—Assyria (the cat), Persia (the stick), Greece (the fire), Rome (the water), the Saracens (the ox), the Crusaders (the slaughterer), and the Turks (the Angel of Death), who at the time of the song's completion (late sixteenth century) still ruled the Land of Israel. *Chad Gadya* concludes with the confident assurance that the Messiah (representing the Holy One) will finally redeem the Jews from this last oppressive ruler.

Is *Hallel* recited in the synagogue on Passover? (N)

An abbreviated *Hallel*, which omits the first 11 verses from Psalm 115 and all of Psalm 116, is recited on the last six days of Passover. The Midrash offers an ethical, humanitarian explanation for limiting the *Hallel* on the last six days of Passover. God is pictured as rebuking the angels who wished to sing praises to celebrate the deliverance of the Israelites: "My creatures are drowning in the sea, and you would sing to Me!" (Yalkut Shimoni 247). Thus, the abridged *Hallel* reflects the mitigation of Israel's joy because of the death of the Egyptians who had pursued them.

For similar reasons, when reciting each of the 10 plagues, Jews traditionally dip their little finger into the wine and spill a drop of it to symbolize their grief at the loss of any human life, even that of their bitter enemies.

Was the Song of Songs uniformly approved by the Rabbis? (N)

One of the five *megillot* and attributed to King Solomon, the Song of Songs (*Shir ha-Shirim*) is usually read on the intermediate Sabbath of Passover. Filled with striking, erotic imagery, it is a series of lyric poems, in which two lovers express to each other the yearnings and delights of their mutual love. Unique in the Bible, the Song of Songs focuses entirely on the love between man and woman. No morals are drawn, no prophesies are pronounced, God is not mentioned, and theological concerns are never discussed. Consequently, there was intense discussion among the Rabbis regarding whether the Song of Songs should be included in the biblical canon. The argument was resolved by R. Akiva, who insisted: "All the Writings are holy, but the Song of Songs is the Holy of Holies." The book subsequently has been interpreted by Jewish tradition as an allegory for God's love of the Israelites.

Is there any special celebration at the end of Passover? (T)

Maimuna is a daylong celebration of Moroccan Jews, which begins immediately after sundown at the conclusion of the Passover holiday. It is characterized by an extraordinary show of hospitality, in which Jews open their doors to friends and neighbors. The table is traditionally set with a white tablecloth and adorned with flowers, fig branches, stalks of wheat, and a fishbowl that may contain a live fish as a symbol of fertility. Dairy foods are eaten, especially pancake-like wafers of fried dough (*muflita*) spread with butter and honey. In Israel, Moroccan Jews celebrate the day after Passover with communal picnics, and a large central gathering is held in Jerusalem.

Is the 49-day Omer period a time of semi-mourning? (T)

From the second day of Passover until the festival of Shavuot, Jews are commanded to count seven weeks to commemorate the period between the Exodus from Egypt and the Revelation at Sinai. This process of counting, known as *sefirat ha-omer* (counting of the Omer), recalls the ancient practice of bringing a sheaf (*omer*) of the newly harvested barley crop (the first grain to ripen) as an offering to the Jerusalem Temple.

The Omer period is observed as a time of semi-mourning. Traditional Jews do not get haircuts or celebrate weddings during this time. Initially, these restrictions may have been related to the anxiety during this critical time when the success of the harvest was determined. According to Talmudic and midrashic sources, during the period between Passover and Shavuot, 24,000 disciples of R. Akiva died of a terrible "plague." This may refer to the overwhelming defeat suffered by the forces of Bar Kochba, whom R. Akiva strongly supported in the unsuccessful rebellion against the Romans.

Are there any days of celebration during this period? (T)

The major exception to the semi-mourning during the *Sefirah* period is Lag ba-Omer, the 33rd day of the counting of the Omer (18th of Iyar), when the plague temporarily ceased. It also may commemorate the brief recapture of Jerusalem, which is traditionally said to have occurred on this date. Relating Lag ba-Omer to Shimon bar Yochai, the reputed author of the mystical *Zohar*, kabbalists and Hasidim in Israel hold a festive celebration at the sage's grave in the village of Meron, near Safed, studying mystical texts and singing and dancing around bonfires. As marriages and cutting one's hair are generally prohibited during the Omer period, on Lag ba-Omer many weddings are performed and it became customary for three-year-old boys to have their first haircut.

Other days that are exempted from the restrictions of the Omer period include the two modern holidays of Yom ha-Atzma'ut (Israel Independence Day) and Yom Yerushalayim (Jerusalem Day), as well as Rosh Chodesh (New Moon) of the month of Iyar.

Is there any special food eaten on Lag ba-Omer? (T)

It is traditional to eat foods made from carob on this day, because the fruit of a carob tree sustained Shimon bar Yochai and his son during the 12 years they hid from the Romans in a cave.

During the Omer period, is it traditional to study a special tractate of the Mishnah every Sabbath? (T)

A popular custom is to study *Pirkei Avot* (Ethics of the Fathers) every Sabbath during the Omer period. Beginning the Sabbath after Passover, one of the six chapters of *Pirkei Avot* is studied following the afternoon service. In this way, the final chapter dealing with the Torah is read just before Shavuot, the festival commemorating the Revelation at Mount Sinai. Sephardim still continue the custom of reading *Pirkei Avot* only during this period, though most Ashkenazic congregations repeat the six chapters three times until the Sabbath before Rosh Hashanah.

Is the festival of Shavuot a harvest festival? (N)

Literally meaning "weeks," Shavuot occurs in the late spring (Sivan 6), 50 days after the beginning of Passover. It is also known as Yom ha-Bikurim (Day of the First Fruits), when joyful pilgrims would march to Jerusalem to offer up baskets of their first ripe fruits and bread baked from the newly harvested wheat (Bik. 3:2–4). During rabbinic times, however, the festival was transformed into the anniversary of the giving of the Torah on Mount Sinai (Pes. 68b). In the synagogue, it is traditional to read the Book of Ruth on Shavuot, because the story takes place at harvesttime (2:23). Moreover, as a proselyte, Ruth accepted the Torah just as Israel did at Mount Sinai.

Is it traditional to stay up all night on Shavuot? (T)

The kabbalists introduced the custom of observing an all-night vigil— *Tikun leil Shavuot* (lit., "The prepared [texts] of the night of Shavuot")— devoted to study of passages from the Bible, Talmud, and *Zohar*. In some communities, the Shavuot eve study session is climaxed with the only sunrise service of the Jewish year, which may symbolize the light of the Torah. [77]

Are all normal activities permitted on the days before Tisha b'Av? (F)

The Three Weeks refers to the period of mourning that extends from the 17th of Tammuz through the 9th of Av (Tisha b'Av). Also known in Hebrew as *bein ha-meitzarim* (lit., "between the straits"; i.e., the two fasts), it commemorates the destruction of the First and Second Temples in Jerusalem. The traditional mourning rituals during the Three Weeks include abstention from weddings and other joyous celebrations (*simchas*), as well as public musical entertainment; and the prohibition against the purchase or wearing of new clothing or the eating of new fruit, for which the S*hehecheyanu* blessing (an expression of joy) must be recited. [78]

Beginning with the first of Av, the mourning customs become intensified. Eating meat and drinking wine are forbidden, except for Sabbath meals. Also prohibited are cutting hair, shaving, bathing (except for basic cleanliness), swimming, or any activities that could bring joy—such as attending a concert or the theater or redecorating a room.

Were the destructions of the Temples the only catastrophes to befall the Jewish people on Tisha b'Av? (F)

According to the Mishnah (Taan. 4:6), Tisha b'Av was also the date of several other disasters for the Jewish people: the 10 spies delivered their negative report about the Land of Canaan to Moses, condemning the Israelites to spend 40 years wandering in the wilderness until they were permitted to enter the Promised Land; and the Bar Kochba revolt was finally crushed when Betar, the last stronghold, was captured by the Romans in 135 C.E. According to tradition, Tisha b'Av was also the date of the expulsions of the Jews from England (1290) and Spain (1492).

According to Jewish tradition, will Tisha b'Av always be a day of mourning? (F)

Tisha b'Av, the ninth day of the month of Av (July/August), is the saddest day in the Jewish calendar. It is a major fast day marking the anniversary of the destruction of the First Temple by the Babylonians in 586 B.C.E. and the

Second Temple by the Romans in 70 C.E. Nevertheless, there is a tradition
that the Messiah will be born on Tisha b'Av, reversing the centuries of travail
and suffering that have been the lot of the Jewish people.

NOTES

1. Garfiel, 127–28.
2. Donin, *To Pray as a Jew*, 321.
3. Ibid., 322.
4. Millgram, *Jewish Worship*, 299.
5. Hertz, 632.
6. Chill, 337–38.
7. Heschel, *The Sabbath*, 13.
8. Witty and Witty, 193.
9. Kolatch, *The Jewish Book of Why*, 166.
10. Telushkin, 600.
11. Ibid.
12. Hertz, 277.
13. Maimonides, *Mishneh Torah*, Shabbat 27:17.
14. Telushkin, 484.
15. Witty and Witty, 187.
16. Maimonides, *The Commandments*, 165.
17. Trepp, 77.
18. Donin, *To Pray as a Jew*, 333.
19. Ibid., 331.
20. Millgram, *Sabbath*, 21–22.
21. As is Ramadan in the Islamic lunar calendar.
22. In the 3rd, 6th, 8th, 11th, 14th, 17th, and 19th years of the cycle.
23. Nisan, Iyar, Sivan, Tammuz, Av, Elul, Tishrei, Cheshvan, Kislev, Tevet, Shevat, and
Adar.
24. Greenberg, 303.
25. *Stone Chumash*, 683.
26. Maimonides, *The Commandments*, 300.
27. Chill, 278.
28. Donin, *To Be a Jew*, 210–11.
29. Millgram, *Jewish Worship*, 210–11.
30. Frankel and Teutsch, 141.
31. Strassfeld, 93.
32. Kolatch, *The Jewish Book of Why*, 227–28.
33. Strassfeld, 98.
34. Kolatch, *The Jewish Book of Why*, 237–38.
35. Sperling, 224.
36. Steinsaltz, 183.
37. This shofar blast was designed to "proclaim liberty throughout the land and to all the
inhabitants thereof" (Lev. 25:10)—words selected by the American patriots to be inscribed on
the Liberty Bell, which announced the signing of the Declaration of Independence and the birth
of their new free land.
38. Frankel and Teutsch, 156–57.
39. Hammer, *Entering the High Holy Days*, 71–72.
40. Ibid., 72.
41. Strassfeld, 219.
42. Hammer, *Entering the High Holy Days*, 67.
43. Ibid., 92.

44. It also is reminiscent of Isaiah's prophesy of Divine forgiveness (1:18): "Though your sins be red as scarlet, they shall become white as snow." Many wear a *kitel* (white robe), also donned at a wedding, which may instill a sense of purity. As the shroud in which one will ultimately be buried, the *kitel* may be worn as a foretaste of death—in view of the imminent Divine decision as to who will live and who will die—or possibly even be a ruse to fool the Angel of Death into thinking that the person has already departed this life.

45. Strassfeld, 219.

46. *ArtScroll Yom Kippur Reader*, 67.

47. This is the source of the custom in many communities, immediately preceding the recitation of *Kol Nidrei*, of worshipers walking around the synagogue and asking forgiveness from one another for offenses committed during the past year.

48. According to the Talmud (Yoma 87a), this is based on the triple repetition of the word "please" in the message that the brothers, fearful of Joseph's exacting revenge after Jacob's death, contended was given to them by their father just before he died (Gen. 50:17) (*Etz Hayim*, 1493).

49. Hammer, *Entering the High Holy Days*, 104.

50. Witty and Witty, 248.

51. Ibid., 266.

52. Steinsaltz, 169.

53. Kolatch, *The Jewish Book of Why*, 248.

54. It must have a minimum of three walls (38 inches or higher), at least two of which must be complete. The *sukkah* may be constructed of any material, though it is usually of wood or canvas suspended on a metal frame.

55. From this service until the first day of Passover, when the Prayer for Dew is said, the sentence *mashiv ha-ruach u-morid ha-gashem* (Who causes the wind to blow and the rain to fall) is included in every *Amidah* prayer at the beginning of the second benediction.

56. *ArtScroll Siddur*, 783–84.

57. Waskow, 108.

58. Frankel and Teutsch, 133.

59. Waskow, 118.

60. Witty and Witty, 377.

61. Sperling, 265.

62. Strassfeld, 191.

63. Frankel and Teutsch, 49.

64. Strassfeld, 12.

65. "Ask the Rabbi: Rice and Beans," n.d., Aish.com, http://www.aish.com/atr/Rice_and_ Beans.html (accessed January 30, 2015).

66. Strassfeld, 16.

67. The phrase, "They believed in God and Moses His prophet," occurs only in later Ashkenazic manuscripts; the custom was to only quote the first two words of the verse, which eliminated the name of Moses.

68. Other examples are "Pour out your wrath" (eliminated in most contemporary Haggadahs) and *Chad Gadya*, which is treated as merely a cute song to end the seder.

69. "I will *bring you out* [from under the burdens of the Egyptians]," "I will *deliver you* [from their bondage]," "I will *redeem you* [with an outstretched arm and with great judgments]," and "I will *take you* [to Me for a people]." However, the next verse contains a fifth expression, "And I will *bring you* [into the land that I vowed to Abraham, to Isaac, and to Jacob]," but this was not considered as warranting an extra cup.

70. *ArtScroll Haggadah Treasury*, 138.

71. Donin, *To Be a Jew*, 231.

72. *ArtScroll Haggadah Treasury*, 43.

73. Frankel and Teutsch, 103.

74. Gross, 73–74.

75. Joan Michel (ed.), *The Hadassah Jewish Holiday Cookbook*. New York: Universe Publishing, 2003.

76. *ArtScroll Haggadah Treasury*, 124.

77. Frankel and Teutsch, 153.
78. Strassfeld, 87.

Chapter Eight

Synagogue and Prayer

Have you ever wondered . . .

1. Is *synagogue* the official Jewish word for a house of worship?
2. Did the synagogue as a site for prayer develop before the Second Temple was destroyed and the sacrificial rites ended?
3. Is there a single traditional style of synagogue architecture?
4. Should a synagogue be constructed on a hill?
5. Is a synagogue required to have windows?
6. Did the biblical Ark of the Covenant hold a Torah scroll?
7. Is the *bimah* typically situated in the front of the synagogue?
8. Has moving the *bimah* to the front of the synagogue affected Jewish prayers?
9. Has the role of the *hazzan* changed substantially since Talmudic days?
10. Was the first half of the twentieth century known as the "Golden Age of *Hazzanut*"?
11. Can a woman be a cantor?
12. Is the *mechitzah* separating men and women during prayer a Jewish tradition?
13. Does the *ner tamid* represent the Menorah in the Temple?
14. Have rabbis always been paid for being the spiritual leaders of their congregations?
15. Has the role of the rabbi changed dramatically over time?
16. Are there different levels of *semichah*?
17. Is *semichah* conferred through laying of hands on the recipient?
18. Was there ever an attempt to reinstitute the ancient practice of *semichah*?

19. Is the weekly Sabbath morning sermon a time-honored Jewish tradition?
20. Is the *siddur* a uniform prayer book that was developed by a committee of rabbinic scholars and cannot be changed?
21. Does the earliest *siddur* date from the rabbinic period?
22. Is there a uniform version of the *siddur*?
23. Are the crown or silver finials placed on top of the Torah scroll for decoration?
24. Are Torah scrolls covered with cloth mantles?
25. Is there special significance of the wrapping to bind the Torah scroll?
26. Can anyone write a Torah scroll?
27. Is a woman permitted to write a Torah scroll?
28. Is there a single type of script used in writing a Torah?
29. Is the Torah written from right to left?
30. Can someone other than a trained *sofer* write a part of a Torah scroll?
31. Can errors made when writing a Torah scroll simply be erased?
32. Is there any significance to the flourishes over some letters in a Torah scroll?
33. When writing a Torah scroll, does the *sofer* have artistic freedom to design its format?
34. Do all parts of the Torah scroll look alike?
35. Is prayer primarily asking something of God?
36. Do people pray for themselves?
37. Were there any prayers in ancient Israel?
38. Were there formal communal prayers during biblical times?
39. Is there a biblical basis for Jews praying three times each day?
40. Can anything be added to the standard prayer text in the *siddur*?
41. Is Hebrew the language for Jewish prayer?
42. Are some prayers inappropriate and invalid?
43. Do Jews pray to the east?
44. Has music always been an important aspect of Jewish prayer?
45. Is the playing of instrumental music now accepted as part of the Sabbath and festival services?
46. Was ritual swaying during prayer a Hasidic innovation?
47. Is praying alone at home just as good as praying in a synagogue?
48. Is a rabbi or cantor required for a prayer service in the synagogue?
49. Are prayers recited only to praise and thank God and plead for Divine help?
50. Are the authors of prayers anonymous?
51. Is a *minyan* necessary for Jewish prayer?
52. Is a *minyan* needed at other times?
53. Are only men counted in the *minyan*?

54. Does the requirement for 10 members of a *minyan* come from the Ten Commandments?
55. Before each service, is one person responsible for counting to 10 to make certain that there is a *minyan*?
56. To constitute a *minyan*, do all 10 people have to be praying?
57. During the repetition of the *Amidah*, must there always be a *minyan*?
58. Is a traditional Jewish man required to cover his head at all times?
59. Does the type of head covering indicate something about the wearer?
60. May a worn-out *kippah* be thrown into the garbage?
61. If a man does not have a *kippah* handy, may he simply use his hand to cover his head?
62. Is a married woman required to cover her hair?
63. Is a *tallit* worn at night?
64. In Orthodox synagogues, do all Jewish males 13 years or older wear a *tallit*?
65. Does the *tallit* have a standard appearance?
66. Is the *tallit* worn so that it rests on the shoulders?
67. Is the collar of the *tallit* merely decoration?
68. On days when *tefillin* are worn, are they put on after the *tallit*?
69. Although the Bible requires that there be a thread of blue on each corner of the *tallit*, is this still observed?
70. Is there a standard pattern to the threads of the *tzitzit*?
71. Does a woman wear a *tallit*?
72. Do Jews only wear a *tallit* for prayer services?
73. Is there anything written in the *tefillin*?
74. Are *tefillin* worn for morning services?
75. Are *tefillin* put on the left arm?
76. Are there a large number of blessings in Judaism?
77. Do blessings have a uniform formula and structure?
78. Are blessings recited for good things?
79. Is the blessing formula grammatically incorrect?
80. Is "amen" an ancient word with no intrinsic meaning?
81. Are there rules for when and how "amen" should be said?
82. Is there more than one *Kaddish*?
83. Has the *Kaddish* always been an important part of the synagogue service?
84. Is the original *Kaddish de-Rabbanan* still recited in synagogue?
85. Does the *Mourner's Kaddish* focus on death?
86. Is the *Kaddish* recited for less than a full 12 months after death?
87. May only sons recite the *Mourner's Kaddish*?
88. Is there a standard melody for all synagogue services?
89. Was the opening prayer of the morning service written by a non-Jew?
90. Were the morning blessings (*Birchot ha-Shachar*) once much shorter?

91. Do the preliminary morning blessings have a standard wording?
92. Is the *Ashrei* an alphabetical acrostic?
93. Does the term *Shema* refer to a single verse in Deuteronomy?
94. After the first verse of the *Shema* is recited in the synagogue, is the response said aloud?
95. After the complete *Shema* is recited in the synagogue, does the prayer leader proceed immediately to the next prayer?
96. Is the first verse of the *Shema* recited more than once on Sabbath morning?
97. Is the first verse of the *Shema* read differently from other prayers?
98. Must the first verse of the *Shema* be recited in Hebrew?
99. Because of the importance of the prayer, is the *Shema* traditionally read standing?
100. Is the first blessing in the prayers immediately before the morning *Shema* a direct biblical quote?
101. Is the *Amidah* known as the *Shemoneh-Esrei* (18) since it has that number of blessings?
102. Is the "silent" *Amidah* ever recited aloud?
103. Should the *Amidah* be said in a loud voice to affirm one's faith?
104. Are the feet traditionally placed in a specific position when reciting the *Amidah*?
105. Is the *Amidah* repeated at all services?
106. Is the repetition of the *Amidah* different from the silent prayer?
107. Does the *Amidah* contain a prayer for life-giving rain?
108. Was there a theological reason for the addition of a partial repetition of the *Amidah* at the Friday evening service?
109. Are personal prayers permitted during the *Amidah*, with no suggested rabbinic text?
110. Is taking steps backward and forward at the beginning of the *Amidah*, as well as bowing at the end, more than mere custom?
111. Is the *Kedushah* a prayer praising the holiness of God?
112. Is there a "short" version of the *Amidah*?
113. Is the Priestly Blessing recited by *kohanim* on the three major pilgrimage festivals?
114. Does the congregation respond "amen" after each part of the *Birkat ha-Kohanim*?
115. Do those in synagogue gaze with awe at the *kohanim* during the Priestly Blessing?
116. Does the appearance of the hands of the *kohanim* have any application outside of the synagogue?
117. Do Jews recite the words of the Priestly Blessing in any other context?
118. Is there a single version of the prayer for peace?

119. Are the Thirteen Attributes of Mercy recited in the synagogue the same as those in the Bible?

120. Are the Thirteen Attributes of Mercy also recited at any other time?

121. On a weekly basis, is the Torah read only on Sabbath morning?

122. Is the triennial cycle for reading the Torah a modern innovation?

123. Has the Torah always been divided into chapters and verses?

124. Do Jews throughout the world always read the same Torah portion on a specific Sabbath?

125. When the Torah is taken around the synagogue before being read, is there a tradition regarding how and in what direction the Torah is carried?

126. Is only one Torah scroll removed from the ark to be read?

127. Can there be Torah readings from more than two Torah scrolls?

128. Are there always seven people called up to the Torah?

129. Can there ever be more than seven *aliyot* on Sabbath mornings?

130. Are there different ways to approach the *bimah* when called for an *aliyah*?

131. When congregants say *yasher ko'ach* to a person returning from an *aliyah* to the Torah, does that mean "congratulations"?

132. Is calling up two people for the same *aliyah* a generally accepted practice?

133. Is there a prohibition against close relatives having adjacent *aliyot*?

134. Is a *kohen* always given the first *aliyah*?

135. Is there a difference between the "prestige" of different *aliyot*?

136. Is the selection of who is given an *aliyah* at a specific service random?

137. When two or more people are observing the same occasion, is a visitor given the honor of an *aliyah*?

138. Is the recitation of one blessing before the Torah reading and one after it the standard Jewish practice?

139. Is the first Torah blessing grammatically inconsistent?

140. Is there controversy whether the Torah scroll should be rolled closed or left open while the Torah blessings are being recited?

141. Does the *baal korei* (master of the reading) read the entire Torah portion?

142. Is the musical cantillation for chanting from the Torah written in the scroll?

143. Are the symbols and melodies the same for all readings?

144. Does the person reading the Torah read exactly what is written in the scroll?

145. If the Torah script is faded, is the decision as to whether the scroll can continue to be used for the reading based solely on the observation of a trained rabbi?

146. Is a woman permitted to read from the Torah?

147. Should congregants stand when the Torah is read?

148. Are portions of the Torah read in different ways?

149. Was there ever a custom to have a verse-by-verse translation of the Torah reading into the vernacular?

150. Does each person called for an *aliyah* receive a blessing after their portion?

151. Do the *gabbaim* serve as an "honor guard" on either side of the Torah scroll as it lies on the reading table?

152. At the end of the reading, is the Torah scroll simply lifted up so that it can be covered?

153. Are there different traditions among Jewish communities regarding when the Torah is raised and what words are recited?

154. Have there always been two people responsible for taking care of the Torah scroll after it has been read?

155. In some communities are there special individuals who perform the role of *hagbah*?

156. Is there a *haftarah* after the Torah reading?

157. Has the *haftarah* followed the Torah reading since the second century B.C.E.?

158. Does the earliest reference to the reading of the *haftarah* occur in the Talmud?

159. Are the *haftarot* related thematically to the Torah reading?

160. Is the *maftir* portion one of the seven obligatory readings for the Sabbath?

161. Do Jews recite a prayer for the country in which they live?

162. Is *Ein Keloheinu* (There is none like our God) merely a popular hymn of praise?

163. In this prayer, was the order of the words to describe God chosen for a specific reason?

164. Has the *Aleinu* always been recited at the end of each prayer service?

165. Has the text of the *Aleinu* been the subject of controversy?

166. Have changes been made to the *Aleinu*?

167. Is *Adon Olam* part of the bedtime prayers?

168. Is *Yigdal* a polemical hymn?

169. Does the blessing *ha-motzi lechem min ha-aretz* (Who brings forth bread from the earth) apply to products made from wheat?

170. Does the blessing *borei pri ha-etz* (Who creates the fruit of the tree) apply to bananas, melons, strawberries, pineapples, and tomatoes?

171. For wine, is the correct blessing *borei pri ha-gafen*?

172. Are there different forms of the Grace after Meals?

173. Is there an Aramaic version of the *Birkat ha-Mazon*?

174. Was the *Birkat ha-Mazon* written during the biblical period?

175. Is the *Shehecheyanu* blessing said for all things that are new?
176. Is it a Jewish custom to give a small sum of money to one setting out on a journey?
177. Should *Birkat ha-Gomel* be recited after an airplane flight?

Is *synagogue* the official Jewish word for a house of worship? (N)

The synagogue is considered by many Jews to be the most important institution in Judaism. However, the word itself is of Greek origin and means "to bring together." The three Hebrew designations for the synagogue indicate its major functions—*beit knesset* (house of assembly); *beit tefillah* (house of prayer); and *beit midrash* (house of study). The Yiddish term for a synagogue is *shul*, from a German word meaning "school," reflecting the fact that Jewish worship and learning most often take place in the same building. Early Reform Jews chose the term "temple" for their synagogues, indicating that in the post-Enlightenment age they no longer yearned for a return to the Land of Israel and the rebuilding of the Temple in Jerusalem, instead considering the country of their citizenship to be their everlasting homeland. [1]

Did the synagogue as a site for prayer develop before the Second Temple was destroyed and the sacrificial rites ended? (T)

Historically, the synagogue represents the site of the first communal worship divorced from sacrifice. Unlike the Temple, which could only be in Jerusalem and was run by a specifically sanctified clergy born to the task (*kohanim* assisted by *levi'im*), the synagogue could be housed anywhere (not necessarily in a spot with some sacred connotation), did not have to adhere to a rigid architectural pattern, and had prayer leaders and teachers whose roles were not determined by birth, ancestry, or socioeconomic level. [2]

Virtually all scholars agree that the synagogue as an institution originated during the Babylonian Exile following the destruction of the Kingdom of Judah in 586 B.C.E. With the Temple destroyed, the Israelites were suddenly cut off from traditional methods of seeking Divine assistance, gaining forgiveness from sin, thanking God for merciful salvation, and celebrating the holy days. [3] Not only were the exiles deprived of their Temple, but they also were forbidden to build an altar and offer sacrifices outside the Land of Israel. Had this prohibition not been in effect, the exiles would probably have returned to the previous situation of erecting multiple sacrificial shrines throughout the Diaspora. In contrast to pagans, who believed that their gods were exclusively associated with a given land, the exiles were convinced that the Divine Presence, later termed the *Shechinah*, was with them in Babylonia. Although sacrifice to God was forbidden outside of the Land of Israel, the Torah did not prohibit the worship of God *without sacrifice* on foreign soil.[4]

At this stage, there was no precedent for people assembling for joint prayer services. However, during the years of exile, it appears likely that groups of Israelites periodically gathered together for mutual support and consolation and to maintain their connection with fellow Jews and the God of Israel. In time, these informal meetings became routine religious functions of the community, and the prayers became organized into a synagogue liturgy.[5] After the destruction of the Second Temple in 70 C.E. and the end of the sacrificial rites, the synagogue became the center of Jewish communal and spiritual life.

Is there a single traditional style of synagogue architecture? (F)

Synagogue architecture has been extremely diverse, usually reflecting the popular styles of the dominant culture in which Jews lived. Some structures, such as the synagogues in Florence and Budapest, are extremely elaborate and no less impressive than Christian cathedrals or grand mosques, although Christian laws in medieval Europe generally mandated that synagogues have modest exteriors that would not rival the splendor of churches.[6] After the Cossack slaughter of the mid-seventeenth century, Polish Jews built synagogues with thick walls, heavy buttresses, and crenellations for sharpshooters along the roof.[7]

Should a synagogue be constructed on a hill? (N)

Traditionally, the synagogue was built on the most elevated site in the city so that it was the tallest building in town. However, Jews frequently have been unable to comply with this law in both Christian and Muslim countries, which reserved this prerogative for their churches and mosques.[8] Indeed, in many places synagogues were deliberately built low, so as to be as inconspicuous as possible to non-Jews. To increase the height of the interior space, the floor of the synagogue often was dug below street level, fulfilling the verse: "Out of the depths I call you, O Lord . . ." (Ps. 130:1).[9]

Is a synagogue required to have windows? (T)

According to *halachah*, a synagogue must have windows. This derives from the description of Daniel having "had windows made in his upper chamber looking toward Jerusalem" (Dan. 6:10) where he prayed. According to Rashi, windows are required because they allow the worshiper to see the sky, which inspires reverence and devotion during prayer. Some have recommended that there be 12 windows in a synagogue, corresponding to the Twelve Tribes of Israel. Each has a special angel who carries its prayers through a particular "window in heaven" (reflecting the distinct spirit and soul of the tribe) directly to the Throne of God.[10] The modern synagogue at

Hadassah Medical Center in Jerusalem has 12 vibrantly colored windows designed by Marc Chagall, each of which represents one of the tribes.

Did the biblical Ark of the Covenant hold a Torah scroll? (F)

Although the Torah scrolls in a modern synagogue are kept in an ark, the biblical Ark of the Covenant housed both the broken First Tablets and the intact Second Tablets of the Ten Commandments, an *omer* of manna (Exod. 16:32), and the rod of Aaron (Num. 17:25). The Ark of the Covenant was carried by the Israelites on their trek through the wilderness as a visible reminder of the covenant between God and the people, providing assurance that the Divine Presence was always with them on their journey.

Is the *bimah* typically situated in the front of the synagogue? (N)

The *bimah* (lit., "elevated place") is the raised platform that contains the table on which the Torah scroll is placed when it is read. It is traditionally located in the center of the synagogue, emphasizing the central role of the Torah in the worship service. In some Ashkenazic synagogues, there is a separate reading stand immediately in front of the *bimah* and facing the ark, from which the *hazzan* leads the service.

In the nineteenth century, the Reform movement introduced the radical innovation of locating the *bimah* in front of the ark, a layout modeled on the church pulpit. Although Joseph Caro had ruled three centuries earlier that it was not essential to place the *bimah* in the center of the synagogue, the Reform decision was met with intense hostility. Some major traditional rabbis even issued proclamations prohibiting their followers from worshiping in a synagogue that did not have a central *bimah*. Nevertheless, locating the *bimah* in front of the ark is now the dominant architectural style in North America among liberal and even many Orthodox congregations.

Has moving the *bimah* to the front of the synagogue affected Jewish prayers? (T)

This arrangement makes it more conducive for congregants to become spectators rather than full participants in the service. Placing the *bimah* in front of the sanctuary disregards the traditional custom of respectfully facing the ark and praying eastward toward Jerusalem. To solve this dilemma, some contemporary synagogues have either eliminated the *bimah* or returned to earlier architectural models by focusing prayer toward the center of the worship space.

Has the role of the *hazzan* changed substantially since Talmudic days? (T)

Initially, the term *hazzan* referred to a communal official who performed certain duties in the synagogue, serving as a professional superintendent of the house of prayer responsible for bringing out the Torah scrolls for readings (Sot. 7:7–8) and blowing three blasts of a trumpet to announce the time to stop work at the approach of the Sabbath and festivals (Shab. 35b). He also recited the blessings at marriages (Ket. 5b), presided at funerals, blessed and consoled those in mourning, and recited *Kaddish* for their dead (Sof. 19:12). At times he led services and read from the Torah, like any other knowledgeable members of the congregation, but these functions were incidental to his other duties and there was no permanent cantor in the modern sense.

As the liturgy became more complex and general knowledge of Hebrew decreased during the geonic period, the role of *hazzan* transformed into that of a permanent *shaliach tzibbur* (emissary of the congregation), who was responsible for leading the congregation in prayer rather than praying on their behalf.

Was the first half of the twentieth century known as the "Golden Age of Hazzanut"? (T)

With the massive immigration of Eastern European Jews to the United States after the turn of the twentieth century, traditional *hazzanut* became firmly transplanted in America. Large congregations competed to secure one of the celebrated names among *hazzanim*, who filled synagogues to overflowing and made guest appearances at other synagogues and concert halls. Some even became equated with great opera stars. With the development of sound recordings, some cantors achieved international reputations of legendary proportions. However, among more liberal congregations in America, the last half century has seen the virtual demise of classical *hazzanut*, with a strong trend toward active congregational singing.

Can a woman be a cantor? (N)

Kol isha (lit., "voice of a woman") is a Hebrew term used in the context of the prohibition against men hearing a woman singing, which was deemed too provocative for male worshipers. This traditionally precluded the possibility of a woman leading the congregation in prayer. Today, however, the Conservative, Reform, and Reconstructionist movements in America have accepted women as cantors.

Is the *mechitzah* separating men and women during prayer a Jewish tradition? (N)

Literally a "partition," *mechitzah* is the Hebrew term used for the physical separation in an Orthodox synagogue between the space reserved for men and that for women. Contrary to popular belief, separation of the sexes in the synagogue is not an ancient tradition. The Jerusalem Temple had a special Women's Court (*Ezrat Nashim*), but this generally was open to both men and women. The sole exception was the water drawing ceremony on Sukkot, when the sexes were separated to prevent the ecstasy of the occasion from leading to promiscuity. By the thirteenth century, separate sections for women in the synagogue were widespread, and this practice soon became the universally accepted rule.[11] In the early nineteenth century, the Reform movement abolished the *mechitzah*, arguing that the Bible does not command the separation of men and women during public worship or assemblies. In Conservative, Reform, and Reconstructionist synagogues today, there is no *mechitzah* and men and women sit together.

Does the *ner tamid* represent the Menorah in the Temple? (N)

The *ner tamid* (perpetual or eternal lamp) in the synagogue is a continuously burning light, which usually hangs in front of the ark. In the Temple, the "eternal light" is thought to have been the central or westernmost arm of the Menorah in the Temple, which was constantly supplied with oil so that it burned at all times (Exod. 27:20; Lev. 24:2) and was used to kindle the other six branches that were extinguished daily to be cleaned.[12] According to the Rabbis, the *ner tamid* symbolizes God's Presence, which dwells among the congregation of Israel (Shab. 22b). It may also refer to the Torah, which rests in the ark below the *ner tamid*, and is associated with light: "The commandment is a lamp and the Torah is a light" (Prov. 6:23).

After the Temple was destroyed, an oil lamp was put by the western wall of the synagogue as a symbolic reminder of the Menorah. Eventually, however, the *ner tamid* was moved above the ark, despite the objection of some authorities that this was a Gentile custom (in churches, there is a perpetual light above the altar). In modern times, an electric light is used in place of an oil lamp, and the *ner tamid* is usually made of glass and placed in a circular metal container.

Have rabbis always been paid for being the spiritual leaders of their congregations? (F)

Until the late fourteenth century, the rabbinate was not a profession, partly because it was deemed inappropriate for someone to receive money for teaching Torah. Eventually, however, it became necessary for a community to support its rabbi. The development of a professional rabbinate was bolstered by Christian persecutions in Spain, which forced distinguished rabbis, many of whom had earned their livings as physicians, to flee to countries where they had no opportunity to pursue their professions. To avoid the problem of paying a rabbi for teaching Torah, a legal fiction was instituted (still in force today) whereby a rabbi was paid for the time he was forced to take away from Torah study in order to fulfill his rabbinic duties.

Has the role of the rabbi changed dramatically over time? (T)

Until late medieval times, the major role of the rabbi was to exercise scholarly wisdom in judging matters related to Jewish law. In large communities, rabbis headed *yeshivot* and served as *dayanim* (judges) in rabbinical courts. As civil courts came under government control in the modern age, rabbis have assumed more pastoral, social, and educational responsibilities.

Today, congregational rabbis preach, teach, and act as the spiritual leaders of their congregations, often leading the worship services. Rabbis also counsel, officiate at life cycle events, visit the sick, represent their congregations at Jewish and non-Jewish community events, and engage in fund-raising.

Are there different levels of *semichah*? (N)

Semichah (literally meaning "laying of hands") is the traditional ceremony of ordination required before a rabbi can decide practical questions of Jewish law. Although today each denomination of Judaism confers a uniform *semichah*, during the Talmudic era there were a number of levels of ordination. These allowed the recipients to perform different functions, ranging from the lowest level of only deciding religious questions to the highest degree that permitted one to judge criminal cases (Sanh. 5a). The complete formula of ordination was *Yoreh Yoreh, Yaddin Yaddin, Yattir Yattir* (May he decide? He may decide. May he judge? He may judge. May he permit? He may permit).

Is *semichah* conferred through laying of hands on the recipient? (N)

The practice of laying of hands derives from the Divine command to Moses to ordain Joshua by placing his hands on his successor, thus "investing him with some of his authority" (Num. 27:18–20; Deut. 34:9). However, the laying of hands was abandoned after the time of Hadrian (second century C.E.), with ordination bestowed merely by referring to the ordained as "Rabbi." Interestingly, the laying of hands was retained by the Christians as a way of symbolically passing on authority. In order to ensure that the Land of Israel remained the center of Jewish life, the Rabbis only permitted ordination there, based on the verse: "For out of Zion shall go forth the Law, and the word of the Lord from Jerusalem" (Isa. 2:3). Thus the Babylonian *amoraim* were referred to as "Rav." With the death of the last patriarch in the Land of Israel in the fourth century, the original *semichah* was discontinued.

In medieval times, ordination of rabbis became an academic degree (similar to those given at Christian universities), which was awarded to a student who had mastered sufficient learning and possessed the qualifications of character and piety to such an extent that he had the right to serve as a judge and teacher. It did not involve the traditional "laying of hands." Today, the requirements of rabbinical seminaries and *yeshivot* differ widely. Although rabbinic ordination is still known as *semichah*, it merely certifies that the graduate is competent to serve as a rabbi in that Jewish denomination.

Was there ever an attempt to reinstitute the ancient practice of *semichah*? (T)

In the sixteenth century, Jacob Berab of Safed tried to reinstitute the ancient *semichah* (laying of hands) by relying on Maimonides's opinion that this could be accomplished if all the rabbis of the Land of Israel agreed.

Berab ordained four rabbis, including Joseph Caro, the author of the *Shul-chan Aruch*. However, the rabbis of Jerusalem vehemently objected that they had not been consulted, and the movement to reinstate traditional *semichah* ended when Berab died.

Is the weekly Sabbath morning sermon a time-honored Jewish tradition? (N)

The Pharisees and their rabbinic descendants were masters of the art of preaching. However, during the persecutions of the sixth and seventh centuries designed to suppress Jewish practice, the church prohibited homilies on the Scripture during synagogue services. Even when these restrictions were eased, the time constraints related to congregants earning a livelihood tended to seriously restrict the preaching of the medieval Ashkenazic rabbi. Consequently, rabbis generally delivered only two annual addresses to the congregation—on the Sabbath before Passover (*Shabbat ha-Gadol*), which dealt with the technical legalities of the Passover observance; and on the Sabbath before Yom Kippur (*Shabbat Shuvah*), which focused on issues of repentance and greater piety.

Only in nineteenth-century Germany did the sermon become a regular feature of the synagogue service. The early Reform preachers consciously modeled their sermons on those of the Protestant clergy, focusing on a single central theme that they developed in an orderly fashion, without the academic digressions characteristic of earlier periods. Today, especially in the United States, the sermon is generally an integral part of Jewish worship, in which the rabbi conveys to the congregation moral, ethical, and religious values that are often thematically linked to the Torah portion.

Is the *siddur* a uniform prayer book that was developed by a committee of rabbinic scholars and cannot be changed? (F)

The *siddur*, also known as *seder tefillot* (order of prayers), is the collection of prayers designated for public and private worship for weekdays, Sabbaths, festivals, and fast days. The development and maturation of the *siddur* was far from an orderly process. Rather than appearing as a completed text that was logically organized by a committee of scholars, the *siddur* is the culmination of centuries of liturgical additions, each reflecting the theology, culture, and history of its period. Unlike the Bible and Talmud, which once completed were permanently closed and only could be enhanced through commentaries and glosses, the *siddur* has always remained open to new prayers in response to the ever-changing needs of the Jewish people.

Does the earliest *siddur* date from the rabbinic period? (F)

The earliest *siddurim* were compiled in the geonic period, starting about 850 C.E. As the number of prayers increased steadily during the Middle Ages, in the early sixteenth century the *siddur* was first published in two volumes—one containing the daily and Sabbath services, which retained the original name, and a second consisting of prayers for the festivals, which Ashkenazim called the *machzor*.

Is there a uniform version of the *siddur*? (F)

There is no uniformly accepted version of the *siddur*. Ashkenazim and Sephardim have different *siddurim*, which are also regionally specific, and each Jewish denomination within these groups has its own variant. With the development of desktop publishing, individual congregations now can produce custom-made *siddurim*.

Are the crown or silver finials placed on top of the Torah scroll for decoration? (N)

The beginning and end of the parchment scroll are attached to two carved wooden rollers called *atzei chayim* (trees of life), which allow the Torah to be opened, closed, and rolled to any part of the scroll without any need for the hands to touch the parchment. Atop the *atzei chayim* is either a crown (*keter*) or a pair of silver finials called *rimonim* (lit., "pomegranates"). These are often adorned with bells, which tinkle during the procession and are reminiscent of the High Priest's robe, which was hemmed with golden bells and blue, purple, and scarlet balls shaped like pomegranates. The bells of the Torah ornaments serve the practical purpose of informing those seated in the back of the congregation that a Torah is in procession. Therefore, they can fulfill the requirement of rising with reverential respect whenever the Torah is removed from the ark.

Are Torah scrolls covered with cloth mantles? (N)

In the Ashkenazic tradition, the Torah scroll is covered by a cloth mantle. This sheath of silk or velvet is usually embroidered with gold or silver threads and may be richly decorated with images of lions, crowns, pomegranates, the columns of Jachin and Boaz, and various implements of the Temple service.

In the East and the Sephardic traditions, however, the Torah is enclosed in a cylindrical or octagonal case (*tik*), which is made of wood or metal, divided into two pieces, and hinged in the back. The *tik* originated in tenth-century Iraq and is usually elaborately decorated and inscribed. It opens like a book to reveal the scroll, which is not removed and is read in an upright position.

Is there special significance of the wrapping to bind the Torah scroll? (T)

Prior to being read, the scroll is unwrapped and laid down on a reading stand. After the Torah reading, the scroll is rolled together and kept tight. Since antiquity, this has been accomplished by scarves in the East and by a long, wide ribbon (wimpel) in Europe. In some congregations. it is still customary to cut the linen cloth on which a boy was circumcised and sew it into an elaborately embroidered or painted wimpel, which is presented to the congregation on the child's first visit to the synagogue and later used to secure the Torah from which the boy reads when he becomes bar mitzvah and before he marries. This practice symbolizes his "binding" himself to the Torah and to the Jewish community.[13]

Can anyone write a Torah scroll? (N)

Torah scrolls (*sifrei Torah*) must be meticulously written with care by a specially trained scribe known as a *sofer*. This is a shortened form of the title *sofer stam*, with the last word an acronym for "*sefer Torah, tefillin*, and *mezuzot*"—the three items containing texts that the *sofer stam* writes. Literally meaning "one who counts," the name *sofer* probably reflects the fact that some of the early scribes used to count all the letters, words, and verses of the Torah to make certain that none were inadvertently added or omitted. Working full-time, it takes a skilled *sofer* about nine months to complete the 5,888 verses and 79,976 words in the Torah.[14]

Is a woman permitted to write a Torah scroll? (N)

Traditionally, the accepted rule is that a woman may not write a Torah scroll; if she does, the scroll is invalid for public use. This is based on a Talmudic dictum, "Whoever cannot serve as the representative of the public in religious matters is not permitted to write a scroll of the Torah" (Sof. 1:13), and women in post-Talmudic times were not permitted to read the Torah before a congregation. However, women recently have become trained as scribes and written Torah scrolls for congregational use.

Is there a single type of script used in writing a Torah? (F)

The Torah is written in a square script, and the precise shape, form, and method for writing each letter is prescribed. There are two basic styles of script—the Ashkenazic, which resembles that described in the Talmud, and the Sephardic, which is identical to the printed letters of the Hebrew alphabet currently used in sacred texts. Regardless of the script used, care must be taken to ensure that each letter is clear and distinct.

Is the Torah written from right to left? (N)

Although Hebrew is written and read from right to left, each individual letter of a word in the *sefer Torah* is written from left to right.

Can someone other than a trained *sofer* write a part of a Torah scroll? (N)

Interpreting the biblical verse, "Now, therefore, write this song for you . . ." (Deut. 31:19), which was originally a Divine command to Moses and Joshua to write down the final farewell hymn of joy that Moses spoke to the children of Israel just before his death (Deut. 32:1–43), the Rabbis deduced that every Jew is commanded to write a Torah scroll. Based on the

Talmudic statement, "Even if he corrected but one letter [in a *sefer Torah*] he is regarded as if he had written it [the entire Torah]" (Men. 30a), in recent centuries the custom has developed for the scribe who completes the writing of a Torah scroll to merely trace the outline of the letters of the first verses in Genesis and the last verses in Deuteronomy. At a festive celebration, various members of the congregation, often selected by auction, purchase a letter, thus symbolically participating in the writing of a Torah scroll.

Can errors made when writing a Torah scroll simply be erased? (N)

When writing a new Torah, the scribe is forbidden to rely on his memory and must have before him a correct scroll or printed Pentateuch to serve as his guide, for any incorrect word or obliterated letter makes a scroll unfit for use (*pasul*). Despite all precautions, however, mistakes are inevitable due to the difficulty of the scribe's task. Most simple errors may be corrected by scratching out the incorrect writing with a sharp blade and pumice stone. The most serious error—the omission or misspelling of the Name of God—cannot be corrected since the Divine Name cannot be erased. Therefore, the entire sheet of parchment must be discarded. When a mistake is found in a Torah, a cloth ribbon is tied around the mantle as a sign that it is *pasul* and cannot be used until the appropriate correction is made. A scroll that cannot be repaired must be placed in an earthenware container and buried in the cemetery.

Is there any significance to the flourishes over some letters in a Torah scroll? (N)

Seven letters (*shin, ayin, tet, nun, zayin, gimel, tzadi*) are embellished with decorative crowns (*ketarim*) or flourishes (*tagin*, Aramaic for "daggers") whenever they occur. According to the Talmud, God affixed the *tagin* to the letters of the Torah before Moses ascended Mount Sinai to receive it (Men. 29b). However, some modern scholars believe that these calligraphic flourishes were introduced by early scribes to enhance the beauty of the Torah lettering. Although Maimonides[15] considered the inclusion of *tagin* an "exceptionally beautiful fulfillment of the *mitzvah*," he also maintained that a scroll without them was still valid if all the letters and words were written clearly. Ashkenazic authorities disagreed and deemed such a scroll *pasul*. Kabbalah stresses the mystical meaning of the *tagin*, considering every additional stroke or sign as a symbol revealing extraordinary secrets of the universe and Creation.

When writing a Torah scroll, does the *sofer* have artistic freedom to design its format? (F)

Detailed regulations were established regarding the layout of the Torah so that the words are beautiful to view. The text is set out in columns of 42 lines, representing the numerical value of the Hebrew word *bam* in the phrase *ve-*

dibarta bam (And you shall speak *of them*) in the first paragraph of the *Shema*. This precise number of lines per column also allows for the scroll to have a script size that can be read easily yet without being too large or too heavy to carry. Traditionally, each sheet of parchment contains three columns of script. There must be two inches between each column of script—plus an extra inch where sheets are to be sewn together—and margins of three inches on the top and four inches on the bottom (which is subject to more wear). A space of four inches is required between each of the Five Books of Moses. [16]

Do all parts of the Torah scroll look alike? (F)

The Masoretes, who designed the layout of the Torah, thought certain portions of the text to be so significant that they must have a unique appearance in the scroll. *Shirat ha-Yam* (Song at the Sea; Exod. 15:1–19) is written in three sections with intervening white space that symbolizes the two walls of water between which the Israelites passed to safety on a dry path. Other sections of the Bible that are written to have special visual effects include both versions of the Ten Commandments (Exod. 20:1–14; Deut. 5:6–18) and the Song of Moses (*Ha-azinu*; Deut. 32:1–43).

Is prayer primarily asking something of God? (N)

Many people associate prayer with requesting something from God. Indeed, the English word derives from the Latin root *precare* meaning "to beg or entreat." However, in the Jewish concept, prayer can take the form of praise, petition, thanksgiving, and confession. All of this is encompassed in the most common Hebrew word for prayer, *tefillah*, and the corresponding verb, *hit'pallel*, which come from a root meaning "to judge." When praying we often present our needs and desires to God with the hope that these requests will be deemed worthy of receiving favorable Divine judgment. [17]

In prayer we recognize how much we depend upon God and realize that every blessing, even life itself, is not earned but rather a generous Divine gift. Prayers express our deepest feelings, a response that Abraham Joshua Heschel termed "radical amazement." As Heschel wrote, "to pray is to take notice of the wonder, to regain a sense of the mystery that animates all beings, the Divine margin in all attainments." [18] As he also observed, "Prayer may not save us, but it makes us worthy of being saved."

Do people pray for themselves? (F)

Jewish prayers, even those that are petitionary, are always recited in the plural. In this way, worshipers do not pray exclusively for themselves, but also for the entire community, as indicated in the Talmudic dictum: "A man should always associate himself with the congregation" (Ber. 29b–30a). Congregational prayers in the plural always have been considered the ideal in Judaism, for the well-being of the individual is inextricably linked with that of the entire community of Israel. According to the Talmud, even one who is far removed from a congregation, praying on a lonely road for his personal safety, must pray for the group and not for himself alone (Ber. 29b). [19]

Were there any prayers in ancient Israel? (T)

Biblical prayers are simple and spontaneous human reactions to personal events or experiences. They range in length from the brief five-word plea of Moses to heal his sister, Miriam (Num. 12:13), to the extended prayer of Solomon at the inauguration of the Temple (1 Kings 8:15–21; 23–53). Biblical figures prayed for a variety of reasons. Abraham prayed for Sodom to be spared if 10 righteous men could be found in this depraved city (Gen. 18:23–33). Jacob prayed for protection on his flight from Esau's wrath (Gen. 28:20). The barren Hannah, who became a model of Jewish prayer, beseeched God for a son (1 Sam. 1:11). The tortured Samson prayed for the strength to tear down the pillars to which the Philistines tied him (Judg. 16:28). The prophets begged for Divine forgiveness of the sins of the people (Jer. 14; Amos 7:2), and Daniel asked for the restoration of Israel (Dan. 9:3–19). Praise, a common element of prayer, is exemplified by the prayer of the *levi'im* (Neh. 9).

Were there formal communal prayers during biblical times? (N)

The only formal prayers during the biblical era were the confessions to be recited when bringing the firstfruits and the tithe (Deut. 26:5–15), and that of the *Kohen Gadol* on Yom Kippur, which had no prescribed formula (Lev. 16:21). In the Temple, the *kohanim* recited a short liturgy consisting of a blessing, the *Shema* and the Ten Commandments, three additional benedictions, and the Priestly Blessing. However, there was no communal prayer, and those laymen present for the sacrifices participated in the ritual merely by prostrating themselves and, at appropriate pauses, chanting such responses as, "Praise the Lord, for He is good" (Ps. 136:1).

Is there a biblical basis for Jews praying three times each day? (N)

The Talmud cites two major reasons for the rabbinic decree that Jews pray three times a day (Ber. 26b). According to one opinion, the three services correspond to the daily sacrifices in Temple times—the morning and afternoon prayers to the *Shacharit* and *Minchah* offerings; and the evening (*Ma'ariv*) prayers to the nighttime burning on the Altar of all the fat and organs of the daily offerings. The other attributes the establishment of the three daily services to the patriarchs, based on three biblical references— Abraham "rose up early in the morning and hurried to the place where he had stood [in the presence of the Lord]" (Gen. 19:27), and "standing" always means "praying"; Isaac went out "to meditate in the field toward evening" (Gen. 24:63); and Jacob prayed before he went to sleep on his stone pillow and dreamed of angels ascending and descending a ladder connecting the earth to Heaven (Gen. 28:11).

Can anything be added to the standard prayer text in the *siddur*? (N)

The prophets strongly condemned mechanical worship, as did their successors, the Rabbis of the Talmud. They realized that rote recitation of established formulas of prayer could reduce them to mere outward performance of a religious duty (Ber. 4:4). Consequently, canonization of the early synagogue prayers met with intense opposition because of the danger that strict regulation of prayer would severely limit spontaneity. Nevertheless, most Rabbis recognized that fixed forms of prayer and regularity of worship were essential to a person's religious life. While waiting for the rare flash of inspiration conducive to prayers of self-expression, a person could forget the art of prayer, be incapable of praying even when that rare spiritual instant arrived, and end up never praying at all![20]

Nevertheless, the Rabbis did permit private prayers within the structure of the prescribed services. At the end of the silent *Amidah*, the worshiper was urged to add a personal prayer. Although the Talmud records several prayers that the sages composed for their private use (Ber. 16b–17a), with that of Mar ben Ravina being incorporated into the service, most ordinary worshipers were satisfied to recite the standard prayers with deep feeling.[21]

Is Hebrew the language for Jewish prayer? (N)

Hebrew has always been the preferred language of Jewish prayer (JT Sot. 7:2). Some Rabbis of the Talmudic era even opposed the use of Aramaic in prayer. Despite the fact that Aramaic was considered a semi-holy tongue because several of the books of the Bible (Daniel, Ezra, Nehemiah) are largely written in this language, the Rabbis asserted that the Ministering Angels do not understand that language and thus cannot transmit these prayers to God (Sot. 33a). However, this extreme view did not prevail, and prayer in other languages was permitted. A number of Aramaic prayers were admitted into the liturgy, such as the *Kaddish* and *Kol Nidrei*. The Mishnah ruled that the *Shema* and the *Amidah*, which form the core of Jewish worship, "may be recited in any language" (Sot. 7:1).

Until modern times, using the vernacular in prayer posed little problem, because virtually all Jews could understand the prayers in Hebrew. Unfortunately, in most communities this is no longer the case. Some argue that if *kavanah* (conscious purpose) is essential, the prayers should be in the vernacular lest the words be merely "mysterious incantations." Defenders of the tradition maintain that translating prayers into the vernacular strips them of their historic significance and diminishes their powerful appeal to the collective heart of the people.

According to Maimonides, the Rabbis mandated prayer in Hebrew because they foresaw the danger of Jews being dispersed throughout the world and speaking different languages. Formulating the prayers in pure Hebrew would allow all Jews to worship together. Even today, the Jew who can pray in Hebrew is able to attend a synagogue anywhere in the world and feel at home in the worship service. [22]

Are some prayers inappropriate and invalid? (T)

The Mishnah labels a supplication to God to change the past as a "vain prayer" (Ber. 3b). Examples include a husband praying that his pregnant wife will bear a male child, and a person returning from a journey who "hears cries of distress in the town and says, [God] grant that this is not in my house." Moreover, it is impossible for God to positively answer the conflicting prayers of various individuals. This is clearly indicated in the prayer of the *Kohen Gadol* on Yom Kippur, who before the rainy season that was so vital for the harvest in Israel, used to pray that God reject the supplications of travelers seeking fair weather (Yoma 53b).

Do Jews pray to the east? (N)

From Temple times to the present, Jews have always faced Jerusalem when they pray. According to the Talmud, a person praying in the Diaspora must turn toward the Land of Israel; in the Land of Israel, toward Jerusalem; in Jerusalem, toward the Temple; and in the Temple, toward the Holy of Holies. "In this way, all Israel will be turning their hearts [in prayer] towards one place" (Ber. 30a).

Consequently, although Jews in North America do pray toward the east, those situated to the east (Russia), north (southern Europe), and south (South Africa) of Jerusalem and the Land of Israel pray in the direction appropriate to their locale.

Has music always been an important aspect of Jewish prayer? (N)

Music has always added to the beauty of prayer and enhanced its emotional and spiritual depth. In the Temple, a choir of *levi'im* sang the appropriate psalms accompanied by musical instruments. After the Temple was destroyed, however, the use of musical instruments on the Sabbath and festivals was banned as a sign of mourning. The sages believed that no Jewish prayer service should approximate the glory of worship in the ancient Sanctuary. Musical instruments were also prohibited because they might lead to work (forbidden on the Sabbath and festivals), such as the repair of a broken string on a violin. [23]

Is the playing of instrumental music now accepted as part of the Sabbath and festival services? (N)

In its early stages, the Reform movement introduced the organ into the worship service. More traditional Jews rejected this practice, arguing that the organ was so closely associated with worship in Christian churches that it was a prohibited "imitation of gentile custom" (*chukat ha-goy*) to play it in the synagogue. Today, Reform and some Conservative synagogues do permit the playing of instrumental music on the Sabbath and festivals, rationalizing that the prohibition of music as a sign of mourning for the destruction of Jerusalem included vocal no less than instrumental music. Moreover, they argue that since the use of instrumental music in the church is itself a borrowing from the Temple, there is no reason to prohibit something as a "Christian" custom that was originally adapted from Jewish practice.

Was ritual swaying during prayer a Hasidic innovation? (N)

Ritual swaying (*shuckling*, from the Yiddish word meaning "to shake"), typically forward-and-back but also side-to-side, is a characteristic of worshipers in traditional synagogues. Although many erroneously believe that these bodily movements originated with the Hasidim in the seventeenth century, they merely accentuated a practice dating back to geonic and even Talmudic times to produce deeper concentration and more intense devotion in prayer. Indeed, the Talmud relates that when R. Akiva prayed privately, his repeated "genuflexions and prostrations" were so vigorous that he would begin in one part of the room and finish in another (Ber. 31a).[24]

However, ritual swaying is not a requirement during prayer. The critical element is intense concentration, which some find easier to achieve when standing still rather than when in motion.

Is praying alone at home just as good as praying in a synagogue? (N)

Communal worship has always been a distinctive feature of Jewish prayer. Although an individual Jew can fulfill the *mitzvah* of prayer privately, joining others as part of a congregation is a particular virtue. Indeed, a person who cannot be present at a service should try to pray privately *at the same time* as the congregation.[25] Consequently, many of the major parts of the worship service (*Barchu*, repetition of the *Amidah* with *Kedushah*, Torah reading, Priestly Benediction, and *Kaddish*) require the presence of a *minyan*.

Is a rabbi or cantor required for a prayer service in the synagogue? (F)

The person leading the communal worship is known as the *shaliach tzibbur* (emissary of the congregation). The prayer leader does not have to be a professional cantor (*hazzan*) or an ordained rabbi; any adult male (or female, in liberal congregations) may assume this role. The Talmud stresses that the *shaliach tzibbur* is not an intermediary between the congregation and God, but simply an agent who recites the prayers on behalf of the worshipers.[26]

Are prayers recited only to praise and thank God and plead for Divine help? (N)

While all these are the motivations behind most Jewish prayers, some have a polemical purpose and were initially designed to attack dissidents and sectarian minorities within the community. For example, the second blessing of the *Amidah* repeats six times the doctrine of resurrection, which was denied by the Samaritans and Sadducees. The verse "Who forms light and creates darkness, makes peace and creates all things" (Isa. 45:7) attacks the dualist Persian (Zoroastrian) religion, which believed that the world was created and preserved by two opposing forces, light and darkness, that manifest their existence in good and evil. Several polemics were introduced against the Karaites, who followed the literal meaning of the Bible and denied rabbinic interpretation of the text. The Rabbis introduced a special blessing over the Sabbath lights, and the *geonim* inserted into the Friday evening service a recitation of *Ba-meh madlikin* (With what may we light), a *mishnah* that discusses which types of wick and oil should be used to provide the home with light on the Sabbath (Shab. 2:1). These practices, in direct opposition to the Karaite ritual of extinguishing all lights before the Sabbath and spending the day without heat or light, were designed to indicate unequivocally that having lights burning in one's dwelling was not merely permitted but a positive commandment.[27]

Are the authors of prayers anonymous? (N)

Although generally true, several major prayers contain hints as to the name of their authors. *Nishmat kol chai* (The soul of every living being [shall bless Your Name]) is the poetic glorification of God that is recited during Sabbath and festival morning services at the end of *Pesukei de-Zimra*. The initial letters of the second words of the four verses starting with *Be-fi yesharim* (by the mouth of the upright) spell out the Hebrew word *Yitzhak*, suggesting that Isaac was the name of the composer of the prayer. In addition, the third letters of each of the verbs in these verses (if rearranged, as in the Ashkenazic High Holy Day liturgy) form the word *Rivkah* (Rebecca). This has led some to speculate that the author was none other than the patriarch Isaac, the husband of Rebecca. In the Sephardic ritual, the verbs are rearranged and the words Isaac and Rebecca are printed in bold type so that everyone can see the name of the presumed author. Other scholars have discovered acrostics of the name *Shimon* (Simon) in previous verses, giving rise to speculation that *Nishmat* might have been written by R. Shimon ben Shetach (around 100 B.C.E.), or even by the apostle Peter, whose Hebrew name was *Shimon*.[28]

In the next prayer, *Yishtabach* (Praised), the first letters of the second, third, fourth, and fifth words spell the name *Shlomo* (Solomon), giving rise to speculation that this was the name of the unknown author or that the prayer was written in honor of King Solomon.

A final example is *Lechah Dodi* (Come, my beloved), the poem that is the climax of the *Kabbalat Shabbat* service. The initial letters of the first eight stanzas spell out Shlomo ha-Levi, the name of Solomon ha-Levi Alkabetz, the best-known liturgical poet of the Safed circle of kabbalists in the early sixteenth century.

Is a *minyan* necessary for Jewish prayer? (N)

A *minyan* (lit., "number") is the term for a quorum, traditionally composed of 10 adult males (13 years of age or over), which is necessary for *congregational* worship and certain other religious ceremonies. It is required for the following sections of the public synagogue service—*Barchu*, repetition of the *Amidah* with *Kedushah*, Torah and *haftarah* readings, Priestly Blessing, and *Kaddish*. However, all other daily prayers, including the *Shema* and the silent *Amidah*, can be recited with less than a *minyan*, or even alone.

Is a *minyan* needed at other times? (T)

A *minyan* is also necessary for the rites of comforting the mourners, the recital of the *Sheva Berachot* at wedding ceremonies, and the special invitation (*zimun*) including the word *Eloheinu* preceding the *Birkat ha-Mazon* (Grace after Meals).

Are only men counted in the *minyan*? (N)

Traditional Orthodox congregations do not count women as part of the *minyan*, because they are not required to attend public prayer services—an exemption related to their essential time-dependent responsibilities toward home and family. In liberal synagogues today, in which women have full religious equality with men, the requirement is for 10 *people* to constitute the *minyan* needed for a public prayer service.

Does the requirement for 10 members of a *minyan* come from the Ten Commandments? (F)

The Talmud derives the number 10 as constituting a congregation from the word *edah* (community), which in the Torah is applied to the 10 spies (termed a "wicked community") who gave a negative report on the land of Canaan (Num. 14:27) and thus condemned the people to 40 years of wandering in the wilderness (Meg. 23b). Others have related the requirement for a quorum of 10 to Abraham's plea to God to save Sodom if at least 10 righteous men were found there (Gen. 18:32); to the 10 elders mentioned in the Book of Ruth (4:2); or to the verse, "Bless God in congregations" (Ps. 68:27), in which the Hebrew word *b'machalot* (congregations) has the same numerical value as *b'asarah* (with 10). On the basis of the first verse in Psalm 82—"God stands in the congregation of Divine beings"—the Talmud concluded that if 10 men pray together, the Divine Presence is with them (Ber. 6a).

Before each service, is one person responsible for counting to 10 to make certain that there is a *minyan*? (N)

There is a long tradition of not using actual numbers when counting to see if there are enough people to make a *minyan*. Therefore, several different counting customs developed to determine whether a *minyan* is present. Some use verses from Psalms that consist of 10 Hebrew words—*Hoshia et amecha u-varech et nachalatechah, u-r'eim v'nas'eim ad olam* (Save Your people and bless Your inheritance, tend them and elevate them forever; Ps. 28:9); *Einay chol eilecha y'sabeiru, v'ata notein la-hem et achlam b'ito* (The eyes of all look to hopefully to You, and You give them their food in its proper time; Ps. 145:15); and *Va'ani b'rov chasdechah avo veitechah, eshtachaveh el heichal kodshechah b'yiratechah* (As for me, through Your abundant kindness I will enter Your house, and bow low toward Your holy Temple in awe of You; Ps. 5:8). A different approach is to say "not one, not two . . ." and thus pretending that one is not actually counting.

To constitute a *minyan*, do all 10 people have to be praying? (F)

As long as a majority of six people are actively praying, the other four may merely be present and respond "amen" to the blessings. This situation may arise when the four have already completed their prayers but remain in the synagogue so that the others may recite those parts of the service, including the *Mourner's Kaddish*, which require a *minyan*.

During the repetition of the *Amidah*, must there always be a *minyan*? (N)

The repetition of the *Amidah* during the daily morning (*Shacharit*) and afternoon (*Minchah*) services and the additional (*Musaf*) service for Sabbaths and festivals may not begin unless at least 10 people are present. However, once begun, the prayer leader may complete the repetition even if one or more people leave the service, as long as the majority of the *minyan* (i.e., six) remains. However, the congregation may not start the next prayer that requires a *minyan* unless 10 people have reassembled.

Is a traditional Jewish man required to cover his head at all times? (N)

The head covering worn by Jews in modern times, known as a *kippah* (Hebrew), *yarmulke* (Yiddish), or skullcap (English), has become a universally recognized symbol of Jewish identity. However, there is no explicit biblical commandment to cover one's head for prayer or other religious functions. In ancient Rome, free men went bareheaded, and the wearing of a head covering stigmatized a person as a servant. To stress that they were loyal servants of the Lord, Jews in Talmudic times adopted the practice of covering their heads while reciting prayers and during any activity when blessings including the Divine Name were said, such as eating. Eventually, Jews began to cover their heads at all times to demonstrate their awesome respect for God.[29]

Nevertheless, the Talmudic sages ruled that it was optional for men to cover their heads and only a matter of custom to do so for prayer (Ned. 30a). Medieval French and Spanish rabbinic authorities took a similar approach, but the Babylonian rabbis disagreed, viewing covering of the head as an expression of the "fear of Heaven" (*yirat Shamayim*) (Shab. 156b; Kid. 31a). Therefore, the current requirement among traditional Jews that all men cover their head during prayer and Torah study and while eating meals is comparatively recent. Indeed, some have argued that the custom was based on the verse, "You shall not follow their laws" (Lev. 18:3), and essentially represented a reaction to the Christian practice of immediately taking off their hats when entering a church or other building. Therefore, it became the normative Jewish tradition to worship and even walk around with the head covered, so that being bareheaded became equated with showing insolent disrespect for God.[30]

Does the type of head covering indicate something about the wearer? (T)

Head coverings come in various materials, from plain cloth to satin, velvet, fur, crochet, and leather. The style of head covering often provides a clue as to the type of religious observance of the wearer—from the stringent "black hat" of the ultra-Orthodox to the knitted *kippah* of the modern Orthodox. The early Reform movement virtually eliminated the practice of covering the head during services, but now the wearing of a *kippah*, though considered optional, is increasingly encouraged.[31]

May a worn-out *kippah* be thrown into the garbage? (T)

Although traditional Jews cover their heads during prayer, Torah study, and eating, unlike a *tallit* or *tefillin*, the head covering has no intrinsic religious sanctity. Therefore, a worn-out *kippah* may be disposed of in an ordinary fashion, including throwing it into the garbage.

If a man does not have a *kippah* handy, may he simply use his hand to cover his head? (F)

Covering one's head with another part of the body is not considered a covering, which must be something external to one's body. Instead, it would be better to cover the head with a clean handkerchief or napkin or even a flat piece of paper.

Is a married woman required to cover her hair? (N)

Although there are no explicit biblical references to the tradition of women wearing head coverings, by Talmudic times it was accepted practice. A married woman who dared to walk bareheaded in the street could be summarily divorced by her husband without paying her *ketubah*. Explaining why this violation was so serious, the Talmud compared a woman's hair to her "private parts." Despite being deemed as "sexually exciting," head coverings were only required for married women (Ket. 2:1).

Toward the end of the eighteenth century, some women began wearing a wig (*sheitel*), a "radical innovation" that was vehemently opposed by some ultra-traditional rabbis. Because high-quality wigs look as good, or even better, than real hair, some argue that wearing one is not consistent with the underlying goal of a modest appearance, recommending instead a scarf or hat. Although only strictly Orthodox women now cover their hair at all times, many married women still cover their head in synagogue. In egalitarian congregations, some Jewish women—single as well as married—have opted to wear a *kippah* as a manifestation of their religious equality. Moreover, some of these synagogues require that a woman wear a *kippah* (and *tallit*) in order to lead services or to be called up to the Torah for an *aliyah*.

Is a *tallit* worn at night? (N)

Because the explicit purpose of the *tzitzit* (ritual fringes) attached to the *tallit* is "that you may *see* them [and recall all the commandments of the Lord and obey them, so that you do not go astray after your own heart and eyes]" (Num. 15:39), as a general rule the *tallit* is only worn during the day. However, there is one exception—Yom Kippur, when the *Kol Nidrei* service actually starts just before evening and the *tallit* adds sanctity to the occasion.

In Orthodox synagogues, do all Jewish males 13 years or older wear a *tallit*? (N)

Some Orthodox synagogues follow the Eastern European tradition in which a *tallit* is worn only by a married man. This is based on the fact that the phrase, "If a man marries a wife," immediately follows the repetition of the commandment concerning *tzitzit* (Deut. 22:12). However, all men wear a *tallit* when leading the congregation in prayer or called up for an *aliyah* to the Torah.

Does the *tallit* have a standard appearance? (F)

The *tallit* is usually woven of wool, cotton, or silk and is typically white, although various color combinations are increasingly popular in keeping with individual aesthetic tastes. Many *tallitot* have stripes, either black to symbolize mourning for the destroyed Temple or blue to represent the fringe of that color worn in ancient times. Many Jews wear only a small scarf-like *tallit*, while others prefer a large *tallit* that covers most of the body.

Is the *tallit* worn so that it rests on the shoulders? (N)

Most people pray with the *tallit* resting on their shoulders. However, some prefer to have the *tallit* covering their head—especially during the *Shema*, *Amidah*, and *Kedushah*, and when called up to the Torah—to eliminate distractions and increase their concentration at these major portions of the service. Being enfolded by the *tallit* is regarded as being surrounded by the holiness of the commandments of the Torah, symbolically indicating total obedience to the Divine Will. *Kohanim* always cover their heads with their *tallitot* when bestowing the Priestly Blessing upon the congregation.

Is the collar of the *tallit* merely decoration? (N)

The *tallit* has a reinforced band of cloth called an *atarah* (crown), which is usually decoratively embroidered or inscribed with the blessing for putting on the garment. Although today the *atarah* is generally considered primarily a decoration, it may have developed to mark the top of the completely sym-metric *tallit*, since as a religious act it should be put on the same way every time. Another explanation is that the weight of the *atarah* helps to keep the *tallit* on the wearer's shoulder, preventing it from slipping.

Although the most ornamented part of the *tallit*, the collar is not the most important. If the collar is torn off, the *tallit* may still be used. However, if one of the four corners of the garment with the fringes (*tzitzit*) is torn off, it can no longer be used as a *tallit*.

On days when *tefillin* are worn, are they put on after the *tallit*? (T)

The *tallit* is always put on first, consistent with the general principle that when two *mitzvot* are to be performed at the same time, the more frequent one takes precedence. The *tallit* has priority because it is also worn on Sab-baths and festivals, when *tefillin* are not worn. According to the Talmud, another reason for giving priority to the *tallit* is that the commandment of *tzitzit* is equal to all the *mitzvot* of the Torah, since it reminds the wearer of them (Men. 43a).[32]

Although the Bible requires that there be a thread of blue on each cor-ner of the *tallit*, is this still observed? (N)

The last half of the Torah verse commanding the wearing of *tzitzit* man-dates that on each corner there be seven white threads and one of blue (*techeilet*). In ancient times, this blue was made from a precious dye, which was extracted from a sea snail (*chilazon*) by a few families on the Mediterra-nean coast. After the destruction of the Second Temple, the secret of obtain-ing this exact shade was lost, and the use of the blue thread in the fringes was discontinued. Recently, researchers claim to have discovered a close relative of the snail, and *tallitot* with blue fringes are now available.

Is there a standard pattern to the threads of the *tzitzit*? (N)

In each collection of eight threads on the four corners of the *tallit*, one is longer than the rest and is wound around the remaining seven threads in either of two different ways. Among Ashkenazic Jews, there are four series of rings winding 7, 8, 11, and 13 times around. The sum of these numbers equals 39, the numerical value of the Hebrew words *YHVH echad* (God is One). Thus, when looking at the fringes, one is constantly reminded of the fundamental Jewish principle of monotheism. Among Sephardic Jews, the pattern of windings is 10, 5, 6, 5, numbers that represent the letters *YHVH*.

Does a woman wear a *tallit*? (N)

Women have traditionally been exempt from the commandment to wear *tzitzit*. According to the Talmud, women are not required to observe laws that must be performed at a specific time of day ("time-bound *mitzvot*"), since their primary obligation is considered to be to their home and family. Since the *tzitzit* must be worn at a specific time—during daylight hours—the wearing of the *tallit* is not incumbent on women. Another explanation is that garments with four corners on which fringes were hung were originally considered to be male attire, and the Bible forbids a woman from wearing a man's clothing, and vice versa. Nevertheless, some women are known to have worn *tallitot* during Talmudic and later times. For example, R. Judah ha-Nasi, the editor of the Mishnah, is described as having personally attached fringes to his wife's apron. Maimonides[33] maintained that a woman may wear a *tallit*, but should not recite the blessing. Conversely, Rabbenu Tam, a leading French scholar, permitted women to make blessings upon performing commandments from which they are exempt. The *Shulchan Aruch* supports the view of Maimonides, while the great Ashkenazic legal authority Moses Isserles agreed with Rabbenu Tam.

In liberal synagogues, some women choose to wear a *tallit* for worship.

Do Jews only wear a *tallit* for prayer services? (F)

In addition to the *tallit* worn during morning prayer services, some traditional Jews also wear fringes on a *tallit katan* (little *tallit*), a light undergarment that is fitted over the neck and shoulders so that the *tzitzit* hang down and are visible throughout the daylight hours. Use of the *tallit katan*, also called *arba kanfot* (four corners), developed when it became awkward and inconvenient to wear an outer garment with fringes throughout the day, especially when changes in fashion dictated that clothes no longer always had four distinct corners.[34] Furthermore, wearing fringes on an inner garment shielded from view (i.e., not hanging down far enough to be seen) was a safer alternative in those communities in which exposed *tzitzit* identifying the wearer as a Jew might single him out for persecution.[35]

Is there anything written in the *tefillin*? (T)

Tefillin are two small black leather boxes that are bound by black leather straps to the forehead and arm. Also known as phylacteries, they contain parchments on which are written the four sets of biblical verses that mention the commandment to wear them as "a sign upon your hand and as frontlets between your eyes" (Exod. 13:1–10, 11–16; Deut. 6:4–9; 11:13–21).

Are *tefillin* worn for morning services? (N)

Tefillin are worn for each weekday morning service, but not on the Sabbath or on festivals (Men. 36b). The reason is that, like the Sabbath (Exod. 31:17) and circumcision (Gen. 17:11), *tefillin* are a sign of the covenant between God and Israel, the Divinely chosen people. Therefore, wearing *tefillin* would be considered superfluous because these days are also symbols of holiness. Moreover, just as Jewish law requires the testimony of two witnesses to convict someone of any offense, so a man requires two witnesses to attest to his Jewishness. On weekdays, the *tefillin* and circumcision fulfill that role. On the Sabbath, however, the day itself is the second witness, so that it is not necessary to wear *tefillin*.

Are *tefillin* put on the left arm? (N)

Most people wear *tefillin* on their left forearm, which is closest to the heart. However, the rule is that they should be put on a person's weaker forearm, because the commandment is immediately followed in the Torah by the one to "write them on the doorposts of your house (*mezuzah*)." This led the Rabbis to conclude that the hand that writes must be the hand that wraps—the stronger hand. Therefore, left-handed people wear the *tefillin* on their "weaker" right arm (Men. 37a).

Are there a large number of blessings in Judaism? (T)

The Rabbis formulated blessings for practically every aspect of human existence. These range from common experiences of daily life, such as awakening from sleep, dressing, eating, and drinking, to such unusual occurrences as escaping from danger, recovering from illness, and seeing some marvelous natural event such as lightning or a comet.[36]

Do blessings have a uniform formula and structure? (N)

All blessings (*berachot*) open with the words *Baruch ata Adonai* (Praised are You, O Lord). When the blessing occurs at the beginning of a prayer, the words *Eloheinu melech ha-olam* (Our God, King of the Universe) are added. There are four basic formulas of *berachot*. The simplest is the "short" blessing for experiences of enjoyment, which opens *Baruch ata Adonai, Eloheinu melech ha-olam* and concludes with a reference to the experience that called for the blessing. Thus, in the blessing over bread, one adds *ha-motzi lechem min ha-aretz* (Who brings forth bread from the earth); for wine, the blessing concludes *borei pri ha-gafen* (Who creates the fruit of the vine).

Blessings for the privilege of performing religious commandments open with an expanded formula—*Baruch ata Adonai, Eloheinu melech ha-olam, asher kidshanu b'mitzvotav v'tzivanu* (Who has sanctified us with His commandments and commanded us to . . .)—and conclude with the specific *mitzvah* that is about to be performed. Thus, when lighting the candles on Friday night, one adds *le-hadlik ner shel Shabbat* (to kindle the Sabbath lights). When a *mitzvah* is performed for the first time in the year, one adds the *Shehecheyanu* blessing (Who has kept us alive and preserved us and enabled us to reach this season).

Are blessings recited for good things? (N)

In the Talmud, R. Meir declared that it is the duty of every Jew to recite 100 blessings daily (Men. 43b), expressing thanks for the myriad of Divinely bestowed gifts. Nevertheless, according to the Talmud, "it is incumbent on man to bless [God] for the evil in the same way as for the good" (Ber. 54a). The pious Jew acknowledges God as *Dayan emet* (the true Judge) even when receiving unusually bad news, such as the death of a loved one. As R. Akiva noted, a person should always say, "Whatever the All-Merciful does is for good" (Ber. 60b).[37]

Is the blessing formula grammatically incorrect? (T)

The way in which God is addressed and described in blessings was the subject of a rabbinic controversy that resulted in a grammatical inconsistency. In the third century, Rav maintained that a blessing should begin with the words *Baruch ata*, speaking of God in the second person as "You." His contemporary, Samuel, thought this too familiar for the relationship between mere mortals and the Divine. The sages ruled in favor of Rav, but decided to combine both opinions in what became the approved formula. The opening of every blessing stresses the nearness of God to each worshiper by addressing God as "You," and many references are made to God as our "Father," who is merciful and compassionate toward His creations. When we refer to God as *melech ha-olam* (King of the universe), we assume a more formal and respectful tone. The remainder of the every blessing switches into the third person, as in "Who sanctified us by *His* commandments . . ." and "Who creates the fruit of the vine."[38]

Is "amen" an ancient word with no intrinsic meaning? (N)

"Amen" is an ancient response of affirmation that originated in the Torah and has now become a word in almost every language. Saying "amen" affirms agreement that what another has said is the truth. By saying "amen" a worshiper is considered as having actually recited the prayer or blessing (Ber. 53b);[39] when said after a petitionary prayer, "amen" is the equivalent of "so may it be."[40] During Temple and Talmudic times, when most congregants were unfamiliar with the text of the prayers, responding "amen" was the primary way for them to participate in the service. Moreover, the format of public worship at the time generally consisted of a prayer leader who spoke the words and everyone else who merely offered the response.

According to the Talmud (Shab. 119b), "amen" is an acronym for *El melech ne'eman* (God, the faithful King), the same phrase that precedes the reading of the *Shema* when recited in the absence of a *minyan*. As such, saying "amen" acknowledges acceptance of the yoke of the Divine Kingdom.

Are there rules for when and how "amen" should be said? (T)

According to *halachah*, an individual who hears another recite a blessing is required to respond "amen." However, "amen" is not said after a blessing that one has personally recited (Ber. 45b). Numerous rules are given concerning how "amen" should be said. The Talmud states that it must be said with a strong clear voice, but not in a louder tone than the blessing itself (Ber. 45a),[41] and only after the preceding blessing has been completed. It is forbidden to respond "amen" to a blessing that is unnecessary and thus takes the name of the Lord in vain, but it may be said when hearing a blessing recited by a non-Jew. A person should not say "amen" if he or she did not actually hear the blessing or know what it was (Ber. 47a). However, it is permitted to join in the congregational "amen" if one knows the blessing to which they are responding.

Is there more than one *Kaddish*? (T)

Although most associated as the prayer recited by those in mourning or to commemorate the anniversary of the death of a close relative, the *Kaddish* appears in four distinct forms in the synagogue ritual. The simplest is the so-called "half" *Kaddish* (*Hatzi Kaddish*), which is recited by the prayer leader after each subdivision of the service. In the morning, it is recited after the introductory psalms (*Pesukei de-Zimra*), the *Amidah* (or *Tachanun*), and the Torah reading. The "full" *Kaddish* (*Kaddish Shalem*) is recited by the prayer leader after the *Amidah* and concludes each service. It contains a special verse beginning with the word *titkabeil* (Let be accepted [the prayers and supplications of the whole house of Israel by their Father in Heaven; and let us say "amen"]) as well as two prayers for peace. In the *Kaddish de-Rabbanan*, the *titkabeil* verse is replaced by several lines praying for the teachers of Israel, their disciples, and all who study the Torah. The *Mourner's Kaddish* (*Kaddish Yatom*; lit.,"Orphan's *Kaddish*"), which contains the full text except for the *titkabeil* verse, is recited after the *Aleinu* at the end of each service and may be repeated after the reading of additional psalms. It is also said in the morning service at the beginning of *Pesukei de-Zimra*, just before *Baruch she-Amar*.

Has the *Kaddish* always been an important part of the synagogue service? (F)

Although it now closes every public service as well as the individual sections within it, the *Kaddish* was originally not even a part of the synagogue ritual. Instead, it was a formal prayer that was recited by the preacher or teacher at the conclusion of a discourse on the Torah. Addressed to the assembly in the Aramaic vernacular, the *Kaddish* proclaimed God's greatness and holiness and expressed the hope for the speedy establishment of the Divine kingdom on earth.

Is the original *Kaddish de-Rabbanan* still recited in synagogue? (T)

The ancient custom of a teacher dismissing the assembly with the words of the *Kaddish* is still preserved in the *Kaddish de-Rabbanan* (*Kaddish* of the Rabbis), which is recited in the synagogue after communal study. It includes several lines praying for the teachers of Israel, their disciples, and all who study the Torah. However, instead of being uttered by the teacher, the *Kaddish de-Rabbanan* is now recited in traditional synagogues by mourners.

Does the *Mourner's Kaddish* focus on death? (F)

Although the *Kaddish* is recited by mourners, it contains no mention of death. Instead, it sanctifies and glorifies God, extolling the Divine sovereignty, and ends with a prayer for peace. The practice of mourners reciting the *Kaddish* probably began during the thirteenth century, when Jews in Germany were suffering severe persecutions at the hands of the Crusaders.

Is the *Kaddish* recited for less than a full 12 months after death? (T)

Mourners actually recite the *Kaddish* for only 11 months, based on a Talmudic statement implying that only the wicked are judged in purgatory for a full 12 months—and no child would want to designate a parent as wicked (Shab. 152b).

May only sons recite the *Mourner's Kaddish*? (N)

Jewish law requires only sons of the deceased to recite the *Mourner's Kaddish*, even when there are no sons and only daughters among the survivors. Traditionally, the daughter honored her deceased parents by merely saying "amen" at the appropriate times during the prayer. Although a majority of halachic scholars have forbidden women from reciting the *Kaddish*, some prominent contemporary authorities have permitted it, even ruling that a woman may recite *Kaddish* in a synagogue in the presence of a *minyan* of 10 men, whether or not a man is saying *Kaddish* along with her. As the recitation of *Kaddish* becomes halachically permissible, this obligation has been assumed by an increasing number of Orthodox women. In liberal egalitarian congregations, women are encouraged to stand with male mourners and recite the *Mourner's Kaddish*.

Is there a standard melody for all synagogue services? (F)

The Hebrew word *nusach* refers to the collection of musical motifs that differentiate one service from another and have been handed down through the generations. Specific modes and melodies characterize the weekday, Sabbath, festival, and High Holy Day services. Certain biblical books, such as the five *megillot* (Esther, Ruth, Song of Songs, Ecclesiastes, and Lamentations), have their own *nusach*. The musical tradition also differs regionally, often reflecting the music of the country of origin.

Was the opening prayer of the morning service written by a non-Jew? (T)

Mah Tovu (How goodly [are your tents, O Jacob, your dwelling places, O Israel]) is the opening prayer of the morning service and is recited upon entering the synagogue. This biblical verse (Num. 24:5) was initially uttered by the Gentile prophet, Balaam, who was hired by Balak to curse the Israelites but blessed them instead. According to tradition, Jacob's tents refer to the houses of prayer, while Israel's dwellings represent houses of study. Balaam also was amazed at how each tent (*ohel*) in the Israelite encampment was constructed so that everyone's privacy was respected, and no one could see into his neighbor's home (BB 60a). [42]

Were the morning blessings (*Birchot ha-Shachar*) once much shorter? (T)

The initial prayer section of the morning service contains a greater variety of prayers, blessings, and Torah study passages than any other part of the *siddur*. Many of the prayers and blessings were intended to be said privately at home prior to the synagogue service, to be recited with each act of rising and getting ready for the day's work. However, they became widely neglected because many Jews did not know the blessings by heart and, as part of the Oral Law, it was forbidden to write them down. Therefore, the Rabbis decided to transfer these morning blessings to the beginning of the synagogue service, where the prayer leader recited them aloud to provide an opportunity for the less knowledgeable in the congregation to hear them and respond with the traditional "amen." [43]

Do the preliminary morning blessings have a standard wording? (N)

Each of the 15 blessings that are traditionally said upon arising begin with the standard blessing formula—"Praised are You, Lord our God, King of the universe"—and concludes with a specific instance of the Divine role in all that one does in life and the satisfaction of every human need. The Conservative movement has revised the classic second and third blessings ("Who did not make me a Gentile" and "Who did not make me a slave") into affirmative statements ("Who has made me an Israelite" and "Who has made me a free person"). It has also transformed the original fourth blessing ("Who did not make me a woman") into "Who made me according to His will."

Is the *Ashrei* an alphabetical acrostic? (N)

The *Ashrei* (Happy are they), which consists of Psalm 145 plus two introductory verses (Pss. 84:5; 144:15) and one concluding verse (Ps. 115:18), is read twice in the morning service (in the *Pesukei de-Zimra* and toward the end), and at the beginning of the afternoon service. Although a Hebrew alphabetical acrostic, it is missing a verse beginning with the letter *nun*. According to the Talmud (Ber. 4b), this is because that letter may suggest the Hebrew word *naflah* (fallen) and thus imply a reference to a prophetic verse that speaks of the destruction of Israel (Amos 5:2). However, a verse beginning with *nun* may have once been used, since one of the Dead Sea Scrolls includes the line "*ne'eman Elohim bi-d'varav, ve-chasid be-chol ma'asav*" ("God is faithful in His words, and gracious in all His works").

Does the term *Shema* refer to a single verse in Deuteronomy? (N)

Shema Yisrael Adonai Eloheinu Adonai Echad (Hear, O Israel: the Lord is our God, the Lord is One) is the basic declaration of faith of the Jewish people in the unity and oneness of God and their acceptance of the yoke of the Kingdom of Heaven. The term *Shema* may refer either to a single verse in Deuteronomy (6:4) or to the prayer composed of three biblical passages—Deuteronomy 6:5–9 (*v'ahavta*) and 11:13–21, and Numbers 15:37–41—that is recited daily in the morning and evening services.

After the first verse of the *Shema* is recited in the synagogue, is the response said aloud? (N)

When the people assembled in the Temple courtyard heard the first line of the *Shema*, they responded, "*Baruch Shem k'vod malchuto l'olam va-ed*" ("Praised is the Name of His glorious kingdom forever and ever"). Since rabbinic times, however, it has been customary in more traditional circles to recite the Temple response silently. The Rabbis offered two reasons for this practice. When Jacob (Israel) lay on his deathbed, his twelve sons declared their loyalty to God by reciting the *Shema*. Jacob responded "Praised is the Name . . .", but he was so weak that his words could barely be heard. The other explanation is that Moses heard this phrase recited by the ministering angels and brought it down to earth to teach the Children of Israel. The sages compared this to a man who stole a valuable ornament from the palace of the king and gave it to his wife, on the condition that she wear it only at home and never in public. As sinful humans, we dare not say aloud an angelic formula. The sole exception is on Yom Kippur, when Israel elevates itself to the pure and sin-free level of angels.[44] Consequently, today the Temple response is said aloud several times on the Day of Atonement, after the first verse of the *Shema* and during the *Avodah* service in response to the three confessions of the *Kohen Gadol* and his utterance of the holy Name of God (Tetragrammaton). In Reform synagogues, the response is usually said aloud at all services where the *Shema* is recited.

After the complete *Shema* is recited in the synagogue, does the prayer leader proceed immediately to the next prayer? (F)

The Rabbis taught that the 248 positive commandments equal the number of organs in the human body, symbolizing that it is essential to dedicate one's entire body to the service of God and fulfilling the *mitzvot*. Because the total number of words of the *Shema* (together with "Praised is the Name . . .") is 245, in public worship it is customary for the prayer leader to repeat the last two words of the *Shema* (*Adonai Elohaichem*; The Lord, your God) and the first word of the following benediction (*emet*; true). This brings the total number of words up to 248, echoing the parallel phrase in Jeremiah (10:10): "The Lord God is true" (Ber. 2:2). When the *Shema* is recited in private, or if there is no *minyan*, the total of 248 is achieved by first reciting, "*El melech ne'eman*" ("God, faithful King"). These three words were chosen because their initial Hebrew letters spell *amen*, thus testifying that the worshiper is firmly convinced that the words about to be recited are completely true.[45]

Is the first verse of the *Shema* recited more than once on Sabbath morning? (N)

In the middle of the fifth century, a fanatical Persian king was offended by the Jewish emphasis on the unity of God and forbade the recitation of the *Shema* at synagogue services. To ensure that the Jews would not disobey his decree, guards were stationed in the synagogue for the first quarter of the day, when the *Shema* must be read. As a countermeasure, the Rabbis ruled that the first verse of the *Shema* be recited on two occasions, which fulfills the obligation when there is an extreme emergency. They composed a short prayer unit, with the first verse of the *Shema* at the center, which was to be read privately at home before coming to the public services. The other recitation was inserted into the *Kedushah* of the *Amidah* for the *Musaf* (additional) service on the Sabbath, at a time when the government inspectors sent to enforce the prohibition had already left the synagogue, satisfied that the *Shema* had not been recited. Even after the king was killed, his decree lifted, and the *Shema* with its blessings restored to its traditional place in the service, the extra two abbreviated recitations of the *Shema* were retained as part of the regular ritual to commemorate this event. The home recitation became part of the introductory prayers, where it has remained to this day. [46]

Is the first verse of the *Shema* read differently from other prayers? (T)

According to the Rabbis, the *Shema* should be recited with full concentration on the meaning of the words. To prevent distractions, it is customary to follow the practice of Judah the Prince and place the right hand over the eyes while saying the first verse. The *Shema* should be recited loud enough to be heard by the ear, since it is written "*Hear*, O Israel" (Ber. 15a).

Must the first verse of the *Shema* be recited in Hebrew? (F)

Any language can be used—because it is crucial that the worshiper understand what he or she is affirming—as long as one enunciates the words clearly (Sot. 32b).

Because of the importance of the prayer, is the *Shema* traditionally read standing? (F)

Unlike the *Amidah*, which must be recited while standing, the *Shema* is said while standing or sitting, or even while traveling (stopping only to recite the first verse). For a long time, the Jews in Israel stood up for the *Shema*, both because of its importance and because it was an act of witnessing God (and testimony in a Jewish court is always given while standing). In ninth-century Babylonia, however, the Karaites argued that standing for the *Shema* meant that the Jews considered only these three passages (and the Ten Commandments) to be fundamental tenets of the faith and of Divine origin. To counteract such views, the rabbis ruled that the *Shema* be recited while seated, and this remains the prevailing custom today. [47]

Is the first blessing in the prayers immediately before the morning *She-ma* a direct biblical quote? (N)

Focusing on the concept of light, since the morning service was usually held at sunrise, this blessing thanks God for the sunrise as well as for the other miracles of Creation. Although based on the verse from Isaiah (45:7), "I form light and create darkness, I make peace and create woe," the blessing was put in the third person and the last word changed to "all things." Not only did the Rabbis deem this a "euphemism" or "more appropriate language," but the new wording also emphasized that God is the sole source of Creation. This served as a polemic against the once-prevailing dualistic doctrine that day and night, and good and evil, were created and ruled by different deities.

Is the *Amidah* known as the *Shemoneh-Esrei* (18) since it has that number of blessings? (N)

Literally meaning "standing" prayer, the *Amidah* is the highlight of the Jewish prayer service, referred to by the Talmudic rabbis as simply *ha-Tefillah* (The Prayer). The paradigmatic prayer, it contains the primary elements of praise, petition, and thanksgiving. The Hebrew name comes from an early version, which consisted of 18 blessings. Today, however, the *Amidah* has an additional 19th benediction, which according to tradition was added by Rabban Gamaliel as an attack against the *minim*—sectarians such as the Sadducees, Essenes, and especially the early Christians, who posed a threat to the precarious existence of the Jewish people. Any reader who failed to recite this benediction, or any worshiper who failed to respond to it with the customary "amen," was immediately recognized as a heretic. In this way, these sectarians were effectively eliminated from the synagogue.[48]

Fragments from the Cairo Genizah have confirmed that Gamaliel's *Amidah* consisted of only 18 blessings, which included a pre-existing attack against separatists and heretics. Therefore, the expansion to 19 blessings appears to be a third-century Babylonian creation, in which the single combined blessing in the Land of Israel for "David, builder of Jerusalem" was expanded into the current pair of separate blessings of David as builder of Jerusalem and forerunner of the Messiah.[49] Although the specific sects against whom it was addressed no longer existed, the Rabbis retained the benediction against *minim* in the *Amidah* because the danger of non-believers and heretics persists in every generation.[50]

Is the "silent" *Amidah* ever recited aloud? (T)

According to Jewish tradition, even the "silent" Amidah, the core of the prayer service, is read loud enough to hear it oneself, but not so loud that it is audible to others and disturbs their concentration. This requirement is based on the famous prayer of Hannah, in which she "spoke in her heart, only her lips moved, but her voice could not be heard" (1 Sam. 1:13). Saying the prayers aloud, even if they cannot be heard by others, is associated with an emotional component and spiritual experience that cannot be matched by reading them rapidly and silently.

Should the *Amidah* be said in a loud voice to affirm one's faith? (F)

Conversely, a person should not shout out the prayers in an overly loud voice. In addition to disturbing the prayers of others, one who loudly declaims the *Amidah* so that it can be heard was deemed by the Rabbis as being "small of faith," for this implies that God cannot hear the soft voice that barely escapes the lips.

Are the feet traditionally placed in a specific position when reciting the *Amidah*? (T)

The *Amidah* is recited with feet together, based on emulating either Ezekiel's description of the ministering angels ("And their feet were as a straight foot"),[51] or the position of the *kohanim* when ascending the Altar, who respectfully shuffled along so slowly that their legs were hardly separated as they placed one foot in front of the other;[52] or because the numerical value of *Tefillah* (*Amidah*) equals that of *yesharah* (straight).[53]

Is the *Amidah* repeated at all services? (F)

In congregational worship, but only during the morning and afternoon service, the prayer leader repeats the *Amidah* out loud following the personal recitation of the prayer. This practice was devised to allow illiterate people to fulfill their prayer duty by reciting "amen" to each of the blessings.

Is the repetition of the *Amidah* different from the silent prayer? (T)

Various additions are made to the *Amidah* when it is recited aloud in the congregational service. The most significant is the *Kedushah*, a prayer in which the community of Israel joins with the heavenly hosts to proclaim the holiness of God. While the reader intones the 18th benediction (*Modim anachnu lach*; we give thanks to You), the congregation recites a different prayer of thanksgiving in an undertone. Also, the Priestly Blessing is included whenever the *Amidah* is repeated.

Does the *Amidah* contain a prayer for life-giving rain? (N)

Mashiv ha-ru'ach u-morid ha-geshem (Who causes the wind to blow and the rain to fall) is the Hebrew phrase praying for rain, which is added at the beginning of the second blessing of the *Amidah* at all services from Shemini Atzeret until the first day of Passover. During the rest of the year, *Morid ha-tal* (Who causes the dew to fall) is recited instead.

Was there a theological reason for the addition of a partial repetition of the *Amidah* at the Friday evening service? (F)

Magen Avot (Shield of [our] fathers) are the opening words of an abridged form of the intermediate blessings of the *Amidah*, which is recited aloud by the prayer leader at the Friday evening service. It summarizes the seven blessings said quietly by each congregant. In Talmudic times, when synagogues were generally outside the town limits, it was dangerous to walk home alone after dark. Some scholars have suggested that reciting this extra prayer gave latecomers time to complete their prayers so that all the worshipers could return to town together.

Are personal prayers permitted during the *Amidah*, with no suggested rabbinic text? (N)

At the end of the silent recitation of the formal *Amidah*, it has become customary for the individual to add a personal prayer. The Talmud specifically mentions the supplications generally added by 11 prominent sages (Ber. 16b–17a). The petition of Mar ben Ravina, a fourth-century Rabbi, became a favorite and found its way into the prayer book. Opening with the verse from Psalms (34:14), "My God, guard my tongue from evil, and my lips from speaking guile," it beseeches God to keep the worshiper from spreading falsehoods and gossiping (*lashon ha-ra*), a sin that the Talmud regarded as especially serious.

Is taking steps backward and forward at the beginning of the *Amidah*, as well as bowing at the end, more than mere custom? (T)

Before beginning the *Amidah*, one humbly takes three steps backward and then moves three paces forward to symbolically draw nearer to God, just as Moses rose through three levels of holiness when ascending Mount Sinai.[54] Another interpretation is that it reflects the three ancestors whom the Bible records as having "stepped forward"—Abraham, when bargaining with God for the lives of the inhabitants of Sodom (Gen. 18:23); Judah, when he pleaded with Joseph to allow him to be kept hostage instead of his brother Benjamin, fearing that otherwise it would lead to the death of their father Jacob (Gen. 44:18); and Elijah, when he asked for Divine help in defeating the prophets of Baal (1 Kings 18:36).[55] At the conclusion of the *Amidah*, the worshiper takes three paces backward so as to not turn his or her back on the Divine King.[56]

The *Amidah* ends with a recitation of *Oseh shalom* (He who makes peace [in His high heavens]). Before beginning these words, the worshiper takes three steps back (starting with the left foot), and then bows to the left, right, and center, as though leaving one's teacher or departing from the presence of royalty (Ber. 34a; Maimonides). Another interpretation is that as we bow to the left we face the angel Michael, who symbolizes God's spirit of Mercy and stands at the right of the Divine throne. The bow to our right is toward the angel Gabriel, who stands at the left of the throne and represents the Divine quality of strict justice. Finally, we bow forward, directly toward God, who alone can harmonize these two disparate Divine manifestations and establish lasting peace, both in Heaven and on earth.[57]

Is the *Kedushah* a prayer praising the holiness of God? (N)

Meaning "holiness" or "sanctification" in Hebrew, the *Kedushah* refers to the proclamation of God's holiness and glory in the third blessing that is recited during the repetition of the *Amidah* when a *minyan* is present. It contains the verse "*Kadosh, Kadosh, Kadosh*" ("Holy, holy, holy [is the Lord of hosts; the whole world is full of His glory]"), which is taken from Isaiah's vision of the angels surrounding the Divine throne and proclaiming the holiness of God (Isa. 6:3). This became a source of conflict with the Christians, who realized that the Jews did not consider the threefold repetition of "holy" as a reference to the trinity. Instead the Jews were using the verse as both an assertion of God's unity and an implied repudiation of core Christian doctrine. When the Christians prohibited the recitation of the *Kedushah*, the Jews simply inserted it into another prayer, *Uva Le-Zion Go'el* (A redeemer shall come to Zion). This had the advantage of being recited at a time when the government censors were not in attendance—at the conclusion of the homily when the congregation reassembled for the afternoon service.

Is there a "short" version of the *Amidah*? (T)

An abbreviated version of the *Amidah* can be used when there is not enough time to recite the full text. Known as *Havineinu* (Grant us understanding), the initial word of the middle section, it consists of the first and last three paragraphs plus a brief restatement of the main ideas of the other paragraphs (Ber. 29a).

Is the Priestly Blessing recited by *kohanim* on the three major pilgrimage festivals? (N)

These three biblical verses with which the *kohanim* conveyed the Divine blessing to the people—"May God bless you and keep you; may God shine His face on you and be gracious to you; may God lift up His countenance on you and give you peace" (Num. 6:23–26)—became the last significant remnant of the priestly cult after the destruction of the Second Temple.

Today, local customs differ as to the time (morning or additional service) for the recital of the Priestly Blessing, which requires a *minyan*. The general Ashkenazic custom is to recite it only during the *Musaf Amidah* on the High Holy Days and the three pilgrimage festivals of Passover, Shavuot, and Sukkot (exclusive of *chol ha-mo'ed*). In Israel and among Sephardic Jews everywhere, the *kohanim* go up to recite the Priestly Blessing every day in accordance with the ancient Temple practice—during the *Amidah* of the morning service or, whenever there is an additional service, during the *Musaf Amidah*. In all communities, if the *kohanim* do not recite the Priestly Blessing, the prayer leader recites the text during the repetition of the *Amidah*, just before the final blessing.

Does the congregation respond "amen" after each part of the *Birkat ha-Kohanim*? (N)

Initially, congregants listened silently to the Priestly Blessing. Today, it is customary to respond with "amen" after each of the three sections when said by the *kohanim*, but with "*kein ye-hi ratzon*" ("so may it be Your will") when recited by the prayer leader.

Do those in synagogue gaze with awe at the *kohanim* during the Priestly Blessing? (F)

While chanting the Priestly Blessing, the *kohanim* cover their heads with prayer shawls and stretch both arms and hands out at shoulder height with their hands touching at the thumbs and their palms forward. The second and third fingers of each hand are separated from the fourth and fifth to produce a fan-like appearance. The congregation stands quietly, with head bowed and eyes cast down as a sign of respect and humility, carefully listening to every word spoken by the *kohanim*. The Talmud forbids a person from looking at the hands of the *kohanim* while they are pronouncing the Priestly Blessing, lest their "eyes become dimmed" (Hag. 16a). Rashi explains that this is due to the glow of the Divine Presence in the synagogue radiating from the fingers of the *kohanim*. In many communities, a father draws his children to himself and covers them with his *tallit*.

Does the appearance of the hands of the *kohanim* have any application outside of the synagogue? (T)

Outstretched hands have become symbolic of the *kohanim*, and it is common to find this representation engraved on tombstones of members of priestly families. More recently, Leonard Nimoy (Mr. Spock) used the characteristic appearance of the hands of the priests as the Vulcan greeting in the classic science fiction series, *Star Trek*.

Do Jews recite the words of the Priestly Blessing in any other context? (T)

On Sabbath eve, it is a custom for parents to bless their children with the Priestly Blessing, after first saying either "May God make you like Ephraim and Menashe" (for sons) or "May God make you like Sarah, Rebecca, Rachel, and Leah" (for daughters).

Is there a single version of the prayer for peace? (F)

The final blessing of the *Amidah* appears in two versions—*Sim Shalom* (Grant peace) and *Shalom Rav* (Abundant peace). Since these prayers for peace coexisted in different localities, instead of choosing one and rejecting the other, the Rabbis made a compromise and retained both.[58] Among Ashkenazim, *Sim Shalom* is recited only at the morning and *Musaf* services, while *Shalom Rav* is used in the afternoon and evening services. Sephardic Jews use *Sim Shalom* in all services.[59]

Are the Thirteen Attributes of Mercy recited in the synagogue the same as those in the Bible? (N)

The Thirteen Attributes of Mercy are the core of the *Selichot* prayers (before the High Holy Days). These are traditionally the exact words that God taught Moses for the people to use whenever they needed to beg for Divine compassion. In the Bible, they are found after the incident of the Golden Calf, when God threatened to destroy the people of Israel rather than forgive them (Exod. 32:10). The Thirteen Attributes of Mercy are based on two verses in Exodus (34:6–7)—"The Lord! The Lord! God, Compassionate and Gracious, Slow to anger and Abundant in kindness and truth, Preserver of kindness for thousands of generations, Forgiver of iniquity, willful sin, and error, and Who cleanses [but does not cleanse completely, recalling the iniquity of parents upon children and grandchildren, to the third and fourth generations]."[60] The Rabbis ingeniously cut off the end of this verse, thus changing the meaning to indicate that God does forgive all sins! This remarkable midrashic transformation has become the standard format whenever this Torah verse is used in a synagogue service.

Are the Thirteen Attributes of Mercy also recited at any other time? (T)

The kabbalists introduced the current custom of reciting the Thirteen Attributes of Mercy before taking the Torah from the ark during the three pilgrimage festivals of Passover, Shavuot, and Sukkot, unless they occur on the Sabbath.

On a weekly basis, is the Torah read only on Sabbath morning? (F)

After the return from Babylonian Exile, Ezra the Scribe introduced the practice of also publicly reading the Torah on the market days of Monday and Thursday (BK 82a). This was established for the convenience of those living in isolated areas, who were unable to attend a local prayer meeting on the Sabbath. As the time when villagers congregated to do their shopping and trading, market days were ideal for gathering the people to teach them Torah. This eventually became the custom even in larger towns where a regular Sabbath reading of the Torah took place. For the sake of the town merchants, who had to protect their wares and thus could not leave their stalls when the Torah was being read on Mondays and Thursdays, Ezra instituted an extra reading of the Torah on Sabbath afternoon, which also became common practice.[61]

Is the triennial cycle for reading the Torah a modern innovation? (F)

Initially, the head of the congregation or the Torah reader selected biblical passages that were thematically appropriate for the planned homily or occasion. There was no systematic order for the substance and length of the public Torah readings until the Rabbis established the practice of consecutive readings.

In the Land of Israel, the text was divided into 155 portions, which were read on each Sabbath in the synagogue so as to cover the entire Torah in three years (Meg. 29b). In effect, what now is considered the weekly Torah portion—called *parashah* by Ashkenazim and *sidrah* by Sephardim—was read over three successive weeks.

The large and influential community of Jews in Babylonia developed the custom of completing the entire Torah in a single year, and this rule eventually became the generally accepted practice throughout the world. The Babylonian tradition divided the Torah into 54 sections, making it inevitable that two portions be read on some occasions to complete the entire Torah during the year (especially since the regularly scheduled weekly portion is postponed for a week when a major festival falls on a Sabbath). [62]

Some American Conservative synagogues have returned to a triennial cycle, though they read only one-third of each *parashah* every year. Thus, the initial third of a given portion is read in the first year, the middle third in the second year, and the final third in the third year—resulting in the entire Torah being read every three years. This practice has become increasingly popular, though it means that the Torah is no longer read consecutively, so that narratives and bodies of biblical legislation are interrupted.

Has the Torah always been divided into chapters and verses? (F)

The Torah scroll has no punctuation, but the printed *Chumash* has the text subdivided into chapters and verses. This division was a thirteenth-century Christian innovation designed to aid missionaries and those engaged in public theological disputations with the Jews to quickly find quotations to support their specious arguments. Thus, it became necessary for the rabbis to use the same system of chapters and verses so that they could find the references used by their enemies and offer effective rebuttals to the Christian version of the Jewish text. [63]

Do Jews throughout the world always read the same Torah portion on a specific Sabbath? (N)

The cycle of Torah readings begins with the first Sabbath following Simchat Torah and ends with the final reading on Simchat Torah itself. Most of the time, all Jewish communities throughout the world read the same Torah portion. However, the observance of Passover and Sukkot for seven days in Israel and eight days in the Diaspora occasionally results in different Torah portions being read. This continues until there is a portion that can be added to another to form a "double" portion that is read in Israel, allowing the Torah portions throughout the world to again be in sync.

When the Torah is taken around the synagogue before being read, is there a tradition regarding how and in what direction the Torah is carried? (T)

The removal of the Torah from the ark and its return after the reading has been completed is the most ceremonial ritual of the synagogue service, especially on the Sabbath and festivals. It clearly demonstrates the centrality of the Torah and its teachings in the Jewish tradition. The Torah should be carried with the right arm and received on the right when handed from one person to another, probably reflecting the fact that most people are right handed and have a stronger right arm. Because the right side symbolizes the majesty and power of God, the Torah is traditionally taken first to the right side when carried in procession around the synagogue before being read. [64]

Is only one Torah scroll removed from the ark to be read? (N)

On most Sabbath mornings, all the *aliyot* are read from a single Torah scroll. However, it is traditional to use a different scroll for every extra Torah reading that is required on special occasions. When Rosh Chodesh or a festival falls on the Sabbath, a description of the appropriate sacrifices is read as the *maftir* portion from the second scroll. Employing a separate scroll for each special reading, rather than using a single scroll and simply rolling it to the next passage to be read, is based on the principle of *k'vod ha-tzibbur* ([regard for the] honor of the congregation) (Yoma 70a). For similar reasons, the Torah scroll is always prepared in advance, rolled to the proper place before the service begins.

Can there be Torah readings from more than two Torah scrolls? (T)

Occasionally, readings are made from three separate scrolls, as when the Sabbath of Chanukah coincides with the New Moon of the month of Tevet. When this occurs, the ordinary weekly portion is read from the first scroll, the special portion for Rosh Chodesh from the second, and the section for Chanukah from the third (Meg. 29b).

Are there always seven people called up to the Torah? (F)

Seven people are called up to the Torah on Sabbath morning, but the number of *aliyot* varies widely on other occasions (Meg. 4:1–2). Three people are called to the Torah on Monday and Thursday mornings, on Sabbath afternoons and the *Minchah* service on Yom Kippur, on the festivals of Chanukah and Purim, and on all fast days. There are four *aliyot* on Rosh Chodesh and on the intermediate days (*chol ha-mo'ed*) of Passover and Sukkot; five on Rosh Hashanah and the festival days of Passover, Shavuot, and Sukkot; and six on the morning of Yom Kippur.

Can there ever be more than seven *aliyot* on Sabbath mornings? (T)

Some congregations take advantage of a provision in Jewish law that permits dividing the Torah portion into more, but not less, than the required number of *aliyot*. This is not permitted on Mondays, Thursdays, or other midweek occasions such as Rosh Chodesh, Chanukah, and fast days, because of the principle of *bittul melachah*, wasting the time of people who have to go to work. Termed *hosafot*, these extra *aliyot* allow one or more additional persons to have the honor of being called up to the Torah.[65]

Are there different ways to approach the *bimah* when called for an *aliyah*? (T)

There are two traditional customs. One is to ascend on the right and descend from the left, in accordance with the practice of approaching the Altar in the Temple (Zev. 63a–b). Moreover, the entrance to the Temple Mount was also from the right (Mid. 2:2). The other tradition is to ascend to the *bimah* by the shortest route and descend by the longest, thus demonstrating that one is eager to be called for an *aliyah* and reluctant to leave. According to the *Shulchan Aruch* (OH 141:7), if it is necessary to choose between these two traditions, one should take the shorter route even if this requires going up from the left.

When congregants say *yasher ko'ach* to a person returning from an *aliyah* to the Torah, does that mean "congratulations"? (N)

In Ashkenazic synagogues, other worshipers typically congratulate the person returning from having an *aliyah* by saying "*yasher ko'ach*" ("may you grow in strength" or "may your strength be directed in the right path"), to which the reply is "*Baruch t'hiyeh*" ("may you be blessed"). This custom may reflect the Talmudic belief that intense study of the Torah, symbolized by the Torah reading, "weakens the strength of man" (Sanh. 26b). Among Sephardim, the expression used is "*Hazak u-varuch*" ("be strong and be blessed") or "*Baruch t'hiyeh*" ("may you be blessed"), to which the person returning from having an *aliyah* replies, "*Hazak ve-ematz*" ("be strong and of good courage").

Is calling up two people for the same *aliyah* a generally accepted practice? (N)

In some liberal congregations, two or more people are sometimes called up for the same *aliyah*, especially when there is a bar/bat mitzvah. They may either recite the blessings in unison, or have one person recite the blessing before the Torah reading and the other the blessing after it.[66] In more traditional synagogues, however, two people are not called up for the same *aliyah*. This is based on the law requiring that congregants hear every word of the Torah reading distinctly, which is difficult if two persons chant the portion simultaneously. This ruling was extended to prohibit two people from being called up to the Torah together, even if only to recite the blessings, since worshipers unable to hear the words clearly would not be permitted to respond "amen."

Is there a prohibition against close relatives having adjacent *aliyot*? (N)

Traditionally, two blood relatives are not called consecutively to the Torah, either because of fear that the "Evil Eye" will cast a spell upon a family receiving too many blessings or because Jewish law forbids near relatives from testifying together—and those pronouncing the Torah blessings are effectively giving testimony as to the truth of the sacred text. However, it is permitted to have one read the seventh *aliyah* and the other the *maftir* portion.

Is a *kohen* always given the first *aliyah*? (N)

According to the Talmud, a precise system for allocating *aliyot* was developed "for the sake of preserving peace in the congregation" (Git. 5:8). The privilege of the first *aliyah* is given to a *kohen*, as a member of the priestly caste and descendant of Aaron. The second person to be called to the Torah is a *levi*, a descendant of the family that also played a major role in the Temple service. The remaining *aliyot* are distributed among the rest of the congregation, who are classified as "Israelites." If there is no *kohen*, a *levi* has the next priority. If there is no *levi*, an Israelite is called first. In either of these cases, an announcement is made that the individual is being awarded the *aliyah bim'kom kohen* (in place of the *kohen*). If there is no *levi*, the *kohen* who received the first *aliyah* is given the second one as well. However, in the unusual situation in which everyone in the congregation is a *kohen* except for one Israelite, the latter receives the first *aliyah* so as to avoid any possible conflict among the *kohanim* about which of them should be called first.

Some synagogues have abolished the distinction between *kohen*, *levi*, and Israelite because of a belief in the equality of all members.

Is there a difference between the "prestige" of different *aliyot*? (T)

On the Sabbath, the third and sixth *aliyot* are particularly esteemed, and it is customary to give them to learned individuals or to the person who sponsors the refreshments after services. It is an even greater honor to receive the final *aliyah* for each of the five books of the Torah. Other especially honored *aliyot* are *Shirat ha-Yam* (Song at the Sea) and the Ten Commandments, for which the congregation stands while the Torah is being read.

Is the selection of who is given an *aliyah* at a specific service random? (N)

According to an old tradition, those commemorating specific events in their lives are given precedence in receiving the honor of being called to the Torah. In a traditional congregation, priority in the distribution of *aliyot*— those from the third onward—is generally as follows:[67]

1. Bridegroom on the Sabbath *before* his wedding
2. Boy who has turned 13 years of age (bar mitzvah)
3. Father of a newborn infant on the first Sabbath that the mother appears in the synagogue
4. Bridegroom on the Sabbath *after* his wedding

5. Father of a baby girl who is to be named
6. One observing *yahrzeit* for a parent on that day
7. Father of a baby to be circumcised on that day or during the coming week
8. One observing *yahrzeit* for a parent during the coming week
9. One required to recite the blessing of *gomel*
10. One who is about to leave on a long journey or has just returned from one
11. A distinguished guest in the community

Any unclaimed *aliyot* are then distributed randomly.

When two or more people are observing the same occasion, is a visitor given the honor of an *aliyah*? (F)

Priority is generally given to a regular worshiper over one who comes infrequently, and to a member of the congregation over a non-member. [68]

Is the recitation of one blessing before the Torah reading and one after it the standard Jewish practice? (N)

Originally, only two Torah blessings were recited—one by the first person before he began to read and the second by the last person after he had completed his reading (Meg. 21a). Those in between read their Torah portions without reciting any blessings at all. The current practice, in which each person called to the reading of the Torah recites both blessings, is a later rabbinic innovation. According to the Talmud, the reason for this change was "to avoid error on the part of people entering and leaving the synagogue" (Meg. 21b). Otherwise, a person who came in after the reading had begun and saw a new person starting to read the Torah without saying a blessing, might think that no preliminary blessing is necessary. Similarly, one who left before the reading was concluded might think that no blessing at all is necessary after reading the Torah. Another explanation for this practice is that those members of the congregation who arrived after the beginning of the Torah reading, or left before its end, would not be deprived of the chance of hearing both blessings and responding, "amen." [69]

Is the first Torah blessing grammatically inconsistent? (T)

The first blessing, which emphasizes that God chose Israel to receive the Torah, contains a grammatical inconsistency with great theological significance. The first portion of the blessing describes God as *natan ha-Torah* (Who *gave* us the Torah), while the second changes this to *notein ha-Torah* (Who *gives* us the Torah). The Rabbis emphasized that having the second part of the blessing in the present tense indicates that the Torah is not merely a static and lifeless text. Instead, they considered it conclusive proof that

Revelation is a continuing process, with subsequent interpretations of the Torah (Oral Law) also being Divine and thus binding. [70]

Is there controversy whether the Torah scroll should be rolled closed or left open while the Torah blessings are being recited? (T)

The Talmud describes two different procedures that have been adopted by different Jewish communities (Meg. 32a). According to R. Meir, a person called up for an *aliyah* should open the scroll, look at the place where the reading is to begin, roll the scroll closed, recite the first Torah blessing, and then unroll the scroll for reading. His rationale was that if the scroll were left open, an uninformed person might mistakenly think that the blessings are being read from the scroll itself. R. Judah disagreed, arguing that there was no need to close the scroll because no one would be foolish enough to imagine that the blessings were written in it. Ashkenazic Jews generally follow the ruling of R. Meir and close the scroll while the Torah blessings are recited or cover it with the mantle or a cloth. Sephardic Jews usually neither roll the Torah scroll closed nor cover it when reciting the blessings. [71]

Does the *baal korei* (master of the reading) read the entire Torah portion? (N)

Originally, each person called to the Torah read his own portion (Meg. 3:11). If only one person was competent to read from the Torah, he was given all the *aliyot*. This tradition continued through the medieval period and was codified as the norm in the *Shulchan Aruch* (OH 139:1–2). An exception was made if a person who was unable to read his own portion was needed because he was the only *kohen* or *leviamor* present.

As Torah learning among the laypeople declined, in many communities there were numerous Jews who did not know how to read from the Torah scroll and thus were prevented from ever having an *aliyah*. One solution was to allow such a person to recite the appropriate blessings, while a knowledgeable official of the synagogue read the Torah selection. However, this publicly humiliated some members of the congregation by showing that they were so unlearned that they required a substitute to read for them. To solve this dilemma, the rabbis ruled that an official Torah reader would read for everyone, both the ignorant and the scholar. With the person called to the Torah now only required to recite the prescribed blessings, the privilege of having an *aliyah* is available to everyone. [72]

Is the musical cantillation for chanting from the Torah written in the scroll? (F)

Trope is the Hebrew word for the series of musical notations used for chanting the Torah and *haftarah* (as well as the *megillot* on festivals). Although dating back to Talmudic times, the *trope* system was not perfected until the work of the Masoretes in the ninth and tenth centuries. They devised universally accepted symbols that, over the years, were developed into distinctive melodic phrases by various Jewish communities. The Torah reader must memorize the cantillation, since there are no *trope* markings in the scroll. In some congregations, an official standing next to the *baal korei* uses hand signals to cue the reader regarding vocal modulations, the length of specific notes, and the word that ends each verse. [73]

Are the symbols and melodies the same for all readings? (F)

Though the symbols are the same, there are distinct *tropes* for reading the Torah, *haftarah*, the five *megillot*, and the Torah readings on Rosh Hashanah and the morning of Yom Kippur.

Does the person reading the Torah read exactly what is written in the scroll? (N)

The Torah reader is flanked by two members of the congregation, who closely follow from a printed text and quietly correct any mistakes in the reading. However, a millennium ago, the medieval Masoretes noted some spelling errors in the scroll, due to scribal inconsistencies over the centuries, which they regarded as deviations that altered the meaning of the original biblical text. Believing that the Torah had been dictated by God, the Masoretes left the original text intact, but in the margin of texts indicated with vowels how the word should be properly sounded. According to Jewish law, the Torah reader must carefully study the masoretic notes in printed texts and follow these guidelines, which sometimes are different from what is actually written in the scroll.

If the Torah script is faded, is the decision as to whether the scroll can continue to be used for the reading based solely on the observation of a trained rabbi? (N)

Certainly, a rabbi can decide whether the letters in a Torah scroll are too indistinct to be read. An intriguing custom for determining the severity of faded letters, rarely employed today (though the author's young daughter has done it), is to call up a child to view them. If the letters are sufficiently clear that the child is able to read the words correctly, the reading may be continued without substituting another scroll.

Is a woman permitted to read from the Torah? (N)

Although the traditional *halachah* is that a woman may not *write* a Torah scroll for public use, the Talmud explicitly indicates that she may *read* from the Torah at a public service (Meg. 23a). However, the text then says that a woman should not read the Torah because of *k'vod ha-tzibbur* ([respect for the] honor of the congregation). This has been interpreted to mean that, if a woman were to read from the scroll, it would give the impression that there was no male qualified to do so. *K'vod ha-tzibbur* also may refer to the rabbinic fear that a woman reading the Torah could cause sexual distraction during the most significant service of the week. A spurious argument for prohibiting women from publicly reading the Torah is that they may be menstruating and somehow render the scroll ritually impure and unfit for use by touching it. However, the Talmud unequivocally states that "the words of the Torah are not susceptible to ritual impurity" (Ber. 22a). Therefore, a menstruating woman is permitted to hold or kiss a Torah, just as she may touch and kiss a *mezuzah*, which encases a parchment scroll of passages from the Torah. [74] Today, women routinely read the Torah in egalitarian congregations, as well as in Orthodox all-women *minyanim*.

Should congregants stand when the Torah is read? (N)

Although it is customary to stand up when the Torah is removed from or returned to the ark, members of the congregation usually are seated while the Torah is read. A practical reason for this tradition is that it would be difficult for many worshipers to remain standing for the entire Torah reading. Moreover, reading the Torah in the synagogue is considered a form of study, for which students usually are seated. However, congregants do stand when certain especially significant passages are read—the Ten Commandments (Exod. 20:1–14; Deut. 5:6–18), *Shirat ha-Yam* (Exod. 15:1–19), and the last verse of each of the Five Books of Moses. [75]

Are portions of the Torah read in different ways? (T)

Certain Torah verses that describe catastrophic events are traditionally read softly and rapidly, based on the belief that their mere mention may cause them to occur or recur. These sections include the horrible curses (*Tochachah*) that will befall the Israelites if they do not follow the Divine commandments (Lev. 26:14–39; Deut. 28:15–68) and the blasphemy of the Golden Calf (Exod. 32).

Was there ever a custom to have a verse-by-verse translation of the Torah reading into the vernacular? (T)

When the Jews returned from exile in Babylonia, where the vernacular was Aramaic, Hebrew was no longer the spoken language of the masses. The custom developed of having a special synagogue official (*meturgeman*; "interpreter" in Aramaic) provide a verse-by-verse translation of the Torah reading. This was a challenging task because the translator was prohibited from having any written material in front of him, since the translation was regarded as part of the Oral Law. The *meturgeman* was "not permitted to translate word by word, lest he distort the sense of the Torah reading, nor was he permitted to elaborate on the text. His was to be a free, though exact, translation. If he took any liberties with the translation, he was to be 'silenced and admonished.'"[76] Many centuries later, this gave rise to *Targum Onkelos*, the official Aramaic version of the Torah. [77]

Does each person called for an *aliyah* receive a blessing after their portion? (N)

Mi she-Berach (May He Who blessed [our forefathers]) are the initial words of a prayer formula that invokes God's blessings on individuals and the community. Each person called for an *aliyah* generally receives a personal *Mi she-Berach*, though in some congregations a collective blessing is recited after the completion of the entire Torah portion. Those celebrating a special occasion—such as a bar/bat mitzvah, forthcoming marriage, or birth of a child—receive a special version of the prayer that makes reference to the event.

Do the *gabbaim* serve as an "honor guard" on either side of the Torah scroll as it lies on the reading table? (F)

Just as the Torah was transmitted to the Israelites at Sinai through an intermediary (Moses), the Rabbis required there to be at least three persons standing on the *bimah*—the Torah reader (representing Moses, the "agent" through whom the Torah was given), and the two synagogue officials symbolizing God and Israel.

Today, one *gabbai* is responsible for calling people up to the Torah and reciting the special *Mi she-Berach* prayer that is offered after each *aliyah*. The other *gabbai* typically covers the Torah scroll after the second Torah blessing of one *aliyah* is completed and then removes the covering when the next person called for an *aliyah* is ready to begin the first blessing. However, the major duty of the *gabbaim* is to closely follow the Torah reading from a printed text and quietly correct any mistakes. Such errors are easy to make, since the scroll has neither punctuation nor vowel signs. [78]

At the end of the reading, is the Torah scroll simply lifted up so that it can be covered? (F)

The person who lifts the Torah traditionally opens at least three columns of the scroll before raising it up as high as possible and then slowly turning to show the script to all assembled. When the Torah is read at a central *bimah*, with congregants seated in front and in back as well as to both sides, the person lifting the open scroll should move in a full 360-degree circle (or 180 degrees to both right and left) so that everyone in the congregation is able see the text and proclaim, "*v'zot ha-Torah*" ("This is the Torah [that Moses placed before the children of Israel]"; Deut. 4:44). Some worshipers raise the edges of their *tallit* toward the script and then kiss the *tzitzit*, though the halachic requirement is merely to bow toward the open Torah. [79] The precedent for raising an open scroll so that the entire congregation can view the Torah script comes from the practice of Ezra, who "opened the book in the sight of all the people" (Neh. 8:5).

Are there different traditions among Jewish communities regarding when the Torah is raised and what words are recited? (T)

Ashkenazim and Sephardim have developed different traditions for the timing and wording of this dramatic ceremony. In Ashkenazic congregations, the Torah scroll is raised *after* the reading is completed, while Sephardim raise the Torah scroll *before* the reading begins. In addition, in the Ashkenazic rite there is also the recitation of a second verse, "according to the command of the Lord, by the hand of Moses" (Num. 9:23).

Have there always been two people responsible for taking care of the Torah scroll after it has been read? (F)

Hagbah is the term for raising the Torah, which is performed by the *magbi'ah*; *gelilah* is the word for rolling up and tying the Torah scroll and replacing its cover and ornaments, which is done by the *goleil*. The Talmud does not appear to separate these two functions, referring primarily to the latter (Meg. 32a). Indeed, the person who received the last *aliyah* may have initially performed both of these duties. However, the potential danger of the scroll being torn or dropped, if one person were responsible for both holding the Torah and tying the binder around it, presumably led to the decision to have two people share this honor.

In some communities are there special individuals who perform the role of *hagbah*? (T)

In traditional Western Sephardic congregations, there are designated individuals known as *levantadores* (lit., "master lifters [of the Torah scroll]"), who are exclusively honored with the role of *hagbah* so as to minimize the danger of dropping the scroll or handling it in a degrading way.[80]

Is there a *haftarah* after the Torah reading? (N)

There is always a *haftarah*, the reading from the Book of Prophets, after the Torah reading on Sabbath and festival mornings and at the afternoon service on fast days. The only exceptions are on Yom Kippur and Tisha b'Av, when it follows the Torah reading at both the morning and afternoon services. The *haftarah* is not read on a weekday, even if it is Rosh Chodesh or *chol ha-mo'ed* (intermediate day of festivals), nor is it read on Chanukah or Purim. Because work is permitted on these days, the Rabbis did not want to unduly lengthen the morning service.[81]

Has the *haftarah* followed the Torah reading since the second century B.C.E.? (T)

Most scholars believe that the custom of adding a prophetic section after the Torah reading dates back to the days before the Hasmonean revolt of 167 B.C.E., when Antiochus Epiphanes issued a decree banning the public reading of the Torah. Since other public readings in the synagogue were still permitted, the Rabbis added the reading of prophetic verses that related directly or indirectly to the topic of the Torah reading scheduled for that week. Just as it had been traditional to read a minimum of three Torah verses for each of the seven *aliyot* at Sabbath morning services, the Rabbis ruled that a minimum of 21 verses be divided among the seven called up to read from the Prophets. After the Hasmonean victory, the weekly Torah readings resumed. Nevertheless, the custom of reading the *haftarah* persisted, though with only one person called to read the entire prophetic portion.[82]

Does the earliest reference to the reading of the *haftarah* occur in the Talmud? (F)

Ironically, the earliest references to the actual reading of a *haftarah* are found in the Christian Bible. After reading the Torah at a Sabbath service in Nazareth, Jesus is described as being handed a scroll of the Book of Isaiah, from which he found and then read a specific portion. He then rolled up the scroll and handed it to the attendant, before sitting down and expounding on the reading (Luke 4:16–21). Similarly, Paul is described as being invited to deliver a talk "after the reading of the law and the prophets" (Acts 13:15).

Are the *haftarot* related thematically to the Torah reading? (N)

Many of the readings from the prophets have a thematic connection with the weekly Torah reading. For example, for *Parshat Beshalach* (Exod. 13:17–17:16), which contains *Shirat ha-Yam* (Song at the Sea), the *haftarah* reading includes the Song of Deborah (Judg. 4:4–5:31). Similarly, for *Parshat Shelach Lecha* (Num. 13:1–15:41), which describes the incident of the twelve spies sent by Moses, the *haftarah* is an account of the spies sent by Joshua (Josh. 2:1–24). However, about one-third of the Sabbath *haftarot* are determined either by the calendar or by historic circumstances. For 10 successive weeks from the Sabbath before the 17th of Tammuz until the Sabbath before Rosh Hashanah, there are three *haftarot* of tribulation and then seven of consolation. There are also special *haftarot* read on Sabbaths that fall either on or the day before Rosh Chodesh (New Moon) and on the Sabbath during the Ten Days of Repentance (*Shabbat Shuvah*). Finally, there are specific *haftarot* for the four special Sabbaths that precede Passover (Shekalim, Zachor, Parah, and ha-Chodesh), which relate to the special additional Torah portions read on these days. As late as geonic times, different *haftarot* were in vogue in various localities. To this day, certain variations persist between the Sephardic and Ashkenazic rites.[83]

Is the *maftir* portion one of the seven obligatory readings for the Sabbath? (F)

The person who reads the *haftarah* is known as the *maftir* (lit., "one who concludes"), since this individual also is called up for the last part of the Torah portion. However, the *maftir* is not included in the minimum obligatory number of seven persons who must be called up for *aliyot* on the Sabbath.

This is emphasized by the fact that the half *Kaddish*, which traditionally follows the required Torah reading, is recited even before the person is called up for the *maftir aliyah*. Thus, the custom arose for the *maftir* reading to consist of a repetition of a few verses from the end of the seventh portion. On festivals, Rosh Chodesh, and the four special Sabbaths that precede Passover, the *maftir* portion consists of a special reading from a second Torah scroll.

Do Jews recite a prayer for the country in which they live? (N)

Based on the Talmudic principle of *dina d'malchuta dina* (the law of the state is the law), a prayer for the welfare of the government is recited during the Sabbath morning service, immediately after the prayers for the congregation that are said prior to returning the Torah scroll to the ark. In most congregations, a prayer composed by Israel's chief rabbinate for the welfare of the State of Israel is also recited after the Torah reading.

Is *Ein Keloheinu* (There is none like our God) merely a popular hymn of praise? (F)

Few people realize that this simple song of faith, which is sung at the end of the *Musaf* (additional) service on Sabbaths and festivals in the Ashkenazic ritual and on weekdays after the morning service in the Sephardic rite, was formulated in response to a particular need for an additional source of blessings for Sabbaths and festivals. The Talmud teaches that it is meritorious to recite 100 blessings each day (Men. 43b). On weekdays, the bulk of this total is accounted for by the thrice-daily recitation of the *Amidah*, which contains 19 blessings. On Sabbaths and festivals, however, the *Amidah* contains only seven blessings. The first three stanzas of *Ein Keloheinu* contain an acrostic that spells out the word "amen" four times in 12 lines. Since "amen" is a response to a blessing, these 12 "blessings" added to the seven in the *Musaf Amidah* results in a total of 19 blessings to help reach the quota.[84]

In this prayer, was the order of the words to describe God chosen for a specific reason? (T)

In *Ein Keloheinu*, God is designated by four different names, which are arranged in the order in which they appear in the Torah: (a) *Elohim* (God), from the first verse describing the Creation in Genesis; (b) *Adon* (Master), first used by Abraham (Gen. 15:2); (c) *Melech* (King), implied in the phrase "the Lord will *reign* for ever and ever" (Exod. 15:18) but first used directly later (Num. 23:21); and (d) *Moshi'ah* (Deliverer), which is implied when Israel is termed "a people *delivered* by the Lord" (Deut. 33:29).[85]

Has the *Aleinu* always been recited at the end of each prayer service? (F)

The *Aleinu* combines the idea of Israel as a Chosen People, with the challenge that this status demands—that Jews exert all possible efforts to perfect mankind under the kingdom of God (*l'takein olam b'malchut Shaddai*). Although *Aleinu* has been recited at the conclusion of every prayer service since the thirteenth century, it was originally used as the introduction to the *Malchuyot* (Kingship) section of the *Musaf Amidah* on Rosh Hasha-nah, which proclaims God's universal sovereignty and stresses the belief in the coming of the day when all human beings will acknowledge Divine rule over the world.

Has the text of the *Aleinu* been the subject of controversy? (T)

The original version of *Aleinu* contained a sentence that was censored during the Inquisition as an implied insult to Christianity. This verse from Isaiah (45:20)—"For they bow to vanity and emptiness and pray to a god which helps not"—appeared just before "but we bend the knee" and was claimed to be a slanderous reference to the Christian trinity. The Jews coun-tered that the objectionable line could not possibly refer to Christianity, since the biblical phrase was pre-Christian and *Aleinu* was composed either well before the time of Jesus or in a non-Christian country. This defense might have succeeded were it not for a Jewish apostate, who "proved" the anti-Christian sentiment of the prayer by demonstrating the coincidental equiv-alence of the numerical value (316) of the Hebrew words *va-rik* (emptiness) and *Yeshu* (Jesus).[86]

Eventually, the offending line was eliminated from Ashkenazic prayer books. The Sephardim, especially in Eastern countries under Moslem rule, retained the full text, despite the tradition that the numerical value of *la-hevel va-rik* (vanity and emptiness) equals that of *Yeshu u-Muhammad* (Jesus and Muhammad). Even in countries where censorship of Jewish prayers no long-er exists, the expurgated sentence of *Aleinu* has generally not been restored in the Ashkenazic text, though it does appear in parentheses in the *ArtScroll Siddur* and some Israeli prayer books.[87]

Have changes been made to the *Aleinu*? (T)

The early Reform movement made substantial cuts in the first paragraph of *Aleinu*, eliminating the lines "for God has not made us like the nations of the lands and has not placed us like the families of the earth; for God has not assigned our portion like theirs nor our lot like all their multitudes." This was a conscious attempt to deny the existence of a special "Jewish Peoplehood" and to stress that Jews, except for their religious practices, were like all other citizens of the countries in which they lived (e.g., "Germans of the Mosaic persuasion"). Recent Reform prayer books have offered the full *Aleinu* as an option.

Is *Adon Olam* part of the bedtime prayers? (T)

Adon Olam (Lord of the World/Eternal Lord), one of the most popular hymns, is an inspiring song of praise attributed to Solomon ibn Gabirol, an eleventh-century Spanish philosopher and liturgical poet. It is generally sung at the conclusion of the Sabbath and festival *Musaf* (additional) services in a variety of musical settings. However, *Adon Olam* also concludes the bedtime prayers, based on its final verses: "Into God's hand I entrust my spirit when I sleep—and I shall awaken! With my spirit shall my body remain. God is with me, I shall not fear."

Is *Yigdal* a polemical hymn? (N)

Based on the Thirteen Principles of Faith of Maimonides, *Yigdal* (Exalted [be the living God]) contains strong polemics against dissidents and sectarian minorities. For example, the phrase, "He is one, and there is no oneness like His," is clearly aimed at Christianity and its doctrine of the trinity. This is accentuated by the following line, "He has no bodily form or physicality." The verse, "He granted His rich gift of prophecy to the men of His choice, in whom He gloried," stresses the exclusive inspiration of the classical biblical prophets of Israel, thus attacking as false any claims of Muhammad and Islam. The line, "God will never alter or change His law for any other," opposed the Christian Bible and the Koran, both of which were claimed to have supplanted the Torah. The verse emphasizing the belief in the resurrection of the dead was directed at the Karaites, a sect that rejected this fundamental concept of rabbinic Judaism as not having been specifically stated in the Five Books of Moses. Finally, the firm belief in the future coming of the Messiah was an attack on the Christians, who asserted that Jesus had ushered in the Messianic Age.

Does the blessing *ha-motzi lechem min ha-aretz* (Who brings forth bread from the earth) apply to products made from wheat? (N)

In addition to wheat, this blessing also is said before eating bread baked from the flour of barley, oats, rye, and spelt. With wheat, these are the five grains mentioned or alluded to in the Torah as indigenous to the Land of Israel. Reciting the single blessing for bread at the beginning of a meal is sufficient for all kinds of food eaten during the meal, except for wine and fresh fruit, which require separate blessings.

Does the blessing *borei pri ha-etz* (Who creates the fruit of the tree) apply to bananas, melons, strawberries, pineapples, and tomatoes? (F)

The criterion for distinguishing fruits from vegetables in terms of the proper blessing to be recited before eating is whether the plant is an annual or perennial. Unlike apples, pears, stone fruits, nuts, and avocados, for which *borei pri ha-etz* is appropriate, bananas, melons, berries, pineapples, and tomatoes come under the blessing for vegetables, which is *borei pri ha-adamah* (Who creates the fruit of the earth).

For wine, is the correct blessing *borei pri ha-gafen*? (N)

Although grapes themselves are considered a fruit for which the blessing *borei pri ha-etz* is appropriate, before consuming grapes in the form of juice or wine, one says *borei pri ha-gafen* (Who creates the fruit of the vine).

However, this blessing does not apply to the fermented juice of other fruits or vegetables, even if it is called "wine," for which the proper blessing is *she-hakol nih'yeh bid'varo* (through Whose word all things were called into being).

Are there different forms of the Grace after Meals? (T)

The full *Birkat ha-Mazon*, consisting of four blessings, is recited only after a meal at which one has eaten bread of an amount at least equivalent to the size of an olive, approximately one ounce by volume. When bread is not eaten, there are two other forms of the Grace after Meals depending on the type of food consumed. After eating food prepared from the five species of grain that are indigenous to the Land of Israel (wheat, barley, rye, oats, and spelt) not in the form of bread, wine, or fruits (grapes, figs, olives, pomegranates, and dates), one recites a short summary of the *Birkat ha-Mazon* in a single benediction, with insertions for the type of food eaten and for special occasions such as the Sabbath or a festival. For any other food, the Grace after Meals consists of a brief benediction generally known by its first two words, *Borei nefashot* (Who creates living things).

Is there an Aramaic version of the *Birkat ha-Mazon*? (T)

The Talmud (Ber. 40b) has transmitted the formula of a blessing of a shepherd named Benjamin, who lived in Babylonia at the beginning of the third century. Possessing no knowledge of Hebrew, he was unable to recite the prescribed Grace after Meals. Instead, he substituted a brief prayer in Aramaic, "Blessed be the All-Merciful, the owner of this bread," which is known today as *B'rich rachamanah*. The Talmud relates that this is the minimum one may recite if strapped for time, as in the example of one who is being pursued by robbers on the highway.[88]

Was the *Birkat ha-Mazon* written during the biblical period? (N)

According to the Talmud, the four blessings of the Grace after Meals arose from different sources (Ber. 48b). The first, which praises God for providing food for all creatures, is attributed to Moses upon receiving manna from Heaven. The second, which expresses thanks for the good land (of Israel) that God has given us, the redemption from Egypt, the covenant of circumcision, and the Revelation of the Torah, was composed by Joshua when he conquered the land of Canaan. The third blessing, consisting of a plea for God's mercy, the rebuilding of Jerusalem, and the restoration of the ancient Temple and the Davidic kingdom, was written by David and Solomon because of their respective roles in making Jerusalem the capital of the Israelite state and building the Temple. The core of the fourth blessing, *ha-Tov v'ha-Meitiv* (Who is good and Who does good) was added by the Rabbis of the Talmud after the unsuccessful rebellion led by Bar Kochba in the second century C.E., in gratitude both for the corpses at Betar not decaying and spreading disease, and for the Romans finally granting the Jews permission to bury them. The last blessing also includes a number of general supplications beginning with the word *ha-Rachaman* (May the Merciful One) and ends with the same prayer for peace (*Oseh Shalom*) that concludes the full *Kaddish*—for only when at peace is it possible to truly enjoy all the other Divine blessings.

Is the *Shehecheyanu* blessing said for all things that are new? (N)

One of the best-known blessings, the *Shehecheyanu* prayer is recited on a variety of joyous occasions and thanks God for having "kept us in life, sustained us, and permitted us to reach this time." It is also said whenever one does something "new" in a given year, such as eating a fruit for the first time in the season, moving into a new house, acquiring new clothes or household effects, or having a reunion with a dear friend whom one has not seen for some time. As an expression of thanksgiving for being alive, however, this blessing was regarded as inappropriate if one's pleasure resulted from harm to animals, whose welfare is an important Jewish principle. Consequently, a *shochet* does not recite *Shehecheyanu* the first time he performs the *mitzvah* of ritual slaughter, since this act requires taking the life of an animal. Similarly, it is customary not to say this blessing when wearing any article made of leather for the first time. [89]

Is it a Jewish custom to give a small sum of money to one setting out on a journey? (T)

This practice transforms the traveler into a *shaliach mitzvah*, an agent responsible for carrying out the *mitzvah* of delivering charitable funds when arriving at his destination. As promised in the Talmud, "Those sent to perform a *mitzvah* are not harmed on their way to do a *mitzvah* or on their return" (Pes. 8b).

Should *Birkat ha-Gomel* be recited after an airplane flight? (N)

Birkat ha-Gomel (He who bestows [good]) is a thanksgiving blessing recited by a person who has been saved from a life-threatening situation. According to the Talmud, it must be said by anyone who has recovered from a major illness, has completed a sea voyage or a hazardous land journey, or has been released from prison or captivity (Ber. 54b). It can also be said by an entire community that has been delivered from a potential calamity.

In modern times, there is debate over whether one should recite *Birkat ha-Gomel* after every airplane flight. Proponents of this view argue that air travel, like a sea voyage, entails separation from the earth (with its increased inherent dangers), so that it is appropriate to offer a prayer of thanksgiving for arriving safely. Other authorities object to everyday use of this blessing, preferring to reserve *Birkat ha-Gomel* for when a person wants to thank God for being saved from a dangerous situation.

NOTES

1. Trepp, 15.
2. Hammer, *Entering Jewish Prayer*, 62.
3. Millgram, *Jewish Worship*, 63.
4. Hammer, *Entering Jewish Prayer*, 65–70.
5. Millgram, *Jewish Worship*, 64–67.
6. Frankel and Teutsch, 167.
7. Millgram, *Jewish Worship*, 551.
8. Ibid., 336.
9. Steinsaltz, 197.
10. Sperling, 83.
11. Millgram, *Jewish Worship*, 340.
12. Kolatch, *This Is the Torah*, 82–83.
13. Frankel and Teutsch, 179–80.
14. Cohen, 170.
15. Maimonides, *Mishneh Torah*, Sefer Torah 7:9.
16. Kolatch, *This Is the Torah*, 106–9.
17. Hammer, *Entering Jewish Prayer*, 8.
18. Heschel, *Man's Quest for God*, 13.
19. Millgram, *Jewish Worship*, 31.
20. Ibid., 26–27.
21. Ibid., 28.
22. Ibid., 32–34.
23. Trepp, 23.
24. Millgram, *Jewish Worship*, 359.
25. The Rabbis interpreted the phrase *eit ratzon* (favorable time [for prayer]) in Ps. 69:14 as meaning that God is most receptive to prayer "when the congregation is praying."
26. Donin, *To Pray as a Jew*, 14–16.
27. Cohen, 46–48.
28. Millgram, *Jewish Worship*, 611.
29. Donin, *To Be a Jew*, 180.
30. Sperling, 20.
31. Frankel and Teutsch, 91.
32. The Rabbis noted that the numerical value of the Hebrew word *tzitzit* (fringes) is 600. When combined with the eight threads and five knots on each fringe, this adds up to 613—the precise number of *mitzvot* in the Torah. Thus, by looking at the fringes we are to "remember all the Lord's commands and obey them" (Num. 15:39).
33. Maimonides, *Mishneh Torah*, Tzitzit 3:9.
34. Kolatch, *The Jewish Book of Why*, 105.
35. *Etz Hayim*, 1469.
36. Millgram, *Jewish Worship*, 91.
37. Once R. Akiva came to a certain town and looked for lodgings but was everywhere refused. Consequently, "he went and spent the night in the open field. He had with him a cock, an ass, and a lamp. A gust of wind came and blew out the lamp, a weasel came and ate the cock, a lion came and ate the ass. He said: 'Whatever the All-Merciful does is for good.'" Later, R. Akiva learned that on the same night some robbers came and carried off the inhabitants of the town!
38. Donin, *To Pray as a Jew*, 66.
39. Maimonides, *Mishneh Torah*, Berachot 1:13.
40. Donin, *To Pray as a Jew*, 227.
41. The person who recites the original blessing and the one who responds "amen" are considered equal partners in praising God. By raising his voice, the latter would be unjustifiably attempting to assume a more important role in the partnership.
42. Shlomo Riskin, "From Curse to Blessing," *International Jerusalem Post* (July 6, 2001), 39.

43. Millgram, *Jewish Worship*, 144.
44. *ArtScroll Siddur*, 91; Sperling, 42.
45. *ArtScroll Siddur*, 90.
46. Ibid., 28.
47. Donin, *To Pray as a Jew*, 147–48.
48. Millgram, Jewish Prayer, 105–6.
49. Cohen, 40.
50. *ArtScroll Siddur*, 107.
51. Donin, *To Pray as a Jew*, 71.
52. Cohen, 11.
53. Gelbard, 18.
54. *ArtScroll Siddur*, 99.
55. Gelbard, 10.
56. Millgram, *Jewish Worship*, 358–59.
57. *ArtScroll Kaddish*, 46.
58. Millgram, *Jewish Worship*, 139.
59. Ibid., 608.
60. There is no unanimity among scholars as to the precise correlation of the Thirteen Attributes with the biblical text.
61. Cohen, 190.
62. Because of their relative length, Torah portions from the Book of Genesis are never combined, since this would extend the service unduly and violate the Jewish legal principle against imposing unnecessary inconvenience on the congregation.
63. Cohen, 181–82.
64. Kolatch, *This Is the Torah*, 74.
65. Cohen, 186–87.
66. Kolatch, *This Is the Torah*, 167–68.
67. Ibid., 350.
68. Ibid.
69. Millgram, *Jewish Worship*, 110.
70. Ibid., 109.
71. Kolatch, *This Is the Torah*, 188–89.
72. Millgram, *Jewish Worship*, 183–84.
73. Kolatch, *This Is the Torah*, 137, 144–45.
74. Ibid., 46, 135.
75. Ibid., 131–32.
76. Millgram, *Jewish Worship*, 113–14.
77. Cohen, 190.
78. Donin, *To Pray as a Jew*, 248.
79. Cohen, 199.
80. Ibid., 196–97.
81. Donin, *To Pray as a Jew*, 242.
82. Kolatch, *This Is the Torah*, 199.
83. *Etz Hayim*, 1486–90.
84. Witty and Witty, 181.
85. Ibid., 214–15.
86. Millgram, *Jewish Worship*, 455–56.
87. *ArtScroll Siddur*, 158–59.
88. "Brich rachamana," August 21, 2008, http://velveteenrabbi.blogs.com/blog/2008/08/brich-rachamana.html (accessed January 19, 2015).
89. Cohen, 134.

Chapter Nine

Life Cycle Events

Have you ever wondered . . .

1. Is circumcision performed on the eighth day of life?
2. Is there a medical reason to perform a circumcision on the eighth day?
3. Is a professional *mohel* necessary to perform a circumcision?
4. Is a male child not Jewish until he is circumcised?
5. Are godparents an essential part of the circumcision ceremony?
6. In some traditional homes, is there a special ceremony the night before a circumcision?
7. Is circumcision the only celebration within the first eight days after the birth of a male child?
8. Do some Jews celebrate the birth of a girl with a *Simchat Bat*?
9. Did Jews have no family names until the Emancipation?
10. In Jewish tradition, is a child named for a person who has died?
11. Is a male baby named at his *brit milah* (circumcision ceremony)?
12. Do Jews never change their names?
13. Are firstborn sons required to have a *pidyon ha-ben*?
14. Is the religious status of an adopted child based on that of the adopting family?
15. Is bar mitzvah a biblical ritual?
16. Is a boy permitted to lead a service or be called up to the Torah prior to his bar mitzvah?
17. Does the bar mitzvah take place in the month in which the boy was born?
18. Can a bar mitzvah ceremony occur at a time other than a Sabbath morning?

19. At a traditional bar mitzvah, does the father give thanks that God will no longer punish him for the misbehavior of his son?
20. Does a man who did not have a bar mitzvah at age 13 need an "adult bar mitzvah"?
21. Is bat mitzvah a modern American tradition?
22. Is confirmation a ceremony rooted in Talmudic tradition?
23. Is the confirmation ceremony held on a special Sabbath?
24. Is wishing that someone will live to 120 based on the life span of Abraham, the first Jew?
25. Does *halachah* discourage conversion to Judaism?
26. When approached by persons who wish to convert to Judaism, are most contemporary rabbis supportive?
27. Is it permitted to convert in order to marry a Jew?
28. Is there a uniform practice for Jewish conversion?
29. Are there special rules for conversion of a child to Judaism?
30. If a woman converts while pregnant, does the child require conversion?
31. Are converts to Judaism treated as second-class citizens?
32. Do converts to Judaism have special names?
33. Is a Jew who adopts another religion no longer a Jew?
34. Did the Rabbis believe that celibacy was a higher state than marriage?
35. Is there a Jewish tradition that "marriages are made in Heaven"?
36. Was it once the custom for the marriage ceremony to occur on more than one day?
37. Is *kiddushin* the equivalent of a betrothal?
38. Does *kiddushin* involve the giving of a ring?
39. Are there other ways to perform *kiddushin*?
40. May the groom use his mother's wedding ring for *kiddushin*?
41. Does the groom place the wedding ring on the fourth finger of the bride's left hand?
42. Is the *bedeken (di kalla)* ceremony an ancient custom?
43. Are weddings performed in venues other than the synagogue?
44. Is Sunday the ideal day for a Jewish wedding?
45. Are there other times when weddings are not performed?
46. Is the *aufruf* before the wedding principally designed to give the groom an *aliyah*?
47. Do Jewish grooms traditionally have a bachelor party on the night before the wedding?
48. Is all music appropriate for the wedding procession?
49. Is the tradition for the bride to make a circle around the groom based on magic?
50. Is throwing rice and sweets at the newly married couple a Jewish tradition?

51. Is the *ketubah* a mere formality with no legal significance?
52. In rabbinic times, were cedar and pine trees associated with weddings?
53. Does breaking the glass under the *chuppah* at the wedding ceremony commemorate the destruction of the Temple?
54. Must a rabbi be present for a marriage to be legally binding under Jewish law?
55. Is a *minyan* required for a wedding?
56. Does the newly married couple consummate their marriage immediately after the ceremony?
57. Would some biblical marriages be invalid according to current Jewish law?
58. Is sex in marriage something that a husband demands and a wife must fulfill?
59. Does the husband have any other obligations toward his wife?
60. Does the word *mamzer* mean someone born out of wedlock?
61. Does Jewish law forbid bigamy?
62. Are there exceptions to the prohibition of bigamy?
63. Is a surviving brother obligated to marry the widow of his brother who died without having sired children?
64. Is levirate marriage the preferred solution?
65. Is intermarriage legal under Jewish law?
66. May the parents in a mixed marriage choose whether their children are considered Jews?
67. Has the principle of patrilineal descent affected the rate of conversion to Judaism?
68. Does Jewish law forbid birth control?
69. Are women obligated to have children?
70. Can failure to procreate lead to a divorce?
71. Is artificial insemination permitted under Jewish law?
72. Is it a biblical duty to honor one's parents?
73. Is the order of the parents the same in both versions of the Ten Commandments?
74. Does Judaism correlate the relationship with parents to that with God?
75. Should a child violate the Sabbath to fulfill a parental request?
76. May a doctor perform surgery on a parent?
77. According to the Talmud, does a father have specific obligations toward his son?
78. Does Jewish law permit a parent to favor one child more than another?
79. To obtain a divorce, does the couple have to go before a religious court?

80. Is having the husband give a *get* to his wife all that is required for a Jewish couple to be divorced?
81. Can a woman sue for Jewish divorce?
82. Can a woman be divorced against her will?
83. Are the rules of divorce on the grounds of adultery different for men and women?
84. According to rabbinic courts, is custody of the children usually awarded to the mother after a divorce?
85. According to Jewish law, are both parties free to marry anyone they wish after a divorce?
86. Are the parties free to marry at any time after a divorce?
87. May an amicably divorced couple remain together in their house?
88. Does delivery of a *get* immediately end the marriage?
89. After three years, is a missing husband presumed dead so that his wife is permitted to remarry?
90. Are two witnesses required to establish that a missing husband has died?
91. Is circumstantial evidence sufficient in the case of a husband suspected of being deceased?
92. Is a rabbi required to officiate at a funeral?
93. According to Jewish law, should the dead be buried in their best clothes?
94. To honor the dead, is an expensive, water-tight coffin used?
95. Except for the body of the deceased, are Jewish coffins empty?
96. Can burial traditionally be performed at any time after death?
97. Is viewing the body a Jewish practice?
98. Is sending flowers to the bereaved a Jewish practice?
99. Is there an obligation to do anything as a funeral procession passes by?
100. At the cemetery, does the funeral procession stop as it proceeds to the grave site?
101. Once the coffin is placed into the grave, should those present remain?
102. Is anything said to the mourners at the grave site?
103. May a *kohen* participate in a funeral?
104. Do pregnant women attend funerals?
105. Are Ashkenazic and Sephardic tombstones different?
106. Is there a standard epitaph for Jewish tombstones?
107. Is the ceremony unveiling the headstone an old custom?
108. Is there a specific time for consecrating the grave marker?
109. Should mourners wear black clothing?
110. Is *keriah* an ancient tradition?
111. Is *keriah* performed at the moment of death?

112. Does the mourning period last seven days?
113. Is the meal of consolation after the funeral prepared by the bereaved family?
114. Are there special foods appropriate for the meal of consolation?
115. Do mourners primarily observe *shivah* to honor the dead?
116. Must all the shoes and clothing of the deceased be thrown out?
117. Does *shivah* last seven days?
118. May friends of the bereaved visit them any time during the *shivah* period?
119. Do mourners sit on low stools or benches during *shivah* so that they are uncomfortable during this period of intense mourning?
120. When making a *shivah* call, are visitors expected to greet the mourners with words of sympathy?
121. May a mourner leave the house during *shivah*?
122. Is there a *shivah minyan* for all seven days?
123. Is a *shivah minyan* different from the service in the synagogue?
124. Should a mourner who is mistakenly called up to the Torah during *shivah* refuse the *aliyah*?
125. Does Jewish law require that mirrors be covered in a house where mourners are sitting *shivah*?
126. Does the *yahrzeit* correspond to the day of death on the secular calendar?
127. Is *Yizkor* a communal service?
128. Is recitation of the *Kaddish* a part of the *Yizkor* service?
129. Should those whose parents are alive leave the synagogue for *Yizkor*?
130. Does Jewish law forbid an autopsy after death?
131. May the ashes of a cremated person be buried in a Jewish cemetery?
132. Is a person who commits suicide denied a Jewish burial?
133. Are suicides buried in a special section of the cemetery?
134. Is euthanasia forbidden under Jewish law?
135. Can any amount of medication be administered to relieve pain?
136. Is assisted suicide permitted in Jewish law?
137. Does Jewish law permit organ donation?
138. According to Jewish thought, does cessation of brain function indicate the time of death?
139. Is Judaism concerned only with this life, not with what may happen after one dies?
140. Is the concept of resurrection a Christian belief and not part of Jewish thought?
141. Is there a Jewish belief in transmigration of souls?
142. Is faith the basic requirement for entry into the World to Come?

143. Does the Talmud specify requirements for entry into the World to Come?

144. According to Jewish tradition, while still alive is it possible to have a foretaste of the World to Come?

~~~

Is circumcision performed on the eighth day of life? (N)

Circumcision (*brit milah*) is traditionally performed on the eighth day, with the day of birth counting as the first day. This is the case even if the eighth day falls on the Sabbath, Yom Kippur, or a festival, though if the boy was born by caesarean section, the circumcision is postponed to the next weekday. The primary reason for delaying circumcision is the health of the infant. A delay also may be justified by the unavailability of a *mohel* on a Sabbath or holiday because of the need to travel. If the baby is premature or in poor health, it is necessary to delay the circumcision until seven days after he has recovered, though in this case it is not performed on the Sabbath or a holiday.

Is there a medical reason to perform a circumcision on the eighth day? (T)

Although observed as a Divine commandment, there actually is a good medical reason for this practice. In a newborn, the factor that allows blood to clot does not mature until about the eighth day. Performing a circumcision before this time could result in the infant bleeding to death. [1]

Is a professional *mohel* necessary to perform a circumcision? (F)

According to Jewish law, the father is responsible for having his son circumcised, and thus would be the best person to perform the procedure. However, because most Jewish fathers do not have the technical expertise, it is usually necessary to hire a professional *mohel* who is specially trained in the medical procedure and is familiar with the Jewish ritual. In more liberal or more remote communities where *mohalim* are not readily available, a physician may be called on to perform the circumcision while a rabbi conducts the ritual. However, circumcision may be performed by any Jew, including a woman if no male is available. [2]

Is a male child not Jewish until he is circumcised? (N)

Circumcision is not a requirement for membership in the Jewish people. Any male child born of a Jewish mother is a Jew, whether circumcised or not. The Hebrew word *brit* means "covenant," and thus circumcision is the procedure that formally symbolizes the entry of the infant boy into the covenant that God made with the patriarch Abraham almost 4,000 years ago.

Unlike a child born to a Jewish mother, an uncircumcised male candidate for conversion to Judaism cannot be considered Jewish until he is circumcised. If he has already been circumcised, or cannot undergo the procedure for health reasons, a drop of blood is taken from the penis as a symbol of circumcision (*hatafat dam brit*; "shedding the blood of the covenant").

Are godparents an essential part of the circumcision ceremony? (F)

As a prelude to the circumcision ritual, the child is brought into the room by the *kvater* and *kvaterin*, Polish-Yiddish terms often translated as godfather and godmother. However, the idea of godparents in the Western sense is foreign to Judaism, which does not have the Christian concept of godparents as individuals who are responsible for the spiritual upbringing of the child in the church.

In some traditional homes, is there a special ceremony the night before a circumcision? (T)

Leil Shimurim (Night of Watching) is a home ceremony the night preceding a circumcision. It probably developed because friends and relatives, who were visiting the new parents, commonly joined the *mohel* on his rounds as he checked on the health of the infant. Later, this custom reflected the perceived need to guard the newborn throughout the night against malevolent spirits, especially Lilith. In the glow of candlelight (because evil spirits were said to avoid light), a festive meal featuring cooked beans and peas (to scare away demons) was eaten, and the participants held a vigil around the crib reciting prayers and studying Torah.

Is circumcision the only celebration within the first eight days after the birth of a male child? (F)

Shalom zachar (lit., "peace to the male child") is the Hebrew term for a joyous celebration in some traditional Ashkenazic households on the first Friday evening after the birth of a boy. Guests visit the new baby's home to join the family in prayer, a festive meal, and Torah study.[3] According to the Talmud, the ceremony of *shalom zachar* developed during the Roman Empire, when Jews were forbidden to circumcise their sons. A feast was held shortly after the child's birth in an attempt to convince the Romans that no circumcision was to follow on the eighth day.

Do some Jews celebrate the birth of a girl with a *Simchat Bat*? (T)

Literally "Rejoicing for a Daughter," this custom of celebrating the birth of a girl on her eighth day of life (or later) in a home gathering has developed in liberal and some modern Orthodox circles. In the absence of established ritual, the parents often design a personalized celebration. Many include passages from Song of Songs and Psalms, as well as biblical selections featuring such famous women as the four matriarchs (Sarah, Rebecca, Rachel, and Leah) and the seven prophetesses (Sarah, Miriam, Deborah, Hannah, Abigail, Huldah, and Esther), followed by a special blessing over wine and a festive meal.[4]

Did Jews have no family names until the Emancipation? (T)

Before the Emancipation, Jews possessed only the Hebrew name given to a boy on the occasion of his *brit milah* (circumcision) and to a girl when her father was honored with an *aliyah* in the synagogue shortly after her birth. A person's complete Hebrew name is his or her first name (and middle name) followed by *ben* (son of) or *bat* (daughter of) and then the first (and middle) name of the father (and in some instances, with inclusion of the mother's Hebrew name). If the father is a *kohen* or *levi*, the child's name ends with the word *ha-Kohen* or *ha-Levi*. Even today, these Hebrew names are used during Jewish ceremonies and rituals—when called to the Torah for an *aliyah*, on the *ketubah* (marriage document), and in a special memorial prayer at the funeral and later engraved on the gravestone in the cemetery.[5]

In Jewish tradition, is a child named for a person who has died? (N)

Ashkenazim generally name a child for a deceased relative, both to perpetuate that person's memory and in the hope that the child will manifest the spiritual qualities of the beloved who is no longer alive. In contrast, among Sephardim it is customary to name children after living relatives, particularly the grandparents.

Is a male baby named at his *brit milah* (circumcision ceremony)? (N)

Traditionally, a Jewish boy is named at his circumcision on the eighth day of life. However, at times the *brit milah* must be delayed for health reasons, such as when the baby is premature or suffers from severe neonatal jaundice. In these cases, the baby may be given a name before the circumcision. This practice allows for prayers for his speedy recovery to be recited in the baby's name.

Do Jews never change their names? (F)

In the *shtetls* of Eastern Europe (and even today), when a person was seriously ill, members of the community would change the person's name as a last desperate measure. They reasoned that if God had ordained that a person by the name of David was to die, the Divine judgment might not extend to an individual by the name of Moses. (Another reason for this practice was an attempt to confuse the Angel of Death.) A copy of the Hebrew Scripture would be opened at random, and the sick person would be given the name of the first meritorious Jew that appeared. Charity would be donated on behalf of the invalid, along with a blessing for recovery. If the patient recovered, the individual would continue to carry the new name. Although a superstition, this practice reflected the Jewish belief that God was waiting for only a loophole to extend Divine mercy.[6]

Are firstborn sons required to have a *pidyon ha-ben*? (N)

As a consequence of the miracle of the 10th plague, when God killed all the firstborn males in Egypt but passed over those of the Israelites, the firstborn son was to be dedicated to God and perform religious services for the *kohanim* in the Temple (Num. 3:13). However, it was possible to free a firstborn male from this obligation by redeeming him through the payment to the *kohen* (as the representative of God) of five silver coins, originally *shekels* but today most often five silver dollars or coins of the country. *Pidyon ha-ben* (redemption of the firstborn) takes place on the 31st day after the child's birth (with the day of birth counting as the first day), or the next day if the 31st day falls on the Sabbath or a festival, when all business transactions are prohibited.

Pidyon ha-ben is performed only if the firstborn son "is the first to open the mother's womb" (Exod. 13:1). Thus, this ritual does not apply to a boy who was delivered by Caesarean section, or to a second boy who was subsequently delivered normally. Similarly, it is not performed if the mother had previously miscarried or had an abortion of a fetus that existed more than 40 days *in utero*. The first son of a Jewish mother must be redeemed, even if he has an older half-brother born to the father from a previous marriage. Conversely, it is not necessary to redeem a son who is the firstborn of the father but not the mother. Thus, if a man marries a woman who already has a child from a previous marriage, any son issuing from their marriage need not be redeemed.

The redemption ceremony of *pidyon ha-ben* is not performed if the father or the maternal grandfather is a *kohen* or *levi*, since in this case the child would have been obligated to serve in the Temple and could not be exempted.

Is the religious status of an adopted child based on that of the adopting family? (F)

According to Jewish religious law, the status of an adopted child is entirely hereditary and based on the natural (not the adopting) parents. Although adopted children may assume the name of their new family, the privileges and obligations of being a *kohen* or a *levi* depend solely upon birth. Conversely, children born to a *kohen* or *levi* retain this classification regardless of the status of their adopted family. An adopted child who is not definitely known to be Jewish must undergo formal conversion to be considered a Jew.

Is bar mitzvah a biblical ritual? (F)

The special synagogue observance of the bar mitzvah as it is known today did not exist during biblical or rabbinic times. In the Bible, the age of 13 was not even recognized as a major milestone in a boy's life. Instead, the primary age of significance was 20, when a male was fit for military service, counted in the census, and obligated to give a half *shekel* for the upkeep of the Temple.

Is a boy permitted to lead a service or be called up to the Torah prior to his bar mitzvah? (N)

Today, a boy is first allowed to participate in and perform the various rituals associated with full membership in the Jewish community (wearing *tallit* and *tefillin*, leading the congregation in prayer, or being called up for an *aliyah* to the Torah) at his bar mitzvah. In earlier times, however, a child under 13 was permitted to perform these rituals if he understood their significance and was considered capable of doing them. The Talmud explicitly states: "If a minor knows how to wrap himself in the *tallit*, he is subject to the obligation . . . if he knows how to look after *tefillin*, his father must acquire them for him" (Ar. 2a). Similarly, if knowledgeable, he was qualified to be called up to read from the Torah. Therefore, many young boys had performed these activities on numerous occasions before their 13th birthdays, so that there was effectively no religious distinction between minor and adult in Talmudic times. At some time during the Middle Ages, however, minors were deprived of these religious rights. This served to heighten the significance and momentous nature of reaching the age of 13.

Does the bar mitzvah take place in the month in which the boy was born? (N)

Traditionally, the bar mitzvah takes place on or soon after the boy's 13th birthday according to the Jewish calendar, which is based on the cycles of the moon (lunar) rather than the secular solar calendar. Consequently, a child born in one month of the secular calendar may have his 13th birthday in the month preceding or following it. In synagogues with large numbers of bar (and bat) mitzvahs each year, the event may take place several months from the boy's 13th birthday.

Can a bar mitzvah ceremony occur at a time other than a Sabbath morning? (T)

A bar mitzvah ceremony usually occurs on Saturday morning, since it features the boy being called up to the Torah for his first *aliyah* to read the *maftir* portion and then chant the *haftarah*. However, it can take place whenever the Torah is read. Therefore, a bar mitzvah can be celebrated on Saturday afternoon, Monday or Thursday morning, Rosh Chodesh (New Moon), or a festival when reading the Torah takes place (though there is no *haftarah* reading on Saturday afternoon or on Monday or Thursday morning).

At a traditional bar mitzvah, does the father give thanks that God will no longer punish him for the misbehavior of his son? (T)

After the bar mitzvah boy concludes the second Torah blessing, it is customary in Orthodox synagogues for his father to declare: "Praised is

[God] who has relieved me from punishment because of this child [when he misbehaved]" (Gen. R. 63:10). The reason for saying this blessing (known as *baruch she-petarani*) is that before age 13, it is the responsibility of the father to make certain that his son studies Torah and performs *mitzvot*. However, once the boy reaches the age of maturity, this becomes the son's personal responsibility. Thereafter, if the son fails to pursue Torah studies, the father is exempt from any spiritual punishment resulting from this sin of omission.[7]

Does a man who did not have a bar mitzvah at age 13 need an "adult bar mitzvah"? (N)

It has now become common for Jews who were denied religious training in their childhood to celebrate a bar mitzvah (or bat mitzvah) as adults as a symbol of their full membership in the Jewish community. Although these ceremonies are moving experiences, and the extensive preparatory study is praiseworthy, the essence of the bar (or bat) mitzvah is only the *age* of the individual. The transition to legal and religious responsibility is automatic and does not depend on any special initiation rites that provide a public declaration of that status.

Is bat mitzvah a modern American tradition? (N)

The first bat mitzvah celebrated in conjunction with a worship service occurred in 1922 and featured Judith Kaplan, the daughter of Rabbi Morde-cai Kaplan, then a professor at the Jewish Theological Seminary and later the founder of the Reconstructionist movement. In contemporary egalitarian congregations, most young women at age 12 or 13 have a ceremony identical to the bar mitzvah for boys.

In Orthodox synagogues, where women do not have the same ritual obligations and privileges as men (such as being counted in the *minyan* or being called up to the Torah for an *aliyah*), there traditionally was no need for girls to have a formal ceremony like the bar mitzvah.[8] Nevertheless, by the nineteenth century, some families celebrated a girl's 12th birthday, according to the Jewish calendar, with a special meal (*se'udat mitzvah*) and other non-synagogue rituals. Among modern Orthodox today, girls may have a Bat Torah and perform synagogue rituals for a women's *minyan*.

Is confirmation a ceremony rooted in Talmudic tradition? (F)

For centuries, the bar mitzvah celebrated a boy's 13th birthday (according to the Jewish calendar), when he officially attained his legal and religious majority. Upon reaching this age, he was obliged to fulfill all the Divinely mandated commandments and observe the religious duties incumbent on a Jew. With the dawning of the Enlightenment and the rise of the Reform movement in Germany in the early decades of the nineteenth century, the cultural assumptions changed radically. The classic ritual observances of the commandments were denounced as "obsolete oriental rites" and no longer considered the essence of Judaism. Instead, the focus of Reform was solely on the ethical and moral tenets of Judaism. Consequently, they eliminated the bar mitzvah based only on physical age and replaced it with a coming of age on intellectual grounds. They adopted the Lutheran idea of confirmation as a new life cycle event commemorating the mastery of the basic beliefs of the faith that enable the young adult to become a full member of the community.

Unlike bar mitzvah, confirmation was conceived as a group ceremony celebrated by both male and female religious school students at the completion of their studies at age 16. Today, especially in the United States, confirmation has been adopted in some synagogues as a supplement to, rather than a substitute for, the bar/bat mitzvah ceremony. The main intention of confirmation is to extend Jewish education by several years, enhancing the commitment of young people to Judaism. Some religious schools attempt to have confirmation around age 18 to coincide with the senior year of high school.

Is the confirmation ceremony held on a special Sabbath? (F)

The confirmation ceremony is generally held on Shavuot, the holiday celebrating the giving of the Torah on Mount Sinai, since confirmation students symbolically accept the Torah during the ceremony and publicly declare their devotion to Jewish ideals.

Is wishing that someone will live to 120 based on the life span of Abraham, the first Jew? (F)

Abraham lived for 175 years (Gen. 25:7–10). The popular expression wishing another person to live "until 120" is based on the life span of Moses (Deut. 34:7). To reach this age is to be granted not only the great gift of length of days, but also the supreme honor of being linked to the life of the most revered figure in Jewish history. [9]

Does *halachah* discourage conversion to Judaism? (N)

Throughout much of its history, Judaism has always been open to accepting converts. However, there has been significant variation in the extent to which conversions took place and the response of the established Jewish community to these new Jews-by-Choice.

The Talmud and Midrash make multiple references to conversion, demonstrating both positive and negative attitudes to the practice. Rabbi Eliezer states, "When a person comes to you in sincerity to be converted do not reject him, but on the contrary encourage him." [10] As the Talmud (Pes. 87b) notes, "the Holy One, Blessed be He, exiled Israel among the nations so that proselytes might join them." One passage praises those who have converted to Judaism as "dearer to God than all of the Israelites who stood at Mount Sinai. Had the Israelites not witnessed the lightning, thunder, quaking mountain, and sounding trumpets, they would not have accepted the Torah. But the convert, who did not see or hear any of these things, came and surrendered to

God and accepted the yoke of Heaven. Can anyone be dearer to God than such a person?"[11]

Nevertheless, some authorities were extremely opposed to the concept of conversion. The Rabbis expressed concern about the true motivation of potential converts, indicating that none were accepted during the reigns of King David and King Solomon because it was suspected that they might be converting only for financial gain. The bitter experience of Jews with proselytes in times of war and revolt influenced the negative attitude to conversion. Proselytes and their offspring became renegades and informers, often slandering their new religion and denouncing the Jewish community and its leaders to foreign rulers. The Midrash urged that Jews "not trust a convert, even to the 24th generation, because the inherent evil is still within him" (Ruth Zutra 1:12). One sage went so far as to state that "converts are as hard for Israel [to endure] as a sore" (Yev. 47b).

During the Middle Ages, most Jews resided in countries dominated by Islamic or Christian rule. Both of these monotheistic religions strongly condemned those who abandoned their faith, regarding it as a capital offense. Thus conversion to Judaism decreased substantially. With the Emancipation in the nineteenth century, most Jewish communities were reluctant to accept converts, especially since the laws of many European countries prohibited this practice. In the twentieth century, North American Jews took a more tolerant view of those wishing to convert. This initially was most evident among Reform Jews and later spread to all movements. The increased acceptance of converts reflected both the significant rise in the rate of intermarriage and the tolerance of the general society toward Judaism. Converts to Judaism are now commonly referred to as Jews-by-Choice, stressing that they freely elected to join the Jewish people. This avoids the terms "convert" and "proselyte," which can be viewed as derogatory or as being associated with Christianity.

When approached by persons who wish to convert to Judaism, are most contemporary rabbis supportive? (N)

Many rabbis follow the tradition of discouraging potential converts three times by pointing out the difficulties they might face as a Jew, the obstacles to be overcome in casting their lot with the Jewish people, and the new responsibilities they would have to assume (Yev. 47b; Ger. 1:1–2).[12] According to the Midrash (Ruth R. 2:1), this threefold act of discouragement is based on the three times that Naomi tried to dissuade Ruth, the most famous biblical convert, from returning with her to the Land of Israel. However, if potential converts still persist they are received, for one should "always discourage with the left hand and draw near with the right."[13] Other rabbis prefer to be more encouraging to a prospective Jew, while at the same time asking many questions to determine the person's sincerity.

228   *Chapter 9*

Is it permitted to convert in order to marry a Jew? (N)

Many of those wishing to convert to Judaism do so in order to marry a Jew. Traditionally, this has been considered an invalid motive. Rabbis only permitted conversion to those seeking admission to the Jewish people on the basis of sincere conviction, who pledged full and unreserved commitment to all the laws of Judaism.[14] Although some rabbis still refuse to convert a person whose decision is based solely on an upcoming marriage to a Jew, most rabbis will agree to work with the individual if they are convinced that he or she has a strong desire to become Jewish.

Is there a uniform practice for Jewish conversion? (N)

The conversion process consists primarily of a period of study, ranging from several months to a few years, which includes private or group classes on Jewish history, beliefs and prayers, holidays, life cycle ceremonies, and home rituals. Many rabbis require that a convert learn basic Hebrew; in Orthodox conversions, there is an emphasis on the specific requirements of Jewish law. In addition to study, prospective converts begin to adopt a Jewish lifestyle, such as attending synagogue services; observing the Sabbath, festivals, and dietary laws; and performing acts of *tzedakah* and *gemilut chasadim*.[15] Traditionally, the prospective convert appears before a *beit din*, a court of three rabbis, which asks the candidate a variety of questions to test basic Jewish knowledge and commitment to Jewish beliefs, ethics, and ritual observances. In Orthodox and Conservative conversions, the next steps in the process are the rituals of circumcision for males and immersion in the *mikveh* (ritual bath) for both men and women (Yev. 46). If a man has already been circumcised, a drop of blood is taken from the penis as a symbol of circumcision (*hatafat dam brit*). Neither circumcision nor immersion in the *mikveh* is required by the Reform movement. In Israel, conversions may be performed only by Orthodox rabbis.

Are there special rules for conversion of a child to Judaism? (T)

As with adults, conversion consists of immersion in a *mikveh* and, for boys, circumcision or *hatafat dam brit*. However, conversion must be voluntary, and a young child obviously cannot knowingly choose. Therefore, the rabbis ruled that the child of a non-Jewish mother who is adopted by Jewish parents is converted *al da'at beit din* (by the advice and consent of the court). The *Shulchan Aruch* allows this practice, considering it a "privilege" for a child to be converted to Judaism (YD 268:7). However, at the age of bar or bat mitzvah, any child may choose to annul the conversion, though it must be done promptly (Ket. 11).[16]

If a woman converts while pregnant, does the child require conversion? (F)

The child of a woman who converts while pregnant does not require conversion, even if the conception occurred before the conversion, since at the time of birth the mother was already Jewish.[17] *Klein*   *260*

Are converts to Judaism treated as second-class citizens? (F)

A Jew-by-Choice has virtually the same rights as a Jew by birth[18] and becomes a full member of the Jewish community. It is forbidden to taunt converts by reminding them of their non-Jewish past and suggesting that this makes them unfit to study God's Torah. As the *Sifra* states: "Do not say to him: 'Yesterday you worshiped idols, and now you have come under the wings of the *Shechinah* [Divine Presence].'"[19]

Do converts to Judaism have special names? (T)

One difference from a person born a Jew is that the Hebrew name a convert selects includes the phrase *ben* (son of) or *bat* (daughter of) *Avraham*, the first Jew (some congregations use *Avraham Avinu* [our father]. Those communities that include the name of the mother also insert *ben* or *bat* Sarah. This indicates that the person is a convert who has terminated all formal family ties and "is considered a newly born child" in the religious sense (Yev. 48b).

Is a Jew who adopts another religious no longer a Jew? (N)

A Jew who has rejected Judaism and converted to another religion is termed an apostate. Judaism differentiates between a person who voluntarily abandoned the faith and one who was forced to convert. Whether the former still remains a Jew has been the subject of intense controversy. The standard precedent for centuries has been the Talmudic dictum, "A Jew, even if he has sinned, remains a Jew [according to *halachah*]" (Sanh. 44a). According to this view, Jewish identity is not a matter of personal choice. Nevertheless, many authorities totally rejected this view, convinced that a person who has left Judaism and joined another religious faith can no longer be considered a Jew. Even if apostates technically remain Jews, in certain respects they are treated as if they were no longer Jewish. For example, according to Jewish law, apostates are not considered reliable witnesses (since they have renounced the authority of the Torah), and they cannot inherit their father's estate. Their Jewish relatives do not observe the laws of mourning for them.

Did the Rabbis believe that celibacy was a higher state than marriage? (F)

Unlike the Christians of the rabbinic era, who regarded celibacy as the ideal and marriage as merely a concession to humankind's weakness and libidinous nature, the Rabbis championed marriage, including its sexual aspects, as the essential human relationship and basic to a healthy life. As the Talmud observes, "One who does not have a wife lives without joy, without blessing and without goodness" (Yev. 62b). Sexual desire, when properly channeled in the marriage relationship, was a powerful positive force, rather than an emotion that was inherently shameful or evil: "Were it not for the *yetzer ha-ra* ['evil inclination'; used here for the sexual urge], no man would build a house, marry a wife, or beget children" (Gen. R. 9:7). The person at risk for transgression was rather the unmarried man who "spends all his days in sinful thoughts" (Kid. 29b).

Is there a Jewish tradition that "marriages are made in Heaven"? (T)

According to the Talmud, marriages are preordained by Heaven. "Forty days before the birth of a child, a voice in heaven announces: 'The daughter of so-and-so will marry the son of so-and-so'" (Sot. 2a). The mystical *Zohar* maintained that each soul is created both male and female, divided before birth and ultimately reunited when a man and woman marry.[20] The Yiddish term *bashert* (lit., "fate" or "destiny") refers to this concept of a destined spouse or perfect mate. It also can refer to any fortuitous coincidence that seems to have been fated to occur.

Was it once the custom for the marriage ceremony to occur on more than one day? (T)

According to Jewish law, marriage consists of two separate acts—*kiddushin* (or *erusin*) and *nisuin*. Until the twelfth century, the two parts of the marriage ceremony were separated by as much as a year in order to give the bride time to prepare her trousseau. However, because of the possibility of sexual intimacy between the time of the betrothal ceremony and the marriage, especially in the frequent situation where a poor groom was housed by his wealthier in-laws, the rabbinic authorities decided to combine *kiddushin* and *nisuin* on the same day.

Is *kiddushin* the equivalent of a betrothal? (N)

Although this Aramaic term is often translated as "betrothal," it does not correspond to the modern conception of the word. Instead, *kiddushin* creates a special legal and personal relationship between a man and woman before *nisuin* (the actual marriage), which can be dissolved only by divorce or the death of either party. During *kiddushin*, cohabitation between the couple is strictly prohibited, and the formal duties between husband and wife are not yet incumbent upon them. The prospective bridegroom is not liable for the maintenance of his future bride, and she has no *ketubah*.

Does *kiddushin* involve the giving of a ring? (N)

According to the Talmud, the betrothal component of the marriage ceremony is accomplished by the bridegroom transferring to the bride any material of "solid value" that is worth at least one *perutah* (the lowest coin at that time). The term "solid value" meant that the object must have a clear worth that is not subject to misinterpretation, reflecting the ancient understanding of marriage as essentially a business transaction, in which the groom "acquired" his bride and sealed the deal by the payment of a gold or silver coin. Today, this is usually an unadorned ring, typically of gold, without jewels or ornaments.

Are there other ways to perform *kiddushin*? (N)

In ancient times, there were two other ways to effect *kiddushin*: *shetar* (deed) and *bi'ah* (cohabitation) (Kid. 2a). In *shetar,* the bridegroom handed his bride a written document listing the names of the parties and other relevant details. Just as divorce was accomplished by the husband handing his wife a writ (*get*), so the Rabbis reasoned that a woman could become a man's wife by a formal document ratifying the marriage. The other way to effect *kiddushin* was *bi'ah*, a word derived from two common biblical euphemisms for sexual intercourse. Both of these methods of betrothal have long been obsolete.

May the groom use his mother's wedding ring for *kiddushin*? (N)

As a sentimental symbol of continuity of the generations, it would seem a heartwarming custom for the groom to give his mother's wedding ring to his new bride. This is certainly permitted if he has inherited the ring after his mother's death, so that he has the right to use it as he wishes. However, there are serious problems if his mother is still alive and merely loaned it to him temporarily to use under the *chuppah*. According to Jewish law, the ring must *belong* to the groom, since it is being used to seal a legally binding action. The permanence of the relationship established at the wedding would appear to be seriously compromised if the bride had to return the ring to her mother-in-law as soon as the ceremony concluded.

Does the groom place the wedding ring on the fourth finger of the bride's left hand? (F)

During the wedding ceremony, the groom places the wedding ring on the index finger of the bride's right hand and then recites the marriage formula: "Behold, you are consecrated to me with this ring, according to the law of Moses and Israel." The ring is placed on the forefinger, the most prominent digit that is used for pointing, so that witnesses to the ceremony can clearly see that the groom has performed this act.[21] Only after the ceremony is the ring transferred to the fourth finger of the left hand, a traditional practice that may be based on the ancient belief that a vein runs directly from this finger to the heart.[22] *2- book of why*

Is the *bedeken* (*di kalla*) ceremony an ancient custom? (T)

Translated as "covering the bride," this is an old Jewish tradition in which the groom lets down the veil over the face of his bride before the marriage ceremony. The major reason for the *bedeken* ceremony is that it permits the groom to clearly identify his bride before she is veiled, so that he is not fooled as was Jacob when he received Leah instead of his beloved Rachel

(Gen. 29:23–28). Another reason for this tradition is that Rebecca immediately veiled herself after seeing her future husband, Isaac (Gen. 24:65), so that Jewish brides throughout the ages have worn this symbol of female modesty during the marriage ceremony.

Are weddings performed in venues other than the synagogue? (T)

Although marriage is a sacred act that would seem to be most appropriately performed in a synagogue, most traditional authorities prefer that the ceremony not take place in a house of prayer. Most commonly, it takes place in the hall where the subsequent festivities are to be held. Ultra-Orthodox Jews, Hasidim, and Ashkenazim in Israel usually hold wedding ceremonies outdoors after nightfall. This relates to the Divine assurance to Abraham that God would "make your descendants as numerous as the stars in the heaven" (Gen. 22:17).

Is Sunday the ideal day for a Jewish wedding? (N)

In the West, the most popular day for weddings is Sunday because of the convenience of the guests. However, traditional couples often select Tuesday, because the phrase "And God saw that it was good" (Gen. 1:10–12) is repeated in the biblical account of Creation on that day. Conversely, Monday is generally avoided because this phrase does not appear. Some prefer Thursday, since the blessing for fruitfulness was given on the fifth day of Creation. However, any day of the week is valid except the Sabbath, when legal transactions are forbidden and work and travel are not permitted.

Are there other times when weddings are not performed? (T)

Weddings also are not celebrated on major festivals, the three weeks (mourning period) between the 17th of Tammuz and Tisha b'Av, and the *sefirah* period between Passover and Shavuot (with the exception of Lag ba-Omer). Conversely, Rosh Chodesh (even during the *sefirah* period) traditionally was considered a propitious time for weddings, since the waxing moon was a symbol of growth and fertility.

Is the *aufruf* before the wedding principally designed to give the groom an *aliyah*? (N)

Literally meaning "calling up," the Yiddish term *aufruf* refers to the Ashkenazic custom of honoring a bridegroom by calling him up to the Torah on the Sabbath before his wedding. On this day, the bridegroom has precedence over all others, including a bar mitzvah, in being called for an *aliyah*. (Both the bridegroom and the bride are called to the Torah in liberal synagogues.) In the synagogues of medieval Europe, however, the *aufruf* was an opportunity to publicly announce the forthcoming wedding and to make certain that no congregant was aware of anything that would invalidate the marriage.

Do Jewish grooms traditionally have a bachelor party on the night before the wedding? (F)

There is a custom for brides and grooms to fast on the day of their wedding, which includes the night before. In some communities, both bride and groom fast; in others, only the groom does so. According to one explanation, if the groom were not required to fast he might go out with friends on the night before the wedding (i.e., a bachelor party) and become so drunk that he could not recover in time to properly carry out the legal formalities involved in the wedding ceremony. In contrast, the bride is not required to fast since it was thought less likely that her friends would encourage her to drink to excess. [23]

Is all music appropriate for the wedding procession? (N)

Since ancient times, when it was customary to play a flute before the bride and groom, it has been traditional to perform music at a wedding. Processional music usually begins with a single melody and then often changes to heighten the drama just before the entrance of the bride. Couples often select classical music, though many rabbis specifically request that it not be either of two of the most conventional selections in American weddings—Wagner's *Lohengrin* and Mendelssohn's *Midsummer Night's Dream*—pieces written by, respectively, a notorious anti-Semite and a Jew who converted to Christianity. [24]

Is the tradition for the bride to make a circle around the groom based on magic? (N)

Among Ashkenazim, it is customary for the bride to be led in seven circuits around the groom, based on the phrase, "a woman shall go around [encompasses] a man" (Jer. 31:21). In medieval times, this practice was thought to produce a magic circle of protection for the groom to keep away evil spirits. Some believe that this tradition was related to the custom of defining and securing ownership of real property by walking around it. [25] The number seven comes from the times in the Torah where it is written, "And when a man takes a wife." [26]

Is throwing rice and sweets at the newly married couple a Jewish tradition? (T)

In many Jewish communities, it is customary to throw rice, wheat, nuts, and candies at the groom during the wedding and when he is called to the Torah on the preceding Sabbath. Rice and nuts are considered symbols of fertility in many cultures, and throwing these items expresses the hope that the couple will "be fruitful and multiply."

Is the *ketubah* a mere formality with no legal significance? (F)

The *ketubah* (lit., "written document"), which the groom gives to his bride, is the Jewish marriage contract. Written in Aramaic, it sets forth in detail the financial obligations that a husband undertakes toward his wife as her inheritance should he die, or as her alimony should he divorce her (Shab. 14b, 16b). If either of these events occurred, the woman would have money and resources of her own and not be made destitute without any financial support. Today, a standardized *ketubah* is read before the bridegroom and two non-relative witnesses and signed by them. Just as the bridegroom is forbidden to cohabit with his bride after marriage unless he has written and delivered the *ketubah* to her, so the husband is forbidden to live with his wife for even one hour if she no longer has it in her possession. Therefore, if the *ketubah* is lost or destroyed, the husband is obliged to write a new one with the same terms as in the original.

In rabbinic times, were cedar and pine trees associated with weddings? (T)

The Talmud states: "It was the custom when a boy was born to plant a cedar tree and when a girl was born to plant a pine tree. When they married, the trees were cut down and a canopy (*chuppah*) made of the branches" (Git. 57a).

Does breaking the glass under the *chuppah* at the wedding ceremony commemorate the destruction of the Temple? (N)

At the conclusion of the wedding ceremony, the groom traditionally crushes a glass under his right foot. The most popular explanation is that this is a sign of mourning for the destruction of the Temple in Jerusalem. It also serves as a reminder that unbridled joy can be suddenly erased by over-whelming grief.

However, this custom actually dates back to an incident reported in the Talmud. When the guests at his son's wedding ceremony were rejoicing excessively, a great scholar shocked them into silence and sobriety when he took an expensive crystal and deliberately smashed it on the floor (Ber. 31a). This action also may have been related to the ancient belief that it is wise to temper joy to prevent disaster.

The original motivation for breaking the glass may have been to create a loud noise to frighten away evil spirits and demons. This belief is consistent with traditions in many cultures, including such current practices as the ringing of church bells and the smashing of a bottle against the hull of a ship before it is launched.[27]

Must a rabbi be present for a marriage to be legally binding under Jewish law? (N)

In America, most states have enacted laws requiring that ordained clergy officiate at a Jewish marriage ceremony. However, this is not necessary according to Jewish law. The only strict requirements are the bride and groom, an item of value (typically the wedding ring), the *ketubah* (marriage document), two reliable witnesses who are unrelated to each other or to the couple, and two cups of wine for the recitation of the appropriate blessings. The role of the rabbi is not to "pronounce" the couple as husband and wife, but to supervise the marriage ceremony and ensure that the legal documents have been written in keeping with Jewish tradition.

Is a *minyan* required for a wedding? (N)

Although a valid wedding can take place with a minimum of four people (groom, bride, and two witnesses), it is strongly preferable that there be a *minyan* present. This is required for recitation of the full *Shevah Brachot* (seven marriage benedictions). In the absence of a *minyan*, only the first blessing (said over a cup of wine) may be recited (there is a debate about the seventh). The other blessings praise God for Creation (particularly of human beings), invite Jerusalem (Zion) to rejoice as her children marry, and speak of the joy and happiness of the bride and groom The *Shevah Brachot* are considered so important that, if for some reason it was not possible to assemble a *minyan* for a wedding, they must be recited as soon as the bride and groom are in the presence of a *minyan*.

Does the newly married couple consummate their marriage immediately after the ceremony? (N)

Today, the bride and groom traditionally remain alone for a short period following the wedding ceremony. Known as *yichud* (joining, union), the couple break their fast and spend a few quiet moments together to validate their marriage before rejoining their families and friends for the wedding feast and celebration. However, in ancient times, this private act included sexual consummation.

Would some biblical marriages be invalid according to current Jewish law? (T)

According to the Rabbis, before the Revelation at Sinai, the only relationships that were prohibited were those between a man and his mother, his father's wife, a married woman, and a sister on his mother's side. Therefore, Abraham was permitted to marry his half-sister Sarah (the daughter of his father); Jacob could wed two sisters, Rachel and Leah; and Amram was allowed to marry his aunt Yocheved (the parents of Aaron, Moses, and Miriam)—all marriages that would be prohibited today.

Is sex in marriage something that a husband demands and a wife must fulfill? (F)

According to the Talmud, the opposite is true. The Rabbis regarded it a husband's duty to give his wife sexual pleasure, even developing a schedule of minimal sexual activity for men based on their occupations: "The times for conjugal duty prescribed in the Torah [Exod. 21:10] are as follows: for men of independent means [i.e., who have no need to pursue an occupation to earn their living], every day; for laborers [e.g., tailors, weavers, and build-ers],[28] twice a week; for donkey-drivers,[29] once a week; for camel-drivers [merchants who travel longer distances from their homes], once every 30 days; for sailors [whose sea voyages take them away for many months at a time], once in six months" (Ket. 5:5).

Does the husband have any other obligations toward his wife? (T)

According to traditional Jewish law, a man who marries becomes obligat-ed to his wife for 10 things in addition to the statutory *ketubah*. Of these, three are biblical in origin—food, clothing, and conjugal rights (Exod. 21:10). The other seven obligations are rabbinic: "to treat her if she falls ill; to ransom her if she is captured; to bury her if she dies; to provide for her maintenance out of his estate after his death; to let her dwell in his house after his death for the duration of her widowhood; to let the daughters sired by him receive their maintenance out of his estate until they become es-poused; and to let her male children sired by him inherit her *ketubah*, in addition to their share with their half-brothers in his estate."[30]

Does the word *mamzer* mean someone born out of wedlock? (F)

Contrary to popular misconception, a *mamzer* (often mistranslated as "bastard") is not someone born out of wedlock. Instead, a *mamzer* is the child of a sexual relationship between a man and woman whose marriage could never be valid under Jewish law (Kid. 3:12). Examples include the offspring of a union between a brother and sister or some other incestuous relationship, a child born to a married woman by some man other than her lawful husband (adultery); and a child born of a woman who had remarried without having obtained a valid divorce (*get*) from her first husband. According to the Bible, a *mamzer* and all of his or her descendants may never marry a Jew (Deut. 23:3). However, a marriage between two *mamzerim* is permitted. Realizing that this law was overly harsh and unfair to both *mamzerim* and their descen-dants, the Rabbis eventually allowed a *mamzer* to marry a convert as a way of becoming more quickly integrated into the Jewish community.

Except in regard to marriage, the personal status of a *mamzer* is not adversely affected in any way. He can be called up to the Torah, has rights of inheritance equal to other heirs, and can hold public office. The Mishnah even states that "a *mamzer* who is a scholar takes precedence over a High Priest who is an ignoramus" (Hor. 3:8).

Does Jewish law forbid bigamy? (N)

In biblical law, a man was allowed to have more than one wife at a time, as evidenced by two of the patriarchs (Abraham and Jacob). King David and King Solomon had many wives. After the biblical period, monogamy became the norm but not a legal requirement. This changed at the beginning of the eleventh century, when Rabbenu Gershom issued a decree forbidding a married man from marrying a second woman under threat of excommunication.

However, the effect of Rabbenu Gershom's edict only applied to Jews within the scope of his rabbinical authority. Some Jewish communities, such as those in Morocco, never accepted this ruling. In 1950, the Chief Rabbis of Israel ruled that all Jews throughout the world had to be monogamous, and Israeli law regards polygamy as a criminal offense.

Are there exceptions to the prohibition of bigamy? (T)

Even today, there are two rare exceptions to the rule forbidding bigamy. *Heter nisuin* is a legal document permitting a husband who wishes to remarry to escape any consequences for his wife's refusal to accept a *get* or if she has disappeared without a trace. Although the first marriage remains valid, the court has the power to release the husband from the prohibition against bigamy by granting him exceptional permission to contract an additional marriage. Another legal document is *heter me'ah rabbanim* (lit., "permission of 100 rabbis"), a legal document that allows a husband to marry a second wife to escape the consequences of his wife being mentally incompetent and unable to accept a *get*. In this procedure, a document is drawn up by a *beit din* and circulated to the other rabbis for their signatures. Traditionally, these rabbis should be from at least three different countries; in North America today, it is generally accepted that the rabbis can be from three of the U.S. states or Canadian provinces.[31]

Is a surviving brother obligated to marry the widow of his brother who died without having sired children? (N)

This practice of levirate marriage is a biblical commandment designed to perpetuate the name of the dead brother so that it would not "be blotted out of Israel" (Deut. 25:5–6). It also served to protect the wife, since a widow without children was in a precarious situation with no one responsible to care for her and provide material support.

As an alternative, the surviving brother could perform *chalitzah*. Literally meaning "taking off the shoe," this Hebrew term refers to the biblical ceremony in which the widow would take off the man's shoe (a symbol of mourning, because his failure to perform levirate marriage meant that his brother was now irrevocably dead) and spit on the ground in front of him (a symbol of contempt), declaring that "so shall it be done to the man who does not build up his brother's house" (Deut. 25:9). From then on, the widow was free to marry anyone (except for any of the brothers of the deceased or a *kohen*).

Is levirate marriage the preferred solution? (N)

Whereas in the Torah it is clear that levirate marriage was approved and *chalitzah* a shameful way out, the Talmud preferred *chalitzah* (Bek. 13a).

The two greatest medieval scholars took opposite points of view on this issue, with Maimonides favoring levirate marriage and Rashi preferring *chalitzah*. This led to a split in the *halachah* between the two traditions, with Sephardim following Maimonides and his preference for levirate marriage and Ashkenazim upholding Rashi's view that *chalitzah* supersedes it. Because this dichotomy of views could not be permitted in the State of Israel, the Chief Rabbinate ruled in favor of *chalitzah*, thus effectively outlawing levirate marriage. The situation is similar in the United States, where Sephardic rabbis do not permit levirate marriage and require *chalitzah* in all cases. [32]

Is intermarriage legal under Jewish law? (F)

Intermarriage is the union of a non-Jew and a Jew—one born of a Jewish mother or who has converted in accordance with Jewish law. Since biblical days, intermarriage has been opposed because it weakens the stability of the family, the essential core of Judaism, and threatens the continuity of the Jewish people. Marrying out of the faith has been one of the most strenuously discouraged and forcefully condemned acts that a Jew could perform.

The Rabbis declared that mixed marriages are not legally valid, because the non-Jewish party is incapable of contracting a marriage with a Jew within Jewish law. Therefore, the Jewish partner of a mixed marriage does not halachically require a divorce before subsequently marrying a Jew.

May the parents in a mixed marriage choose whether their children are considered Jews? (N)

According to Jewish law, the status of children from a mixed relationship is determined exclusively by the faith of the mother. If the mother is Jewish and the father non-Jewish, the children are considered Jewish in every respect; if the father is Jewish but the mother is not, the children are not considered Jews.

In 1983, the Reform movement broke with this tradition and formally adopted the principle of patrilineal descent, which defines a person as a Jew if *either* of his parents is Jewish *and* the person is living a Jewish life or committed to Judaism. This new definition was designed to compensate for demographic decline by broadening the definition of a Jew and extending a welcome and sense of legitimacy to people who otherwise might be lost to the Jewish community. However, by defining Jews differently from traditional Jewish law, this practice has effectively established a new category of people who are deemed Jewish by the standards of some, but not all, Jews.

Has the principle of patrilineal descent affected the rate of conversion to Judaism? (T)

Ironically, the concept of patrilineal descent has led to a dramatic decrease in the number of conversions of those non-Jewish women who marry

Jewish men, since in the Reform movement this is no longer necessary for the children to be considered Jewish.

Does Jewish law forbid birth control? (N)

The only biblical reference to birth control relates to Onan, who was condemned to death because he "spilled his seed on the ground" and let it go to waste to prevent the birth of a child from his levirate marriage to Tamar, the wife of his deceased brother (Gen. 38:8–10).

Although they encouraged large families, the Rabbis agreed that contraception (termed "an absorbent" [*moch* in Hebrew] and composed of "hackled wool or flax") was permissible if pregnancy was likely to be dangerous to the mother: "Three types of women may use an absorbent in their marital intercourse [to prevent conception]: a minor, a pregnant woman, and a nursing mother. A minor, lest she become pregnant and die as a result. A pregnant woman, lest she cause her fetus to abort [lit., 'degenerate into a sandal,' a flat, fish-shaped structure]. A nursing mother, lest she have to wean her child prematurely [due to becoming pregnant with another child] and it die" (Ket. 39a).

Among traditional Jews, birth control may be used solely by the wife if she would face substantial medical risk during pregnancy and nursing, or if she had suffered agonizing pains during childbirth. More liberal views tend to leave the decision on birth control to the individual, taking into consideration social and economic factors as well as medical issues.

Are women obligated to have children? (N)

The first biblical commandment is to "be fruitful and multiply" (Gen. 1:28). According to Hillel, each married couple must have at least one son and one daughter to fulfill this commandment (Yev. 6:6). However, both law and historical practice urge Jews to have as many children as possible. Of course, couples who cannot have children naturally are exempt from the commandment. They may pursue fertility treatments, but are not obligated to do so.[33]

According to the Talmud, the commandment to procreate applies only to men. Therefore, if a husband and wife both deliberately refrain from having children, it is only the man who is culpable. Similarly, only a man is obligated to marry. Whereas a woman is permitted to marry a eunuch, a man must marry a woman capable of being a mother.[34]

Can failure to procreate lead to a divorce? (N)

According to the Mishnah (Yev. 6:6), if a man was married for 10 years without children, "he may not abstain [any longer from the duty of propagation]." However, it does not precisely state what he should do. The *Tosefta* (Yev. 8:5) clearly states that the man must divorce his wife and return her marriage settlement, and the wife was permitted to marry again. Some men

in childless marriages chose to take a second wife to fulfill the commandment to procreate, rather than divorce an apparently infertile spouse (Yev.
65a). Conversely, the Talmud records instances of childless wives who successfully petitioned rabbinic courts to compel their unwilling husbands to
divorce them after 10 years of infertile marriages, based on their fears of an
impoverished widowhood and old age without the support of offspring (Yev.
65b). Aggadic texts generally deplore dissolution of marriages, even when
male procreation is at stake, presenting preservation of a loving childless
marriage as a situation where human needs and feelings overrule legal pre-
scriptions. These midrashic traditions emphasize instead the efficacy of
prayer and the necessity of faith in God (PdRK 22:2; Song R. 4:2).

Is artificial insemination permitted under Jewish law? (N)

In discussing the biblical law requiring a High Priest to marry a virgin
(Lev. 21:13), the Talmud states that he would be permitted to wed a virgin
who became pregnant accidentally after bathing in water containing human
semen (Hag. 14b–15a). Consequently, virtually all rabbinic rulings on artificial insemination by a donor have refused to brand the act as adultery or
regard the resulting child as illegitimate (*mamzer*). Nevertheless, most Orthodox Jewish authorities condemn the practice on various legal grounds (e.g.,
placing into doubt the paternity of the child; the possible risk of an incestuous marriage between blood relations conceived by a common donor; and
mutual rights and duties [maintenance, honor, inheritance] of child and parents). In contrast, artificial insemination using sperm from the husband is
generally accepted as a way to fulfill the duty of procreation, if for some
reason normal conception is impossible.

Is it a biblical duty to honor one's parents? (N)

Although both versions of the Ten Commandments (Exod. 20:12; Deut.
5:16) require one to "honor" parents, there is also a verse in Leviticus (19:3)
to "respect" them. According to the rabbis, *honoring* one's parents means
serving them; providing them with food and drink, clothing, and shelter; and
assisting them when they are too old and infirm to walk. *Respect* for one's
parents forbids any act that might offend them or reduce the esteem in which
they are held. Thus a child may not sit in their regular places, interrupt them,
insolently challenge their statements, or call them by their first names (Kid.
31b). These filial responsibilities extend beyond the grave, for the child is
obligated to say *Kaddish* in memory of a departed parent for 11 months and
on the annual anniversary of his or her death.

Is the order of the parents the same in both versions of the Ten Com-
mandments? (F)

In Exodus, the father is mentioned before the mother and "honor" is the
word used. In contrast, in Deuteronomy the word used can be translated as

"fear" or "revere" and the mother is listed first. This reflects the difference in the relationships between the child and each parent. The father is considered the disciplinarian, while the mother is more associated with kindness and affection. Consequently, it would be natural for the child to "love" the mother but "stand in awe" before the father (Kid. 30b). Therefore, the Torah insists that the child show love (honor) and reverence (fear) to both. [35]

Does Judaism correlate the relationship with parents to that with God? (T)

The Hebrew words used for "honor/love" and "respect/fear" in the biblical verses are the same as those used in describing attitudes that human beings are required to display toward God. For the child, mother and father are more than ordinary mortals. Thus, this commandment serves as the connecting link between the first four of the Ten Commandments (duties toward God) and the final five (duties to other human beings). According to the sages, honoring and revering one's parents are equal to honoring and revering God (Kid. 30b).

Should a child violate the Sabbath to fulfill a parental request? (F)

Although required to honor a parent, this cannot be at the expense of violating a Divine commandment. Consequently, if a parent asks a child to slaughter or cook something and thus desecrate the Sabbath, the child must respectfully refuse, citing the higher duty to fulfill the will of God (Yev. 6a).

May a doctor perform surgery on a parent? (N)

Wounding a parent and drawing blood is considered a capital offense in Jewish law. Therefore, a surgeon is not permitted to operate on a parent since it would cause loss of blood, unless there is no other qualified physician available. [36] This prohibition is psychologically sound, since the innate feelings that a child has for a parent might compromise a doctor's professional skills.

For a similar reason, the rabbis also prohibited a man employed by the court to administer floggings to inflict that punishment on his father. Instead, he was required to find another to replace him.

According to the Talmud, does a father have specific obligations toward his son? (T)

"A father is required to circumcise his son, redeem him [if the firstborn (*pidyon ha-ben*)], teach him Torah, take a wife for him, and teach him a craft. Some also say to teach him to swim [since his life may depend on it] . . . He who does not teach his son a craft, teaches him to be a thief" (Kid. 29a).

Does Jewish law permit a parent to favor one child more than another? (F)

Realizing the potentially devastating consequences of parental favoritism, the Rabbis said: "Never single out one son, for on account of two *selas* weight of silk [the coat of many colors] that Jacob gave Joseph in excess of his other sons, his brothers became jealous of him and the matter resulted in our forefathers' exile into Egypt" (Shab. 10b).

To obtain a divorce, does the couple have to go before a religious court? (N)

Unlike many other legal systems, in Jewish law the mutual consent of the parties is sufficient for dissolution of the marriage and delivery of the *get*, the formal document of divorce that is written by the husband and delivered to the wife. Consequently, there is no requirement for a court to become involved in the process. However, if only one spouse wishes to divorce, the court must decide whether there are specific grounds to compel the husband to give (or the wife to receive) a *get*.

Is having the husband give a *get* to his wife all that is required for a Jewish couple to be divorced? (N)

In Israel, religious and civil divorces are the same, and the rabbinical court is responsible for handling all issues of support and custody. In the Diaspora, however, Jews must also abide by the laws of the land. Both a civil divorce and a *get* are required before either of the parties can enter into a new marriage. The civil and religious formalities are independent, and there is no need to delay preparation of the *get* until the civil divorce has been finalized.

Can a woman sue for Jewish divorce? (N)

This was not permitted under biblical law, and in Talmudic times the decision to divorce also was exclusively that of the man. In addition to being unable to initiate a divorce action, a woman could be compelled to accept a divorce against her will (Yev. 112b). However, the Talmud states that a wife is entitled to demand a divorce in two general situations (Ket. 77a). The first is when her husband is physically repulsive to his wife, because of either a loathsome medical condition (e.g., afflicted with boils and leprosy) or a malodorous occupation (e.g., gathering dog's dung, smelting copper, or tanning hides). It is immaterial whether the offensive condition arose before or after the marriage, for mere knowledge from a distance is not like being forced to live under adverse circumstances every day. A wife may compel her husband to divorce her if he refuses to fulfill to the best of his abilities his marital obligations to provide her with food, clothing, shelter, and conjugal relations. Similarly, she may be granted a divorce if her husband physically or mentally abuses her so that she cannot be expected to continue living with him. Finally, the wife has legitimate grounds for divorce if her husband is unfaithful to her or if he "transgresses the Law of Moses"—for instance, if he causes her to violate the dietary laws knowing that she observes them, or if he has intercourse with her against her will during her menstrual period.[37]

Can a woman be divorced against her will? (F)

Although this was the case under biblical and Talmudic law, a *takanah* (rabbinic enactment) issued by Rabbenu Gershom of Mainz about 1000 C.E. protected a woman so that she no longer was compelled to consent to a divorce against her will. Initially applying only to Ashkenazic Jews in Germany, this ruling was eventually accepted by Sephardim in accordance with contemporary law in the State of Israel.

Are the rules of divorce on the grounds of adultery different for men and women? (T)

According to Jewish law, when a husband commits adultery, the wife has the power to forgive him and continue the marriage. Of course, she also may refuse to forgive his infidelity and insist on a divorce and receive the full marital settlement to which she is entitled. In contrast, when a wife commits adultery, her husband is not permitted to forgive her and divorce is required (Sot. 27b).

According to rabbinic courts, is custody of the children usually awarded to the mother after a divorce? (N)

Rabbinic courts usually put all children under age six in the custody of their mother, for they are primarily in need of the physical care and attention that mothers typically give children at that age. Boys who are older than six years generally are put into the custody of their father, so that he can carry out his obligation to teach his male children Torah. Conversely, girls older than six years typically live with their mother, so that she can instruct them in the ways of modesty.[38]

Nevertheless, these are only general principles. In an individual case, the rabbinic court makes a final custody decision based on what appears to be the best interest of the child. At times, it can even reject a custody arrangement to which the couple has agreed, as when the wife has granted custody to the husband in exchange for a more generous monetary settlement. If there is a conflict, the custody decision of the rabbinic court may be influenced by the testimony of the child, especially if there is any indication of mistreatment by one of his parents.

According to Jewish law, are both parties free to marry anyone they wish after a divorce? (N)

Both men and women who divorce are generally free to remarry anyone they please, unless it is halachically forbidden. The divorced woman is not permitted to marry a *kohen*, nor is she allowed to marry a man with whom she is suspected of having committed adultery. Furthermore, she may not marry any person who served as a witness at the delivery of her *get*.

A man may remarry the woman he has divorced only as long as his former wife has not remarried in the interim. According to biblical law, a divorced woman who has remarried and had her second marriage also terminated (by divorce or death) may not remarry her first husband. If this were not the case, people may feel free to divorce one another at will to sample other mates before subsequently getting together again. One commentator suggested that this prohibition was intended to prevent the possibility of a man conspiring with his wife to leave him, marry another man, and make life so miserable for her second husband that he would agree to make a cash settlement and divorce her, thus enabling her to then return to her first husband with a financial windfall. [39]

If the husband is a *kohen*, he is forbidden under Jewish law from marrying a divorced woman, including his former wife. If the original divorce was due to the wife's adultery, her former husband is also prohibited from remarrying her.

Are the parties free to marry at any time after a divorce? (N)

A woman may not marry within a period of 90 days following the divorce, lest there be doubt about the paternity of her first child from her second marriage. This rule applies regardless of the age of the woman. The only exception to this waiting period is when the woman remarries the man she had divorced; since paternity is not an issue, they can remarry immediately.

May an amicably divorced couple remain together in their house? (F)

To prevent promiscuity, after divorce the parties are forbidden to reside together in their former common home. If owned or rented by one of them, that party is allowed to remain. If the property of both, the wife is required to leave, based on the somewhat questionable Talmudic concept that "moving about is harder for a man than for a woman" (Ket. 28a), though the court has the right to allow the wife to remain if necessary for an equitable settlement of financial disputes between the parties. Continuing to occupy the dwelling jointly (or later returning to it) can have unexpected and serious consequences. According to the presumption in traditional Jewish law that a man should not live with a woman for the sake of promiscuity and since both parties could have validly remarried according to *halachah*, it is inferred that they had intended to enter into a *new* marital relationship! If either or both wish to marry third parties, they must formally divorce again.

Does delivery of a *get* immediately end the marriage? (N)

Although this is generally true, in exceptional cases a *get* may be written and delivered conditionally, designed to take effect only if a specific event occurs. This is usually applicable only in times of severe persecution (such as pogroms or the Holocaust) or war, when husband and wife may become separated and there is a danger of her becoming an *agunah* (see below) if the husband does not return and no one can unequivocally attest to the fact that he has died. Consequently, a soldier preparing for war may issue a conditional *get* that would be effective if he failed to return by a certain date, thus permitting his wife to remarry.[40]

After three years, is a missing husband presumed dead so that his wife is permitted to remarry? (F)

According to *halachah*, a marriage can be dissolved only by divorce or by the death of either spouse. If the husband deserts his wife and disappears, or if he dies but there is no valid testimony to that fact, the woman remains legally married and cannot marry another. Similarly, if a marriage is untenable but the husband either willfully refuses to deliver a *get* (despite the threats and punitive measures of a Jewish court), or is legally incompetent to grant it (usually because of insanity), divorce is not possible. In all of these scenarios, the wife becomes an *agunah* (chained woman)—a woman whose marriage has in fact ended or been suspended, but who legally remains a married woman bound to a husband who no longer lives with her, and thus is unable to remarry.

The *halachah* has long been torn between the need to find a way to permit the *agunah* to remarry and the grave concern of ruling incorrectly and permitting a still-married woman to marry another man. The consequences of allowing an adulterous marriage by mistake are catastrophic—should the first husband eventually turn up, the woman must be divorced by her second husband and is also barred from remarrying the first—so that she is forbidden to *both* men. Moreover, any children she had with the second husband would be branded as *mamzerim*.

Are two witnesses required to establish that a missing husband has died? (N)

Although the testimony of two competent witnesses is generally required to establish any fact, the need to quickly resolve the problem of an *agunah* led the Rabbis to accept testimony that would not be permitted in other cases. Not only is the testimony of a single witness sufficient, but the rabbinic court will accept the evidence of a woman and a relative—classes usually deemed incompetent as witnesses—as well as hearsay evidence (overheard in conversation among non-Jews). Even the woman herself can be a legitimate witness to her husband's death. The rationale for this ruling is that, were she to give false testimony, she would be setting herself up for disaster if the husband she had reported as dead ever returned. However, the woman is deemed a reliable witness only "under normal circumstances," which the Mishnah defines as "when there is peace between him and her and peace in the world" (Yev. 114b). If there has been known marital friction between husband and wife, there would be reason to suspect the woman of deception in an attempt to simply be rid of her husband.[41]

Is circumstantial evidence sufficient in the case of a husband suspected of being deceased? (F)

Despite the general leniency described above, circumstantial evidence is not permitted in the case of a husband suspected of being deceased. Sufficient testimony must include *direct* evidence of his death. A man seen drowning in a large body of water, whose shores are beyond the horizon, cannot be considered to have perished unless his body is found. The reason is the remote possibility that he may have survived and reached land at a point beyond the view of the witness.[42] The problem of obtaining direct evidence of death is particularly severe in cases of war and pogrom. Death of a husband under such perilous conditions often left the widow an *agunah.*

Is a rabbi required to officiate at a funeral? (F)

Although most funerals today are conducted by clergy, primarily because of their experience and pastoral skills, this is not required under Jewish law. Any layperson can deliver a eulogy, which is often given by family members and friends; recite the appropriate psalms; and chant the *El Malei Rachamim* (memorial prayer for the departed).

According to Jewish law, should the dead be buried in their best clothes? (F)

In the early Talmudic period, it became customary for all Jews to be buried in the same type of garment—a simple shroud made of inexpensive muslin, cotton, or linen—to indicate that rich and poor are equal before God. Since the sixteenth century, the accepted color for a shroud has been white, to symbolize purity. Shrouds are made without seams, knots, or buttons and have no pockets, signifying that it is a person's soul, not his or her wealth, which will be judged in the World to Come.[43] This view was diametrically opposite to that of Egyptian and other early civilizations, which were as concerned with death as with life and whose tombs were filled with jewelry, food, and implements for the deceased to use in a new life after death. In contrast, *Pirkei Avot* (6:9) well illustrates the Jewish belief that "when a person departs from this world, neither silver, nor gold, nor precious stones, nor pearls escort him, but only Torah study and good deeds."[44]

To honor the dead, is an expensive, water-tight coffin used? (F)

During Talmudic times, the rich employed such elaborate coffins for burying their dead that the poor felt ashamed, and a law was enacted stating that all be brought out on a plain bier (MK 27a–b). Consequently, traditional Jews use a plain wooden coffin—with no nails, metal, or any decoration—usually made of pine or other inexpensive soft wood that decomposes more rapidly than a hardwood like oak.[45] In Israel today, the common practice is to wrap the body in linen and bury it directly in the ground, a custom popularized by the sixteenth-century kabbalists to literally fulfill the biblical verse, "for dust you are, and to dust you shall return" (Gen. 3:19). In Western countries, however, where local law generally demands that coffins be used, traditional Jews use coffins with loose bottom boards or with holes drilled into them to bring the corpse into direct contact with the earth and allow more rapid decomposition of the body.

Except for the body of the deceased, are Jewish coffins empty? (N)

Some Jews place earth from the Land of Israel in the coffin. This custom arose from medieval Jewish folklore, which maintained that when the Messiah comes at the end of days, the dead will be resurrected on the Mount of Olives in Jerusalem. Since those who are buried outside of Israel will roll underground to that site, earth from the Holy Land will enable the body to know when it has arrived at the proper place. Another tradition is to put into the coffin *sheimot* (sacred books containing the Divine name) that can no longer be used.

Can burial traditionally be performed at any time after death? (F)

As a matter of respect for the dead, Jewish tradition insists on prompt burial, generally within 24 hours after death. Some delay may be justified to allow for preparation of a coffin, for shrouds to be made, and to await the arrival of close relatives, but never for more than three days. Certain delays are unavoidable, because funerals may not take place on the Sabbath, on Yom Kippur, or in many communities, on the first day of festivals. Where there is a need to bury two people at the same time, the interment of a scholar takes precedence over an *am ha-aretz* (average citizen), and the burial of a woman is always performed before that of a man.

Is viewing the body a Jewish practice? (F)

Jewish tradition opposes the practice of viewing the body before burial, considering it incompatible with the principle of showing proper respect for the dead.

Is sending flowers to the bereaved a Jewish practice? (F)

In the past, fragrant flowers and spices were used at funerals to mask the smell of the decaying body. However, Jewish tradition considers this practice, as well as the placing of flowers on the grave, as non-Jewish customs. Instead of sending flowers, it is proper to send a donation in honor of the deceased to a synagogue or to a charity selected by the mourning family.

Is there an obligation to do anything as a funeral procession passes by? (T)

Escorting the dead (*levayat ha-met*), especially deceased scholars, to their last resting place is considered an extremely important symbol of respect that even warrants interrupting the study of Torah. It is called the "true kindness" (*chesed shel emet*), an act of genuine selflessness since one can expect no reciprocation. The minimum duty is to rise as the funeral cortege passes and symbolically accompany it by walking in the direction of the hearse some six to eight feet to indicate respect for the deceased and sympathy for the mourners.

At the cemetery, does the funeral procession stop as it proceeds to the grave site? (T)

In traditional Jewish funerals, the procession pauses at least three times en route to the grave site to recite Psalm 91, indicating the unwillingness of the mourners to part from the deceased.

Once the coffin is placed into the grave, should those present remain? (T)

Those gathered at the cemetery stay to help fill the grave with dirt so that they can physically take part in the *mitzvah* of burying the dead. The practice is often only symbolic, each person adding just a small amount of dirt to the grave. In some communities, however, those attending the burial add enough dirt to cover the coffin or even to completely fill the grave. If a shovel is used, it is customary for each person to place the shovel in the pile of dirt, rather than hand it to the next person. This is a silent symbolic gesture expressing the prayer that the tragedy of death not be "contagious," and that the remainder of the family and friends may live long and peaceful lives. [46]

Is anything said to the mourners at the grave site? (T)

After the traditional *Mourner's Kaddish* or the "burial *Kaddish*," which includes in its first paragraph a reference to God "reviving the dead and raising them to eternal life," those present at the ceremony form two rows. As the mourners walk between them, they are offered words of consolation: "May God comfort you among all the mourners of Zion and Jerusalem."

May a *kohen* participate in a funeral? (N)

Because of the sacredness of his role in the service of the Temple in Jerusalem, for which he was required to be ritually pure, a *kohen* was prohibited from physical contact with the dead or even being under the same roof with a corpse. Since these regulations are still in effect, a *kohen* may not approach nearer than four cubits (about six feet) to a grave. However, these restrictions are lifted when the deceased is one of the close relations for whom the *kohen* has to observe *shivah*—father, mother, son, daughter, brother, unmarried sister, or wife. *Kohanim* are customarily buried in a special row close to the cemetery wall, so that their relatives can visit the graves without entering the confines of the cemetery itself.

Do pregnant women attend funerals? (N)

Although pregnant women are not forbidden to attend a funeral or visit a cemetery, according to Jewish tradition they were discouraged from doing so, both because of superstitious fear of the Evil Eye and the danger that it would be so traumatic an experience that it could lead to a miscarriage. If the latter reason is not a concern, there is no halachic regulation that prohibits a pregnant woman from attending a funeral.

Are Ashkenazic and Sephardic tombstones different? (T)

Sephardic tombstones typically lie horizontal on the grave and often portray events connected with the biblical character whose name was borne by the deceased. In contrast, Ashkenazim have traditionally used symbols illustrating religious status—hands raised in the Priestly Blessing for a *kohen*; a ewer and basin or musical instrument for a *levi*.

Is there a standard epitaph for Jewish tombstones? (N)

Although since First Temple times a commemorative inscription has marked the place of a Jewish burial, the use of Hebrew in epitaphs became universal during the Middle Ages. In most Western countries today, the vernacular has become more common. The inscription is generally headed by the letters *pei nun* (standing for *po nikbar*) for a man and *pei tet* (short for *po timunah*) for a woman, both of which mean "here is buried." Sephardim use the letters *mem kuf*, which stand for *mikom kevurat* (the place of burial of). At the bottom of the tombstone are engraved the letters *tav nun tzadi vet hei*, the abbreviation of the phrase *ti-hee nishmato (nishmatah) tzerurah bitz'ror ha-chaim* (May his [her] soul be bound up in the bond of eternal life). [47]

Is the ceremony unveiling the headstone an old custom? (F)

In Western Europe and especially in the United States at the beginning of the twentieth century, it became the custom to formally "consecrate" the headstone with a service, though there is no religious obligation to do so. Since in the United States the tombstone is covered with a cloth, which is removed by the family during the service, the ritual has been termed the "unveiling."

The real purpose of friends and family gathering together at the cemetery is to honor the memory of the departed. As such, it is more appropriate to use the Hebrew term *hakamat matzeivah*, which literally means "setting up the memorial stone."

Is there a specific time for consecrating the grave marker? (N)

In the Diaspora, it is customary to erect and consecrate the grave marker during the 12th month after death. While many families wait until almost the full year has passed, it may be done sooner. The reason for waiting is that since the deceased is well remembered for the first 11 months after death, when family members say *Kaddish* for him or her, there is no need to erect a tombstone as an additional reminder during that time. A more practical reason to delay the erection of a monument is to allow the earth around the grave a chance to settle, so that the heavy tombstone does not sink into the ground.[48] In Israel, the stone is usually placed on, or soon after, the 30th day (*sheloshim*).

Should mourners wear black clothing? (N)

At a time of grief at the loss of a loved one, subdued colors are appropriate. However, there is no specific obligation for a Jewish mourner to wear only black clothing.

Is *keriah* an ancient tradition? (T)

Keriah, the tearing of a garment as a sign of grief, is a traditional Jewish mourning custom based on the actions of several figures in the Bible. These include Reuben, on finding his brother Joseph missing from the pit (Gen. 37:29); Jacob, upon seeing Joseph's bloodstained cloak and assuming that his favorite son was dead (Gen. 37:34); the brothers, when the goblet was found in Benjamin's sack (Gen. 44:13); David, on hearing of the death of King Saul (2 Sam. 1:11); Mordecai, when he heard news of the decree of genocide arranged by Haman (Esth. 4:1); and Job, on learning of the death of his children (Job 1:20).

Is *keriah* performed at the moment of death? (N)

The Talmud states that *keriah* should be done at the moment of death (MK 25a). However, today the usual practice is to defer it until just before the funeral service or burial.

Does the mourning period last seven days? (N)

Although most Jews are aware of the seven-day period of mourning, the Rabbis distinguished four stages in the mourning period: *aninut*, the period between death and burial; *shivah*, the seven days following burial; *sheloshim*, the time until the 30th day after burial; and the first year.

Is the meal of consolation after the funeral prepared by the bereaved family? (F)

It is the obligation of the community to provide a meal of condolence (se*'udat havrah*) for the mourners on their return from the cemetery. Indeed, the Jerusalem Talmud criticized neighbors who caused the bereaved to prepare their own meal, cursing them for being so callous to the plight of the mourners.[49]

Are there special foods appropriate for the meal of consolation? (T)

It is customary to serve foods that are round, to symbolize the cyclical and continuous nature of life. Among the most common are hard-boiled eggs (a symbol of the close connection between life and death), lentils, garbanzo beans, and bagels. The critical importance of the meal of consolation to the mourners, which was once eaten only by them, is that it is served by friends and other family members who care deeply for them.

Do mourners primarily observe *shivah* to honor the dead? (F)

The purpose of *shivah* is to permit the survivors to face the enormity of their loss and gradually overcome their initial grief so that they can begin to return to a normal life. The survivors honor the deceased when they study Torah, give charity, and perform good deeds in memory of their loved one who has died.

Must all the shoes and clothing of the deceased be thrown out? (F)

There is a widespread custom of throwing out the shoes that the deceased was wearing at the time of death. Not mentioned in the *Shulchan Aruch*, it apparently developed in the nineteenth century based on the superstitious belief that the shoes might contain poisonous material that would be dangerous to anyone wearing them. Even if one accepts this dubious concept, there is no reason to throw away all the shoes of the deceased, or any of his or her clothing. A friend or relative should have no hesitation about wearing them. Rather than discarding them, many give the shoes and clothes of the deceased to a charity that will distribute them to the poor.

Does *shivah* last seven days? (N)

Literally meaning "seven," *shivah* is the most intense period of mourning. In computing the seven days, Jewish tradition follows the principle of deeming a fraction of a day as a complete day. Thus the day of burial is considered the first day, even if the interment was concluded only a few minutes before nightfall. Similarly, the seventh day is considered a full day after the morning service. *Shivah* is suspended for the duration of the Sabbath, though that day is counted as one of the seven days of mourning, because the Sabbath is a day of joy and delight into which not even death may intrude.

If the burial took place before a major holiday (Rosh Hashanah, Yom Kippur, Passover, Shavuot, or Sukkot) and the mourner observed *shivah* for even a short period before the festival, the remainder of the *shivah* period is canceled by the holiday. However, if the burial occurred during *hol ha-mo'ed* (intermediate days of the festival), the entire *shivah* is observed after termination of the festival.

May friends of the bereaved visit them any time during the *shivah* period? (N)

The Rabbis considered the first three days of mourning as the most intense. Therefore, it is a tradition that mourners be left alone with their thoughts and members of their immediate family for the first two days of mourning (after the funeral, which counts as the first day of *shivah*). Consequently, condolence calls are deferred until the third day, unless this will prevent a person from visiting the mourner at all during the *shivah* period.

Do mourners sit on low stools or benches during *shivah* so that they are uncomfortable during this period of intense mourning? (F)

In the past, the practice was to sit on overturned couches or beds; it is now traditional for mourners to sit on low stools or benches. This may be a symbol of the mourner's awareness that life is no longer the same, or the desire to stay close to the earth in which his or her loved one is now buried. [50] Sitting on low stools or benches is not designed to make the mourners feel uncomfortable, for they are suffering enough during the *shivah* period. Elderly people, the physically weak, and pregnant women may sit on normal seats.

When making a *shivah* call, are visitors expected to greet the mourners with words of sympathy? (F)

It is considered an obligation for relatives and friends to visit mourners during the *shivah* period, comforting them and providing them with food and other needs. Based on the actions of the three friends of Job—the classic mourner—who sat with him for seven days without uttering a word (Job 2:13), the Rabbis noted that discreet individuals express their condolences in sympathetic silence. Therefore, visitors are advised not to speak until the mourner begins the conversation. Idle chatter should be avoided, including such customary greetings as "Hello," "Good morning," and "How are you?"[51]

May a mourner leave the house during *shivah*? (N)

The activity of mourners is strictly limited while they are sitting *shivah*. They usually do not leave the house, perform manual labor, or conduct business transactions. A mourner who must leave to conduct urgent business to prevent irreversible financial loss—such as distributing perishable goods that would be unusable if not sold that week—may place a bit of sand or earth in his shoes as a constant reminder of his status as a mourner and the need to return to sitting *shivah* as soon as possible.

Is there a *shivah minyan* for all seven days? (F)

By the end of the Middle Ages, it was a well-established custom to gather a *minyan* in the home for morning and evening prayers so that the mourners could recite the *Kaddish*. If it is not possible to assemble a *minyan* in the home, the mourner may attend the synagogue for services and the recitation of *Kaddish*. On the Sabbath, the mourner attends synagogue and may not show any outward signs of mourning, since the Sabbath is a day of joy and delight into which not even death may intrude. On Friday evening, mourners omit the six psalms of the *Kabbalat Shabbat* service, remaining in an anteroom until the last verse of *Lecha Dodi*, at which time they enter the synagogue from the rear door and join the congregation. The congregation then offers a greeting of consolation: "*Ha-Makom yenachem.*"

Is a *shivah minyan* different from the service in the synagogue? (T)

Out of sensitivity to the those sitting *shivah*, *Hallel* is not recited in the house of mourning on Rosh Chodesh, because it contains such verses as "The dead cannot praise the Lord, nor any that go down into silence" (Ps. 115:17); and "This is the day that the Lord has made—let us exult and rejoice on it" (Ps. 118:24). In some communities, however, it is recited when the mourners leave the room. If Rosh Chodesh coincides with the Sabbath, *Hallel* is recited even if the service is being held in the house of those sitting *shivah*, since no public display of mourning is permitted on this day.

Tachanun (prayers of supplication) is omitted because its theme—"I have sinned before You"—is inappropriate for mourners, since it would make them feel guilty rather than comforted.

Should a mourner who is mistakenly called up to the Torah during *shivah* refuse the *aliyah*? (F)

The mourner is not called up for an *aliyah* during the week of *shivah*, even if the only *kohen* or *levi* in the congregation, because the Torah blessings express a feeling of good fortune that is not in keeping with the person's true emotions at the time. However, a mourner who is accidentally called up to the Torah should not refuse the *aliyah*, since this would be considered public mourning, which is forbidden.

Ironically, the one day on which a mourner may be called to the Torah is Tisha b'Av, a day of intense national mourning for the destruction of the Temples. On Tisha b'Av every Jew is a mourner, so that one observing *shivah* is no different from all other members of the community and thus may be given an *aliyah*.

Does Jewish law require that mirrors be covered in a house where mourners are sitting *shivah*? (N)

In the house of mourning, it is a custom (but not a halachic requirement) to cover mirrors or turn them to the wall. The most popular reason for this practice is that mirrors are a symbol of vanity, and the mourner should not be concerned with personal appearance. Because prayer services are held in the house of mourning, the reflection might distract the attention of the worshipers. Indeed, it is forbidden to pray in front of a mirror, and synagogues are not decorated with them. [52]

Does the *yahrzeit* correspond to the day of death on the secular calendar? (F)

Literally "year time," this Yiddish term is used by Ashkenazic Jews to refer to the yearly commemoration of the anniversary of the death of one's parents according to the Jewish calendar. Many extend it to the other five close relatives for whom mourning is required—brother and sister, son and daughter, and spouse. Hasidic communities observe the *yahrzeits* of the leaders of their specific dynasties as festive occasions celebrating the day that these *tzadikim* ascended to the spiritual realm. In modern times, annual commemorations have been instituted in Israel to mark the death of such prominent figures as Theodor Herzl, Vladimir Jabotinsky, Chaim Nachman Bialik, Rav Kook, and Yitzhak Rabin. A person observing *yahrzeit* recites the *Mourner's Kaddish* at each of the three daily services. A 24-hour memorial candle is lit at home in accordance with the biblical verse, "the soul [spirit] of man is the lamp of God" (Prov. 20:27). *Yahrzeit* is a day for visiting the grave, engaging in Torah study, and doing charitable deeds to honor the memory of the departed.

Is *Yizkor* a communal service? (N)

Yizkor (lit., "May [God] remember") is the memorial service for the departed. In the Ashkenazic ritual, *Yizkor* is recited after the Torah reading during the morning service on the last days of each of the three pilgrimage festivals (Passover, Shavuot, and Sukkot) and on Yom Kippur. Sephardim also recite the memorial service (*Hashkavah*) during the evening service immediately preceding the Day of Atonement. Rather than congregational memorial prayers after the holiday Torah service, Sephardim personally recite a memorial prayer for their relatives when called to the Torah.

Is recitation of the *Kaddish* a part of the *Yizkor* service? (N)

Although Conservative and Reform congregations end the Yizkor service with a communal recitation of the *Mourner's Kaddish*, this is not part of Orthodox practice. Today, the traditional memorial service consists of three prayers that are recited standing and with the Torah scrolls taken out from the ark. The first prayers, *Yizkor Elohim* (May God remember [the soul of] . . .) and *El Malei Rachamim* (God full of compassion), express the mourner's hope that the departed souls of their loved ones will have eternal life in the presence of God. A special prayer is frequently added for the victims of the Holocaust and for Jewish soldiers who have died in war, particularly in Israel. The traditional memorial service concludes with the recital of *Av ha-Rachamim* (Father of Mercy), a memorial prayer for Jewish martyrs and martyred communities. Anonymously composed during the First Crusade that began in 1096, it requests that God choose how and when to exact punishment upon those who forced Jews to die *al Kiddush ha-Shem*.[53]

Should those whose parents are alive leave the synagogue for *Yizkor*? (N)

It is a custom, but not required under Jewish law, for those whose parents are still alive to actually leave the sanctuary until the *Yizkor* service has concluded. Rising and remaining silent when others are praying for their deceased parent(s) may seem awkward, and it may be potentially embarrassing to be the focus of envy for still having one's parents alive.[54] Nevertheless, some have strongly opposed leaving the synagogue if one's parents are alive as a mere superstitious practice, arguing that it is contrary to the original intent of *Yizkor* as an opportunity for the community to honor the martyrs of Judaism. Moreover, it ignores the need to commemorate the millions who died in the Holocaust but have no living relatives to remember them. [55]

Does Jewish law forbid an autopsy after death? (N)

Whether autopsies are permitted is an extremely controversial issue among traditional Jews, bringing into direct opposition two fundamental principles—*kavod ha-met* (reverence for the human body after death) and *pikuach nefesh* (preservation of life). Many rabbis have argued that the biblical requirement for burial as soon as possible (Deut. 21:22–23), combined with the prohibition against desecrating the corpse (*nivul ha-met*), forbids mutilation of the body for post-mortem examination. However, the trend among modern halachists is that reverence for the corpse must yield to the superior value of life and its preservation, which overrides all but the three Torah commandments of idolatry, adultery, and murder. Consequently, autopsy is permitted if finding the cause of death in a post-mortem examination may save the lives of others. There is a universal consensus of opinion permitting autopsies in the case of violent or accidental death, or when a crime is suspected.

May the ashes of a cremated person be buried in a Jewish cemetery? (N)

Disposal of the dead body by burning is forbidden because it interferes with the natural decay. Because "burning" was one of the four biblical types of capital punishment meted out for a number of offenses, cremation was considered a humiliation inflicted on criminals (Josh. 7:15, 25; Isa. 30:33). The Rabbis regarded the burning of a corpse to be an idolatrous practice, an affront to mankind as the highest form of creation, and a denial of the belief in bodily resurrection. [56]

According to traditional Jewish practice, cremated ashes may not be buried in a Jewish cemetery. Furthermore, those who choose not to be buried in the ancient Jewish manner, as a final defiance of tradition, are not to be mourned. [57] Although rabbis of more liberal denominations also discourage cremation in favor of the traditional practice of burial, some will attend a memorial service for a person who has been cremated and permit the ashes to be buried in the cemetery. [58]

Is a person who commits suicide denied a Jewish burial? (N)

Because the duty of preserving life (*pikuach nefesh*), including one's own, is of paramount importance in Judaism, suicide is prohibited. The formal laws regarding suicide first appear in the late post-Talmudic tractate, *Semachot*. These mandate that no rites be performed in honor of the dead (e.g., *keriah*; eulogy). However, a distinction is made between suicide while of sound mind (*la-da'at*), to which these severe restrictions apply, and suicide while of unsound mind (*she-lo la-da'at*), to which they do not apply. In most cases, a suicide is considered as being of sound mind only when there is clear evidence of deliberate intent. According to *halachah*, however, a person who takes his or her own life is *presumed* to do so without the necessary premeditation, whether from pathological depression, substance abuse (liquor, narcotics, barbiturates), or duress.

Are suicides buried in a special section of the cemetery? (N)

It was, and in some places still is, the custom to bury suicides in a special section of the cemetery, near its outer limits and at least six feet from other Jewish dead. In recent years, however, there is a growing tendency to remove this stigma from those who take their own lives.

Is euthanasia forbidden under Jewish law? (N)

At times, the sanctity of human life and the idea that every second is unique and of equally infinite value comes into direct conflict with the fundamental principle of preventing pain and suffering and preserving human dignity. According to Jewish law, although a person is forbidden to do a positive act to *hasten* death, one is also prohibited from performing an act that would *delay* the death of a moribund person (*goses*; one who is expected to die within 72 hours) by artificial means when he or she has no hope of living. This prohibition against needlessly prolonging the dying process is dramatically illustrated by the ruling that those attending at the moment of death are forbidden to cry, lest the noise restore the soul to the deceased. The general conclusion is that it is permissible to withhold or withdraw "heroic" methods to prolong a lingering life if there is no reasonable hope of recovery, especially if the person is in severe pain.

A classic Talmudic text concerning the martyrdom of Chananiah ben Teradion encapsulates the rabbinic view of euthanasia (Av. Zar. 18a). When the renowned sage was to be burned at the stake, the Romans secured tufts of wet cotton around his heart to prolong his suffering. As the fire raged, the rabbi's disciples urged him to "open your mouth so you can end it quicker." However, he refused, saying that only God who gave him life could take it away. This is the primary argument against *active* euthanasia, any attempt to accelerate death by taking a step that would terminate life faster than it would naturally cease. However, the rabbi did permit removal of the wet cotton around his heart, which was applied only to sadistically prolong his suffering. This is interpreted as meaning that in some circumstances *passive* euthanasia is permitted, the removal of artificial life support keeping alive a person who will soon perish (i.e., not shortening life, but rather removing any impediment to the natural process of dying, especially if one is in severe pain).

In modern practical terms, most Jewish authorities would permit the withholding or disconnecting of artificial respirators and other machines that maintain the vital bodily functions of a *goses* but do not offer any reasonable chance of cure, reasoning that these treatments merely prolong the dying process and do not serve the interests of the patient. This would include cardiopulmonary resuscitation, surgery, dialysis, chemotherapy, and radiation therapy if they are merely palliative, especially if they increase pain and suffering or if the patient does not consent. However, the majority would not permit the removal of artificial nutrition and hydration from one who is terminally ill and cannot or will not ingest food and liquids through the mouth, making a distinction between "unusual" medications and the nutrition and hydration that are required by everyone. A minority would disagree, claiming that intravenous or enteral nutrition and hydration are not providing food and water in the "usual" sense, which we must do, and thus are similar to medications that are effectively prolonging the dying process. One is also required to administer beneficial procedures for complications that any other patient would willingly accept, such as antibiotics for pneumonia and blood replacement for severe hemorrhage.

Can any amount of medication be administered to relieve pain? (N)

The amount of medication that can be given to alleviate pain is a highly controversial issue. Some argue that a physician may give whatever is necessary, even if it may hasten a person's death, as long as the intention is to relieve pain. Others take the opposite approach, maintaining that as long as a physician knows that the dose is strong enough to kill the patient, he would be liable for injuring the patient indirectly even if the primary intent was to relieve pain. However, all would agree that if the primary intent is to cause the patient's death, it is forbidden to give that amount of medication, even at the request of the patient.

Is assisted suicide permitted in Jewish law? (F)

Since suicide is forbidden in Jewish law, so is assisting one to end his or her own life. This applies even if one merely hands an overdose of pills to an individual or sets up a machine so that a person can administer a lethal substance intravenously (i.e., so that once provided with a mechanism to commit suicide, the person acts completely on his or her own). This ruling is based on the biblical prohibition against "putting a stumbling block before the blind," which the Rabbis interpreted as extending to misleading those whose medical conditions are causing them such suffering that they think that a prohibited act is permissible. By actively making it possible for a person to do what is forbidden, the assistant is also guilty of the more serious crime of "strengthening or aiding those who commit a sin." An assistant who knowingly administers a lethal dose of medication or poison with the intent to bring about the person's death has committed murder, even if the ultimate motive was benign. [59]

Does Jewish law permit organ donation? (N)

As with autopsy, the issue of organ donation revolves around the often-conflicting principles of *kavod ha-met* (reverence for the human body after death) and *pikuach nefesh* (preservation of life). In this instance, however, these two basic tenets are in agreement, for it is assumed that deceased persons would be honored if their organs were used to preserve the lives of others. Enabling a person to live through the donation of an organ is also a supreme act of *chesed*, loving-kindness to one's fellow human being. Despite the predominant opinion that delaying burial to permit organ transplantation does not diminish, but rather enhances, respect for the dead, some rabbis have limited this practice to varying degrees. Others object based on the belief that one must be buried intact to be resurrected whole. Nevertheless, except for the most extreme branches of Orthodoxy, virtually all rabbis agree that saving a life in this world unequivocally takes precedence over whatever one believes about future resurrection.

According to Jewish thought, does cessation of brain function indicate the time of death? (N)

A precise definition of the moment of death is a major issue in obtaining permission for organ transplantation among traditional Jews. According to classical Jewish sources, two criteria determined when death occurred. The majority rule was the breath test, in which a feather was placed beneath the nostrils and lack of movement signified death. A minority view in the Talmud maintained that the cessation of heartbeat was also required. Later codifiers insisted on both respiratory and cardiac manifestations of death. Acknowledging the difficulty of accurately distinguishing death from a fainting spell, Moses Isserles argued that even after the cessation of breath and heartbeat, one should wait a period of time before assuming that a person is dead. In a 1988 ruling approving heart transplantation, the Chief Rabbinate of Israel effectively accepted the modern definition of death as a completely flat electroencephalogram (both cortical and brainstem function), which indicates the cessation of spontaneous brain activity.

Is Judaism concerned only with this life, not with what may happen after one dies? (F)

Judaism is often regarded as a religion of this world, with Christianity being focused on what occurs after death. However, Judaism has always maintained a strong belief in an afterlife, though there has been a broad spectrum of views in different historical eras concerning the nature of the World to Come (*olam ha-ba*).

Is the concept of resurrection a Christian belief and not part of Jewish thought? (F)

According to the older books of the Hebrew Scripture, the sojourn of a human being on earth is followed by a descent to *She'ol*, a kind of Hades, a gloomy netherworld where the dead live an ethereal, shadowy existence. An explicit biblical formulation of the doctrine of the resurrection of the dead occurs in the Book of Daniel (12:2): "Many of those that sleep in the dust of the earth will awake, some to eternal life, others to reproaches, to everlasting abhorrence." However, the most dramatic portrayal of this bodily resurrection is found in the Valley of the Dry Bones prophecy in Ezekiel (37), which envisions the future redemption of Israel.

During the Talmudic period, the concepts of immortality of the soul and resurrection of the body were contentious issues between the Pharisees, who accepted them, and the Sadducees, who rejected them. Some viewed the future life as a world of purely spiritual bliss, where "there is neither eating, nor drinking, nor propagating, no bargaining or jealousy or hatred or strife. All that the righteous do is to sit with their crowns on their heads and enjoy the light of the [Divine] Presence" (Ber. 17a). However, most believed that the souls would be restored into the bodies of the resurrected, who would rise from their graves fully clothed (Ker. 111b). In the eschatological Paradise, the righteous will sit at golden tables (Taan. 25a) or under elaborate canopies and participate in lavish banquets (BB 75a), in which they will feast on the flesh of the mythical creatures, Leviathan and Behemoth (Lev. R. 13:3). Rabbinic (and later liturgical) texts viewed the afterlife as a "Torah academy on high,"[60] an eternal house of study that reflected the highest values of the Jewish people.

Is there a Jewish belief in transmigration of souls? (T)

Given that some individuals are born disadvantaged, either physically or mentally, it would seem unjust to expect that everyone would reach the same level of achievement. Consequently, a popular mystical response was that each soul deserves more than one opportunity at life and therefore is placed in a variety of bodies to realize its potential. The body to which the soul is assigned in any given life reflects the moral quality of its former existence. When fully developed, the soul breaks out of the wheel of transmigration and returns to its Divine source. Some kabbalists believed that, after death, the soul does not necessarily go into a new human body. The worse the sins committed, the lower the life form to which the soul is assigned. Some mystics even made detailed lists of which sins led one to come back as which animal.

Is faith the basic requirement for entry into the World to Come? (F)

The afterlife has traditionally been viewed as a time of ultimate judgment and reckoning, with each person held accountable for his or her own actions. Thus, instead of serving as a way to moral and social escapism (i.e., since this world is not the essential, why be concerned with moral and social responsibility), the opposite is true. Accountability in the *future* world is based on one's actions in *this* world, which can be seen as a preparation for the World to Come. In Judaism, mere "faith" is not sufficient.

Does the Talmud specify requirements for entry into the World to Come? (T)

The Talmud describes a scenario in which a person goes before the heavenly tribunal for a final day of judgment and is asked five questions (Shab. 31a). Rather than the questions one might expect—Did you keep the Sabbath? Did you maintain a kosher home? Did you give to charity?—they are (1) Were you honest in your business dealings? (2) Did you set aside time to study Torah? (3) Did you have children? (4) Did you hope for redemption? and (5) Did you search for wisdom? The sages have related these questions to the innate human desire to perpetuate the self beyond the grave in terms of honestly gained wealth, wisdom, and experience; children as "biological" redemption; and perpetuation of one's hopes and dreams.

According to Jewish tradition, while still alive is it possible to have a foretaste of the World to Come? (T)

Even if we did have some information concerning the afterlife, we would be incapable of comprehending it, since the World to Come would have a different dimension of existence beyond time or space and thus be beyond our ability to describe it or even conceive of it. Nevertheless, Jewish tradition assures us that, even in this life, one can experience a sample of the World to Come. As the Talmud states, "three things give us a foretaste of the World to Come—the Sabbath, a sunny day, and sexual intercourse" (Ber. 57b).

[handwritten margin note: Islam says similar: "70 sloe-eyed virgins"]

NOTES

1. Rosen, 203.
2. Maimonides, *Mishneh Torah*, Milah 2:1.
3. Klein, 205.
4. Strassfeld and Strassfeld, 30–37.
5. Dosick, 289.
6. Trepp, 323.
7. Donin, *To Pray as a Jew*, 249.
8. Dosick, 294.
9. Blech, 202.
10. Mechilta Amalek 3.
11. Tanchuma, ed. Buber, Lech Leacha 6 f., 32a.
12. Klein, 440.
13. Ibid.
14. Trepp, 248.
15. Kadden and Kadden, 46–47.
16. Klein, 445.
17. Ibid., 446.
18. One exception is that a female convert may not marry a *kohen*, unless she became Jewish at age three or younger (Yev. 60b). In the Talmudic period, a convert generally could not be appointed to any public office or serve as a judge in a criminal court.

19. Maimonides, *The Commandments*, 240.
20. Kadden and Kadden, 61.
21. Diamant, 175.
22. Kolatch, *The Jewish Book of Why*, 42.
23. Ibid., 34.
24. Diamant, 101.
25. Kadden and Kadden, 66.
26. Greenberg, 226.
27. Kolatch, *The Jewish Book of Why*, 43–44.
28. Although they are home every night, their work is so strenuous that they lack the strength to cohabit more frequently (Maimonides).
29. They must travel during the week to bring grain to sell in the market and were typically away from home for six days at a time.
30. Maimonides, *Mishneh Torah*, Ishut 21:1–4.
31. Strassfeld and Strassfeld, 117–18.
32. Biale, 116–18.
33. *Etz Hayim*, 10.
34. *Sefer Ha-Chinnuch*, 228.
35. Hertz, 498.
36. Chill, 70.
37. Riskin, xi–xiii.
38. Dorff, 359.
39. Chill, 478.
40. Haut, 28–29.
41. Biale, 106.
42. Ibid., 105.
43. Frankel and Teutsch, 157.
44. Kolatch, *The Jewish Book of Why*, 53.
45. Ibid., 54–55.
46. Lamm, 65.
47. Kadden and Kadden, 106.
48. Kolatch, *The Jewish Book of Why*, 75.
49. Lamm, 98–99.
50. Kolatch, *The Jewish Book of Why*, 64; Lamm, 112.
51. Kolatch, *The Jewish Book of Why*, 67.
52. Lamm, 102–4.
53. *ArtScroll Siddur*, 456.
54. Sperling, 198.
55. Hammer, *Entering Jewish Prayer*, 286.
56. Rabinowicz, 15–18.
57. Lamm, 84.
58. Kadden and Kadden, 102.
59. Dorff, 183–84.
60. *Yeshivah shel ma'alah*, as in the preamble to the *Kol Nidrei* on Yom Kippur.

Chapter Ten

Food

Have you ever wondered . . .

1. Is kosher food blessed by a rabbi?
2. Are non-Jews the biggest consumers of kosher items in the United States?
3. Do Jews have a natural revulsion for pork?
4. Are four-legged animals other than pigs kosher?
5. Does the Bible list those birds that can be eaten?
6. Is there controversy regarding which fish are kosher?
7. Are all insects not kosher?
8. Are vegetables and fruits always kosher?
9. May a kosher animal killed by a hunter be eaten according to Jewish law?
10. Is any Jew permitted to perform ritual slaughtering (*shechitah*)?
11. Does *glatt kosher* refer to meat that meets the highest standards of *kashrut*?
12. Is "kosher-style" just a marketing term to confuse buyers by making them think the food is kosher?
13. May all parts of a properly slaughtered kosher animal be eaten?
14. Is the prohibition against mixing milk and meat of biblical origin?
15. Are Jews required to wait six hours between meat and dairy meals?
16. Is a cheeseburger kosher?
17. Can milk from any clean animal be consumed?
18. Are eggs kosher?
19. May eggs be eaten with milk?
20. Is it easy to find certified kosher products?
21. Are Jews required to drink wine (or grape juice)?

22. Is all wine kosher?
23. Are gefilte fish and kugel typical Jewish food?
24. Is gefilte fish served to avoid a violation of the Sabbath?
25. May fish and meat be eaten together?
26. Is fish a popular food for Sabbath meals?
27. Does the Bible list certain types of agricultural produce that symbolize the fertility of the Land of Israel?
28. Was wheat used for the *omer* on Passover because it ripens earlier than barley?
29. During biblical times, was barley considered food for the poor?
30. Is the grapevine the first cultivated plant mentioned in the Bible?
31. Is the fig tree the symbol of Messianic redemption?
32. Was olive oil used only for cooking in biblical Israel?
33. Were olives used as a standard of measurement?
34. In the description of Israel as a "land of milk and honey," does this refer to honey from a bee?
35. Was there a controversy regarding whether bee's honey is kosher?
36. Is there a sandwich named for Hillel, the famed rabbinic sage?
37. Are blintzes a popular food for Shavuot?
38. Is the *ha-Motzi* blessing, thanking God for "having brought forth bread from the earth," recited before eating corn bread?
39. Are chickpeas traditionally eaten on Purim?
40. Are chickpeas traditionally eaten on Passover?
41. Are Boston baked beans related to the Jewish dietary laws?
42. Did the Jerusalem Talmud consider garlic an aphrodisiac?

Is kosher food blessed by a rabbi? (F)

A rabbi does not make food kosher by blessing it. The major role of a rabbi (and certifying agencies) in the process is to ensure that processed foods do not contain any prohibited ingredients. Improperly slaughtered meat and forbidden foods (such as pork and shellfish) or food combinations (mixtures of meat and milk) cannot be made kosher simply because they are "blessed" by a rabbi!

Are non-Jews the biggest consumers of kosher items in the United States? (T)

Most people who buy and eat kosher food in America are *not* Jewish. The belief that kosher products are cleaner, healthier, or simply better than non-kosher products has encouraged many non-Jews to buy them. Muslims, who do not eat pork, often prefer purchasing kosher products and buying kosher food if *halal* products are not available. Vegetarians can purchase kosher dairy or *pareve* products knowing that they do not contain meat, while vegans and those who cannot consume milk products can buy items labeled *pareve* and be assured that they contain neither meat nor milk.

Do Jews have a natural revulsion for pork? (F)

The Rabbis stressed that the refusal of a Jew to eat pork should not be based on a personal dislike but on the Divine command: "A man should not say, 'I have no desire to eat swine's flesh'; rather he should say, 'I would like to eat it, but what can I do, seeing that my Father in Heaven has decreed against it'" (Sifra Ked. 11:122).

Are four-legged animals other than pigs kosher? (N)

The Bible divides the "beasts of the earth" into those animals that are permitted for consumption (*tahor*; clean) and those that are prohibited (*tamei*; unclean). To qualify as kosher, a quadruped must both chew the cud (ruminant) and have completely cloven (divided) hooves (Lev. 11:3; Deut. 14:6), meaning that they cannot hold prey and thus are not carnivores. The Torah specifies 10 herbivorous animals (wild and domestic) that meet these criteria—the ox, sheep, goat, deer, gazelle, roebuck, wild goat, ibex, antelope, and mountain sheep (Deut. 14:4–5). The camel, hare, and hyrax chew their cud but are forbidden because they have incompletely split hooves; the pig has a completely cloven hoof but is prohibited because it does not chew its cud (Deut. 14:7–8).

Does the Bible list those birds that can be eaten? (F)

Although kosher quadrupeds and fish are mentioned by characteristics so that their identities are clear, the Torah specifically names 20 non-kosher species of birds (such as the raven, falcon, hawk, and vulture), thus implying that all others are kosher (Lev. 11:13–19; Deut. 14:11–18). Unfortunately, over time the precise identities of some of the biblically prohibited birds became unclear, and it is now forbidden to eat any species of bird (or its eggs) unless there is a well-established tradition that it is kosher (such as chicken, capon, Cornish hen, domestic duck and goose, pigeon, partridge, and peacock). In general, all birds of prey and scavengers that eat carrion are prohibited (Hul. 3:6).

Is there controversy regarding which fish are kosher? (T)

The Bible clearly states that kosher fish must have fins and scales (Lev. 11:9–12). All fish that have scales also have fins, but not all fish that have fins have scales. To be kosher, the scales must be easily scraped off with a knife without removing the skin of the flesh (which excludes creatures with ill-defined scales such as shellfish, shark, catfish, and amphibians).[1] A major controversy concerns the status of swordfish, which has scales when young but then loses them when older. Swordfish are permitted by the American Conservative movement but forbidden by most Orthodox authorities.

Are all insects not kosher? (N)

Although labeling "all winged swarming things that walk on fours" as an "abomination," the Bible specifically permits the eating of four kinds of *chagavim* (locusts/grasshoppers) that have "jointed legs to leap with on the ground" (Lev. 11:20–23). However, because none of these can be unequivocally identified, later rabbis declared all species of insects to be forbidden. Nevertheless, there are some communities, such as Jews from Morocco and Yemen, that have a long-standing tradition regarding the identity of these kosher insects and still eat them to this day.

Are vegetables and fruits always kosher? (N)

Although all vegetables and fruits are inherently kosher, extra care may be required in their preparation to ensure that there are no tiny worms or insects clinging to them. This can be problematic with leafy vegetables like lettuce and flowery vegetables such as broccoli and cauliflower, and asparagus. Berries also must be carefully checked.

May a kosher animal killed by a hunter be eaten according to Jewish law? (F)

For meat to be kosher, it must be slaughtered by a specially trained *shochet* who, in addition to being a skilled professional, must be a pious individual who is well trained in the technical requirements of Jewish law. Jewish ritual slaughtering strives to prevent unnecessary suffering to the animal. It requires one continuous deep horizontal cut with a perfectly sharp blade with no nicks or unevenness. This severs the windpipe and all of the great blood vessels of the neck so that the animal instantly loses all sensation.

Jewish law prohibits eating the flesh of any kosher animal that has died without kosher slaughter. Termed *nevelah*, this includes an animal that has been killed by hunting or has died a natural death.

Is any Jew permitted to perform ritual slaughtering (*shechitah*)? (F)

The law of Jewish ritual slaughtering, derived from the verse, "you may slaughter any of the cattle or sheep . . . as I have instructed you" (Deut. 12:21), is not spelled out in the Bible and is considered part of the Oral Law. Today, the complex and minute regulations dealing with ritual slaughtering must be performed by a licensed *shochet*, who is both a skilled professional and a pious person well trained in Jewish law.

Does *glatt kosher* refer to meat that meets the highest standards of *kashrut*? (N)

Although the *halachah* permits certain abnormalities in animal lungs that have been determined to be harmless, those Jews who are strictest in their observance declare as kosher only those animals with smooth, lesion-free lungs. This super-inspected meat is called *glatt kosher*, from the Yiddish word for "smooth." Although this term literally refers only to meat, today it has been expanded to apply to food or restaurants that meet the most exacting standards of *kashrut*.

Is "kosher-style" just a marketing term to confuse buyers by making them think the food is kosher? (T)

"Kosher-style" is a meaningless term, since a product is either kosher or not kosher. Indeed, the term is highly misleading since it "tends to confer credibility upon merchants doing business in the Jewish community by attaching a quasi-religious label to their wares, when in fact no kosher status exists."[2] It is important to remember that so-called "Jewish foods"—such as challah, gefilte fish, blintzes, kugel, latkes, and even chicken soup—are not inherently kosher. Even though they are associated with Jewish traditions, in order to be kosher these items must still be prepared from kosher ingredients according to the dietary laws.

May all parts of a properly slaughtered kosher animal be eaten? (F)

The sciatic nerve and its associated blood vessels must be removed before the hindquarters of any quadruped can be prepared for consumption. This nerve extends from the rear of the spinal column and runs down the inner side of the leg. Although some expert butchers can perform the difficult task of cutting out the sciatic nerve, in general the process is so time-consuming and costly that many kosher butchers do not handle the hindquarters at all. Packinghouses usually sell the hindquarters of kosher-slaughtered animals to the general market for non-kosher cuts of meat, such as sirloin or T-bone steak and filet mignon.[3]

The prohibition against eating the sciatic nerve is an eternal reminder of the wrestling match between Jacob and the "stranger," which took place as the patriarch was returning to the Land of Israel after dwelling 20 years with his father-in-law, Laban (Gen. 32:25–32). During this titanic struggle, which resulted in Jacob's name being changed to Israel since he had "struggled with God," the attacker injured Jacob's thigh, resulting in a residual limp.

The fat portions (*chelev*) surrounding the kidneys, liver, stomach, and intestines of oxen, sheep, and goats, which were sacrificed on the Altar in biblical and Temple times, are also forbidden for consumption (Lev. 7:23).

Is the prohibition against mixing milk and meat of biblical origin? (N)

The prohibition against mixing milk and meat derives from the verse, "You shall not boil a kid in its mother's milk" (Exod. 23:19; 34:26; Deut. 14:21). Since it became impossible to determine which baby goat and which mother's milk were related, the law was extended so that no animal (meat) could be cooked in any milk (dairy). The Rabbis interpreted the threefold repetition of this verse as defining three separate prohibitions—cooking meat and milk together; eating such a mixture; and deriving any benefit from it (such as savoring the aroma or feeding it to a pet) (Hul. 115b). In order to create a "fence around the Torah," the Rabbis decreed that the separation of meat and milk must be as complete as possible. Thus, it is necessary to use separate utensils (pots, pans, dishes, and flatware) for dairy foods and meat, which are known respectively in Yiddish as *milchig* and *fleishig*.

Are Jews required to wait six hours between meat and dairy meals? (N)

Because meat takes a long time to digest, or due to residual meat particles or fatty residues caught in the teeth or their taste remaining on the palate, Jewish law rules that one must wait a designated period after eating a meat meal before ingesting milk products. Customs range from one hour for Jews of Dutch ancestry to three hours for German Jews and six hours for those from other European countries.

The waiting time between milk and meat is much shorter. One is generally permitted to eat meat almost immediately after a milk meal, after thoroughly rinsing the mouth and eating a piece of bread or some other "neutral" solid. After hard cheese, however, it is customary to wait a longer period (up to six hours in some traditions) before eating meat.

Is a cheeseburger kosher? (N)

A traditional cheeseburger is obviously not kosher due to the forbidden mixture of milk and meat. However, today there are numerous *pareve* imitation dairy products (derived from soybeans, coconuts, almonds, hazelnuts, rice, and oats) that can be used with meat. Similarly, substitutes for meat (such as beans, grains, tempeh, tofu, and seitan) can be used with dairy products. So it is now possible to have a kosher cheeseburger with meat and *pareve* soy cheese or real cheese and a non-meat patty.

Can milk from any clean animal be consumed? (N)

Milk from cows, sheep, and goats is generally permitted, though the Talmud prohibited Jews from drinking "milk which a heathen milked without an Israelite watching him," because of the fear that a non-Jew may have inadvertently mixed it with milk from an unclean animal (Av. Zar. 2:16). Consequently, today some strictly observant Jews will only drink *chalav Yisrael*—milk obtained and bottled under the supervision of a Jew. Nevertheless, many rabbinic authorities permit the consumption of milk even if a Jew did not supervise the milking, basing this decision on the existence of laws that strictly forbid the adulteration of milk.

Are eggs kosher? (N)

According to the Talmud, "That which emerges from the clean [animal] is clean" (Bek. 1:2), meaning that the eggs of clean birds are permitted for food. The passage continues by saying "that which emerges from the unclean [animal] is unclean," meaning that the eggs of forbidden birds are prohibited. However, even eggs of permitted birds are forbidden if they have a spot of blood, indicating that they have been fertilized (Hul. 64b). An exception is an egg that comes from a chicken in an area where there is no cock. Because it could not have been fertilized, the egg may be eaten after the spot itself has been removed.

May eggs be eaten with milk? (T)

A Talmudic principle prohibits eating part of a living animal or eating meat (or fowl) with milk. However, the Rabbis concluded that the hard shell of the egg is formed before it has been laid, so that the egg is regarded as "complete on its issue." As an entity separate from the fowl that laid it, an egg is not subject to either of the prohibitions against being eaten with milk (Betz. 6b).

Is it easy to find certified kosher products? (T)

Keeping kosher has become much easier in recent years, since at least 75 percent of prepackaged products and most major brands now have some type of kosher certification indicated by a *heksher*. Coming from the same Hebrew root as the word "kosher," a *heksher* is a symbol indicating that the product has been certified as kosher by a specific rabbi or organization. In addition to a *kashrut* symbol, many kosher certifying organizations add the letter "D" (or the word "dairy") as appropriate. For *pareve* products, the word itself is added, since the letter "P" is used to indicate that a product is kosher for Passover.

Are Jews required to drink wine (or grape juice)? (T)

The drinking of wine has long been an essential element of Jewish ceremonial celebrations. The Sabbath and festivals are greeted and conclude with blessings over a cup of wine (*Kiddush* and *Havdalah*), and four cups of wine are drunk at the seders on Passover and Tu b'Shevat. Wine is also included at circumcisions and weddings. Jewish tradition appreciates the positive qualities of wine and its capacity to "gladden the heart" (Ps. 104:15). However, it permits drinking only in moderation and in the context of holiness and community.

Is all wine kosher? (F)

To be considered kosher, wine must be produced under rabbinic supervision. Only Sabbath-observant Jews are permitted to handle the wine or operate the wine-making equipment from grape crushing to consumption. This prohibition against Jews drinking wine prepared by Gentiles was initially instituted lest some of it may have been used as a libation in pagan ceremonies connected with idol worship. In rabbinic times, this decree remained in effect to prevent Jews from fraternizing with Gentiles in social situations, which could lead to assimilation or intermarriage.

A partial exception is wine that is *mevushal*. Literally "boiled," and meaning "pasteurized," this Hebrew term refers to wine that is heated to the boiling point so that air bubbles are brought to the surface with some loss of liquid due to evaporation. This is required according to the laws of *kashrut* for a wine to retain its kosher status once it has been opened and poured by a non-Jew, such as a waiter. Thus, a wine that is produced in this manner retains its religious purity regardless of who opens or pours it.

Are gefilte fish and kugel typical Jewish food? (N)

These are characteristic foods of Ashkenazic Jews, who are of Western and Northern European origin and spread to Central and Eastern Europe. However, these are not typical of Sephardic cuisine originating around the Mediterranean in the Middle East and North Africa and extending to Asia. The differences in these two styles of cooking are closely related to the climate, soil, and locally available produce. The Ashkenazim ate cold, hearty vegetables such as potatoes, carrots, cabbage, and mushrooms, as well as freshwater fish (especially carp) and salted herring. The Sephardic ate peppers and eggplant, zucchini and tomatoes, a diet featuring "sensual, aromatic, and colorful" cuisine of herbs and spices, olive oil, rice, cracked wheat, beans, lamb, and saltwater fish.[4]

Is gefilte fish served to avoid a violation of the Sabbath? (T)

A Yiddish word literally meaning "stuffed," *gefilte* refers to deboned, ground fish mixed with seasonings, which is stuffed or rewrapped in its skin and poached to produce what became the quintessential Sabbath dish in Eastern Europe. It originated around the fourteenth century as a way to avoid the need to remove bones from a piece of fish on the Sabbath, which would violate the prohibition against "winnowing." Although it is permitted to eat around the bones of a non-filleted piece of fish, this is a tedious task that detracted from the joy of the Sabbath meal. The solution was to prepare in advance a boneless piece of fish that could be eaten without fear of violating the Sabbath laws or choking on a bone.

May fish and meat be eaten together? (N)

For the purposes of *kashrut*, fish is considered *pareve*—so that it theoretically could be eaten or cooked with meat or milk. However, the Rabbis prohibited eating or cooking fish and meat together, because they were convinced that this mixture was dangerous for one's health. However, after eating fish it is not necessary to wait before eating meat; all that is required is to rinse the mouth or chew something else. In the United States today, Orthodox communities generally still prohibit cooking and eating meat and fish together, while the Conservative movement permits this practice.

Is fish a popular food for Sabbath meals? (T)

Fish has long been a featured food for meals on the Sabbath. In the biblical account of Creation, three things were blessed after they were created—fish, humans, and the Sabbath. In addition, the Talmud states that the

Sabbath is a foretaste of the World to Come, in which the righteous will feast on Leviathan, the legendary sea monster. Finally, the numerical value of *dag*, the Hebrew word for fish, equals seven, and the Sabbath is the seventh day of the week.

Does the Bible list certain types of agricultural produce that symbolize the fertility of the Land of Israel? (T)

The Bible lists seven agricultural products that represent the fertility of the land—wheat, barley, grapes, figs, pomegranates, olive oil, and honey (Deut. 8:8). According to R. Akiva, these were the "first fruits" (*bikurim*) that the Israelites were commanded to bring as offerings to the *kohanim* in Jerusalem (Bik. 3:9).

Was wheat used for the *omer* on Passover because it ripens earlier than barley? (F)

Although both wheat and barley were sown in the Land of Israel at the beginning of winter, wheat develops more slowly. Therefore, the first barley crop served as the *omer*, which was brought to the Sanctuary on Passover. The "first fruits of the wheat harvest" were offered seven weeks later on Shavuot (Exod. 34:22).

During biblical times, was barley considered food for the poor? (N)

One of the most ancient cultivated grains and able to resist drought, barley was the grain used in the bread, cakes, and porridge that constituted the staple of the Israelite diet. Wheat initially was the food of the rich, but became the common source of flour as it became more plentiful with improvements in agricultural methods. Consequently, barley was relegated to the poor and as food for livestock.

Is the grapevine the first cultivated plant mentioned in the Bible? (T)

Immediately after the Flood, Noah planted grapevines, though he soon "drank of the wine and became drunk" (Gen. 9:20–24). Grapes have long been considered symbolic of the fertility of the Land of Israel. When the 12 spies returned from Canaan, two of them were required to carry a single cluster of grapes on a pole (Num. 13:23), an image that is used as an advertisement promoting tourism to the modern State of Israel.

Is the fig tree the symbol of Messianic redemption? (N)

The fig tree and grapevine are mentioned together in the prophet Micah's vision of the future Messianic Age: "Each man will dwell under his own vine and fig tree, and none will be afraid" (Mic. 4:4). They also are used to symbolize fertility, peace, and security in the Land of Israel (1 Kings 1:5; Zech. 3:10).

Was olive oil used only for cooking in biblical Israel? (F)

In addition to its use in cooking, olive oil served as a fuel for lamps (including the menorah in the Sanctuary), a major element in the meal offering (*minchah*), and for anointing priests, prophets, kings, and holy places.

Were olives used as a standard of measurement? (T)

Although the fruit of different varieties come in different sizes, the olive was considered a common standard of measurement. The term *ke-zayit* (like an olive) was often used to indicate the minimum amount required to fulfill a ritual obligation.

In the description of Israel as "a land of milk and honey," does this refer to honey from a bee? (F)

The biblical phrase (Exod. 3:8) actually refers to syrup made from dates (or figs or grapes), rather than bee's honey, which was much less common in the area.

Was there a controversy regarding whether bee's honey is kosher? (T)

During the Talmudic period, honey came to refer specifically to honey from a bee. In view of the principle, "that which goes forth [issues] from the unclean is unclean" (Bek. 1:2), the question arose whether bee's honey should be forbidden, since the bee is considered an unclean insect. However, the Rabbis concluded that this honey was permitted, since it is not produced by the bee but rather comes from the nectar of a flower and is merely stored in the body of the insect (Bek. 7b).

Is there a sandwich named for Hillel, the famed rabbinic sage? (T)

There is a "Hillel sandwich" (*korech*) made of *matzah* and *maror*, which is eaten at the Passover seder just before the festive meal. It is a reminder of Hillel's practice in Temple times, based on the verse: "They shall eat it [the Passover sacrifice] with unleavened bread and bitter herbs" (Num. 9:11).

Are blintzes a popular food for Shavuot? (T)

Thin crepes filled with cheese and topped with sour cream or fruit sauce are frequently served on days when it is customary to eat dairy dishes. They are especially appropriate on Shavuot, which commemorates the giving of the Torah, since two blintzes placed side by side resemble the two tablets of the commandments that Moses received at Mount Sinai.[5] Other reasons offered for eating dairy dishes on Shavuot include: the promise that the Israelites would live in a "land flowing with milk and honey"; the numerical value of *chalav* (milk) is 40, the number of days Moses was on Mount Sinai; the abundance of available dairy products at Shavuot, which occurs when the lambs and calves born in the spring are suckling; and when accepting the Torah, the Israelites were obligated to observe the laws of *kashrut*, but had not yet learned the rules of animal slaughter.

Is the *ha-Motzi* blessing, thanking God for "having brought forth bread from the earth," recited before eating corn bread? (F)

This special blessing is only said before eating bread from one of the five species of cereals grown in the Land of Israel—wheat, barley, spelt, oats, and rye.

Are chickpeas traditionally eaten on Purim? (T)

According to legend, Queen Esther observed the laws of *kashrut* in the palace of King Ahasuerus by eating only vegetarian foods. These included legumes such as chickpeas, which have long been a dietary staple of Mediterranean Jews.

Are chickpeas traditionally eaten on Passover? (N)

Although Sephardic Jews eat most legumes on Passover, some Middle Eastern Jews do not eat chickpeas. This is based on the similarity between its Hebrew name (*himtzah*) and *hametz*, which is forbidden during the festival. Ashkenazic Jews do not customarily eat chickpeas, since they are considered *kitniyot*.

Are Boston baked beans related to the Jewish dietary laws? (N)

Cooking was one of the 39 categories of creative work forbidden on the Sabbath. In order to get around this prohibition and have a hot meal to enhance the enjoyment of the Sabbath lunch, on Friday morning Jewish women throughout medieval Ashkenazic Europe would fill a large pot with beans and potatoes, seasoned with meat and spices, cover and seal it with a flour and water paste, and keep it simmering overnight in a central communal oven until retrieved after synagogue on Saturday. This was known as *cholent*, from an Old French word (*chald*) meaning "hot." A similar slow-simmering dish for Sabbath lunch developed among Sephardic Jews. In the United States, the Pilgrims refrained from cooking on Sunday, their day of rest. After being exposed to the customs of Sephardic Jews who had settled in Holland after being expelled from Spain, the Pilgrims adopted the concept of a slow-cooking Sabbath stew. However, they substituted maple syrup and pork for some of the Jewish ingredients. Leaving the pot in the oven Saturday night, the Pilgrims had a warm lunch to eat after church—the forerunner of the classic American dish of Boston baked beans.[6]

Did the Jerusalem Talmud consider garlic an aphrodisiac? (T)

The Jerusalem Talmud recommends eating garlic on Friday evenings, since "it promotes love and arouses desire" (Meg. 4:1). The rabbis also taught that garlic "satiates, keeps the body warm, brightens up the face, increases semen, and kills parasites in the bowels [intestinal worms]" (BK 82a).

NOTES

1. *Stone Chumash*, 599.
2. Witty and Witty, 429.
3. Kolatch, *The Jewish Book of Why*, 94.
4. Roden, 15–17.
5. Marks, 224.
6. Shostek, 122.

Chapter Eleven

Plants and Animals

Have you ever wondered ...

1. Does Judaism support ecology?
2. Does *bal taschit* refer to destroying fruit-bearing trees during war?
3. Are Jews traditionally indifferent to animals?
4. Is there a Talmudic story that illustrates how a Rabbi learned about the need for mercy toward animals?
5. Has "sabra" become a proud nickname of native-born Israelis because it grows taller than any other type of cactus?
6. Can animal behavior serve as a model for proper human conduct?
7. Does the Talmud suggest that the chicken comes before the egg?
8. When the Bible prohibited the Israelites from eating "flesh torn by beast in the field" (and thus not kosher), did it command to "cast it to the dogs" (Exod. 22:30) because they were the favorite type of pet?
9. Did the Rabbis approve of dogs as pets?
10. In biblical times, was the donkey considered a symbol of royalty?
11. Is a Jew forbidden from gaining any benefit from a pig?

Does Judaism support ecology? (T)

The Jewish attitude toward nature is based on the belief that the universe is the work of the Creator, and its natural order reflects the Divine covenant with God's creations. Love of God includes love of all aspects of Divine creation, encompassing all humanity, plants and animals, and the inanimate world. When God placed Adam in the Garden of Eden, the first man was commanded to "work it and guard it" (Gen. 2:15). The deep Jewish concern

275

for ecology is exemplified in the regulations concerning the Sabbatical Year, and in the prohibitions against wanton destruction (*bal taschit*) and cruelty to animals (*tza'ar ba'alei chaim*). The need to preserve the natural balance of creation is the underlying rationale for forbidding the mingling of fabrics (*sha'atnez*). A famous comment of R. Yochanan ben Zakkai (first century C.E.) illustrates the importance with which the Rabbis viewed preservation of the natural world: "If you are planting a tree and you hear that the Messiah has come, finish planting the tree and then go greet him" (ARN 31).

Does *bal taschit* refer to destroying fruit-bearing trees during war? (N)

Although the concept of *bal taschit* derived from the biblical prohibition against destroying fruit-bearing trees when laying siege to a city (Deut. 20:19), the Rabbis expanded it to forbid the wanton destruction of anything valuable to human existence, including vessels, clothing, buildings, springs, and food. Destruction for a positive purpose, such as cutting trees to construct a dwelling, is permitted.

Are Jews traditionally indifferent to animals? (F)

Tza'ar ba'alei chaim (lit., "pain of living things") is a fundamental Jewish value prohibiting cruelty to animals. It is based on the concept that human beings are responsible for all God's creatures. Not only is cruelty to animals forbidden, it is a positive commandment for human beings to show compassion and mercy to them. Judaism's sensitivity to animals is strikingly illustrated in the rabbinic prohibition against reciting the festive blessing *Shehecheyanu* before the act of ritual slaughter or before putting on new leather shoes. As explicitly stated in the Ten Commandments, animals as well as human beings must be allowed to rest on the Sabbath (Exod. 20:10; Deut. 5:14). The Rabbis understood several commandments as explicitly related to the prohibition against cruelty to animals—*shechitah* (kosher slaughtering); not working with two animals of unequal strength (Deut. 22:10); not muzzling an animal as it threshes (Deut. 25:4); sparing the mother bird (Deut. 22:6–7); and relieving an animal of its burden (Exod. 23:5). One of the seven Noahide laws is the prohibition of eating flesh cut from a living animal.

Is there a Talmudic story that illustrates how a Rabbi learned about the need for mercy toward animals? (T)

According to legend, once when Judah ha-Nasi, the famed editor of the Mishnah, was studying Torah, a calf being taken to the slaughterhouse begged the sage to save him. "What can I do for you?" he shrugged. "For this you were created." As punishment for his insensitivity, Judah suffered from a toothache for 16 years. One day, a weasel ran past the sage's daughter, who was about to kill it. Judah admonished her to let the animal live, citing the verse from Psalms (145:9), "The Lord is good to all; and His mercy is upon all His works." Because Judah's compassion prevented the suffering and death of the harmless animal, his toothache ceased (BM 85a).

Has "sabra" become a proud nickname of native-born Israelis because it grows taller than any other type of cactus? (F)

Originally imported from Mexico in the 1600s, the prickly pear cactus known as sabra now grows abundantly in the Land of Israel. The name has been applied to native-born Israelis as a description of their national character—prickly and hard on the outside (to withstand the perils of living in an often-dangerous part of the world), but soft and sweet on the inside.

Can animal behavior serve as a model for proper human conduct? (T)

According to R. Yochanan, "If the Torah had not been given [to guide us], we could have learned modesty from the cat [which covers its excrement], honesty from the ant [which does not take the food of another], chastity from the dove [which is faithful to its mate], and good manners from the rooster [who first courts and then mates]" (Er. 100b).

Does the Talmud suggest that the chicken comes before the egg? (T)

According to the passage, "All [the works of] Creation were brought into being with their full stature, their full capacities, and their full beauty" (RH 11a), thus the Talmud appears to favor the view that the chicken came first. [1]

When the Bible prohibited the Israelites from eating "flesh torn by beast in the field" (and thus not kosher), did it command to "cast it to the dogs" (Exod. 22:30) because they were the favorite type of pet? (F)

According to Rashi, this was a reward for dogs remaining quiet on the night of the Exodus from Egypt. Had they barked or howled, the dogs might have terrified the escaping Israelites. Consequently, God decreed that any food deemed not kosher (*treif*) could be given to the dogs. [2]

Did the Rabbis approve of dogs as pets? (N)

Although the Bible considered the dog a potentially dangerous animal that was often trained to attack passersby (Ps. 22:17), several rabbinic stories tell of how dogs saved their masters from violence and death. Nevertheless, the potential ferocity of dogs made the Rabbis wary of them. "Anyone who raises a vicious dog in his house keeps loving-kindness away from his house," since this makes poor people afraid to enter the house to ask for charity (Shab. 63a). R. Eleazer strongly opposed raising dogs in the Land of Israel, declaring that "he who breeds dogs is like one who breeds swine" (BK 83a). However, this practice was permitted in a town on the frontier, as long as the owner agreed to "keep it chained during the day and let it free only at night." One early sage even stated that a person should not live in a town "in which no horses neigh or dogs bark," based on the rationale that dogs raise the alarm and the robbers are pursued on horseback (Pes. 113a).

In biblical times, was the donkey considered a symbol of royalty? (T)

The Bible describes Saul, David, Solomon, and Absalom as riding on donkeys. Zechariah prophesized that, at the end of days, the Messiah will ride into Jerusalem "triumphant and victorious, [yet] lowly [humble], and riding on a donkey" (Zech. 9:9). In addition, according to the Talmud, "if one sees a donkey in a dream, he may hope for salvation" (Ber. 56b).

Is a Jew forbidden from gaining any benefit from a pig? (F)

The Rabbis made a distinction between items prohibited for food (*treif*) and those from which no benefit can be enjoyed (such as *chametz* on Passover). Therefore, although it is strictly forbidden to eat the flesh of swine, it is permitted to wear pigskin shoes (even in the synagogue), carry a pigskin wallet, and even bind religious books in pigskin.[3] Moreover, Jews suffering from diabetes can be treated with insulin derived from pigs.

NOTES

1. Toperoff, 47.
2. Toperoff, 50–51; *Stone Chumash*, 433.
3. Toperoff, 195.

Chapter Twelve

Symbols of Jews and Judaism

Have you ever wondered . . .

1. Does the term "Jew" occur in the Bible?
2. Does *B'nai Yisrael* mean "Children of Israel"?
3. Does being the "Chosen People" mean that Jews are superior and receive special privileges?
4. Is God's choice of the Jewish people stressed in the synagogue and the home?
5. Was the melody of *Hatikvah* written expressly for the Israeli national anthem?
6. Was there once more than one Jewish flag?
7. Did Theodor Herzl design the flag of the modern State of Israel?
8. Do the blue and white colors of the Israeli flag have any biblical allusion?
9. Does the Magen David have a long history as a religious symbol in Judaism?
10. Does the word *mezuzah* refer to the wood or metal case placed on the door of a Jewish home?
11. Is the *mezuzah* placed in a slanted position for aesthetic reasons?
12. Is anything written on the back of the parchment?
13. Can a mistake in a *mezuzah* be fixed by a scribe?
14. Must a house of prayer have a *mezuzah* on its doorpost?
15. Should a Jew place a *mezuzah* on the outside of any place where he sleeps?
16. When moving out of a house, should a Jew remove the *mezuzot*?
17. Is the *mezuzah* thought to have magical properties?

18. Does the word "menorah" refer to the eight-branched candelabrum used on Chanukah?

Does the term "Jew" occur in the Bible? (F)

This general term for a member of the Jewish community does not occur in the Bible, where the covenantal people are termed B'nai Yisrael. The word "Jew" derives from the Latin *Judaeus*, which in turn comes from the Hebrew *Yehudah* (Judah, the fourth son of Jacob). It was first used by the Greeks and Romans to describe someone from the province of Judea (Judah), which had become the dominant tribe after the fall of the Northern Kingdom and the dispersion of the 10 lost tribes.

Does *B'nai Yisrael* mean "Children of Israel"? (N)

Although often translated literally as "Children of Israel," the term is best rendered simply as "Israelites." According to Hebrew grammar, the root *ben* in a compound word does not mean "son of," but rather implies class membership (i.e., a member of the group known as "Israel," the covenantal community). Similarly, *ben adam* means a human being, rather than "son of man," and *b'nai mitzvah* means class membership in those obligated to observe the commandments, rather than the literal "sons of the commandments."

Does being the "Chosen People" mean that Jews are superior and receive special privileges? (F)

The concept of being a "Chosen People," with a unique relationship to God that imposes special responsibilities, has been a central tenet of Jewish thought throughout the centuries. It derives from the series of Divine choices throughout the biblical narrative—the selection of one man (Abraham) to spread the word of the One God; one family (the Children of Israel) to carry on that tradition; one High Priest (Aaron) and family of priests (*levi'im*); one king (David, after the failure of Saul); one land (Israel); and one permanent site for the Sanctuary (Jerusalem). Each of the chosen individuals and groups are responsible for certain tasks and are required to assume particular roles. As Moses stated to the Israelites in his farewell address: "For you are a people consecrated to the Lord your God, who chose you out of all the nations on earth to be His treasured people [or 'special possession'])" (Deut. 7:6).

Israel is to be "a light unto the nations" (Isa. 49:6), spreading the ideas of monotheism, God's relation to humanity, and Divine salvation to the ends of the earth. The selection of Israel, which was sealed by several covenants, was not motivated by its size and strength ("the smallest of peoples"), but solely by Divine love (Deut. 7:7–8). However, there is no concept of a relationship between chosenness and national origin, since King David and ultimately the Messiah himself are descendants of Ruth, the Moabite who converted to Judaism.

The Bible emphasizes that the doctrine of election does not imply the conferring of special privileges, but instead imposes extra obligations and responsibility. It calls for a reciprocal human response, with Israel obligated to "keep His statutes, and observe His laws" (Ps. 105:45). Failure to live up to this responsibility will incur Divine punishment: "You alone have I singled out of all the families of the earth, which is why I call you to account for all your iniquities" (Amos 3:2). Israel's election to spread the Divine message even encompasses the task of vicarious suffering for the nations, as God's "tortured servant" (Isa. 52:13–53:12). Nevertheless, although the wickedness of the people may incur heavenly wrath and punishment, the Divine love underlying the initial choice of Israel is unconditional and will preclude any absolute rejection by God.

For much of the non-Jewish world, the ironic notion that the seemingly despised Jews could conceive of themselves as the Chosen People was summed up in Hilaire Belloc's jingle, "How odd of God to choose the Jews," to which later was added the retort, "It was not odd—the Jews chose God!"

Is God's choice of the Jewish people stressed in the synagogue and the home? (T)

Critical moments in the service reinforce the idea of the Jewish people as having been chosen by God. In the festival *Amidah*, it is written: "You have chosen us from all peoples; You have loved us and taken pleasure in us, and have exalted us above all tongues; You have hallowed us with Your commandments, and brought us near to Your service." Each person honored with an *aliyah* to the Torah expresses gratitude to God: "Who has chosen us from all the nations and sanctified us with His commandments." A similar view is expressed in the *Aleinu*, in which Jews thank God for having "not made us like the nations of the lands nor placed us like the families of the earth . . . [or] made our lot like that of the multitudes." In the Friday evening *Kiddush*, Jews thank God for "having chosen and hallowed us above all other nations," while in the *Havdalah* ceremony at the end of the Sabbath, they praise God for making the distinction "between Israel and the [other] nations."

Was the melody of *Hatikvah* written expressly for the Israeli national anthem? (F)

The melody for *Hatikvah*, the national anthem of the State of Israel, is based on an Eastern European folk song called *Carul cu Bo* (Cart and Ox). It had previously been used by the classic Czech composer Bedrich Smetana in *The Moldau*, part of his *My Fatherland* suite. Samuel Cohen, an immigrant from Moldavia, arranged the music, and it was combined with the poem *Tikvateinu* (Our Hope), written by Naphtali Herz Imber. The simple text of

Hatikvah is a stirring expression of the age-old Zionist dream, to which the Jewish people clung during their almost two millennia of dispersion in the far-flung Diaspora: "As long as deep in the heart, the soul of a Jew yearns, so long as the eye looks eastward toward Zion, our hope is not lost—the 2,000-year hope to be a free people in our land, the land of Zion and Jerusalem"—a hope that was finally realized with the birth of the State of Israel in 1948.

Was there once more than one Jewish flag? (T)

During their wanderings in the wilderness after the Exodus from slavery in Egypt, the Israelites raised banners and flags in their camps to signify their tribal identities. According to tradition, each tribal prince had a flag of a unique color, corresponding to one of the 12 precious stones in the breast-plate of Aaron, the High Priest.

Did Theodor Herzl design the flag of the modern State of Israel? (N)

The flag of the modern State of Israel—a white rectangle with two blue stripes along its entire length and a Star of David in the center made up of six stripes forming two equilateral triangles—reflects a variety of influences. Theodor Herzl's first design for a Zionist flag was seven gold stars (representing the "seven working hours" of the day) on a white background (standing for "our new and pure life"). Although other Zionist leaders convinced him to accept the Star of David, Herzl insisted that six stars appear opposite the six points of the Magen David with a seventh star above it. This design, with the inscription *Aryeh Yehudah* (Lion of Judah) embroidered in the center, became the first Zionist flag.

Do the blue and white colors of the Israeli flag have any biblical allusion? (N)

The combination of blue and white as the colors of the Israeli flag was derived from an 1860 poem (*Judah's Colors*) by Austrian Ludwig August Frankl, which explained that the blue symbolized "the splendors of the firmament" while the white represented "the radiance of the priesthood." The blue stripes on the Zionist flag also were inspired by the stripes on the *tallit*, which provided a religious and ritual symbolism of Jewish life guided by precepts of the Torah, while the Star of David reflected the unity of the Jewish people. The dark blue stripes in the original flag were later lightened to enhance visibility at sea.

Does the Magen David have a long history as a religious symbol in Judaism? (F)

Literally "Shield of David" and popularly known as the "Star of David" or "Jewish Star," the Magen David has become the most distinctive and universally recognized symbol of Judaism and Jewish identity, even though it has no special religious significance. The Magen David is a six-pointed star (hexagram) formed by two equilateral triangles that share the same center and are placed in opposite directions. During the Middle Ages, hexagrams appeared frequently on seals and in churches, but rarely in synagogues or on Jewish ritual objects.

In 1354, Emperor Charles IV granted the Prague Jewish community the privilege of displaying its own flag with a six-pointed star. Known as the Magen David, it became part of the official seal of the community. Following the French Revolution, the politically emancipated Jews selected the Magen David as the identifying symbol of Judaism, similar to the cross that represented Christianity.

Theodor Herzl selected the Star of David to be the symbol for the new Zionist movement, probably because it had achieved wide circulation among Jewish communities yet did not evoke any definite religious associations. During the Holocaust, the Nazis selected the yellow star as a badge of shame to be worn on the garments of all Jews. After the war, Jews turned this badge of humiliation and death as the central image on the flag of the State of Israel.

Today, the Star of David is widely used on religious articles, as well as on necklaces and other jewelry as a secular symbol of Jewish identity. It also is the emblem of the Magen David Adom, the Israeli equivalent of the Red Cross.

Does the word *mezuzah* refer to the wood or metal case placed on the door of a Jewish home? (N)

The distinctive mark of a Jewish home and a reminder of the Divine Presence, the Hebrew word *mezuzah* actually refers to the piece of parchment, made from the skin of a clean animal, upon which a scribe has written the first two paragraphs of the *Shema* (Deut. 6:4–9 and 11:13–21), the affirmation of faith in Judaism. These include the commandment, "And you shall write them upon the doorposts [*mezuzot*] of your house and upon your gate," which was the meaning of the word in biblical Hebrew. The parchment is rolled up and enclosed in a special wood or metal case, since it has the status of a Torah scroll and cannot be touched directly. Although the case may be a work of art, it is the parchment within that is the essential part of the *mitzvah*.

Is the *mezuzah* placed in a slanted position for aesthetic reasons? (F)

Among Ashkenazim, the case is fastened at an angle (upper end pointed inward) to the upper third of the doorpost on the right side of the outside door, as well as to the doorpost of every living room in the house excluding bathrooms, storerooms, and kitchen. The positioning reflects a compromise between the views of two prominent medieval sages—Rashi, who argued that the *mezuzah* should be affixed vertically, and his grandson (Rabbenu Tam), who maintained it should be horizontal. Among Sephardim, the custom is to affix the *mezuzah* in a vertical position, pointing upward to the heavens.

Is anything written on the back of the parchment? (T)

The Hebrew word *Shaddai* (Almighty) is written on the back of the parchment, which is inserted into the case in such a way that the word can be seen through a small opening near the top of the container. According to the Zohar, this Divine Name is used in the *mezuzah* because its three Hebrew letters (*shin, dalet, yud*) are an acronym for *Shomer Daltot Yisrael* (Guardian of the doors of Israel). Since at least the thirteenth century, written upside down at the bottom of the back of the *mezuzah* is a seemingly meaningless combination of Hebrew letters—*Kozu be'Mochsaz Kozu*—which is a cryptogram formed by substituting the next letter of the alphabet for *YHVH Eloheinu YHVH* (the Lord, God, the Lord).

Can a mistake in a *mezuzah* be fixed by a scribe? (N)

According to Jewish law, the portions of the Torah that are on a *mezuzah* (and *tefillin*) must be written by a skilled *sofer* in the correct order. If a mistake is found in the last line or two, these words can be erased and then rewritten—as long as what follows does not include the name of God (that may not be erased), which occurs in the next-to-last line. A *mezuzah* (or *tefillin*) that cannot be fixed is termed *pasul* and must be buried, which means that hours of work by the *sofer* were wasted.

Must a house of prayer have a *mezuzah* on its doorpost? (N)

Strictly speaking, a place that is used only for prayer does not require a *mezuzah*, since it is not a "dwelling place," and one is not permitted to eat in a room designated for prayer. However, since most synagogues also contain rooms for eating, meetings, and other activities—purposes for which a *mezuzah* is required—they typically do have *mezuzot* on their entry doors.

Should a Jew place a *mezuzah* on the outside of any place where he sleeps? (N)

The commandment to affix a *mezuzah* applies only to permanent structures in the home. It does not apply to temporary or casual places, such as a *sukkah*, a camping tent, or an automobile.

When moving out of a house, should a Jew remove the *mezuzot*? (N)

A Jew who moves into a new home is expected to put a *mezuzah* on the outer door immediately, or at least within the first 30 days. A Jew who sells or rents a home to a fellow Jew is required to leave the *mezuzot* in place, but must remove them if the purchaser or lessee is a non-Jew. If one leaves a house before a buyer or renter is found, the *mezuzot* should be removed when vacating the premises.

Is the *mezuzah* thought to have magical properties? (N)

The *mezuzah* may relate to the ancient custom of marking the doorposts of the house to protect against evil spirits. Indeed, this practice appears to be reflected in the Passover story, when the Israelites daubed blood on their doorposts to keep away the Angel of Death, who was killing the firstborn of Egypt in the 10th plague. Despite rationalist attacks on the use of a *mezuzah* as an amulet, it is clear that this protective function has always been part of its appeal. Indeed, some modern Jews wear a *mezuzah* (lacking the inner parchment) around the neck as a good luck charm or as an affirmation of Jewish identity.

Does the word "menorah" refer to the eight-branched candelabrum used on Chanukah? (N)

Although many Jews apply the term "menorah" to the eight-branched candelabrum used for the Chanukah lights, this is actually a *chanukiah*. The menorah is the seven-branched structure, fashioned from a single mass of pure gold, that once stood in the Jerusalem Temple and has become one of the most beloved and enduring symbols of Judaism and the emblem of the State of Israel. The menorah was a common symbol during the rabbinic period, especially in synagogue mosaics and in various amulets, seals, and rings. For the kabbalists, the menorah symbolized the Tree of Life, and its seven branches the lower seven *sefirot*; the oil in the menorah was seen as a symbol of Divine abundance flowing to humankind. Today, the menorah is often a prominent feature in decorations for Torah mantles and the ark. In Israel, the menorah is reproduced frequently on stamps, coins, and souvenirs. A large sculptured menorah depicting major events of Jewish history stands outside the Knesset in Jerusalem, a symbol of the miraculous rebirth of the Jewish people after almost 2,000 years of exile.

Chapter Thirteen

Folkways

Have you ever wondered . . .

1. Does Judaism reject astrology?
2. Are there traces of astrology in Judaism?
3. Did Jews worship the sun?
4. Were the sun and moon originally of equal size?
5. Is there a special blessing for the sun?
6. Do most major Jewish festivals begin on the new moon?
7. Are stars mentioned in God's promise to Abraham?
8. Did the Rabbis of the Talmud believe in the significance of dreams?
9. Did the Rabbis recommend what to do after a bad dream?
10. Do Jews reject amulets and belief in the "Evil Eye"?
11. Do Jews have characteristic superstitious practices?
12. In Jewish lore, is there any significance to sneezing during a conversation?
13. Is there a recognized way to pull the ears after sneezing?
14. Is knocking on wood a Jewish practice?
15. Is 13 an unlucky number?
16. Does the Hebrew term *am ha-aretz* have negative connotations?
17. Is there a Jewish tradition that a living man can be created by human hands?
18. Can anyone create a golem?

Does Judaism reject astrology? (N)

287

Astrology is the ancient study of the connection between the cycles of heavenly bodies and human behavior. Although indirectly condemned in the Bible and rejected by Maimonides, many Rabbis appeared to believe that celestial bodies were powerful determinants of human affairs: "Length of life, children, and sustenance [earning a livelihood] depend not on merit but rather on *mazal* [the stars]" (MK 28a). Others deemed that this only applies to Gentiles, arguing that "Israel is immune from planetary influence [lit., 'Jews have no stars']" (Shab. 156a). That page of Talmud goes into meticulous detail as to the effect of the day and month of birth on the character of the individual. For example, a person born in the constellation of Mars will be "a shedder of blood." However, given the free will of the individual, the person has the power to direct this trait either to evil ways (murderer) or in a positive direction (surgeon, ritual slaughterer, or circumciser).

Are there traces of astrology in Judaism? (T)

Some vestiges of astrology remain in Jewish folklore. *Mazal tov* (good luck; lit., "good constellation") has become the most common expression of congratulations among Jews. A person who succeeds in all his endeavors is known as a *bar mazal* (son of luck), while one who fails at everything is scorned by the Yiddish term *shlimazal*.

Did Jews worship the sun? (N)

Although worshiped as a deity by its pagan neighbors, the sun was, for the Jews, merely "the greater light to rule the day," which was formed on the fourth day of Creation (Gen. 1:16). Nevertheless, sun worship was introduced into Judah by the evil King Manasseh. King Josiah then abolished the cult, destroying his grandfather's altars as well as chariots that had been dedicated to sun worship at the entrance of the Temple (2 Kings 23:5). Hellenized Jews renewed worship of the sun and even wore amulets blasphemously referring to Helios (the Greek sun god) as "God in the Heavens." Mosaic floors in some ancient synagogues, especially Beit Alpha in Galilee, depicted Helios as a handsome youth riding in a chariot drawn by the four horses of the sun placed in the center of the signs of the zodiac.[1]

Were the sun and moon originally of equal size? (N)

To counteract popular fascination with the sun and to prevent any straying from strict monotheism, the Rabbis developed a tale that personified the sun and the moon. According to the *aggadah*, the sun and moon initially were of equal size. In one version, jealousy led each to claim to be greater than the other, and it was necessary to reduce the size of one of them. The moon was chosen to be degraded because it had unlawfully intruded into the domain of the sun, by sometimes remaining visible while the sun was still above the horizon (Gen. R. 6:3). The other version explains that the moon asked God: "Can two kings share a single crown?" When God responded that the moon should make itself smaller, the latter replied: "Because I presented a proper claim, must I be diminished?" Recognizing the justice of the moon's plea, God compensated the moon by decreeing that only it would be seen both day and night. Moreover, the moon would have an honor guard of stars and the Jewish people would calculate the months and years by its phases (Hul. 60b).[2]

Is there a special blessing for the sun? (T)

Once every 28 years, at the vernal equinox early on the first Tuesday of the month of Nisan, the sun begins a new cycle. According to tradition, at that time the sun is situated at the exact same position as at its creation. After the morning service on Wednesday, Jews traditionally recite the Blessing of the Sun (*Birkat ha-Hamah*). The blessing thanks God for creating the sun and for its continued beneficence. At the conclusion of the ritual, worshipers express the hope that they will be privileged to live until the coming of the Messiah, to witness the fulfillment of the prophecy of Isaiah (30:26): "and the light of the sun shall be sevenfold, as the light of the seven days." The next occasion for the *Birkat ha-Chamah* service will be in 2037.

Do most major Jewish festivals begin on the new moon? (F)

With Rosh Chodesh considered only a minor holiday, Rosh Hashanah is the only major Jewish festival that begins on the new moon. Passover, Shavuot, and Purim all begin on the full moon, as do the midwinter holiday of Tu b'Shevat and the midsummer festival of Tu b'Av. The only festival that begins during the waning moon is Chanukah, though it continues for several days after the appearance of the new moon.[3]

Are stars mentioned in God's promise to Abraham? (T)

As a biblical symbol of limitlessness, the Divine promise to Abraham was that his descendants would be "as numerous as the stars of Heaven and the sands on the seashore" (Gen. 22:17).

Did the Rabbis of the Talmud believe in the significance of dreams? (N)

The Rabbis expressed a wide range of views about dreams, although most were convinced that they were significant. Dreams were described as a "variety of prophecy" (Gen. R. 17:5) or "a sixtieth part of prophecy" (Ber. 57b)—a way in which God communicated with human beings. Some were more cynical, noting that one professional would give a favorable interpretation of a dream to one who paid him, but to one who did not pay him, would give an unfavorable interpretation of the same dream (Ber. 56a). Others completely rejected the veracity of dreams, arguing that "dreams neither help nor harm" (i.e., they have no significance) (Hor. 13b).

Did the Rabbis recommend what to do after a bad dream? (T)

Based on the statement, "fasting is potent against a dream," some sages observed a "dream fast" after a bad dream. This took place even on the Sabbath or a festival, if the dream was especially troubling. In another intriguing ritual based on Talmudic teaching, the dreamer asks three close friends to gather on the morning after an apparent bad dream to encourage the dreamer to interpret the dream for good. The three friends open the ritual by reciting in unison, "Do not interpretations belong to God?" This is followed by the responsive recitation of various verses, some of which are repeated three times. It is recommended, but not required, that the dreamer fast and repent on the day of the ritual.[4]

Do Jews reject amulets and belief in the "Evil Eye"? (N)

Although the Bible explicitly forbids divination and magic, the Talmud refers to a variety of amulets and belief in demons, the Evil Eye, and the significance of dreams.

The belief in amulets gradually diminished with the emancipation of European Jewry, though their use remained widespread in Eastern Europe until World War II. They are still popular among Jews of Middle Eastern and North African descent, especially in Israel, where they have aroused controversy during political campaigns when distributed by certain ultra-Orthodox parties under the auspices of prominent rabbis. Although many consider belief in the power of the Evil Eye and various ways to combat it as superstitious, the idea still exerts substantial influence in some communities. Even modern rationalist Jews in the Western world pay heed. Among Yiddish-speaking Ashkenazic Jews, it is customary to temper any praise with the phrase *keyn ayen horeh* (without the Evil Eye), which is generally shortened to *keynahora*. A popular hand-shaped amulet in Sephardic cultures is the *hamsa*, which frequently has a single eye set in the middle of the palm. This symbolizes the ever-vigilant eye of God or is a means to deflect the malevolent intentions of the Evil Eye.

Do Jews have characteristic superstitious practices? (T)

As in all cultures, Jewish folklore contains practices applicable to a variety of occasions. Some of the most popular are spitting three times (literally or figuratively) to prevent tragedies and ward off the Evil Eye; chewing on thread when wearing a garment on which someone is sewing a button or repairing a seam; pulling one's ears after sneezing; closing books that have been left open; and placing salt in pockets and corners of the room to drive away demons, especially in new clothes or a new home.

In Jewish lore, is there any significance to sneezing during a conversation? (T)

Rather than a response to irritation of the nasal passages, a sneeze in ancient times was deemed a grave omen of impending death. Indeed, this may be the underlying reason for the development of the custom of saying "long life" and "good health" to one who has sneezed. A traditional belief is that when a person sneezes during a conversation, whatever has just been said will occur, based on the concept of "sneezing on the truth." While not as foolproof as direct prophecy, it is said to indicate that events that are rational and plausible will actually come to pass, or that an event that has already occurred really happened just as the story related.

Is there a recognized way to pull the ears after sneezing? (F)

Especially common among Jews from Galicia and Lithuania, this super-stitious practice has engendered heated arguments as to whether one ear or both should be pulled and whether it should be pulled up or down.

Is knocking on wood a Jewish practice? (F)

Knocking on wood for protection from evil is a completely *non*-Jewish practice, even though many Jews do it. Many connect this action to Christian beliefs that relate wood to slivers of the cross, which were believed to bring good luck. However, this practice has a more universal, pantheistic origin. Long before the time of Jesus, some cultures regarded trees as gods. Believers were convinced that touching (or knocking on) wood could produce magical results.

Is 13 an unlucky number? (F)

Although 13 is an unlucky number in some cultures (as in Friday the 13th), it has many positive connotations in Judaism. Thirteen is the age of bar mitzvah, when a boy reaches his religious and legal maturity and becomes responsible for fulfilling all the *mitzvot*. After the disastrous episode with the Golden Calf, God revealed to Moses the Thirteen Attributes of Mercy. In the Talmudic period, Rabbi Ishmael developed 13 hermeneutical principles with which to explain the Torah. The Thirteen Principles of Faith were compiled by Maimonides. The fringes (*tzitzit*) of the *tallit* contain 5 knots binding 8 threads for a total of 13, which is also the numerical value of the Hebrew letters in the word *echad* (one) that is used in the *Shema* to indicate the Unity of God.

Does the Hebrew term *am ha-aretz* have negative connotations? (N)

Literally "people of the land," this phrase is used in the Bible to refer to the Jewish masses. In Talmudic times, *am ha-aretz* was applied to the common people who did not observe rabbinic ordinances. Eventually, it became a derogatory term to denote an ignoramus who lacked knowledge of Jewish tradition and laws; a vulgar, boorish, ill-mannered person; or a country bumpkin.

Is there a Jewish tradition that a living man can be created by human hands? (T)

A *golem* is a legendary creature made of dust and clay by human hands in a magical, artificial way to serve its creator. The legend of the *golem* became fully developed during the Middle Ages, under the influence of non-Jewish European folklore and Kabbalah. According to *Sefer Yetzirah* and other mystical books, it is possible to create living beings out of earth, by using esoteric combinations of the letters of the Hebrew alphabet, the names of the 10 *sefirot*, and the secret Name of God. The most famous legend involves the sixteenth-century Rabbi Judah Loew of Prague, who created a *golem* to protect the Jews of his city against a false charge of blood libel.

Can anyone create a *golem*? (F)

According to the Talmud, "if the righteous desired it, they could [by living a life of absolute purity] be creators . . . Rava created a man and sent him to R. Zeira, who spoke to him and, receiving no answer, said to the man, 'You are a creature of the magicians. Return to your dust'" (Sanh. 65b). However, making a *golem* was considered a hazardous endeavor, which should be attempted only by those who were extremely pious and deeply immersed in the Divine mysteries. The fear was that the creator would lose control of the *golem*, which would then run amok.

NOTES

1. Frankel and Teutsch, 166.
2. *Etz Hayim*, 7–8.
3. Frankel and Teutsch, 166.
4. Witty and Witty, 491–92.

Glossary

Adonai. Literally, "my Lords," the current pronunciation of the holiest and most distinctly Jewish name of God, written in the Hebrew Bible with the four consonants *YHVH.*

Agunah (chained woman). One whose marriage has in fact ended, but who legally remains a married woman (bound to a husband who no longer lives with her) and thus is unable to remarry.

Aliyah (pl., *aliyot*). Literally meaning "ascent," this Hebrew word is used to describe the honor of being called up to the *bimah* to read a portion from the Torah.

Amidah (standing [prayer]). Core of the prayer service since the destruction of the Second Temple. Traditionally, the *Amidah* is said silently and then repeated (with some additions) by the prayer leader if there is a *minyan.*

Aramaic. Ancient Semitic tongue that was the official language of the Persian Empire and became the vernacular of the Israelites who were exiled to Babylonia after the destruction of Jerusalem in 586 B.C.E. During the Second Temple period, Aramaic replaced Hebrew as the medium of everyday speech.

Ashkenazim. Designation first used in the Middle Ages for the Jews living in northwest Europe (northern France and western Germany) and the religious and cultural traditions they followed. Today, it refers to Jews of Northern and Eastern European (including Russian) background, with distinctive liturgical practices and religious and social customs that are contrasted with the Sephardim, Jews whose roots trace back to Spain, the Middle East, and the Mediterranean region.

Babylonian Talmud. A compendium of the wide-ranging discussions and elaborate interpretations of the Mishnah by scholars known as *amoraim* (Aramaic for "explainers") in the great academies of learning in Babylonia.

Baruch. Opening word of all blessings. Although often translated as "blessed," in context the word is the equivalent of "praised," for it would be impossible for humans to add anything to God's powers or possessions.

Beit din. Literally "house of judgment," the rabbinic term for a Jewish court of law. Classically composed of three rabbis who arbitrated disputes among Jews on a variety of issues in civil law, today it primarily focuses on religious matters, such as the granting of a *get* (divorce) or decisions regarding conversion.

Bimah (elevated place). Raised platform that contains the table on which the Torah scroll is placed when it is read.

Blood libel (blood accusation). Allegation that Jews used the blood of murdered Christian children to bake *matzot* and prepare wine for Passover and other rituals.

Chametz. Hebrew term for leavened products, which are explicitly prohibited on Passover.

Chanukah. Literally meaning "dedication," this joyous eight-day festival begins on the 25th of Kislev (December) and commemorates the victory of Judah Maccabee and his followers over the army of the Greek-Syrian ruler, Antiochus Epiphanes, and the rededication of the defiled Temple in 165 B.C.E.

Chol ha-mo'ed. Hebrew term for the intermediate days of the weeklong holidays of Passover and Sukkot.

Chumash. Book containing the Five Books of Moses (Torah), the first of the three divisions of the Bible.

Chuppah. Hebrew word referring either to the wedding canopy, which is usually made of beautiful fabric and supported by four poles, or to the marriage ceremony itself.

Covenant. The special relationship between God and the Jewish people, which is a major foundation of the theology of Judaism. The classic covenant between God and Israel took place at Mount Sinai, less than two months after the Exodus from Egypt.

Dayan. Judge of a rabbinic court.

Etrog. Yellow citrus fruit, usually larger than a lemon with a tangy taste and smell, which is one of the four species used as part of the celebration of the festival of Sukkot.

Gabbai. Hebrew word for each of the two synagogue members who serve as an "honor guard" on either side of the Torah scroll as it lies on the reading table. Their major duty is to closely follow the Torah reading from a printed text and quietly correct any mistakes, which are easy to make since the scroll has neither punctuation nor vowel signs.

Gelilah. Hebrew word for rolling up and tying the Torah scroll and replacing its cover and ornaments, actions performed by the *goleil*.

Gemilut chasadim. Literally "the giving of loving-kindness," a core social value that the Rabbis considered a quintessential and distinctive attribute of the Jew.

Genizah. Literally meaning "hidden away," this Hebrew term refers to a special storeroom in a synagogue that is set aside for the disposition of torn prayer books, Bibles, and other holy texts, as well as religious articles such as *tefillin* and *tzitzit* that have deteriorated and can no longer be used, so as to show respect for the name of God contained within them.

Get. Talmudic term for the formal divorce document that is signed by the husband and then delivered to his wife.

Haftarah. Literally meaning "concluding portion," a selection from the biblical books of the Hebrew prophets that is read after the Torah reading on Sabbaths, major festivals, and fast days.

Hagbah (lifting). Hebrew word for the honor of raising the Torah in the synagogue (by the *magbiah*) after it has been read, so that the congregants can see the writing on the parchment scroll.

Haggadah. Literally meaning "telling" (of the Exodus), this book contains the prayers and blessings, stories, legends, commentaries, psalms, and songs that are traditionally recited at the Passover seder.

Halachah. Literally meaning "walking," this all-inclusive term refers to the body of law (rules, prohibitions, requirements) that govern every aspect of Jewish life and constitutes the essence of Jewish religious and civil practice.

Havdalah. Literally meaning "separation," an ancient ritual ceremony that marks the conclusion of the Sabbath (or a festival).

Hazzan (cantor). The synagogue official who leads the congregation in prayer and song.

High Holy Days. Inclusive term applied to Rosh Hashanah, Yom Kippur, and the Ten Days of Repentance between them. Also known as the "Days of Awe" (*Yamim Noraim*), during this solemn period of introspection, repentance, and prayer the Jew endeavors to merit being inscribed and sealed in the Book of Life for the coming year.

Kabbalah. A Hebrew word derived from a root meaning "to receive," Kabbalah is the Jewish mystical tradition.

Kaddish. Aramaic prayer that closes every public service as well as the individual sections within it. Recited only in the presence of a *minyan*, the *Kaddish* proclaims God's greatness and holiness and expresses the hope for the speedy establishment of the Divine kingdom on earth.

Kashrut (dietary laws). From a Hebrew root meaning "fit" or "proper," the collective term for the Jewish regulations and customs that specify what types of food are permitted for consumption and how they are to be prepared.

Kavanah. Hebrew word meaning "devotion, intent, conscious purpose," which describes the state of mind required for praying or performing a *mitzvah*. In the context of prayer, *kavanah* implies total concentration on the act of prayer and the intent to come ever closer to God.

Kedushah. A Hebrew word meaning "holiness" or "sanctification," it refers to the proclamation of God's holiness and glory in the third blessing that is recited during the repetition of the *Amidah* when a *minyan* is present.

Ketubah. Literally meaning "written document," it is the Jewish marriage contract that is written in Aramaic and stipulates the financial and other obligations of the husband toward his wife.

Kiddush (sanctification). Prayer recited over a cup of wine in the home and the synagogue to consecrate the Sabbath or a festival.

Kippah. Head covering that has become a universally recognized symbol of Jewish identity.

Kohen (pl., **kohanim**). Member of the hereditary priestly caste, the descendants of Aaron and exclusively male. During biblical times, the *kohanim* performed four sacred functions: (1) serving the cultic center; (2) deciphering signs and messages from God (i.e., revealing God's will, somewhat like a diviner in other traditions); (3) treating defilement (purification) and diseases (resulting from impurities); and (4) dispensing justice and teaching the law.

Kohen Gadol. High Priest responsible for conducting the special rites on Yom Kippur.

Levi (pl., **levi'im**). Descendant of the tribe of Levi (third son of Jacob and Leah), who were consecrated by Moses to serve in the Tabernacle and Temple as gatekeepers, musicians, teachers, and assistants to the priests.

Lulav. Branch of the date palm that is part of the four species used on Sukkot, which are collectively called *lulav* from its largest member.

Lurianic kabbalah. System of Jewish mysticism based on the teachings of Isaac Luria, the sixteenth-century master of Kabbalah who settled in Safed.

Ma'ariv. The evening service.

Machzor. Prayer book for the major festivals of the Jewish year, with the best known used for the High Holy Days (Rosh Hashanah and Yom Kippur).

Maftir. Literally meaning "one who concludes," the person who is called up for the final *aliyah* on the Sabbath and festivals. After the Torah is raised and bound, the *maftir* chants the *haftarah*, the reading from the prophets.

Mamzer. Contrary to popular misconception, a *mamzer* (often mistranslated as "bastard") is not someone born out of wedlock. Instead, a *mamzer* is the child of a sexual relationship between a man and woman whose marriage could never be valid under Jewish law.

Manna. Food that nourished the Israelites during their 40 years of wandering in the wilderness.

Masoretes. From a Hebrew root meaning "tradition" or "that which has been transmitted," textual scholars of the seventh through tenth centuries who determined and preserved the authentic (masoretic) text of the Torah.

Mechitzah. Literally "partition," the physical separation in an Orthodox synagogue between the space reserved for men and that for women.

Megillah. Hebrew word meaning "scroll," it usually refers to *Megillat Esther*, the reading of which is the main feature of the festival of Purim.

Megillot. Literally "scrolls," the fourth through eighth books of the Writings section of the Bible. They are often grouped together because of the custom of reading them on festivals—Song of Songs on Passover; Ruth on Shavuot; Lamentations on Tisha b'Av; Ecclesiastes on Sukkot; and Esther on Purim.

Menorah. Seven-branched candelabrum that once stood in the Jerusalem Temple. One of the most beloved and enduring symbols of Judaism, the menorah is the emblem of the State of Israel. The term "Chanukah menorah" is also applied to the eight-branched *chanukiah*.

Mezuzah. The distinctive mark of a Jewish home and a reminder of the Divine Presence, it consists of a piece of parchment, made from the skin of a clean animal, on which a scribe has written the first two paragraphs of the *Shema*. The case is fastened to the upper third of the doorpost on the right side of the outside door, as well as to the doorpost of every living room in the house (excluding bathrooms, storerooms, and kitchen).

Midrash. Deriving from a Hebrew root meaning "to search out," the word can refer to either the process of interpreting the Bible, or the genre of rabbinic literature that has collected these interpretations.

Mikveh. Literally "a collection [of water]," the Hebrew term for a ritual bath.

Minchah. The afternoon service.

Minyan. Literally "number," the term for the quorum of 10 adult males (or persons, in egalitarian congregations) necessary for congregational worship and certain other religious ceremonies.

Mishnah. Literally meaning "repetition" or "teaching" in Hebrew, the earliest major rabbinic book and the basis for the Talmud. It was compiled in the early third century by Judah ha-Nasi (Judah the

Prince, known simply as "Rabbi"), who sifted through, evaluated, and edited the vast number of legal opinions constituting the Oral Law that had been expressed over the centuries in the academies of learning, primarily in the Land of Israel.

Mishneh Torah. By far the greatest medieval legal code, compiled by Maimonides in the twelfth century.

Mitzvah (pl., **mitzvot**). Derived from a Hebrew root meaning "command," these religious obligations are the foundation for Jewish law and guidelines for Jewish behavior. In common usage, *mitzvah* has also come to mean a "good deed." There are 613 *mitzvot* in the Bible and seven rabbinic *mitzvot* that were not based on any biblical verses in the Torah.

Musaf. Literally "additional," it refers to the service added after the morning service on those days when an additional sacrifice was offered in the Temple—Sabbath, New Moon, the three pilgrimage festivals (Passover, Shavuot, Sukkot), New Year (Rosh Hashanah), and the Day of Atonement (Yom Kippur).

Musar. Orthodox movement, founded by Rabbi Israel Salanter in Lithuania during the mid-nineteenth century, which focused on ethics, moral instruction, and self-reflection.

Nusach. Collection of musical motifs that differentiate one service from another and have been handed down through the generations.

Omer, counting of the. From the second day of Passover until the festival of Shavuot, Jews are commanded to count seven weeks. Except for the 33rd day of the Omer (Lag ba-Omer), the Omer period is observed as a time of semi-mourning during which traditional Jews do not get haircuts, celebrate weddings, or attend concerts. Two modern holiday exceptions are the celebrations of Yom ha-Atzmaut (Israel Independence Day) and Yom Yerushalayim (Jerusalem Day).

Passover. Spring pilgrimage festival, also known as the "Feast of Unleavened Bread," which commemorates the redemption of the Jewish people from bondage and the Exodus from Egypt.

Pasul. Ritual object that is unfit for use.

Pikuach nefesh. Literally "preservation of life," the rabbinic term applied to the obligation to save an endangered human life. The concept of *pikuach nefesh* supersedes all laws except those prohibiting murder, idolatry, and incest.

Purim. A Hebrew word literally meaning "lots," the joyous festival on the 14th of Adar that celebrates the deliverance of the Jews from the plot of the Persian villain Haman to kill them.

Rosh Chodesh. Literally "head of the month," the first day of the month that correlates with the sighting of the crescent new moon.

Rosh Hashanah. Literally "head of the year," the first and second days of the month of Tishrei (September), which are celebrated as the beginning of the Jewish New Year and the anniversary of the Creation of the world.

Sabbath. The seventh day of the week and a time of rest and spiritual renewal, the Jewish Sabbath (*Shabbat* in Hebrew) begins at sunset on Friday evening and ends on Saturday evening when three stars are visible in the sky.

Seder. Literally "order," the home celebration held on the first night of Passover (also the second in the Diaspora) that fulfills the biblical injunction that parents tell their children about the miraculous deliverance of their ancestors from slavery in Egypt.

Sefirot. According to Kabbalah, the 10 emanations of God that represent the unfolding of the Divine personality, the inner life of God.

Semichah. Literally meaning "laying [of hands]," the traditional ordination required before a rabbi can decide practical questions of Jewish law.

Sephardim. From the Hebrew word *Sepharad* (Spain), the inclusive term for Jews and their descendants from Spain, Portugal, the Mediterranean region, North Africa, and the Middle East.

Seudat mitzvah. Festive meal eaten after religious ceremonies and celebrations, such as weddings, circumcisions, and bar/bat mitzvahs, or to mark the completion of a tractate of the Talmud (*siyum*).

Shaliach tzibbur. Literally "emissary of the congregation," the Hebrew term for the person leading the communal worship.

Shavuot. The second of the pilgrimage festivals, it occurs on the sixth of Sivan (plus the seventh in the Diaspora). Literally meaning "weeks," which reflects the seven weeks of the counting of the Omer that separate it from Passover, Shavuot is a harvest festival that in rabbinic times became observed as the anniversary of the giving of the Torah on Mount Sinai.

Shechinah. Translated as "Divine Presence," one of the rabbinic names for God and often depicted as the feminine aspect of the Deity.

Sheloshim. Literally "30," the period of mourning after the death of close relatives (parents, child, brother, sister, husband, wife).

Shema. Declaration of faith of the Jewish people in the Unity and Oneness of God and their acceptance of the yoke of the Kingdom of Heaven.

Sheva Brachot. Literally "seven blessings," the seven benedictions recited at the wedding ceremony under the *chuppah* after the bridegroom places the ring on the finger of his bride.

Shivah. Literally "seven," the most intense period of mourning that is observed for father, mother, wife, husband, son, daughter, brother, and sister (including half-brother and half-sister).

Shofar (ram's horn). Ancient musical instrument that is the most recognizable symbol of Rosh Hashanah.

Shulchan Aruch (Set Table). Compiled by Joseph Caro in the sixteenth century, the most influential code of law in modern Jewish life and the last comprehensive one to be written.

Siddur. The collection of all the prayers designated for public and private worship for weekdays, Sabbaths, festivals, and fast days.

Sifra. Halachic midrash on the Book of Leviticus, probably written in the second or third century.

Sifrei. Halachic midrash on the Books of Numbers and Deuteronomy (third century).

Simchat Torah (Rejoicing in the Law). Day on which the annual cycle of reading the Torah scroll is completed and immediately begun again.

Sukkah (pl., ***sukkot***). Hastily constructed, insubstantial structure that Jews erect as part of the observance of the fall festival of Sukkot.

Sukkot. Last of the three agricultural pilgrimage festivals, beginning on the 15th of Tishrei (the full moon five days after Yom Kippur), it is a festival of thanksgiving that celebrates the joy of the harvest and commemorates the temporary shelters (*sukkot*) in which the Israelites dwelled as they wandered through the wilderness.

Tallit. Traditional prayer shawl worn during daily morning prayers, to which ritual fringes (*tzitzit*) are attached to each of the four corners.

Talmud. In general use, the term "Talmud" refers to the Babylonian Talmud, though there is also a much smaller Jerusalem Talmud. The Babylonian Talmud is a compendium of the extensive discussions and interpretations of the Mishnah in the great academies of learning by scholars (*amoraim*) from the first half of the third century C.E. (Rav and Samuel) to the editing by Rav Ashi and Ravina around 500.

Tefillin. Two small black leather boxes that are bound by black leather straps to the forehead and arm and worn during each weekday morning service. Also known as phylacteries, they contain parchments on which are written the four sets of biblical verses that mention the commandment to wear them as "a sign [*ot*] upon your hand and as frontlets [*totafot*] between your eyes" (Exod 13:1–10, 11–16; Deut. 6:4-9; 11:13–21).

Teshuvah (repentance). From the Hebrew root *shuv* (return), it encompasses both a turning away from evil and a turning toward the good. A prerequisite for Divine forgiveness, it requires a combination of genuine remorse for the wrong committed plus evidence of changed behavior.

Tisha b'Av. Ninth day of the month of Av (July/August), a major fast day that marks the anniversary of the destruction of the First Temple by the Babylonians in 586 B.C.E. and the Second Temple by the Romans in 70 C.E.

Trope. Series of musical notations used for the chanting of the Torah and *haftarah*, as well as the *megillot* on festivals.

Tzedakah. Literally "righteousness" but often translated as "charity," in Jewish law this is not simply a generous or magnanimous act, but rather the performance of a religiously mandated duty to provide something to which the poor have a right.

Tzitzit. Ritual fringes that are attached to each of the four corners of the *tallit*.

Yahrzeit. Literally "year time," Yiddish term used by Ashkenazic Jews to refer to the yearly commemoration of the anniversary of the death of one's parents according to the Jewish calendar. Many extend it to the other five close relatives for whom mourning is required—brother and sister, son and daughter, and spouse. Hasidic communities observe the *yahrzeits* of the leaders of their specific dynasties as festive occasions, celebrating the day that these *tzadikim* ascended to the spiritual realm.

Yeshiva. From a Hebrew root meaning "to sit" and literally an "academy," the term refers to a Jewish school or seminary of higher learning where students intensively study Torah, Talmud, and rabbinic literature.

Yom Kippur (Day of Atonement). Major fast day on the 10th of Tishrei that is devoted to individual and communal repentance.

Zohar. Known as the "Book of Splendor," the principal kabbalistic book that is the basis for all subsequent Jewish mystical works. Attributed to the second-century C.E. rabbinic authority Shimon bar Yochai and his colleagues and disciples, scholars now believe that the *Zohar* was written in the late thirteenth century by Moses de Leon.

Bibliography

ArtScroll Haggadah Treasury. Brooklyn: Mesorah Publications, 1986.
ArtScroll Kaddish. Brooklyn: Mesorah Publications, 1991.
ArtScroll Siddur. Brooklyn: Mesorah Publications, 1986.
ArtScroll Yom Kippur Reader. Brooklyn: Mesorah Publications, 1989.
Biale, Rachel. *Women and Jewish Law*. New York: Schocken, 1984.
Blech, Benjamin. *More Secrets of Hebrew Words*. Northvale, NJ: Jason Aronson, 1993.
Chill, Abraham. *The Mitzvot*. New York: Bloch, 1974.
Cohen, Jeffrey. *Blessed Are You: A Comprehensive Guide to Jewish Prayer*. Northvale, NJ: Aronson, 1993.
Diamant, Anita. *The New Jewish Wedding*. New York: Fireside, 1985.
Donin, Hayim. *To Be a Jew: A Guide to Jewish Observance in Contemporary Life*. New York: Basic Books, 1972.
———. *To Pray as a Jew: A Guide to the Prayer Book and the Synagogue Service*. New York: Basic Books, 1980.
Dorff, Elliott N. *Matters of Life and Death: A Jewish Approach to Modern Medical Ethics*. Philadelphia: Jewish Publication Society, 1998.
Dosick, Wayne. *Living Judaism: The Complete Guide to Jewish Belief, Tradition, and Practice*. San Francisco: Harper San Francisco, 1995.
Etz Hayim. Philadelphia: Jewish Publication Society, 2001.
Frankel, Ellen, and Betsy Platkin Teutsch. *The Encyclopedia of Jewish Symbols*. Northvale, NJ: Jason Aronson, 1992.
Garfiel, Evelyn. *The Service of the Heart*. New York: Yoseloff, 1958.
Gelbard, Shemuel Pinchas. *Rite and Reason: 1050 Customs and Their Sources*. Nanuet, NY: Feldheim, 1998.
Greenberg, Blu. *How to Run a Traditional Jewish Household*. New York: Simon & Schuster, 1983.
Gross, David C. *The Jewish People's Almanac*. New York: Hippocrene Books, 1988.
Hammer, Reuven. *Entering Jewish Prayer: A Guide to Personal Devotion and the Worship Service*. New York: Schocken, 1994.
———. *Entering the High Holy Days*. Philadelphia: Jewish Publication Society, 1998.
Haut, Irwin H. *Divorce in Jewish Law and Life*. New York: Sepher-Hermon, 1983.
Hertz, J. J. *The Pentateuch and Haftorahs*. London: Soncino Press, 1978.
Heschel, Abraham Joshua. *Man's Quest for God*. New York: Charles Scribner, 1954.
———. *The Sabbath: Its Meaning for Modern Man*. New York: Harper Torchbooks, 1966.
Holtz, Barry. *Back to the Sources*. New York: Summit Books, 1984.
Isaacs, Ronald H. *The Jewish Book of Numbers*. Northvale, NJ: Jason Aronson, 1996.

Kadden, Barbara Binder, and Bruce Kadden. *Teaching Jewish Life Cycle*. Denver: A.R.E. Publishing, 1997.

Klein, Isaac. *A Guide to Jewish Religious Practice*. New York: Jewish Theological Seminary of America, 1979.

Kolatch, Alfred J. *The Jewish Book of Why*. Middle Village, NY: Jonathan David, 1981.

———. *The Second Jewish Book of Why*. Middle Village, NY: Jonathan David, 1985.

———. *This Is the Torah*. Middle Village, NY: Jonathan David, 1988.

Lamm, Maurice. *The Jewish Way in Death and Mourning*. New York: Jonathan David, 1972.

Lutske, Harvey. *The Book of Jewish Customs*. Northvale, NJ: Jason Aronson, 1986.

Maimonides, Moses. *The Commandments*. Translated by Charles Chavel. London and New York: Soncino Press, 1967.

———. *The Guide of the Perplexed*. Translated by Shlomo Pines. Chicago: University of Chicago Press, 1963.

———. *Mishneh Torah*. Translated by Philip Birnbaum. New York: Hebrew Publishing Corp., 1974.

Marks, Gil. *The World of Jewish Cooking*. New York: Simon & Schuster, 1996.

Millgram, Abraham. *Jewish Worship*. Philadelphia: Jewish Publication Society, 1971.

———. *Sabbath: The Day of Delight*. Philadelphia: Jewish Publication Society, 1959.

Preuss, Julius. *Biblical and Talmudic Medicine*. Translated by Fred Rosner. New York: Sanhedrin Press, 1978.

Rabinowicz, Tzvi. *A Guide to Life: Jewish Laws and Customs of Mourning*. Northvale, NJ: Jason Aronson, 1989.

Riskin, Shlomo. *Women and Jewish Divorce*. Hoboken, NJ: Ktav, 1989.

Roden, Claudia. *The Book of Jewish Food*. New York: Knopf, 1997.

Rosen, Dov. *Shema Yisrael*. Translated by Leonard Oschry. Jerusalem: Shema Yisrael, 1972.

Sefer Ha-Chinnuch. Translated by Charles Wengrov. New York: Feldheim, 1978.

Sherwin, Byron. *The Nature of Jewish Ethics*. Dworsky Center for Jewish Studies, College of Liberal Arts, University of Minnesota, 1988.

Shostek, Patti. *A Lexicon of Jewish Cooking*. Chicago: Contemporary Books, 1979.

Sperling, Abraham Isaac. *Reasons for Jewish Customs and Traditions*. Translated by Abraham Matts. New York: Bloch, 1968.

Steinsaltz, Adin. *A Guide to Jewish Prayer*. New York: Schocken, 2000.

Stone Chumash. Brooklyn: Mesorah Publications, 1994.

Strassfeld, Michael. *The Jewish Holidays: A Guide and Commentary*. New York: Harper & Row, 1985.

Strassfeld, Michael, and Sharon Strassfeld. *The Second Jewish Catalog*. Philadelphia: Jewish Publication Society, 1976.

Telushkin, Joseph. *Jewish Literacy*. New York: William Morrow, 1991.

Tigay, Jeffrey H. *The JPS Torah Commentary: Deuteronomy*. Philadelphia: Jewish Publication Society, 2003.

Toperoff, Shlomo Pesach. *The Animal Kingdom in Jewish Thought*. Northvale, NJ: Jason Aronson, 1995.

Trepp, Leo. *The Complete Book of Jewish Observance*. New York: Summit Books, 1980.

Waskow, Arthur. *Seasons of Our Joy*. New York: Bantam Books, 1982.

Witty, Abraham B., and Rachel Witty. *Exploring Jewish Tradition*. New York: Doubleday, 2001.

Index

About the Author

Ronald L. Eisenberg is a professor of radiology at Harvard Medical School and a radiologist at the Beth Israel Medical Center in Boston. A graduate of the University of Pennsylvania and its medical school, he had residency training at the Massachusetts General Hospital and the University of California at San Francisco. The author of 22 books in radiology, he is also a non-practicing attorney, member of the California Bar, and author of *Radiology and the Law*.

Eisenberg holds a doctoral degree in Jewish Studies from Spertus Institute in Chicago and is the author of eight books in the field. These include *The JPS Guide to Jewish Traditions, The Jewish World in Stamps*, and the *Essential Figures* trilogy, comprising *Essential Figures in the Bible, Essential Figures in the Talmud*, and *Essential Figures in Jewish Scholarship*.

CPSIA information can be obtained at www.ICGtesting.com
Printed in the USA
BVOW05*0310100615

403731BV00002B/2/P

9 781442 239463